Subsistence Marketplaces

Madhu Viswanathan

ISBN: 978-0-9897819-4-7

1

Contents

Cover Photo Credits

The collage of photos for the cover of this textbook was arranged by Madhu Viswanathan, Arjun Dutta, and Meagan Hennessey. Credits for individual photos as follows, from left to right:

Top row:

1. Interactions with a small farmer during field immersion, India. Photograph courtesy of students in the course "Product and Market Development for Subsistence Marketplaces."
2. A Portuguese farmer. Photograph by Jose Paulo Carvalho Pereira; Creative Commons licensed image via Fotopedia: http://www.fotopedia.com/items/b1gXYfSmHZw-T6NYInldZ0U.
3. A farmer using a mobile phone in the Philippines to relay messages of a good planting season. Photograph by the International Rice Research Institute; Creative Commons licensed image via Flickr: http://www.fotopedia.com/items/b1gXYfSmHZw-T6NYInldZ0U.

Middle row:

1. A woman pumping water by hand. Photograph by Oxfam International; Creative Commons licensed image via Fotopedia: http://www.fotopedia.com/items/flickr-4642418846.
2. Hill Tribe women at the Laomeng Market, Yunnan, China. Photograph by Alpha; Creative Commons licensed image via Flickr: http://www.flickr.com/photos/avlxyz/2299452961/.
3. Hirsi Farah Ali, village chairman in Waridaad, Somaliland, Africa, who rests under a tree during a drought in 2012. Photograph by Oxfam East Africa; Creative Commons licensed image via Flickr: http://www.flickr.com/photos/46434833%40N05/5758378632.

Bottom row:

1. Local patrons using the internet in the Biblioteca de Camina of Colombia. Photograph by the Gates Foundation; Creative Commons licensed image via Flickr: http://www.flickr.com/photos/gatesfoundation/6046310008/.
2. An instructor explaining concepts and issues of marketplaces to a group of women and men in Tamil Nadu, India. Photograph courtesy of students in the course "Product and Market Development for Subsistence Marketplaces."
3. A family in Haiti using a sun oven for their cooking needs. Photograph by Sun Oven, Inc.

Acknowledgments

I acknowledge with deep gratitude the many individuals and entities who made this journey of more than 15 years possible. This journey has taken us through a variety of research in many different settings where we learned about people who embody the undying human spirit. I acknowledge generous participants in our research who shared the most difficult of life circumstances with us, our extraordinary field team, inspiring community-based organizations, non-profit organizations, and adult education centers, partnering universities, small startups and large companies, the most sincere and dedicated coauthors spanning many disciplines, and students, staff, and faculty at the University of Illinois. Supporting and encouraging me every step of the way have been my wife Deepa, my son Sid, and my parents.

Tom Hanlon, Srini Venugopal, Meagan Hennessey, and Anne McKinney made invaluable contributions through their careful reading and editing, and Arjun Dutta provide able support with images throughout the book. Norma Scagnoli and the eText team provided much needed support and impetus to take the book across the finish line.

Finally, this book is dedicated to the amazing people we met in our journey and who represent the customers, entrepreneurs, families, and communities of subsistence marketplaces around the world. The true measure of this book is not so much in its writing but in whether those who read it in turn are inspired to work toward bettering the world for people living in poverty, one person or family at a time if need be.

Introduction[1]

Image i.01: Hirsi Farah Ali, village chairman in Waridaad, Somaliland, Africa, rests under a tree during a drought in 2012. Photograph by Oxfam East Africa; Creative Commons licensed image via Flickr: http://www.flickr.com/photos/46434833%40N05/5758378632.

Out of the global population of over 7 billion, approximately 2.5 billion live on less than $2 a day. Understanding and alleviating poverty is crucial to the development of sustainable marketplaces. In this book, through an immersive and interactive experience, we aim to a) provide you a fundamental understanding of subsistence marketplaces, b) offer a sense of how solutions can be designed for these marketplaces, and c) explore how these solutions work for different entities. We created this material for multiple audiences—students, educators, managers, and policy makers—and we intend it as a starting point rather than a culmination of learning about subsistence marketplaces.

You'll find rich sets of materials to explore along the way through our web portal, including very comprehensive reports of yearlong projects that serve as intensive case studies, videos produced to provide insights about subsistence

---

[1] This chapter includes material adapted from the following previously published work:

Viswanathan, Madhubalan and Jose Antonio Rosa (2010). "Understanding Subsistence Marketplaces: Toward Sustainable Consumption and Commerce for a Better World," Journal of Business Research, 63(6), 535-537. DOI: 10.1016/j.jbusres.2009.06.001.

marketplaces, and immersion exercises to understand needs and generation ideas for solutions.

We use the term subsistence to cover the broad range of low income, covering individuals who are barely making ends meet. Whereas a number of definitions focus on such metrics as daily income in dollars, our orientation is qualitative in this regard, with the term subsistence emphasizing this focus and allowing for local variations that quantitative metrics aggregate across. As such, we also examine the edges of the phenomenon in terms of sheer survival at one end of the continuum and movement out of poverty into lower-middle class status at the other end. Our perspective is bottom-up, beginning with a nuanced, micro-level understanding of behaviors and contexts. This contrasts with relatively macro-level approaches, such as macro-economic perspectives that examine country- and region-level trends or meso-level business strategy approaches, such as the bottom of the pyramid perspective, which examine issues of business strategy of organizations working in these contexts. Instead, we adopt a micro-level approach and begin with life circumstances at the individual and community level, with a particular focus on marketplace interactions. From this micro-level understanding, we stitch together aggregate-level insights about designing solutions, such as developing products or designing enterprises. (For more on this perspective, see the section titled "Why a Bottom-Up Perspective?" below.)

Our work on subsistence marketplaces over the course of many years has created unique synergies between research, teaching, and social initiatives. In all three arenas, our work involves engagement of students, businesses, and social enterprises as well as a diverse set of faculty and campus entities across different disciplines. The material presented in this book draws on this rich set of experiences.

Why a Bottom-Up Perspective?

Not all subsistence marketplaces are the same. Some exist because of conflict and repression; others because of climate severity; others because of chronic apathy or for other reasons. Therefore, subsistence marketplaces cannot be approached in the same way or be receptive to the same solutions.

That's why we employ a bottom-up approach—one in which we examine consumer, seller, and marketplace behaviors as our starting point. Only when we have a rich understanding at these levels can we begin to design effective business models and technological innovations for these marketplaces.

Visualize it this way: A macro-economic view is like flying above the marketplace at 30,000 feet. A business-strategy perspective might fly closer at 12,000 to 15,000 feet above the ground. A bottom-up approach begins on the ground, learning from sellers, buyers, and communities, being immersed in the cultural, emotional, social, and cognitive contexts of the marketplace.

And it is in this bottom-up approach that we can gain the insights we need to address the marketplace needs of survival and sustainability. After all, why design a solution that works today but that can't be sustained tomorrow?

The approach is bottom-up, emphasizing that we move upward from micro-level understanding to insights for developing solutions at different levels—such as product, enterprise, and sustainable development in general.

How we have laid out the book

We begin this immersive experience with a section on understanding subsistence marketplaces. True to a bottom-up orientation, we begin at the individual level by allowing you to hear the voices of subsistence consumers and entrepreneurs.

Next, we cover needs, products, and markets in subsistence.

This is followed by an in-depth understanding of the subsistence consumer and the subsistence entrepreneur.

Then we delve into designing solutions for subsistence marketplaces. Beginning with developing products, this section covers marketing as well as business issues. Thus, the what of solutions is followed by the how.

The final section of the book is geared to specific audiences, including educators, researchers, business practitioners, social entrepreneurs, and policy makers. This section also provides a window into the research methods that led to the insights discussed in the other chapters.

With the vast literature on poverty and the many different subsistence contexts around the world, it is important to emphasize what this book is based on and what is the intent here. We do not provide an exhaustive analysis of subsistence contexts; instead, we offer an extended study of subsistence marketplaces in India, contrasted with low-literate, low-income consumers in the United States, supplemented with our experiences in marketplaces in Africa and South America. There are many subsistence contexts—some war-torn, some the result of genocide, and we should be very cautious in generalizing across contexts. Nevertheless, the deep study of specific contexts supplemented with our experiences in diverse parts of the world provides us a valuable starting point. This combination of deep engagement in some contexts and broad understanding across contexts provides the basis for this book.

Also noteworthy in delineating our approach is the multifaceted nature of deprivation in subsistence contexts. Our emphasis is specifically on marketplace interactions, but we necessarily cast this within larger life circumstances.

Finally, we believe that subsistence marketplaces are worthy of study in their own right, wherein subsistence describes the current state of individuals and communities. These are preexisting marketplaces we can learn from in order to design solutions for all of us. Thus, our terminology reflects an orientation that is diametrically opposite of viewing these contexts as parallel markets for existing products. Our goal is to understand and enable the progress from subsistence marketplaces to sustainable marketplaces, i.e., marketplaces characterized by sustainable production and consumption that enhance individual and community welfare and conserve natural resources.

Chapter 1
Voices of Subsistence Consumers and Entrepreneurs[2]

The voices of subsistence consumers and entrepreneurs are voices that many of us have not heard before. In this chapter you will hear two such voices. No two such voices are alike, but listening to their stories and perspectives gives you a window into their world.

Image 1.01: An elderly woman shopping for food in Colombia. Photograph by World Bank Photo Collection; Creative Commons licensed image via Flickr: http://www.flickr.com/photos/worldbank/1987288554/.

[2] This chapter includes material adapted from the following previously published works:

Viswanathan, Madhubalan, S. Gajendiran, and R. Venkatesan (2008), Enabling Consumer and Entrepreneurial Literacy in Subsistence Marketplaces, Dordrecht: Springer.

Viswanathan, Madhubalan, S. Gajendiran, and R. Venkatesan (2008), "Understanding and Enabling Marketplace Literacy in Subsistence Contexts: The Development of a Consumer and Entrepreneurial Literacy Educational Program in South India," International Journal of Educational Development, 28 (3), 300-19. DOI: 10.1016/j.ijedudev.2007.05.004

Viswanathan, Madhubalan (2007), "Understanding Product and Market Interactions in Subsistence Marketplaces: A Study in South India," in Product and Market Development for Subsistence Marketplaces: Consumption and Entrepreneurship Beyond Literacy and Resource Barriers, Editors, Jose Rosa and Madhu Viswanathan, Advances in International Management Series, Joseph Cheng and Michael Hitt, Series Editors, 21-57, Elsevier. DOI: 10.1016%2FS1571 -5027%2807%2920002-6

We also have placed additional interviews on our web portal to provide you a glimpse into the lives of many other consumers and entrepreneurs. The interview transcripts from the native Tamil language were translated and minimally edited to preserve authenticity.

Sumitra, a Low-Literate Buyer

Sumitra is a 46-year-old woman with no formal education, who lives in a low-income neighborhood in urban Chennai, India. She has two sons who were of the ages 18 and 16 at the time of the interview. Sumitra's husband expired a few years back, an event that drove the household into deep debt. Her sons had to discontinue their schooling and find work to ameliorate the financial difficulties of the family. Presently, Sumitra works as a housemaid earning Rs. 500 per month. Both her sons work as electricians, earning a wage of Rs. 100 and Rs. 40 per day if they find work. During the interview Sumitra spoke about how she strives to balance the needs of today as well as tomorrow. Despite her efforts, she said, "I struggle and I don't know what would be tomorrow". With regard to her aspirations, Sumitra put it succinctly—"I prefer to live like you (interviewer), I wish to wear clothes like you, as then only people will respect me".

Sumitra's situation illustrates how low-literate, low-income individuals cope and how adult literacy programs can lead to quantum increases in consumer skills. She reported having been abused and controlled by her husband for a long time. Thrust into the role of primary decision-maker after her husband's death, she enrolled in adult literacy classes that had a transformational effect on her. Lacking the ability to read numbers, she would rarely travel.

Due to very low literacy, she used pattern matching to identify bus numbers, at a great cost to her in terms of taking the wrong bus, or in being treated rudely by strangers whom she approached for help. Before he died, her husband would write the bus number on her hand and she would try to memorize it. But sometimes it would be washed away, and she was left to depend on her memory or ask people around her or the bus conductor.

Following are parts of an interview we conducted with her.

> **Interviewer:** Could you check the bus number before you attended the [adult literacy] class?
>
> **Sumitra:** I tried to remember the number, otherwise my husband would write on my hand and advise me not to forget it. Sometimes it would be erased while washing the hand or washing the plate after serving the food. I would notice it after reaching the bus stand, what do I do? I would ask the conductor to give the ticket for the

Periyar road stop [nearest stop to her house], but he would drop me at Liberty [a stop next to the Periyar stop].

Sumitra was forced to travel often in the years preceding her husband's death, when he was in hospitals.

Sumitra: I took him there and admitted him in the hospital. 37D alone would go there; 37 wouldn't. I believed that 37 would go and caught the bus. He [the conductor] told me that it wouldn't go and dropped me halfway. What do I do after getting down midway? When I enquired of people, they would advise me to go to the next bus stop, where the 37D would stop. I would walk with the lunch boxes and luggage in the hot summer. I struggled like this and took lunch to my husband. I visited different hospitals for five years in Madras for the treatment of my husband. If I had the money spent for him, I could have built a big building. I struggled like this without knowing the places and identifying the bus numbers.

Now, it is okay [after attending an adult literacy program]. Now, I go to Genjee [a village located 140 km away]. I visited Cuddalore last Saturday and returned on Sunday. I went alone by train to Cuddalore. I used to be afraid earlier. I would be afraid to go alone at night after 9:00 pm and when it became dark. Now, I do not fear. ... I know the numbers and can speak well. I can say the address, my children's name, and other members' names. Now I know everything. Do I not? Suppose I go there, I could add the letters, read slowly and know the name of the place.

Interviewer: You said that you could not read the number. How did you read, and know what he wrote when your husband wrote the number on your hand?

Sumitra: He wrote 20. He wrote 2 and 0 then the initial ... I would show [the number written on my hand] and ask whether this particular bus would stop here. ... Whether the 37 would stop here or the 27 would stop here. I would show it and ask the people in the bus stand, and then I would catch the bus.

I didn't want to ask anyone in the middle of the journey. ... I wouldn't ask anyone who was standing in the bus stand. First, I would judge the people around, whether they were good, then I would ask them. I could identify the right people from their faces and appearances. ... [The wrong people] wouldn't tell or guide, but criticize. So I would decide that we should not ask such people; instead I should catch whatever bus comes. I would catch the bus and enquire from the bus conductor in the middle of the travel. Suppose he was a good person, he would say that this bus wouldn't go on the route I asked and he would guide me to get down and show the proper stop to catch the right bus. Sometimes, the conductor was not in a good mood or was an irresponsible person, and he would shout at me in anger with filthy words and ask me to get down from the bus.

Difficulties as a Buyer

Sumitra had no formal education, very low income, and little experience as a customer—she primarily had bought basic necessities at the nearest retail store on instructions from her husband. She did not inquire about prices, did not compute her bill, and always shopped at the same outlet. She had been cheated on numerous occasions through unfair weighing and other means, but never took action either by switching stores or by arguing with sellers.

> **Sumitra:** [My husband] didn't ask me anything. Yes, he would give me his weekly salary of rupees [Rs.] 500 to Rs. 600. I would take all the money and buy the necessities. There wouldn't be any balance to spend or save. Sometimes, he used to shout. I used to tell him, "What do I do?," and to check the bill if he needed any clarification. [The local shopkeeper] would have issued the bill with many mistakes. I managed my family in this manner in the past.
>
> Now, it is better. I ask him to give the right weight even when I go to the ration shop. I would fight. I would demand of him to give the full amount, otherwise I wouldn't accept. Now I can speak all the rules. … It was the situation. What do we do? You have to simply accept whatever is given. Now [after adult literacy classes], that is impossible; I could fight. I used to tell him that I would complain to the appropriate authority. The ration supplier says that this is nonsense and that every month I had become a headache, whereas earlier I used to buy and go silently with whatever was given. He says now: "Okay, you take the full amount and don't shout."

Budgeting under Constraints and Uncertainty

Sumitra is faced with the task of managing the household budget in the face of unsteady and inadequate income. Since both her sons are daily wage laborers, the household income is not only inadequate, but also fluctuates based on factors outside of their control. The twin characteristics of income constraints and income uncertainty further compound the problem of managing even basic household needs such as food, soap and toothpaste.

> **Sumitra:** My younger son earns when he attends the job. He gives me his salary, Rs.100, if he attends the job. I could get Rs.3,000 per month if he attends his work in all 30 days. I don't have to worry. He gives Rs.100, supposing he attends the job a day. I use [most of the money] to buy the needs of the day and save Rs.10 from that money. Supposing it is not sufficient, I would reserve Rs.20 for the future.

> My elder son may come and ask Rs.5 or Rs.2 to buy anything to eat. I used to ask him, "Why are you going to buy, when I have in the house?" Sometimes, he may demand the money to buy tender coconut; I won't deny I would give them. Later they would ask the account for the money given to me. I would tell them the expenses incurred, like what I bought: toothpaste, soap, etc. I would ask them how I could have balanced money if they used 3 or 4 soaps in a month, and why they couldn't use less soap.

[Note: as per current exchange rate, one dollar is approximately equivalent to Rs. 50).]

Social Support and Social Pressures

During times of need, Sumitra harnesses the support of individuals in her social network, such as her family back in the village, her sister, or even her employer. The forms of support vary from borrowing money or provisions to using the refrigerator of her employer to store her perishables. However, maintaining the social network also imposes significant financial pressures on her.

> **Sumitra:** Sometimes my relatives from [home] would send oil, groundnut and gingili each 5 kgs during the harvesting seasons. We would share it here. I would take the major share. I would ask my brother-in-law's families to give me more, as my husband is no more and [we have no] sufficient income when compared with them. They too would give me the major share, as I have to manage the family without the support of others. I could manage with these items received from [home] for a maximum of 4 to 5 months. Then, I may face problems, by the time I would borrow money from my sister or aunt and manage... If I buy other vegetables (perishables), I keep them in the [refrigerator] available at the employer's house. They use little space, so I too would use it.

Sumitra: Expenses [sometimes arise when we need] to attend a marriage or funeral or visit the celebration of puberty attainment of any young female relatives. These are all unexpected. We [sometimes] have to visit relatives who are dying. We may have to borrow Rs.100 and go, supposing it is important function. I plan to repay the loan later. Many times I have had to bear these waste expenses. I used to decide at the moment and spend. Sometimes I shouted at my sister, who invited me to attend the relative's function, and asked her to repay the loan when I could not afford it. I would ask them who would be here to support me. Sometimes my sister or her daughter would give Rs.100 to repay the loan. I have been managing like this.

Increased Confidence Through Literacy

The adult literacy classes have transformed Sumitra, increasing her skills and confidence. Before enrolling in the adult-literacy program, her children would check the bills for her; now, she is empowered by checking the bills herself. Her consumer skills were previously extremely low. However, after becoming the primary decision-maker and attending the adult literacy classes that her husband had forbidden her from taking in the past, the difference is night and day.

Now, she argues, bargains, threatens action against sellers who engage in unfair practices, makes inquiries at several shops before buying, purchases wholesale whenever possible, weighs packaged products for accuracy, reads information on packages, avoids high-interest loans, saves money, and takes actions, such as taking her business elsewhere. She is much more confident about effectively managing her purchasing environment through conversation, argument, and action.

Sumitra: [The shopkeeper] would give the bill; I would show it to my children to check it. My younger son doesn't know to calculate; my elder son would calculate the bill. If the bill total shows an extra Rs. 2 or 3, he would ask me why I paid more. I would tell him, "What do I know!"

But now, I am commanding the shopkeeper. I make the calculation the moment I receive the bill. The moment I calculated, I would recall the price for what I bought yesterday and check the discrepancies in today's bill... Nowadays, I am asking with a commanding tone. [The shopkeeper] would tell me that a drumstick was Rs. 2. I would ask him whether he would be ready to sell it for Rs.1; otherwise, I would go to next shop. I would ask everything very assertively and in a high tone...

Interviewer: One month ago you didn't join the [adult literacy] course. At that time, you bought the same vegetables. The situation was the same as it is now. What would have happened?

Sumitra: Nothing. He would have exploited me.

Interviewer: So, you wouldn't have calculated?

Sumitra: I wouldn't have calculated. I wouldn't know the price. It was just what he told me. I have just followed the same [pattern] for the past 36 years. I was 13 years old when I got married. Now, my age is 46 [sic]. I had been buying for the same price that he fixed and stated. I paid the same.

Interviewer: Would you ask the price in other shops?

Sumitra: I wouldn't ask the price.

Interviewer: You wouldn't ask the price in the same shop too?

Sumitra: Now, it has been okay for the past month. I would check and verify as they coached me. I would verify the bill. I know all this. I would ask [the shopkeeper] why he cheated me. It happens in the wholesale shop too. [The local shopkeeper recently] asked why I am not like I used to be earlier. [The wholesale shopkeepers] realize that I have changed. [The local shopkeeper] asked like that. He sells soap for Rs. 11, which is sold for Rs. 10 at the wholesale stores. I would ask him how he could sell like that. I would ask him to justify. He would ask me to pay the wholesale price and not to shout there. He cheats well. It is the place for cheating. We earn hard money. Here, we could earn good money if we know [how to avoid] cheating.

Opening Pathways to New Relationships and a New Life

Attaining literacy changes lives in many ways. In Sumitra's case, the adult literacy program has also changed the way she relates to others and in how she lives.

Sumitra on her employers: Now, [my employers] say to me that I am confident after attending the classes; I may dominate them if I am a literate. Even this morning [my employer] told me, "You are performing at this level though you are unable to read and write well; if you were literate, you would command us."

Sumitra on shopkeepers: They should approach me in a respectable way and inquire politely, and then it is okay. I don't like indecent treatment or rough words. I would slap him, whoever attempted it. I would get angry. Now, I try to reduce [my anger] gradually. But even now I have a little of a bad temper. My employer madam advises me to reduce my anger. I used to slap the moment anyone scolded me or disrespected me and warn him that he should not keep the shop in the vicinity. I did once.

Now, I don't do it. I am quiet and calm, because I have attended the [adult literacy] classes. People wonder whether I am in the house or not, and say that I was seen but they couldn't hear my voice. Today, this is the first time I am talking much in the past month. [My employer] has advised me to talk less, especially in the summer, and suggests that I speak selectively with good people. She told me to talk less when I know well that they are not good people. She said that I have the capacity to analyze and understand whatever she says and adjust, though I am low-literate.

Although she has completely transformed herself since her husband's death using the adult literacy program, Sumitra has not changed some things, living her life the way her husband "would have wanted" her to.

She is sensitive to comments by others that she is now enjoying "luxuries" after her husband's demise. She states that she is living today the way she lived when her husband was alive and the way he would have liked her to live. This is a striking feature of many women we interviewed. Despite psychological and physical abuse, they have an idealistic notion of what it is to be a wife and live by that ideal.

Interviewer: Would you go to a restaurant or films? Do you visit hotels?

Sumitra: We visited, when my husband was alive. Supposing I go now, there is a chance that my neighbors would notice it. If someone noticed me in the restaurant, they would tell others that so-and-so's wife is eating in the restaurant. They wouldn't say that I was in the restaurant to have food because I was hungry. But, they would pass sarcastic comments like "Look at her, she goes to the restaurant instead of cooking at home."

I would get angry if I heard such comments. So, I won't even buy and have a snack from the shop nearby. You could check with others. Even when I am hungry, I prefer to prepare rice porridge and eat it. I don't have the habit of eating in hotels.

Velamma, a Low-Literate Seller

Velamma, a 45-year-old woman with a 5th-grade education, shows how adult education and business training empowered her to successfully run a business and support a family. Having no formal education, minimal experience as a customer, and very poor consumer skills, she managed her household with her husband and two children for many years with next to nothing to eat and substituting regular meals with inexpensive alternatives (e.g., an inexpensive beverage rich in carbohydrates, often used as a last resort).

She never borrows, but lives within very limited means. After 15 years of staying at home, she had to be the primary breadwinner because her husband became dysfunctional. She decided to start a business, buying utensils from stores and reselling them to residents in her community. Early in this endeavor, adult education, business training, and financial assistance from an NGO enabled her to buy a vehicle to transport products, and helped her develop her ability to manage her business.

In one of her initiatives, she runs an installment plan wherein people pay a fixed sum each month for 15 months, at the end of which they choose a large utensil from an assortment of comparably-priced items. She offers gifts to customers who sign up at the beginning of the installment plan and has a monthly lottery witnessed by some subscribers to give out a large utensil to a lucky winner. She also offers an incentive plan for customers to buy large vessels through installments. Such a plan requires considerable skills to implement in a one-on-one environment. It requires upfront planning, witnesses for a monthly lottery, collection of money every month, and a gift at the beginning of the plan, as well as distribution of large vessels at the end.

Following are portions of an interview we conducted with Velamma about her marketplace dealings.

Building Her Clientele

> **Velamma:** I introduced a chit [a savings scheme] in which the members have to pay Rs. 20 per month. There would be 200 members in total. From that, I gained courage. I would give them a prize when they joined the service. Apart from this, we would choose a winner per month through a lottery method. At the end of the 15th month, all members would be given the vessels... Through door-to-door visits, we would enroll people. ... I enrolled those who trusted me or were willing to try. I have been steadily doing this from 1993 onwards. So, everyone joined and paid regularly.

Velamma explains to potential customers the benefits of buying certain items that would be useful during important life events, such as marriage. In this way she gains many new customers and many who want to learn more about the products and the chit.

> **Velamma:** Without any knowledge of the item, they would ask what the price is. Some didn't know the price, so they would ask their husbands. If they asked their husbands, what would they say? They would say that it does not have to be bought. So I would explain to those who don't know anything. I would tell them not to consult their husbands. If they consult the males, they cannot add a single article in their house.

> I would tell them: "See, you should save Rs. 3. When they give Rs. 10 for the family expenses, you could pay me Rs.1, and you save the balance of Rs. 2. You have children. Suppose they get married tomorrow. What would the others ask you? They should say: 'Okay, your talent has saved [the situation] though your husband is an alcoholic.'" When I talk in this manner, they get confidence and courage. They would decide that they should support me and encourage me, who counseled them and gave them the courage.

> I have the skill [to do this]. They would listen to my words and ask me to enroll them. They would appreciate me for encouraging them. They would support me in this manner.

Velamma counters what husbands are likely to say, discusses a hypothetical situation, such as a marriage of a child, and points out that others would commend the woman for having saved despite having an alcoholic husband. She talks at length with customers, but maintains confidentiality. She expects potential customers whom she encouraged to be courageous to then reciprocate and give her business. Velamma works within cultural norms. Being a woman, she deals primarily with women in households.

Dealing with Women

> **Interviewer:** You said that you wouldn't approach the males while enrolling members for the chit.

> **Velamma:** Because women would buy the materials without the knowledge of the males. There could be confusion between them suddenly. Even if the men pay Rs. 50 in the absence of the women, it should not be a problem between them. It is okay if we collect the money when both men and women are in the house. The women

would have bought the item without the knowledge of the men. ... How can I collect the money from the men? It would become a dispute between them. He would ask her how she can buy? "I gave Rs. 50 to the chit women," he would say to her. The next day the women would come and ask me why I received the money? So, I won't collect the money. I would collect the money from the women.

Interviewer: So, if the male paid Rs. 50 first?

Velamma: I won't receive. I won't receive it. So far, I never receive from men. Because I should not give room for the problem between them. She would have bought it without his knowledge. You tell me!

Relevant here is how Velamma's basic interpersonal skills blend into business policies she adheres to. Her business policies reflect the day-to-day context where the separation between private lives and the marketplace is blurred, or even nonexistent. She is sensitive to potential problems that could be created between spouses by some business practices. She adheres to a strict business code of not discussing her judgments of specific customers with other customers. It also gives the seller a sense of control, perhaps stemming from making individual judgments and not worrying about a myriad of opinions from other people. She notes that customers may have bad relationships currently with someone, which may be resolved, at which point any of her opinions may be shared to her detriment.

Interviewer: You are selling to all?

Velamma: Immediately, they would ask how the chit woman [Velamma] gives always to you. A woman would ask, how is she giving always? She would ask me too on what basis I am giving to them [other women]. I would smile rather than responding. I would not reply.

Interviewer: Why?

Velamma: Because we should not discuss it. They may have so many connections with each other. We should not discuss it. I should see how I collect the money from them. So I would pass them with a smile.

Interviewer: When you are a customer, would you speak to others?

Velamma: I won't speak to others and outsiders.

We asked Velamma questions about when she would approach businesspeople as a customer and ask them questions.

Velamma: When we have had exposure and experience, I would talk about the business with business people. If someone called and asked for an item, I would ask for an advance.

Interviewer: But you would talk to others when you are a customer and ask?

Velamma: Yes. I would ask.

Interviewer: But you won't ask [about others] while you are running the business?

Velamma: Wherever they can go, why do we worry? I would have this control. It is important [the business and collection]. They may fight or quarrel with each other now and may join a little later. Then they would say that the chit woman said this and that against you. They may speak behind my back. Is it not a problem? So I won't ask anyone about anything.

The Murky Business of Giving Credit

A constant issue for sellers to deal with is judging creditworthiness and honesty. This is done in a variety of ways, essentially judging people based on appearance, familiarity, on the recommendation of an acquaintance, or from their dwelling. It is a highly personal, subjective judgment made on the basis of available information.

Interviewer: How do you decide when to give credit to someone?

Velamma: It is all based on my assessment and confidence. I won't give [credit] to all. ... Who can pay [me] back? Who goes for housemaid jobs? ... I would first verify. But I won't really ask anyone. I would just make my own assessment.

Velamma makes judgments of creditworthiness and honesty on her own, without consulting others, because word can spread. Moreover, there are many motives for people to speak poorly of others, such as personal animosity. She believes in her judgment and in making it independently and sticking with it.

Velamma: I won't ask anyone [about creditworthiness of specific customers]. I would give products based on my assessment and confidence. They may tell me [if asked], but they may have quarreled [with the potential customers]. So they would tell me not to give products to their neighbors and say that they would move out of the area.

Even the people paying me now would say that they don't know, when I am asking about their neighbors. They would respond without any seriousness...They would come and quarrel with me immediately. They are all fighters. They would ask me not to give to their neighbors. In the end, [the people who asked me not to give to their neighbors] would be the ones who won't pay regularly, but the neighbor would pay regularly. So I won't count on input from individuals. I would decide based on my own confidence.

An integral part of business skills in this context is the ability to judge customers on such attributes as their ability and motivation to repay loans. Credit ratings are fluid, and decisions are made through personal judgments. Velamma maintains confidentiality when individuals have not made appropriate payments.

Getting Paid When Customers are Short of Money

Velamma also maintains cordial relationships and does not shout, although the threat of shouting is an effective mechanism that many individuals fear. For this seller, moral fear, rather than anything else, is effective in getting paid what she is owed.

Interviewer: When you run the business, what are all the things customers do to avoid paying you?

Velamma: They would do nothing, sir. They would say that they will give tomorrow if it is not possible today. Velamma also spoke to the importance of being discreet in her dealings with people who cannot pay on a day they owe. They would say: "Okay, sorry, I would give earlier [if I could]." If I ask them in front of ten people, they would be embarrassed. So I would talk to them individually. If it is not possible today, give to me tomorrow. But don't send the message while hiding. It will become a regular practice in your life. [They would say,] "Okay, chit madam. I feared that you may scold me." I am confident because they have fear.

Interviewer: But you won't shout?

Velamma: I won't shout. However, they have [moral] fear. I won't collect [payments] by shouting.

Dealing with Refund Issues

Velamma operates in an environment where there is a constant threat of someone shouting and creating a scene. Customers asking for refunds on product returns is another facet of running the business.

Interviewer: Has anyone complained that you are not giving a product worth the Rs. 300 they paid for it?

Velamma: Few people are like that. … I would ask them to check the products that were given to others. I would tell them that I gave them the same products that I gave to others. Some may accept what I said and leave quietly, some may shout. I may have to adjust to both situations.

Interviewer: How are you managing such situations?

Velamma: I would invite them to check the quality of products supplied to other customers. The other customers would say that the product given was good and useful. This feedback would cool down their temper and they would leave quietly.

Interviewer: Suppose they say even after the explanation and feedback that the product is not good and that they don't want it?

Velamma: If they don't want, they can choose any other product available with me. But I won't return the money. At any cost, I won't give the money back.

Interviewer: Your principle is not to return the money?

Velamma: I won't give back money, only products.

Interviewer: Could you give them the costly item? Could you give the item worth Rs. 300 because they come and question you?

Velamma: We can't encourage this, others may follow it. They may go and announce to others that she got the money back from the chit woman. So the others would follow suit. Hence, I would give the product only. Whatever item, they can ask, but no money. I would not give the money back.

The Complexities of Managing a Subsistence Business

Velamma resists the sometimes intense pressure to customize terms of business for one person, because if she did customize, then all buyers could make similar demands. In fact, if someone refuses to pay, the seller has to insist that payment be made, whether she expects it or not. The seller cannot waver on the issue of payment, because others will take their cue from it. The seller also must keep the same price for all her customers.

As Velamma's situation demonstrates, managing a business in this environment is no small task. Thrust into this role with almost no financial decision-making experience, she has managed a number of functions, including negotiating and buying from wholesalers, identifying and appealing to potential customers, and coming up with innovative installment plans that make her products affordable to customers while providing liquidity for running the business and for additional income through lending.

She also has to manage relationships with customers and not cause problems among family members; hence, she only accepts orders from the female head of the household. She uses the threat of public humiliation, without actually carrying it out, to induce payments. In an environment where dwellings are extremely close to each other, most, if not all, discussions may not be private. This emphasizes the importance of effectively managing interactions with customers. She is careful not to compromise on the price of the type of utensil that people get; otherwise, the word would get out and cause havoc in her business.

Yet Velamma is flexible in allowing people to join later and catch up on payments. They are, however, given a utensil of lesser value at the end to compensate for their money being available for "rotation" only later in the process. She also uses the money in hand to lend and collect interest. This seller illustrates the context for running a business as well as the unique skills that are needed to be successful.

Conclusion

We conclude this chapter by acknowledging the generosity shown by our informants in sharing so much of their personal lives with us. As researchers, we have learned so much by interacting with them and listening to their voices. Our objective in this chapter was to start by listening directly to the voices of subsistence consumers and entrepreneurs rather than "expert opinions" on poverty. We leave you with these voices as a starting point to reflect on and learn form. In the ensuing chapters, we draw deeper insights from these voices.

Exercises

To further understand the world of subsistence consumers and entrepreneurs, we have created seven assignments. We also have many interviews available on the web portal as well as short-form interviews; these will help you complete the assignments. The link for the web portal is http://www.business.illinois.edu/subsistence/Resources/.

Assignment #1: First-Person Profile of Subsistence

Read an interview on our web portal. Using the first person, write a profile of the person interviewed, detailing your broader impression of living in subsistence. Aim for about four pages, double-spaced.

Here are some emphases for your profile:

- Focus primarily on the person's life circumstances and what it is like to live in subsistence, rather than on the economic realm as it impacts product and market interactions. You can touch on the marketplace realities, but more as a part of the whole life of the person.

- Identify key life-changing circumstances the person has experienced.

- Reflect on what you have learned about living in poverty—e.g., the types and nature of challenges that people face in areas such as food, health, safety, environmental factors, and so on.

Assignment #2: Comparisons of Living in Subsistence

You can complete this exercise with any set of interviews, although we recommend two short forms. Read two interviews and write about your broader impression of living in subsistence. Do this in about two double-spaced pages. Please adhere to the following guidelines:

- Focus not just on the economic realm (the product and market interactions), but more on life circumstances in subsistence, where the marketplace is one part.

- Compare and contrast the circumstances of the two persons in the interviews. Consider levels of poverty, literacy, family situations, and so on.

- Identify key life-changing circumstances for each person.

- Reflect on what you have learned about living in poverty—e.g., the types and nature of challenges that people face in areas, such as food, health, safety, environmental factors, and so on.

- Compare and contrast the circumstances in subsistence marketplaces to those of poverty for low-literate, low-income individuals in the United States.

- Prepare to discuss these issues in class and in subsequent assignments.

Assignment #3: Comparing Across Subsistence Consumers and Entrepreneurs

Read two more interviews covering buyers and sellers and then complete the following in two single-spaced pages. You can choose which two interviews you add.

- Compare people in the three interviews—these two new ones and one you have read before.

- Write a synopsis based on your inferences and interpretations of all three interviews.

- Provide a broader discussion of poverty, based on the three interviews.

- Take the assignment any direction you wish: Highlight turning points in lives, catalog actions taken, and so on.

Assignment #4: Developing Poverty Models

The aim of this exercise is to begin to abstract across interviews to build conceptual maps or big pictures. It can be done individually or in groups. Typically, in a classroom course, model-based assignments are a good way to rotate students between groups of four as a way of meeting the rest of the class.

The model could consist, for instance, of a causal diagram with boxes (with large category titles and a list of factors) and arrows supported by text. But it can take any other form—a collage, a more organic model, a slide presentation (two to three slides are fine, along with a one-page description of the model, how it was developed, and the rationale behind it), and so on. The conceptual maps need to be about people's lives rather than purely economic (entrepreneurship or consumer skills), although the economic element can be part of the larger model.

It could be a model of individual, family, social, economic, and other factors and how they affect daily behaviors, for example. You would have some antecedents and some outcomes. It could be a model of how skills develop. In other words, take an angle and build a broader understanding beyond the individual interviews. Provide a 1-page rationale for the model.

To provide totally unrelated examples of models, please see the figures at the web portal. These are, of course, just arbitrary examples to give you an idea of what we mean by models.

Assignment #5: Developing Models of Needs, Products, and Markets

Develop a model that captures categories of needs, categories of products that satisfy these needs, and market interactions. If you wish to display additional elements beyond these three circles that help express yourself, please feel free to do so. Categorize needs as you see fit, ranging from the physiological to the spiritual. Provide a 1-page rationale for the model.

Assignment #6: Subsistence and Ecology

Examine the intersection of subsistence and ecology. Present your work in a slide presentation (two to three slides are fine). Answer these questions in your slides:

- What are the unique ecological issues that subsistence marketplaces face?

- How do these issues affect the daily lives of those who operate in subsistence marketplaces?

- What are some directions to take to find solutions?

Please be as creative as you wish to be, bringing in images and providing insights. The questions above are merely examples; please take the assignment in any direction you wish.

Assignment #7: Video Analysis

View the videos in the following order:

1. A Day in the Life of Tambuzai—Experience Poverty:
   http://www.youtube.com/watch?v=KX8mmJ3o80Y

2. Malaria claims another African life every 30 seconds:
   http://www.youtube.com/watch?v=mel6PEEhSK8

3. FRONTLINE/World |Kiva | PBS:
   http://www.youtube.com/watch?v=MXk4GUGXNTQ

Use the material in the video and the web portal to illustrate what you learned about subsistence contexts. Write a double-spaced page about the following:

- Compare and contrast the circumstances in the three videos.

- Reflect on what you learned about living in poverty—i.e., the types and nature of challenges that individuals have to face in different areas, such as food, etc.

- List some ideas that businesses could pursue to help people living in poverty while also being economically sustainable.

Chapter 2
Understanding Needs, Products, and Markets for Subsistence Consumers[3]

Image 2.01: Subsistence consumers buying vegetables from a hand cart vendor, India. Photograph courtesy of students in the course "Product and Market Development for Subsistence Marketplaces."

This chapter examines the marketplace activities of subsistence customers in South India. This specific geographic emphasis allows deeper understanding that can then be compared and contrasted with other contexts, while fully recognizing that our insights here are not generalizable to the many different subsistence contexts around the world. The primary objective of this chapter is

---

[3] This chapter includes material adapted from the following previously published work:

Viswanathan, Madhubalan (2007), "Understanding Product and Market Interactions in Subsistence Marketplaces: A Study in South India," in *Product and Market Development for Subsistence Marketplaces: Consumption and Entrepreneurship Beyond Literacy and Resource Barriers*, Editors, Jose Rosa and Madhu Viswanathan, Advances in International Management Series, Joseph Cheng and Michael Hitt, Series Editors, 21-57, Elsevier. DOI: 10.1016%2FS1571-5027%2807%2920002-6

to present a picture of the day-to-day behaviors and interactions of subsistence customers in terms of their needs, the products they purchase and their interactions with sellers and outlets.

We focus on two issues:

- people in a subsistence context as buyers and consumers rather than as sellers, and on

- describing how people relate to products and the marketplace to satisfy their needs.

Such delineation is important in providing focus to phenomena that can and has been approached in many different ways such as expansion of freedoms, exclusion, distributive justice, social marketing and business strategy (cf., Sen, 1992; Hill, Felice, and Ainscough 2007; Narayan and Petesch, 2000; Kotler, Roberto and Leisner 2006; Prahalad 2005). Moreover, we distinguish our focus from alternative foci, such as explaining consumer behavior, or exploring necessary consumer skills and their development, or examining coping strategies to overcome cognitive and economic constraints.

This chapter is based on observations and in-depth interviews over several years in urban and rural South Indian contexts. The aim is not to catalog marketplace interactions for generalizations, but to use our chosen contexts as a starting point to highlight key issues. (For an overview of the issues studied in this chapter, see Appendix 1.)

We organize these insights by product categories relevant to subsistence customers and their economic relationships with the marketplace. We then discuss the key characteristics of the interaction of subsistence customers with products and markets. We incorporate relevant literature into the discussion.

The Context

The typical low-income, low-literate individual lives in a small, usually rented dwelling and spends a high proportion of income on necessities such as food (rice, lentils, vegetables, meat, and spices), clothing, and unexpected expenses (usually for serious illnesses or family commitments due to traditions associated with birth, death, or marriage; for visits by guests; or even for something mundane, like a punctured tire on a bicycle).

The woman is usually responsible for household purchases, with assistance from her husband on some big-ticket items or when considerable travel is involved. The husband's tendency is to delegate most shopping decisions to his wife.

Thus, males sometimes do not know the distribution of the family budgets, nor have the ability to assess the quality of generic products.4

Males sometimes run very small businesses such as street vending, or are employed as construction workers, agricultural laborers, house painters, or other work in which they typically are paid by the hour or the day. In addition to the normal uncertainties of obtaining a regular income, seasonality is a major influence, with the rainy season in particular severely affecting income.

In terms of employment for women, the bottom of the pecking order is to work as a housemaid, with a very low salary usually supplemented with food, clothing on special occasions, and help in need. More and more women are employed outside the home and two-income families are becoming common. Educating children is a high priority. Whereas government schools offer free education, individuals strive to send their children to private schools considered of higher quality, which typically require a fee.

Birth, death, and marriage are events for which tradition is central and typically involve financial expenditure. Others may speak ill of those who do not live up to local traditions, for instance, criticizing an individual for not even giving money when a close relative dies. People usually borrow or find some way to meet expenses and live up to tradition.

Products and Purchases

Here, we discuss the set of products that subsistence individuals use, and we describe purchase options when they are difficult to separate from the product offering itself. A subsequent section examines market interactions in more depth. We present a rough category of needs, products, markets, and budgets for households in subsistence contexts in Table 2.1, and our discussion is summarized in Figure 2.1.

---

[4] A variety of sources of information suggest that alcohol addiction and accompanying by-products characterize a sizable proportion of families. When males who are addicted to alcohol are also the primary breadwinners, they often give a small proportion of their income (if any) to their wives to run the family while using most of the money for alcohol. Some males with an alcohol problem may just not go to work.

Table 2.1: Sample Needs, Products, Sellers, and Expenses in Subsistence Marketplaces

Categories of Needs	Sample Goods and Services	Sample Sellers / Providers	Sample Expenditure Breakdown (for families with monthly income as listed below)*		
			Rs. 6,000	Rs. 9,000	Rs. 14,000
Housing	Mud huts, concrete houses	Homeowner, landlords, government programs	< 1,250	< 2,450	< 3,500
Sanitation	Sanitation service, water	Government services	< 100	< 200	< 250
Food and beverages	Rice, meat, vegetables, spices, grinder, stove	Corner retail store, large reseller, mobile vendors, large markets, government ration shops	< 1,400	< 2,000	< 4,400
Clothing	Saris, lungis (clothing for men)	Larger stores, sidewalk sellers, door-to-door resellers	< 250	< 450	< 600
Personal care and hygiene	Soap, detergent, toothpaste	Retail store, wholesale store	< 300	< 400	< 500
Healthcare	Consultations, allopathic medicine	Government hospitals, clinics	< 300	< 400	< 300
Education	Government schools, private schools, adult education	NGOs, government, private organizations	< 400	< 400	< 900
Entertainment	Televisions, movies, festivals	Theaters, cable stations	< 150	< 200	< 300
Financial services	Retailer credit, pawning jewels, non-collateral loans, savings plans with stores, chit schemes	Retailer, store owner, pawn shop, moneylenders	< 700	< 500	Nil

			< 300	< 650	< 800
Transportation	Walking, bicycle, motorized two-wheeler, public bus, autorickshaws	Government buses, private buses, auto companies	< 300	< 650	< 800
Communication	Cell phones, land lines, phone centers	Private phone centers, cell phone plans sold through retail outlets	< 200	< 300	< 700
Energy	Electricity, fuel for cooking, fuel for two-wheelers	Government utilities, gasoline stations, retail outlets, wholesale outlets	< 300	< 500	< 550
Spiritual / Religious needs	Fruits as religious offerings, new clothes, fairs and carnivals	Temples, retail outlets, community-based organizations	< 100	< 200	< 500
Social obligations (customerical & cultural events)	Gifts, parties, function arrangements, hall rentals	Temples, retail outlets, function halls, community-based organizations	< 150	< 200	< 500
Savings	Money savings either weekly or monthly dependent on income pattern	Postal dept., banks, SHGs, chit	< 100	< 200	< 500

Estimates made by SMI research team for Chennai, India, in September 2011; estimates at two earlier points in time available on web portal.

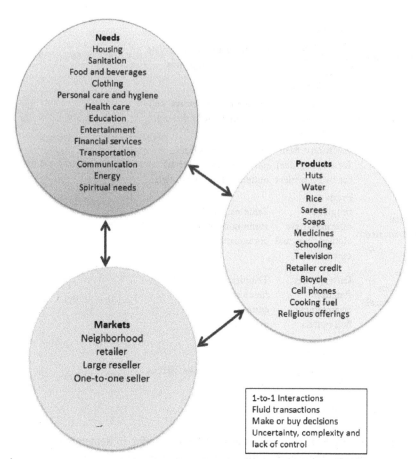

Needs
Housing
Sanitation
Food and beverages
Clothing
Personal care and hygiene
Health care
Education
Entertainment
Financial services
Transportation
Communication
Energy
Spiritual needs

Products
Huts
Water
Rice
Sarees
Soaps
Medicines
Schooling
Television
Retailer credit
Bicycle
Cell phones
Cooking fuel
Religious offerings

Markets
Neighborhood
retailer
Large reseller
One-to-one seller

1-to-1 Interactions
Fluid transactions
Make or buy decisions
Uncertainty, complexity and
lack of control

Figure 2.1: Product and Market Interactions in Subsistence Marketplaces.

General Background

The typical family lives in a small rented dwelling, often with very poor
infrastructure relating to electricity, water, and sanitation. Housing may range
from mud huts to concrete structures.[5] Transportation is typically by public

---

[5] Many individuals live on (i) encroached private lands without land titles and are not eligible
to get basic amenities, (ii) encroachments on roadsides, canal banks, government wastelands,
treated as unauthorized habitat by governmental authorities, or (iii) the same land as in
(ii) above, which government authorities have subsequently deemed as authorized habitat
by including locations under special schemes and developing minimum infrastructures
and providing minimum facilities such as electricity, water and sanitation. Wherever the
government does not allow people to live in a specific location and eviction is necessitated, it
may provide alternative settlement in exceptional cases. The first two categories suffer from
basic infrastructure problems in terms of electricity, sanitation, and water.

buses, by walking or bicycles or motorized two-wheelers. In rural areas, lack of access is characterized by few transport options to travel to nearby larger towns for medical treatment and for shopping needs. Long-distance communication is accomplished through the use of phone centers for calls, owning landlines, or owning cell phones. Indeed, cell phones are increasingly used, and provide an example of technology being viewed positively when it has clear benefits.

The use of cell phones also illustrates the adaptivity of users to new products. People have increasing exposure to a variety of information and products through television and word of mouth and are willing to try to learn about new products.

Energy needs for cooking include kerosene for stoves and gas cylinders for gas stoves. Electricity is used for lighting and appliances, although power supply is often not reliable.

Children's education is central to parents, with government schools or private schools as the two choices. People are willing to make sacrifices to enable their children to have a good education. Parents value schools with English as the medium of instruction. Similarly, many parents strive to send children to college. In rural areas, people typically have access to about the 8th grade or so for basic education, with further education requiring travel to a larger town. This latter constraint can be difficult or impossible for many girls to overcome, because parents are fearful of sending them a long distance from home. A noteworthy generational difference is the higher level of education for younger generations. It is less likely to find people with no education or first or second grade education among the younger generations.

Some expenses are directly related to spiritual and religious needs, such as for making religious offerings of fruits and other items at places of worship. Religious festivals are also occasions for travel and celebration with new clothes. Thus, they are often the single or few occasions in a year when people buy certain products—such as new clothing—by way of celebration.[6]

---

[6] Differences between urban and rural settings are significant and briefly mentioned throughout the chapter. Many of the people we interviewed in urban areas had migrated from villages to the big city. Rural settings are indeed striking in the lack of economic opportunity. Some who grow up in villages have experience from working in fields and from observing or participating in exchanges. The village often appears to be a place of strong relationships and social support, despite severe economic adversity and lack of easy access to goods and services. The city in comparison can initially be viewed as being harsh and frightening in several realms, including the economic. A woman who migrates from a village after marriage may be trained for a year or so by a relative (e.g., mother-in-law), often even staying in the same household and observing how to manage a household and buy products. Such a transitional arrangement appears to be an effective training ground for them independently managing a household in an urban area.

Food

Rice is the staple diet in South India. The word for rice has special meaning in its use synonymously with food, akin to the use of the term bread in other societies. Often, the focus of daily life is to have one square meal of rice a day. Even the poorest may pay a little more to get better quality rice. Lentils are purchased to make liquid dishes with spices and vegetables or meat, to go with rice. Vegetable and meat dishes are also prepared in a dry form to accompany the rice. With relatively higher income, these liquid and dry dishes become viable. The state where we conducted interviews also has an extensive cuisine of snack items that can serve as regular meals. With significant constraints, the only diet may be plain boiled rice with salt. In extreme adversity, food options are even more limited, such as a starch-based drink.

The quality of rice, as well as of other generic food items, depends on agricultural factors, such as the quality of the soil. Many products are generic, needing further processing, such as boiling. This is akin to making bread out of dough versus buying it directly. Trials are needed to determine whether rice boils appropriately. Some buyers may try out small quantities of rice before buying in larger amounts. The quality of rice is an important issue. There are many variables in how cooked rice turns out, and people manage the process of identifying the type to buy and of complaining to sellers. The same rice can be perceived as being of different quality by different people based on such factors as their style of boiling it or the type of water they use. Localized variations exist in factors such as water quality that affect the outcome. Many factors that are generally similar in western societies can affect the processing of food products in this context.

Rice is sold by neighborhood retailers and larger stores who deal in both retail and wholesale distribution, heretofore referred to as large resellers. Moreover, a set amount of rice and other basic necessities may be available through government ration, which is generally of poorer quality. Rice may also be obtained in bulk from villages for some who either own land or have relatives in villages engaged in farming.

Vegetables are usually sold by weight by neighborhood retailers, large resellers, street vendors, and larger markets, the latter being either just retail or both retail and wholesale. Often, lower quality assorted vegetables are sold at a lower price, not by individual weight but as an assortment of vegetables with a specific price. Very poor people often opt for such a purchase. Note that there is segmentation based on price going on at various levels in the value chain, from farmers using their land of different soil quality or farming later versus earlier in the season, to resellers sorting based on quality. Vendors may offer lower prices late in the day to avoid inventory being left over.

Health and Medicine

Medicine can range from homemade treatments to relatively inexpensive country medicine to allopathic medicine based on advice from a pharmacy or corner retail store to consultation with doctors, depending on the seriousness and duration of the illness. Government hospitals are the cheapest option, providing free consultations and medicine, but they have restricted hours.[7] Private doctors, considered to offer better quality health care, usually charge more, with medicine being extra. Medical doctors are identified and assessed for effectiveness, and those perceived as being good or lucky for the patient develop a loyal following. Patients ask their doctors to check filled prescriptions for accuracy, reflecting a one-to-one interactional marketplace. In rural areas, lack of access includes distances to be traveled for medical treatments. Bicycles and public buses are possibilities, but options are often restricted during the night hours, leading some individuals to suffer through the night without medical attention.

One form of capital that people have, often the only form, is their own body. They sacrifice their bodies, often neglecting health concerns until it is too late. There is resignation and acceptance in health-related issues. Only when health is affected to the point of affecting earnings do some seek out medical attention.

The following interviews with individual participants regard their health care options and treatments.

Excerpts from Interview with Rani

Rani is a 30-year-old woman with no formal education.

Interviewer: Where do you go for treatment when you are ill?

Rani: I always go to the government hospital. But I would take the children to private practitioners when they fell ill. The treatment in the government hospital is not very effective. When I take the children to the government hospital, they advise [the children] to take ¼ tablet or ½ tablet when we are supposed to take 1 tablet. So, it won't be cured.

But, I wouldn't prefer a [private practitioner] for myself; I would compromise and go to the government hospital. We get treatment from the private practitioner only for children.

---

[7] Whereas there are no consultation charges in government hospitals, fees may be charged for X-rays and other tests.

Interviewer: Is the private hospital located nearby or at a distance?

Rani: It is situated near my house.

Interviewer: How much do you pay for doctor's fees?

Rani: He would charge Rs.20 and provide drugs, too. When we go for treatment for a cough and cold, [the private practitioner] gives cough medicine, tablets, everything. He prescribes medicine if we feel that the child is too ill and we ask him to prescribe. Otherwise, he won't prescribe. The drugs he provides are sufficient.

Interviewer: It would be cured…if he prescribes.

Rani: I would ask [the practitioner] to prescribe; I can't tolerate when the children are affected by cough and wheezing. Otherwise, there would be high shivering due to fever. They would be crying. I am struggling completely for the children. I should take care of them, so I ask the doctor to prescribe medicines and assure him that I will buy them outside. He would prescribe within Rs.20 to Rs.30.

Interviewer: Where do you buy those medicines?

Rani: There is a medical shop nearby. I would buy them there.

Interviewer: You buy them at the medical shop. OK. Do you check whether they are giving the same medicine prescribed by the doctor?

Rani: Yes. I check. I take it and show it to the doctor. "See doctor, whether the medicines are the right ones." After checking, he would advise doses to be taken and timings in a day.

Here is an example of how things may work in a one-to-one world, with the patient taking the purchased medicine back to the doctor to make sure it is the right one. Here, this lady takes her children to a private doctor while treating her own health at the government hospital, which she views as lower in quality.

Excerpts from Interview with Badri and Sivakami

Badri is a 37-year-old man with a 5th-grade education; Sivakami, who has no formal education, is his 30-year-old wife.

Interviewer: Do you go to the hospital when you are sick?

Badri: If I have the money, I go to the hospital or else I buy medicine from the shop.

Interviewer: Where do you go to buy the medicine?

Sivakami: Medical store.

Interviewer: You buy it from a medical store when you have money.

Badri: If I have the money I take an injection.

Interviewer: Whom do you go to? Badri: Dr. [name of doctor]. Interviewer: What are his fees?

Badri: The fees are Rs.20. I go to him if I have Rs.40 or else I will get medicines for two times.

Interviewer: You go buy the medicines from the medical shop. Do you check the medicines?

Badri: All these things, I don't know sir.

Sivakami: We don't know much about the medicine. We accept whichever medicine they give. We accept it, even for our children.

Interviewer: When do you go to the doctor?

Badri: Only when we are very unwell do we go to the doctor. When we are attacked by fever and are unable to walk, we go. If we get a cough or slight fever, we take the medicine from the shop.

Interviewer: Do you go to the government hospital?

Badri: We have no time to go to the government hospital.

Interviewer: You can't go in time?

Badri: Instead of going to the hospital I go to Dr. [name of doctor] who will clearly see and give medicine, duly telling us how to take the medicine, but it is not so in the hospital, where they will give the medicine without even telling us how to take it. But [name of doctor] will tell us to take porridge or bread and take the pills.

Interviewer: Does he administer injections?

Badri: He administers injections and for that reason I go to him. The injections make us all right.

Interviewer: In which shop do you buy the medicine when he prescribes it?

Badri: Medical shop, sir.

Interviewer: Do they give the correct medicine?

Badri: They give the same medicine which he prescribes.

Interviewer: How do you know that?

Badri: I look at the first letter, sir. It is in English. But there will be a number like 550, 5500. I look at the first number. I ask my children to look at the number.

When going to a doctor, an injection is a hallmark of good treatment. As this person states, he goes to a doctor because the doctor administers an injection, apparently even for common colds. An option here is to go to a government hospital, which has restricted times to see patients, and sparse instruction when compared to a private doctor. In terms of medicine bought at pharmacies, some people do not check, but take whatever is given. Others match the first letter, as Badri mentioned. Some people take the medicine back to the doctor to confirm that it is the right one.

Excerpts from Interview with Kavitha

Kavitha is a 38-year-old woman with a 5th-grade education.

Interviewer: Do you visit the same doctor every time you are ill?

Kavitha: We visit the same doctor.

Interviewer: Why do you visit the particular doctor?

Kavitha: We get cured when he administers the injections, it is healed immediately, and we get an instant remedy. He is a kind of lucky and auspicious person. We are cured if we get treatment from him; hence, we visit him. Other doctors would ask us to visit again and again. He doesn't do this; he administers an injection and tells us that it will be cured in one visit.

Interviewer: Is there any difference in the fees between doctors?

Kavitha: All charge the same fee of Rs.20.

Interviewer: He, too, charges twenty rupees.

Kavitha: However, he charges twenty rupees and prescribes medicines for seventy-five rupees.... If we went to another doctor, he would prescribe costly medicines for one hundred rupees and ask us to visit him again and again for three days. He would administer three injections, too. The fees would cost around 60 rupees and the medicine cost around 100 rupees, so it would cost a total of 160 rupees. But, we visit the same doctor here and try to finish it within 100 rupees.

Interviewer: He administers an injection for which kind of problems? Are the injections for fever?

Kavitha: He would administer an injection if we went with a fever or cough with a cold. Earlier, he provided both the injections and medicines. Now, it is not like that. He injects if we buy the drugs from medical stores and give them to him. It costs around 30 rupees to buy the injection drug.

Interviewer: Now, which medical shop do you use?

Kavitha: There is a medical shop on the main road; we buy there. We go directly from the clinic to the shop and buy the medicine.

Interviewer: The price is less or higher there?

Kavitha: No, it is all same price.

Interviewer: Would you buy any medicine without consulting the doctor, for headaches or similar problems?

Kavitha: Yes, we crush ginger and pepper and boil them with water to prepare a kind of syrup at home; it arrests the cough and fever when we have a glass.

Interviewer: Would you buy any medicines from the shop without going to doctor?

Kavitha: We have. If we tell them that we have a headache or cold with cough and ask them to give us medicine, they give them to us.

Several issues pertaining to medical attention are relevant here. Sometimes, the seller at the pharmacy administers medicine after hearing the symptoms. People usually visit doctors when they are severely affected by an ailment to the point of affecting earnings or when their children suffer from ailments. Otherwise, they may try some home remedy or ask the neighborhood pharmacist for some medicine. When visiting the doctor, they develop a relationship, often considering whether a particular doctor is lucky for them. Perceptions of 'lucky doctors' stemming from past experience play an important role in deciding on doctors. With medicines, people may buy a small, affordable fraction of the total dosage prescribed. Sometimes, individuals may diagnose their own conditions and buy and use medicines prescribed for previous illnesses that appear to be similar.

Clothing and Ornaments

In this mostly warm-weather climate, clothing is often bought from street vendors, at large stores that cater to low-income clientele, or from door-to-door resellers. Whereas sidewalk vendors provide cheaper prices, they usually don't sell matched sets of clothing, and because of their lower quantities of clothes, people must search longer for what they need from vendors, compared to when they shop in stores.

With daily urgency related to basic necessities, other possessions take a back seat or have symbolic value. For example, buying a silk sari (which costs about Rs. 2000 or more) or jewels symbolizes good times, and people treat themselves to these possessions for occasions such as festivals or weddings. But this is distinctly different from the desire to constantly accumulate possessions. Rather, most people are fixated on their next meal, on food and basic necessities, coupled with the occasional, symbolic materialistic purchase to treat oneself to better things, to keep as a reminder of better times, and sometimes to use as an investment to pawn or sell in times of need.[8]

Financial Products

Financial products are, of course, central to day-to-day living in subsistence contexts. The literature has examined the complexities associated with financial

---

[8] Jewels are particularly useful in this regard. Consumers purchase jewelry in good economic times and pawn them in time of need. This is discussed in more detail later.

services for the poor (cf., Rutherford, 2000). We report on a variety of financial services. This discussion is organized into savings and loan alternatives.

Savings Options

Different savings services abound, often motivated by fear of interacting with larger banks. People are anxious about filling out forms due to literacy problems, or because of their perceived need to know English. In some communities, non-governmental organizations (NGOs) or self-help groups run savings services to encourage regular savings, with collection even occurring door-to-door. The neighborhood retailer may also be willing to safeguard money from neighbors, family members, and thieves for a fee.

Stores may also offer "chit" services; an example of this is a Rs. 10-per-day savings requirement over 100 days, with a bulk amount of Rs. 950 returned. Accounts are maintained by marking a card with 100 boxes on it—a pictorial representation equally meaningful to the literate and low-literate. Savings amounts vary and can be as low as one rupee per day. Savings amounts can also vary between visits (e.g., a customer visits with ten rupees, buys items for eight rupees, and leaves the balance towards the savings plan). The record-keeping system varies based on the arrangement.

Some savings services are communal, as when a chit organizer enrolls members into services that vary by maturity period, amount due, and net chit amount received, based on saving capacity of members. If ten members joined in the chit service with a chit sum of Rs. 10,000, the chit conductor would invite bids from the members on a specific date every month to receive the collection for the month. Members who are in need may bid if they are ready to receive something less than the monthly collection of Rs. 10,000, for example Rs. 9,000. This discounted Rs. 1000 would be shared by all members as a benefit of the service and the members can pay just Rs. 900 instead of Rs. 1000 as the due amount for that particular month.

At the same time, the bid amount or discount is a form of interest charged on those receiving the money in advance or prior to the completion of the chit period of ten months. In this order, nine members would get the money in advance and prior to the completion and pay the bid amount, akin to paying interest. The tenth person who receives the money at the end of the tenth month would get the full amount, Rs. 10,000, but would have paid less than the monthly due for the nine months.

Kavitha, the 38-year-old woman who earlier spoke about medical options, responds to the question of whether a chit conductor would visit door to door:

Kavitha: They won't visit; they invite the neighbors and people known to them for the enrollment. They would tell us that [the conductor] is going to start chits and would ask us whether we are interested in joining. We should be present [at the scheme organizer's house/place] promptly on every tenth day [of the month]. We should be ready with the chit amount when the bidding starts. Collected chit money would be available for bidding. Those interested can join in the bidding. Whether you join the bid and take the money or not, you should remit your monthly chit dues immediately to the organizer.

Here, the chit conductor is a de-facto member of the team and fully responsible for collecting amounts from other members and providing funds to the bidder within a reasonable timeframe. The benefit for the chit conductor is that she or he may be able to take the full amount of the second month's collection bidding. Another benefit may be that each month, bidders may pay 2% of the total chit (Rs.10,000) to the chit conductor (Rs.200). Chit services are examples of need-based savings services originating in the community. Peer pressure is an important element in these services.

How Buying on Credit is Viewed

Loan alternatives include buying for credit at the neighborhood store. Following is a quote from Velamma, a 45-year-old woman with a 5th-grade education introduced in Chapter 1, about her thoughts on buying for credit.

Interviewer: Do you make purchases in wholesale shops for cash or any credit?

Velamma: No credit, only cash payment on hand.

Interviewer: Cash on hand purchase?

Velamma: Yes, cash on hand.

Interviewer: Have you bought anything on credit recently?

Velamma avoids credit due to the loss of control over the accuracy of transactions and the possibility of being charged more than she owes. Rani, a 30-year-old woman with no formal education, speaks of the loss of respect that comes with credit purchases.

Interviewer: Do you feel that when you go there to make purchases, the people at the shop respect you, using kind words and enquiring about your needs?

Rani: How can he? If we had money, everyone would respect us… when my husband used to go for jobs. Once when he had a problem, I approached the [local shop owner]. He told me that he was ready to give more credit. I won't buy credit usually. I fear whether we could repay it or not. However, what could I do? [My husband] went without looking for a job for 10 days once. During that time, I got credit for Rs.100.

[The shop owner] harassed me a lot while my husband was there. I felt so sad. Then I got money unexpectedly, and the first thing I did was to settle the credit. From that incident I feared credit. I won't buy on credit from anybody.

Interviewer: So, the local shop owner shouted because you bought on credit.

Rani: He shouted loudly. Why do we need this? We don't want credit.

Interviewer: Will he respect and speak politely, if you don't buy on credit?

Rani: Yes, people respect whoever [pays cash].

Here, the local shop owner disrespects the buyer who purchases on credit. Such disrespect stems from the lower means and income level of the buyer. We also found situations, however, where the relationship is amicable and respectful. The neighborhood retailer will likely exert influence if the buyer who owes money purchases from a different store, such as a large reseller. In some instances, the neighborhood retailer may ask that some items be bought at his or her store and others at the wholesale store.

Loans Without Collateral

There are many forms of loans available. Here is an example of a loan without collateral. Mythili is a 40-year-old woman with a 4th-grade education.

Mythili: [A loan] is borrowed money. I won't borrow for interest. I would borrow for temporary receipt. If no one is there to help me,

I would go for [a high-interest non-collateral loan].... It has a daily repayment arrangement.

Interviewer: How much have you borrowed?

Mythili: I would borrow Rs.1,000 from [a high-interest non-collateral lender]. I would agree to pay Rs.10 daily.

Interviewer: How many days do you have to repay?

Mythili: I have to pay for 90 days.

Interviewer: OK, it is for Rs.1,000.

Mythili: 90 to 100 days.

Interviewer: How much would they deduct when paying you?

Mythili: They would deduct Rs.150.

Interviewer: They deducted?

Mythili: They would give me Rs.850 after deducting Rs.150, which I should repay correctly in 100 days. Rs.1,000 in 100 days.

This is similar to a Rs. 850 loan at an average balance of Rs. 425 over 50 days with a Rs. 150 interest, which works out to an annual interest rate of 258% $[(150/425) \times (365/50)]$. Even higher rates are common. Loans without collateral are usually the ones with high interest rates, often enforced through the threat of public humiliation. Non-collateral lenders enforce payment through public humiliation, using offensive language and expletives outside a person's house when he or she fails to make a payment.

For example, listen to what Sumitra, a 46-year-old woman with no formal education introduced in Chapter 1, says when she is asked if she has had to borrow without collateral:

Sumitra: We had borrowed Rs.30,000 when my husband was ill. The moneylender came once and shouted with filthy words. We felt sad and worried much. My husband felt that the person who came up well [in life] with his support shouted at him because of the credit. So, he instructed that I should not go to [the moneylender], whatever the family situation in the future.

Sumitra was deeply pained about the public humiliation many years later, recounting how her husband was anguished by the event and how the lender had been someone the husband had helped before. There is genuine fear of such humiliation, and it appears to be an effective mechanism in a one-to-one world, where sometimes the only thing that people possess is their dignity. Some avoid taking loans just because of this fear, while others have learned through experience.

Pledging Jewelry

Pledging jewelry is a preferred option for those with the means to make the initial purchase. After relatively large earnings, individuals will often purchase some pieces of jewelry (e.g., gold arm bracelets, pendants) that serve both as adornments and a "rainy day" savings account. They will pledge their jewelry in bad times for a loan, with a year to redeem the jewelry. Whether they actually redeem the jewelry or not, the choice of redemption is one that people like to have.

People often prefer buying jewelry to regular savings. There is symbolic value in owning and using it; it is a remembrance of good times. Moreover, pledging does not require people to commit to regular payments with uncertain future income, as compared to other loan arrangements.

Following are quotes from Murali, a 40-year-old man with an 8th-grade education, and Chandra, a 28-year-old woman with no formal education, about pledging jewelry.

> **Interviewer:** So, you would pledge the jewels when you had money problems and then you would redeem them? You talked about the redemption. What amount would you pledge and what would be the redemption amount?

> **Murali:** Yes sir, it would be less. We buy material for Rs.1,000 or Rs.800. We may have to pledge it for Rs.400. If we don't have a regular job in the subsequent months, we have to lose that article [without redeeming it]. It becomes a big loss to us. We have only those items to manage our crisis situations on time. We have nothing else.

> **Interviewer:** Rainy seasons are difficult times in your profession?

> **Murali:** Yes, we have to suffer on those days.

> **Interviewer:** So, this is an option you have and you adjust?

Murali: Yes, sir.

Interviewer: I mean you buy jewels or articles and pledge it when you are in need.

Murali: Yes, we used to pledge. If we joined in a chit, we may not be in a position to pay it regularly, especially when we don't have a regular job. It would be a problem when we could not pay on time. Hence, we prefer to have articles or jewels [to pledge] and we would adjust.

Chandra: Yes, I have done so even very recently. We have pledged the jewels. Still, we are not in a position to redeem it.

Interviewer: You are unable to redeem it and it is still there. So, sometimes you pledge the jewels and get the money to manage.

Chandra: Yes.

Interviewer: Why do you pledge like that? Few people take loans without pledging any items and few get money after pledging their jewels as capital. Why do you borrow like this?

Chandra: They would come to my house and shout if I got a loan. If I pledge my articles and get money, I can be fearless. I can redeem it whenever I wish. They won't come and shout in front of my house. So we decided that we should borrow after pledging our articles.

Interviewer: How much interest is this? How much do they charge from you as interest if you pledge the jewels and get money?

Chandra: They fix and charge Rs.2.50 or Rs.3.

Interviewer 2: How much would you be charged with interest if you took a loan from someone without pledging any articles?

Chandra: I don't borrow for interest like that... Maybe for temporary cash rotation of about Rs.500.

Here, the rate of interest is Rs.2.50 or Rs.3 per month, per 100 rupees. In addition, Rs.10 may be levied for document charges and a month's interest may be deducted in advance from the loan amount. Loans through pledging valuable items versus loans without collateral, which come with the potential for public humiliation, are often the options that people consider.

Entertainment Options

Movies, either on TV or in theaters, soap operas, and variations on these forms are primary means for entertainment, along with fairs during religious festivals. Televisions are increasingly owned and provide almost all the entertainment. Through installment plans, individuals may buy a black and white television for about Rs. 2,400 (for example, in installments of Rs. 100 a month for 24 months), with cable costing around Rs. 100 per month. Government programs also offer free televisions for households. Some may prefer to buy a newspaper or go to a movie rather than consider buying a television because it involves a longer-term financial commitment.

With severe income constraints, individuals may avoid going to movies or even avoid going out of the home except for work. They may avoid going to a nearby food vendor even to buy and drink tea due to lack of money, either making items or foregoing them altogether. Even under these circumstances, festivals are often celebrated. For certain festivals, people may take a trip to their home village or town or spend some money at a fair.

Market Interactions

The discussion to this point has centered on the set of products purchased by the subsistence customer. Embedded in this discussion were interactions with sellers and the marketplace, which are difficult, if not impossible, to separate from the set of products. This section focuses on interactions of subsistence customers with the marketplace and the primary economic relationships they form.

Neighborhood Retail Stores and Large Resellers

The typical person in these subsistence marketplaces has a primary economic relationship with one store. Usually, in urban areas, this is likely to be a small neighborhood retail store that buys generic products at wholesale rates and sells to the local community. Geographic proximity in terms of a neighborhood and lack of mobility are key considerations, the latter due to cost of travel for longer distances, time constraints due to restrictive work schedules, and just-in-time daily wages (i.e., wages earned by evening, with the need to prepare one meal soon after). The primary relationship may also be with a larger store located farther away that sells to retailers as well as individuals.[9]

---

[9] The term *wholesaler* may be somewhat misleading in that such outlets may be larger stores that resell to retailers and sell directly to end users; hence our use of the term *large reseller*.

Both retailers and large resellers are characterized by their responsiveness to customer needs and a very detailed knowledge of individual customers, akin to and in some ways better than sophisticated databases. They accept product returns, allow exchanges for bad products, adjust supply based on customer complaints, sometimes deliver products to homes, and generally strive to satisfy customers. Customers may often resort to trial and error to try out products, such as a variety of lentils, and provide regular feedback to sellers about products, such as rice varieties.

Due to income constraints, people often buy from neighborhood retailers at higher prices. The retailer is also used for last-minute convenience purchases, such as for a final ingredient during cooking, a common occurrence with daily wages. The large reseller sells to retailers as well and may reserve credit only for customers with large monthly expenditures, beyond what is typical for low-income households.

The neighborhood retailer is more likely to offer credit for low-income residents of the neighborhood. For those with sufficient money at the beginning of the month, the large reseller provides practically all the necessities, responsive service, and refunds or returns. However, with people earning weekly or daily incomes, or receiving payment later in a month for monthly income, the large reseller is often not a viable alternative. People buy from a retailer, who usually charges higher prices, and offers credit. Thus, the customer is tied to the retailer who may likely ask for full repayment if patronage stops or decreases. The retailer is usually responsive to customer needs. Regular customers often receive better treatment in terms of weightings, extras, and discounts. The neighborhood retailer may price higher for credit purchases, usually without explicitly communicating with customers and usually on generic products (e.g., charging Rs.16 for a kg of rice instead of Rs.13 or 14).

By helping in time of need, being responsive, and providing credit, the neighborhood retailer often cements relationships with customers and elicits loyalty. One customer, when asked whether she enquires about the price of a product she is buying from the neighborhood retailer, wondered aloud how he would feel because he helps by providing credit in time of need. In fact, when customers begin to purchase regularly at an outlet, they may tend to stop checking prices even when they are capable of doing so.

Loyalty to Local Stores

A number of factors lead to loyalty to specific outlets, primary among them being credit received in times of need. In a world of geographic proximity, patronage of a different store when owing money to a specific store may not be viable. The fear of needing credit in times of need in the future is a strong motivator. Loyalty to neighborhood retailers is influenced by credit, which represents help in time of need, and a hold over the customer, and by the need to patronize and encourage a local business.

The balance between purchases from a large reseller versus a neighborhood retailer, while triggered by income and credit, also involves other complexities. The retail shop owner provides more customized service than the large reseller in some respects. Purchase patterns are not just due to income management but also due to consumption management. Buying things in larger quantities may not be preferable when consumption may have to be restricted to a minimum down the road. Kavitha, a 38-year-old woman with a 5th-grade education, describes her experiences purchasing in local shops.

> **Interviewer:** Now, you buy from a shop in bulk. Suppose you wish to return anything, would that shop accept it? Do they know who you are?
>
> **Kavitha:** Yes, they know. This is the shop where we always buy. If we didn't want an item or an item were missed in the supplied provision, we would go ask, and they would give [the item] though we don't show the bill. It is a trusted shop.
>
> **Interviewer:** So, you say that every month, first you used to buy from the large reseller. Instead, if you buy the same from the local shop owner [a neighborhood retailer], he will get some income. Now, he loses that income because you visit the large reseller. Would he not be concerned about this?
>
> **Kavitha:** He would ask. I would tell him that I bought the items that he didn't have from the large reseller. He would tell us, "Okay, you buy a few items there and a few here."
>
> **Interviewer:** If you bought from the wholesale shop, you could save Rs.100 or Rs.150 in a month. Why don't you go shop there?
>
> **Kavitha:** Sir, we don't have the money; it isn't available. [My husband] gives me the money daily. I save from this and buy from the nearest shop.

Here, the buyer balances purchases between the large reseller and the neighborhood retailer, essentially providing some business for each. Daily income is a major constraint in buying from the large reseller, which requires having sufficient money but can lead to savings in prices paid. Because of an established relationship, the local retailer is responsive to needs, returns and refunds, adjusting his supplies based on feedback from customers.

Whereas urban areas are characterized by a plethora of stores, lack of mobility makes the neighborhood store a central part of people's economic relationships. In a rural setting, access is severely restricted and a larger nearby town may be miles away with few modes of transportation. Retailers or mobile vendors may charge sizably higher prices due to transportation costs to buy from larger towns.

Installment Plans for Bigger-Ticket Items

Occasional purchases of somewhat big-ticket items are made through installment plans. Individual sellers buy clothing and small appliances (big-ticket items in this context) from retail or wholesale outlets and sell on an installment plan, thus enabling customers to procure products beyond their immediate means, although at very high interest rates. Companies offer much lower interest rates but for much bigger purchases, such as televisions. Thus, the installment seller, often a member of the same community, offers a product and service that caters to the needs of the community. The low-income, low-literate marketplace studied here in some ways can reflect a truly free marketplace with seller and buyer exerting balancing influences.

A number of community-based services include installment plans for relatively more expensive items. Individuals offer services to buy relatively expensive products, such as large vessels, through installments with monthly payments over many months. What constitutes bigger ticket items is, of course, relative. Products like clothing could be bought through installments. Mixies (blenders), cookers, and chairs may also be bought through installments.

Following is from an interview with 37-year-old Badri and his 30-year-old wife, Sivakami. Badri has a 5th-grade education and Sivakami has no formal education.

Interviewer: What are the items you have purchased in installments?

Badri: Clothing for women.

Sivakami: We have bought articles and simple clothing for men and saris.

Interviewer: Have you bought clothing in installments and are these items up to your standard?

Sivakami: We don't know that it is of good standard, but we buy it.

Badri: But due to the circumstances, we buy. We cannot pay in full since we have to meet daily expenditure and hence, we will pay Rs.5 or Rs.10 daily and clear the account.

Interviewer: But the quality is not so good?

Sivakami: No.

Badri: These clothes have been bought this way. We cannot pay the price in full. In a shop, a good [men's clothing item] costs Rs.70 but we cannot pay the price in full. We cannot save that amount, and if we do, there will be some other expenditure to be met.

Interviewer: Do you return the clothing bought in installments if the color goes away?

Badri: They would not take it back, sir.

Interviewer: What would you do?

Sivakami: We would reduce Rs.10.

Interviewer: So you would say that the color has faded and reduce the amount of payment? Have you ever said that you would not wear such clothes bought in installments?

Sivakami: No sir, we would not say that. Even if we said so, the seller would not agree. So we reduce Rs.5 or Rs.10, stating that the color is fading and the clothes are not of good standard and not good clothes. But they would not reduce in full.

Even though products are of lower quality, the installment plan enables low-income individuals to buy them. Installment plans, even for relatively inexpensive products such as clothing or small appliances, are common and make purchases affordable while also forcing people to save appropriately to make payments. With defective products, adjustments are made in the price. In some cases, the buyers may just stop paying.

Buying on installment often leads to the purchase of poorer quality products. Using a fictitious example, a "Malathi" stove may be a well-reputed product. However, a "Malanthi" (emphasis added) stove is not as good but may be sold as the former. Low-literate customers, who match patterns rather than read, are susceptible to such tactics.

Characteristics of Product and Market Interactions

Some important characteristics of this marketplace context, based on the product and market interactions of individuals as customers described earlier, are discussed here.

Uncertainty, Complexity, and Lack of Control

One of the most important factors to understand in gaining insight into the subsistence marketplace is uncertainty and lack of control over many aspects of day-to-day life, whether it is the quality or quantity of water or the availability of electricity. This, of course, follows directly from being resource-poor; with very little resources, the poor have little control over the basic amenities that may be taken for granted by people in higher strata of society.

Overlaying these issues is the level of complexity in a variety of realms of day-to-day life that distinguishes a transitional context such as India from Western societies. Basic services such as transportation are subject to greater variation in India when compared to the West. The level of complexity in a number of domains is very high due to the number of variables involved, the interactions among these variables, and the considerable uncertainty and variation experienced on these variables. Complexity is inherent in meeting basic necessities such as food preparation cooked from generic ingredients, which in turn, is dependent on uncontrollable factors, such as quantity and quality of water and quality of generic ingredients.

One-to-One Interactions

Perhaps the most striking characteristic of the marketplace in subsistence contexts is the network-rich, one-to-one interactional nature, such as the one-on-one relationship between buyers and sellers. This leads to accountability and service considerations on the part of the seller. The environment is characterized by continuous interaction between buyer and seller. The seller knows buyer preferences and there is continuous communication. Price and quantity is negotiated, installments are not paid, prices are adjusted for personal circumstances both to buyer and seller advantages, and community-based service providers balance buyer and seller needs, enforce contracts, and are aware of specific needs and purchasing power.

Credit and help in times of need lead to strong relationships between buyers and sellers. Creditworthiness is determined by the retailer (or by the individual seller on installment purchases or the money-lender for loans). This system is, in some ways, more sophisticated than complex customer databases. Retailers offer additional services, such as credit purchases to people in need. In turn, retailers keep accounts and may overcharge for credit purchases without explicitly informing the customer, although this practice is implicitly known.

Retailers also provide the service of securely keeping customers' savings in return for a charge (for example, a 10 percent negative interest). Customized service and product returns are often the norm, sometimes an almost customer-level democracy in action where accountability is expected or demanded at the grassroots level. Shopkeepers may respond to feisty behavior from customers with better treatment. Small numbers in terms of customers and local ownership, direct interaction, and powerful word-of-mouth, are all pertinent factors. Direct feedback on products leads to appropriate stocking decisions by sellers. Large resellers deliver products, and accept product returns of some regular customers. Savings services reflect the one-to-one interactional marketplace and are characterized by a sense of community.

As discussed, several services are offered that address community needs, such as resellers going door-to-door to sell products on affordable installment plans, although at extremely high interest rates. Buying on installment may sometimes lead to poorer quality products. Customers may always have the power to stop payments for poor products. Refusal to pay subsequent installments for a defective product is one form of redress. Word-of-mouth is very strong, whether among customers or between customers and sellers.

Irrespective of financial constraints, certain traditions during death, marriage or religious ceremonies are usually maintained, even and often by borrowing money. A salient motive here is to avoid being spoken ill of. Maintenance of tradition even in dire financial circumstances follows from the centrality of one-to-one interactions. Medical doctors are identified and assessed for effectiveness, with loyalty usually following. One-to-one interactions include patients asking their doctors to check filled prescriptions from pharmacies for accuracy.

Make-or-Buy Decisions

A key aspect of customer interactions is the decision to make something, buy something, or forego it altogether. The make-or-buy decision applies in several realms, such as visiting a hotel or making ingredients such as powders for cooking. The make option is cheaper, allowing customization even across family members (e.g., making cooking powders with different ingredients depending on age). Following are quotes from interviews—with Badri, a 37-year-old man with a 5th-grade education, and Mythili, a 40-year-old woman with a 4th-grade education—related to this decision.

Interviewer: So you grind these items. What is the difference in going to a shop and purchasing these items versus grinding these items?

Badri: If we bought these items they would not be good. They would not be hot and they would be different. These items are adulterated. I buy chili and [another type of spice] powder from the shop and grind them myself, which is good for health and also very tasty.

Interviewer: What is the price when you buy it outside versus when you prepare it at home?

Badri: In the shop the item would be less, but when we prepare in the house there is more, and the quality would also be good.

Interviewer: When you make the item in the house it will be costly?

Badri: It will be clean.

This is another example of a make-or-buy decision. Here, the make decision happens to be costlier, which is not usually the case, while providing more benefits.

Interviewer: Do you prepare anything at home that is needed for cooking?

Mythili: I would make [chili powder].

Interviewer: Would you grind it yourself?

Mythili: Yes, for chili.

Interviewer: You buy all ingredients and…?

Mythili: We would grind at a machine [flour mill].

Interviewer: Why are you not buying at shops?

Mythili: We would get stomach pain because of it. We don't know what they are mixing in the shop with the chili powder. Last month, we all had stomach pain because we ate the food prepared with the powder bought at the shop.

Interviewer: It was not good?

Mythili: It was not at all good. I don't know why. We don't know what they are mixing and doing. They are talking about [a leading brand], it causes stomach pain. Stomach pain for everyone in our house. So, we always buy chilis and grind them first whether we have anything else or not. Last month, at the end of the month, I had no money. Since I bought it in the shop, it was happening like that.

Interviewer: OK. Is there any price difference between the chili powder bought in the shop and grinding powder in the machine yourselves?

Mythili: It would be little more [quantity] than buying the powder at the shop. The price would be less too. If you spent Rs.100, the price of chili is high. If you spent Rs.100 or Rs.150, it could be used for three months freely. Money could be saved and the item too would be a quality one. We grind it with our supervision. It would be clean and good for everything.

The make-or-buy decision is also related to the idea of consuming natural foods rather than something in a package that may contain contaminants. In fact, hand-ground spices may be preferred to even using a grinder or over-packaged foods that may not be fresh. Small packages may also lead to wastage during transfer, another reason cited for the make option. The make option is more difficult when women work outside the house, leading to more of the buy option. The forego option is, of course, pervasive in many realms, such as in rationing or foregoing medicine and treatment for illnesses.

Transactional Fluidity

Another striking aspect of this subsistence context is the fluid nature of transactions. Pure exchange is not necessarily of the arm's-length variety. The transaction is often fluid, price and quantity are negotiated, installments are not paid, and prices are adjusted for personal circumstances both to buyer and seller advantages. Also, community-based service providers balance buyer and seller needs, enforce contracts, and are aware of specific needs and purchasing power.

Even weighing of products may differ, depending on the negotiated prices, with deliberate variations in the way the weighing balance, and the chain links are held (sometimes, weighing pans are of different weights). If a negotiated price is low, then customers may be shortchanged in the weighing. As one seller said when a relatively low price was negotiated for three pounds of grapes, but the amount seemed to be less by half a pound when weighed elsewhere, "That is the weighing you will get for that price"! Accurate weighing may occur when full price is given. Sellers clearly differentiate products by quality, and price accordingly. Thus, buyers have clear expectations for prices. Following are a few interview excerpts from Chandra (a 28 year-old woman with no formal education) and Mythili (a 40 year-old woman with a daily flower delivery service and a 4th-grade education) on the issue of fluidity of transactions.

> **Chandra:** If we go and ask [the shopkeepers about weighing], they would say, "No, no…it is the same price. I would have given [the other customers] a bit more quantity, that is why I had quoted them a slightly higher price. But, I would have given you a little less in weight, hence, I had given it to you for a lower price."

> **Mythili:** The weight depends on the weighing method. You can do tricks. The person who weighs the scale can keep the fingers open. If they push a finger to the right side it, [that side] would fall down. The innocent would think that they are getting more than the weight and the amount of supply is high and accept it. The experienced person should see the top of the scale.

Conclusion

This chapter summarizes the types, needs, and product and market interactions that characterize subsistence marketplaces, focusing on urban and rural South India. The purpose here is not to assert that these detailed descriptions generalize to other subsistence settings, but to describe subsistence contexts and interactions between individuals and marketplaces in one setting, and thereby distill more abstract traits that are endemic to these marketplaces across settings.

We can organize the set of products purchased by the subsistence customer into several categories (see Figure 2.1). At the surface level, this list does not seem very different from the needs of individuals in other segments of society. But underlying this surface similarity is affordability, with a very narrow range of product options being accessible to subsistence customers, and trade-offs between what the more affluent customer would consider necessities having to be made when crises arise.

In terms of a hierarchy of needs (Maslow, 1970), the lower-level needs— physiological and safety needs—take precedence, but social, esteem, and self-actualization needs are vitally important as well to people in subsistence contexts. Our categorization of needs is at a level appropriate for examining relationships with products and markets. However, we can categorize needs at a number of levels of abstraction to cover social and self-esteem needs.

The tenuousness of life circumstances creates a complex web of interdependencies and interactions between buyers and sellers, and may lead to loyalty to neighborhood retailers who are not the lowest-cost option. Several characteristics of these marketplace interactions are noteworthy, including the one-to-one nature of the environment and the fluidity of transactions. "Bigger ticket items" may include clothing, large utensils, jewelry and appliances, and financial services. Community-based service providers offer many of these services.

The broad context in which the product and market interactions occur is one of uncertainty in basic infrastructure, services, income, and lack of control over many aspects of daily life. In this larger context, product and market interactions are characterized by a network-rich, one-to-one interactional environment that, coupled with product complexity, may lead to experiential evaluation of products and stores. Decisions on which retailers to patronize are closely intertwined with product decisions; often, the two are inseparable. Also important is the make-or-buy (or forego) decision. At a broader level, adaptive strategies in response to adverse conditions require extraordinary adjustments in daily life. What is considered rational in relatively resource-rich environments in light of the certainties and assumptions, would be very different from what is rational for subsistence contexts.

References

Hill, R., W. Felice, and T. Ainscough. 2007. International human rights and quality of life: An ethical perspective. Journal of Macromarketing 27:370-9.

Kotler, P., N. Roberto, and T. Leisner. 2006. Alleviating poverty: A micro/macro perspective. Journal of Macromarketing 26:233-9.

Maslow, A. (1970). Motivation and Personality. New York: Harper and Row.

Narayan, D. & Petesch, P. (2000). Voices of the Poor: From Many Lands. New York, NY: Oxford Univ. Press.

Prahalad, C. K. (2005). The Fortune at the Bottom of the Pyramid. Upper Saddle River, N.J.: Wharton School Publishing.

Rutherford, S. (2000), The Poor and Their Money, OUP: India.

Sen, A. K. (1992). Inequality Reexamined. Cambridge, MA: Harvard Univ. Press.

Viswanathan, M., Gajendiran, S., and Venkatesan, R. (2007). Enabling Consumer and Entrepreneurial Literacy in Subsistence Marketplaces: A Research-Based Approach to Educational Programs. Springer.

Chapter 3
Understanding Subsistence Entrepreneurs[10]

Image 3.01: A vegetable seller and customers in Morocco. Photograph by Rookuzz; Creative Commons licensed image via Flickr: http://www.flickr.com/photos/72283508%40N00/2558609172/Flickr%E2%80%9D.

In this chapter, we describe subsistence entrepreneurs in terms of their day-to-day activities, their strengths, and their vulnerabilities. We describe how subsistence entrepreneurs negotiate three different domains—suppliers,

[10] This chapter includes material adapted from the following previously published work:

Viswanathan, Madhubalan, Jose Antonio Rosa, and Julie Ruth, "Exchanges in Marketing Systems: The Case of Subsistence Consumer Merchants in Chennai, India," *Journal of Marketing*, 74 (May), 1-18 (Lead article; Best Paper Runner-Up, MSI/Paul Root Award, *Journal of Marketing*, 2010, Best Paper Runner-Up, Harold H. Maynard Award, *Journal of Marketing*, 2010). DOI: 10.1509/jmkg.74.3.1

customers, and family—and how they move resources between these arenas. We again take a bottom-up approach in quoting directly from entrepreneurs.

Subsistence entrepreneurs are entrepreneurs who are poor themselves and operate small businesses in contexts of poverty, for the primary purpose of survival. Read the following stories from two subsistence entrepreneurs: Rukmini, a 50-year-old woman with no formal education, and Anita, a 46-year-old woman with no formal education.

> **Rukmini:** On one occasion, my situation became a little worse; my (family) income decreased. I had borrowed from a person against interest. She always intimidated me and sometimes she made forcible demands. In such a context, I decided that I could conduct a chit [financial service], as I could get the second month's collection and settle my debts.

> **Anita**: I did only the agricultural jobs at my native home. Then, once we shifted from there to here, I was wondering, "What should I do? How should I live?" As I was illiterate, I could not do any work at a company. I preferred to do a business on my own instead of bowing to someone and expecting wages. So, I used to make this vadai, bajji, etc. [snack items] and sell these items.

Subsistence entrepreneurs are embedded within the social milieu of their customers and operate their businesses in the face of extreme resource constraints and uncertainty. These uncertainties could arise from personal financial difficulties or external uncertainties such as eviction drives by state authorities.

> **Rukmini:** I have approached someone who is an outsider [for financing] but they are dragging it out and say today, later they say tomorrow, [delaying and postponing it whenever I meet them to seek financing]. We have fixed the date for our daughter's marriage; it is on the 26th of this month. I will be relaxed only when I know I will have sufficient money. I am worrying a lot about it, whether they would provide for me or not.

Poovizhi is a 32 year-old woman with a 2nd-grade education.

> **Poovizhi:** Yes, We had some times like that. There was no business for two or three days. We could not do anything for the children; we could not prepare food to provide for them. Sometimes, I would think about that and feel sad, because we could not do business when the City Corporation people arrived [to evict]. Due to [the

drive to evict encroachment on roadsides], they would take away all materials while we were doing good business. It would be very difficult for us in these times. It would be very tough to manage if they took away all the items. We have to adjust to all the difficulties, and profit and loss in the business.

The Entrepreneur-Supplier Relationship

In interacting with suppliers, entrepreneurs seek credit in light of their limited resources. Read the story of Narayan, a 32-year-old man with a diploma in electrical appliance maintenance, who has been delivering milk and operating a provision shop for seven years.

Narayan: Suppose the bill exceeds 200 rupees [US $4]. I would tell [the primary vendor] that I would give the balance amount of 50 rupees tomorrow. He would say OK and accept it since we buy regularly. He would give us [credit] based on trust. That's all.

Suppliers offer loans to known entrepreneurs, and a history of regular repayment leads to increased loans and cements relationships between primary suppliers and entrepreneurs. Vanita, a 35-year-old woman with 8th-grade education, who has been selling packaged snacks door-to-door for 10 years, says:

Vanita: I wouldn't go to other shops. I buy from that particular shop. I visit Parry's [an alternate vendor] to buy appalam [snacks] if [the primary vendor] is out of stock. [The primary vendor] would give [credit] if we don't have sufficient cash. I would say, "Shopkeeper, today I have no sufficient amount. I have problems. You give the items on credit. I would settle it immediately after the sales." The shopkeeper would accept it and give us. He knows the people who repay promptly. He would consider our request very sympathetically, as we are poor and struggle for life, and give credit to us. We would pay him back immediately after sales. As he is an acquainted person, we should think before changing the shop just because of lower rates [elsewhere]. Because he is an acquainted person, we couldn't just ignore him easily. We too should do something to help him.

Regular repayment is central in nurturing the relationship, with the premium being placed on actual behavior that follows through on verbal commitments. Parvathi, a 32-year-old woman and entrepreneur who has been selling pooja items used in devotional practices for three years, says:

Parvathi: When [the vendors] ask us to pay money on a day when there was nil business, and we tell them that we don't have money now and that [they should] collect it the next day, they shout at us, "Why do you say that you would pay tomorrow, while you have agreed and bought the loan against daily repayment?"

Suppliers in turn depend on and seek to strengthen relationships with small entrepreneurs. The following quotes reflect the importance of prices and product returns in such relationships.

> **Anita:** Since we buy from them regularly, they charge the same rate [each day]. They charge 46 rupees for oil, [but] if we bought the same oil from another place [and they found out], they would charge 47 or 48 rupees. The price would be higher if we bought from other shops.

Anita has been preparing and selling snacks for more than five years.

> **Parvathi:** We became known to each other and buy from there only. They would provide quality coconuts. If we buy here and there [from other vendors], they won't give good coconuts and they won't exchange the rotten ones. Sometimes they may exchange the sizes, but they won't provide other [services]. So, if there were one or two rotten coconuts they would take it back and give us good ones. That is why I buy from the same shop.

When the primary supplier does not have stock or closes business for a few days, entrepreneurs buy from alternate vendors. Mobilizing supplies from elsewhere is a way in which the supplier maintains a primary relationship with the entrepreneur. Mythili, a 40-year-old woman with a 4th-grade education, who has been preparing and selling pooja items for 20 years, describes this:

> **Mythili:** Suppose it was not available [from the primary vendor] and there was no stock. He would mobilize it from somewhere else and supply to us. Even if they couldn't mobilize, they would advise us to buy it from somewhere. In this case we must have identified an alternative shop nearer to us. Always we would have two shops that were located nearer to our place. Suppose the items like coconuts were not available in the shop where we shopped regularly. We would go to another shop that we have identified already.

The Entrepreneur-Customer Relationship

Entrepreneurs similarly build relationships with customers, offering them credit in times of need. Credit and responsiveness to customers work to strengthen the relationship between customers and entrepreneurs.

Anita: Two days, even one week, [regular customers] would take to pay [me]. They are all known people who are living here. They would buy and say that they would pay later. I wouldn't trust those [unknown] people and give [credit to them]. I would give [credit to] those who were living in this area who are known to me.

Such relationships engender positive feelings, allowing for leeway when products don't meet standards. In the words of Preethi, a 32-year-old woman with a 6th-grade education, who has been operating a garment sewing and sales operation for seven years:

Preethi: [Regular customers] won't return [the product]. They might complain that the work was not proper. Then I would assure them that hereafter I would stitch well their orders. Definitely, they would complain if the stitched items were very loose to them. We would alter and stitch it again to get tightness but they wouldn't demand us to take back the stitched [product] and provide them an alternative. It is not like that.

Entrepreneurs maintain relationships with customers and emphasize the importance of loyalty.

Mythili: If you buy a worship plate from me, you should continue to buy from me alone. If you buy here and there and are not buying from me regularly, but visit my shop once and ask me, even though I have [the product] I would say that I don't have [it in] stock. Because [I know] though you come to me today, you would buy from another shop tomorrow. If you have bought from us previously, we treat you with respect. We will even pack your needs in a bag and reserve them for you. If we find you in different shops, we will lose faith. We would supply if we had stock. Otherwise, we would tell [customers caught elsewhere], "Sir, it is not available now. Since you are not coming to my shop regularly I gave it to someone loyal who asked me just before you."

The entrepreneur above ensures that priests receive worship items, even when customers cannot make it but request in advance.

Entrepreneurs may have to customize offerings, while at the same time striving to adhere to general principles and managing communications with customers. This is a substantial challenge, as there are few (if any) private conversations with customers, and entrepreneurs have to address the constant demand for customization.

Janaki, a 34-year old woman with a 6th-grade education, who has been running a milk delivery business for more than 10 years, speaks about this issue:

> **Janaki:** We discussed in advance at the milk distribution depot that we [merchants] were going to raise the delivery charge to 15 rupees since there was a price hike in the market and we could not manage our families with the ten rupees rate. I told my customers that I raised the delivery charge to 15 rupees for the next month. [Some] customers accepted it and a few wouldn't agree, so I would try to retain as many customers as possible and tell the few customers who didn't agree [to] the price hike to continue to pay me at the old rate of ten rupees. I received it confidentially [and] informed the customers that they shouldn't reveal the rate I was collecting from them. I warned them that they would be in for a fight with me if they revealed my rate to others. If I demanded [the higher] rate I might have lost a customer.

If a customer receives a special deal, word can get out and everyone may ask for special deals. This is the tightrope the entrepreneur has to walk in customizing offerings in response to demands from customers.

> **Anita:** I won't give [a price reduction]. Never. If someone like a regular customer would ask me for one extra, I would agree and give. Supposing they buy [ten items] for ten rupees, I would give one extra. [But] I won't [sell] for 75 paise. If we gave to someone at the rate of 75 paise, then everyone would ask for the same price. Everyone in this area would start to ask for 75 paise if I gave it once. Could we afford it? We would incur loss. It would be known to everyone. We can't afford it. I look after the business sincerely. Then I have to cook and wash the clothes for my family. I spend my time like this.

Often, entrepreneurs need a sound rationale to offer special deals that can then be communicated when customers demand the same deal offered to someone else. Preethi explains:

> **Preethi:** I used to charge 22 rupees from the customers who belong to middle-income families, charge 25 rupees from those who come from rich families, and charge 20 rupees from those poor people who are getting low wages. One or two would question me. I would inform these people that I charge them only 20 rupees since they are poor and struggle in their life. I would caution them and inform these ladies not to reveal the rate to others, as I charge them less since they are economically struggling. They would listen to me.

Entrepreneurs often strive to develop a personal relationship with customers, blurring economic and human domains. Mythili notes:

Mythili: I would inquire, "How are you, sir? How is your wife? Do you have children? Do they attend school?" As I ask about them like that, definitely they would come to my shop in their next visit. They wouldn't go to any other shop. ... "How are you and your family members? Are you not feeling well?" If I ask you like that, you would prefer to visit my shop only. You wouldn't go to another shop.

In the context of this personal relationship, entrepreneurs are often candid with customers, such as a flower seller informing customers that she "tied the flowers with a little gap because the price is high in the market."

Figure 3.1 depicts the exchanges that occur between entrepreneurs and customers. Full explanation of this model is available elsewhere (Viswanathan et al., 2010).

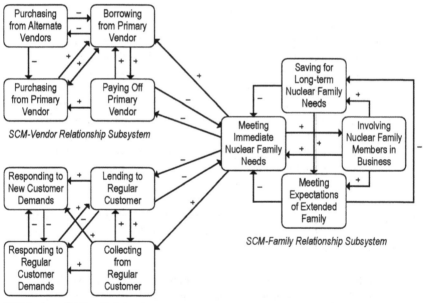

Figure 3.1: Role Performance Activities of Subsistence Consumer-Merchants in Vendor, Customer, and Family Relationship Subsystems, Viswanathan et al, 2010.

Understanding Subsistence Entrepreneurs

The Entrepreneur-Family Relationship

In terms of family, entrepreneurs ultimately run enterprises to survive; they seek well-being for themselves and their families. However, families are the buffer as suppliers and customers take priority and resources are drawn away from the family to meet their demands. Prema, a 36-year-old woman with a 3rd-grade education, who has been preparing and selling tea and tiffin for three years, explains:

> **Prema:** We wake up at five o'clock. Immediately after that, we light the stove, prepare the items, and sell to our customers. My husband and my children join me. All four of us serve the tiffin to customers and simultaneously complete other activities. We prepare lunch for at least 20 people. I slice and cut the vegetables to prepare the lunch while I serve the morning tiffin to our customers. Then, we rest for two hours in the afternoon. Again, we start our work by 4 p.m. We prepare and the tiffin is ready in the late evening. Then, we wash the vessels and grind the grains and make it ready for the next day. Apart from this, we list out and arrange the purchase of items for business on the next day. We make it ready and start the work in the next morning.

Children and other relatives are often central to running the enterprise as illustrated above, in Prema's example, and in Janaki's:

> **Janaki:** Even when I am not feeling well or have a serious illness, I have to go. Even if I request someone else, they can't do it because they don't know the houses to be delivered to. It would be new to them. Only known people can do [it]. As I have children, I take them along with me while I go for milk delivery. As I push the cart and approach the houses, my children take the milk packets and deliver at the homes on the different floors in the housing quarters. I wait at the ground floor and guide them to deliver at which houses.

Inventory is managed on a short-term basis and perishables have to be thrown away or used by the family on bad days. Sita, a 45-year-old woman with a 5th-grade education, who has been preparing and selling tiffin for 20 years, speaks on this issue as well:

> **Sita:** [My husband] buys the needs for our shop on the previous night. We shop in the daytime if we need anything for our family. [If short], I wouldn't prepare tea or coffee at the house. We don't buy in bulk. We buy the day-to-day needs.

Parvathi: Yesterday, since I expected good business, I purchased all items for 500 rupees to 1,000 rupees. But there was no big crowd. I got enough business only for 300 rupees or 400 rupees. [In spite of poor sales], we have to acquire the necessary items for business the next day. We have to throw away the unsold perishable items. We have to adjust and be prepared to meet everything in the business.

After meeting business needs, high priority needs such as children's education take priority, often pushing basic needs to the background.

Sita: We have to meet the family expenses from the business profit. We must pay the rent and electricity bill. My daughter's annual school fee is 3,750 rupees [about US $75]. We remit the remaining balance to the bank account, in little amounts, and save it. As we feel that we would spend it if it were cash on hand, we remit it. When we have a balance amount, then we use it to pay the school fee.

Family members sacrifice needs so the enterprise can survive and to support the family. Commitments with the extended family are also a central consideration for entrepreneurs.

Sita: My husband was working in a coffee shop when I married him. Since his [unmarried] sisters were also in the family, the income was not sufficient. So, he decided to start a small tiffin shop on his own. We used it as a base and gradually improved our life.

As mentioned earlier in the chapter and repeated here for convenience, Poovizhi speaks of the sacrifice that is often called for:

Poovizhi: Yes, We had some times like that. There was no business for two or three days. We could not do anything for the children; we could not prepare food to provide for them. Sometimes, I would think about that and feel sad, because we could not do business when the City Corporation people arrived [to evict]. Due to [the drive to evict encroachment on roadsides], they would take away all materials while we were doing good business. It would be very difficult for us in these times. It would be very tough to manage if they took away all the items. We have to adjust to all the difficulties, and profit and loss in the business.

Whereas customers and suppliers take precedence and families adjust and cope, when emergencies arise (school fees for children, medical emergencies), entrepreneurs delay payment or exert pressure on suppliers for credit or ask customers to repay debts. Thus, when the stress on the family becomes excessive, resources have to be moved from customer and supplier domains. The following quote from a financier illustrates how individuals renegotiate terms with suppliers during times of household financial distress. The quote also illustrates how personal information is exchanged and influences marketplace transactions.

Pankajam: Suppose their situation in a given month is not conducive to repaying the committed due amount, definitely they would try to settle the accumulated due on the next month. In case they can't repay the total amount on the second month as well, they would try to settle a portion on the first month and the rest on the next month by easy installments. They would inform us that their situation is worse and they are not in a position to repay the committed amount at once. They may request that we permit them to repay in two installments at the rate of Rs.500 on each month and be ready to pay the additional due interest. They have paid in such a way, and I too have collected so.

Thus far we have illustrated how subsistence entrepreneurs move their resources across domains to manage their enterprise. These processes act as strengths that enable them to successfully run an enterprise in the face of extreme resource constraints. However, subsistence entrepreneurs also display certain vulnerabilities, such as the inability to pursue bigger business opportunities due to the unavailability of sufficient capital or the reduced ability to protect oneself from risks like customer delinquency. The following quotes from Rukmini, a 50-year-old woman with no education, speak to this point:

Rukmini: I have no big ideas. We can expand it and go further if we have enough money. We can conduct a Rs. 5,000 chit [per month collection from each member] and Rs.10,000 chit. We can organize a Rs.10,000 chit fund. We don't have sufficient money. Supposing a member fails to pay on time, we should pay it immediately to settle the amount to the successful bidder and collect the amount due later on from the respective member. Now, I cannot afford to adjust such big amounts. Hence, I don't collect big chits. We should conduct the fund within our affordable limits. We should not overstep and stretch beyond our limit.

Preethi: As I told you, I have been doing this business for the past four years. Two years ago, a lady bought sarees and absconded. She took three sarees and told me that she would come back after showing it to family members [but never returned].

Conclusion

Our bottom-up approach provides a window into how subsistence entrepreneurs in South India negotiate different domains and move resources between them. The family is often the buffer, as customers and suppliers are paramount. But in an emergency, family needs to come to the forefront. Resources don't necessarily fall into neat compartments, but are moved around in a variety of ways. Thus, categories such as business loans used by service providers from outside these communities may take on less meaning with the demands of day-to-day life that blur differences between the family and the enterprise.

Also evident here is how being an entrepreneur and being a customer are two sides of the same coin in this environment of intense one-to-one interactions. We have referred to such entrepreneurs as subsistence consumer-merchants elsewhere. These and other themes will be elaborated in subsequent chapters.

References

Viswanathan, Madhubalan, José A. Rosa, and Julie A. Ruth (2010), "Exchanges in Marketing Systems: The Case of Subsistence Consumer-Merchants in Chennai, India," Journal of Marketing, 74 (3), 1–17.

Chapter 4
Consumer and Entrepreneurial Strengths and Vulnerabilities in Subsistence Marketplaces[11]

Image 4.01: A garam chai tea stand at Gol Park in South Kolkata, India. Photograph by Eric Parker; Creative Commons licensed image via Flickr: http://www.flickr.com/photos/ericparker/2242661174/.

[11] This chapter includes material adapted from the following previously published works:

Viswanathan, Madhubalan, S. Gajendiran, and R. Venkatesan (2008), *Enabling Consumer and Entrepreneurial Literacy in Subsistence Marketplaces*, Dordrecht: Springer. Reproduced with kind permission from Springer Science+Business Media B.V..

Viswanathan, Madhubalan, S. Gajendiran, and R. Venkatesan (2008), "Understanding and Enabling Marketplace Literacy in Subsistence Contexts: The Development of a Consumer and Entrepreneurial Literacy Educational Program in South India," *International Journal of Educational Development*, 28 (3), 300-19. DOI: 10.1016/j.ijedudev.2007.05.004

Viswanathan, Madhu (2011), "Consumer Behavior Across Literacy and Resource Barriers," in Wiley International Encyclopedia of Marketing, Volume 3—Consumer Behavior, Richard Bagozzi and Ayalla A. Ruvio, Volume Editors, Jagdish N. Sheth and Naresh K. Malhotra, Editors in Chief, 44-54. DOI: 10.1002/9781444316568.wiem03058

This chapter presents a discussion of consumer and entrepreneurial strengths and vulnerabilities in subsistence marketplaces. We cover the vulnerabilities and innovative practices of subsistence customers and entrepreneurs, and the development of consumer skills. We contrast skill development in these contexts with those of low-literate, low-income customers in the USA, reserving the term subsistence for contexts where poverty is more extreme and widespread.

Vulnerabilities and Innovative Practices of Subsistence Consumers and Entrepreneurs

Our research provided rich insights into the lives and marketplace interactions of low-literate, low-income buyers and sellers. The buyers and sellers we interviewed informed us of many innovative practices, as well as many pitfalls that buyers and sellers deal with. Vulnerabilities ranged from lack of awareness of rights to lack of confidence or lack of skills for day-to-day customer tasks. Tasks such as planning, creating shopping lists, checking prices, checking products, or requesting a bill were often not undertaken.

Following are quotes that illustrate the approach to, and thinking behind, behaviors of consumers and entrepreneurs.

Difficulty Calculating Costs

Malini, a 35-year-old woman with no formal education:

> **Malini:** We don't know how to calculate and account. … We know a little based on our assumptions. Suppose I visit a shop regularly and buy the items every day…I try to change the shop I buy from when I feel that the rate is high. I try to change the shops and buy from different shops to gain one or two rupees. I search and see whether I could get items for a lower price and visit shops that are nearby. If I had a good education and knowledge I could visit shops anywhere or shops with high standards. I could go for any job. Since I have no education, I hesitate to approach others and shop wherever I go. I hesitate to approach others freely. This is why I feel sad.

Fear of Shopping Situations Due to Lack of Literacy

Gauthami, a 28-year-old woman with a 3rd-grade education:

> **Gauthami:** The neighbors used to tell me that [the sellers] would quote Rs. 5 [for a product] and scold us if we didn't buy, compelling us to buy. … They would ask us, "Won't you buy, if the price is

little higher? Would you buy only when the price is less?" [The neighbors] say that [the shopkeepers] scold in this manner. I would have all this in my mind and have a kind of fear that they may scold me like that as well.

Seeking Help and Corrections from Shopkeepers

Menaka, a 32-year-old female with a 3rd-grade education:

Menaka: [The shopkeepers] would give the bill. They would calculate the amount and issue the bill for purchased items. I would bring it and show it to my daughter. If the bill was accurate, I would leave it. If she found any error in the calculation or bill, I would show it to the shopkeepers and discuss it. As I would visit the school the next day [to pick up my son], I would go to the shop on the way to the school and clarify the errors. The shopkeeper would recheck it and return the amount even if the difference or error was one or two rupees.

Planning Purchases and Checking Products, Prices, and Bills During Shopping

Kavitha [a 38-year-old woman with a 5th-grade education]: They issue the bill while they deliver the items. So, we can check the items in the bill one by one.

Interviewer: Do you have any difficulties in this?

Kavitha: I can't identify the moment I look at it. … I would think about it and verify the details after reaching my home. It would be in grams, and I would feel sad at that time.

Checking Accuracy of Product Purchase, Matching Patterns

Bhuvanesh [a 31-year-old man with no formal education]: Whether the medicine written and given by the doctor is the same [as the medicine sold in the medical store] must be compared and seen, must it not? Mostly, his handwriting cannot be understood, and we don't know English. So we send our children to the medical store to buy it. [The shopkeepers] sometimes even change the medicine and give the wrong medicine. But when we ask, they will say that the company is the same and that there is no difference. So I may buy the changed items.

Interviewer: Will they give the correct medicine?

Bhuvanesh: They will give the same medicine which he prescribes.

Interviewer: How do you check that?

Bhuvanesh: I will see the first letter sir.

Interviewer: How will you find out that the items bought by you are of good quality?

Bhuvanesh: How do I know? It is a good shop and the things that are there seem to be good and so I buy them. That is all I can say.

Choosing Between Neighborhood Retailer and Large Reseller

Kavitha: If I have more money or a sufficient amount of it, I can buy in bulk and stock up. Because we don't have money, we have to buy a little in bulk purchases and use it for 10 or 15 days…again we have to buy one or two kilograms for urgent need from the nearby shops, and when we get money. What do we do? The local shops also buy from [the wholesale shop] and sell it to us; they would get a profit of Rs. 1 or Rs. 2. When we buy, it is a loss to us, is it not?

Bargaining, Comparing Products

Rani [a 30-year-old woman with no formal education, food shopkeeper]: If it is a high price, we would bargain. Why is the rate this much here, while it is less there? [The shopkeeper] buys the vegetables in the market and knows the market price. Suddenly, how could he raise the price in the nearby shop? We would visit the market, when there was no sufficient stock of items like green chilies at the nearby shop. When we buy those at the market, we would compare the prices in both places. The price would be higher here [at the local shop]. We would ask the shopkeeper: "Why are you charging Rs. 2 per 50 grams of green chili while the price of a kilogram is Rs. 6 only at the market?" The shopkeeper would ask us: "Who is selling for such a low price?" We would say we visit daily and buy this product. "Don't we know even this." We would tell them that it is unfair and unjust. The local shopkeeper will get angry. Then I will come back quietly.

Making Versus Buying Decisions

Kamala [a 44-year-old woman with an 8th-grade education]: Yes, I will crush even chili powder. Crushed chili powder is sold in the market, but I will not buy it. I will crush chili and dhania [ingredients] in my house. I will crush and prepare even turmeric powder.

Interviewer: So you gain from doing this?

Kamala: Yes, I gain. It will also be clean. When we do this, we will be satisfied because [the shops] may also adulterate the product. We will watch the process when chili powder is crushed in the machine. When chili and dhania are crushed in the shop, they add rice powder. I have seen this. What we make ourselves is good for health. Seragam, pepper, and dhal are added to crush chili powder. They are not added in the [chili powder made at the] shop.

Assessing Quality of Products

Kavitha: First, I would buy a kilogram of rice as a sample to cook and test it. Suppose we find the cooked rice is good and tasty, then we would buy 5 kg or more and prepare the regular food. Our local shopkeeper also used to buy the rice [from wholesale] and sell. If we tell the local shopkeeper, "I bought this rice from this particular shop and it is good, so you buy the same and stock it for selling to us," he would comply with our request and would be prepared to supply whenever we need it.

Weighing

Sumitra [a 46-year-old woman with no formal education]: Yes, while weighing he shakes [the balance] and uses some technique to balance the needle of the scale and push down the plate. He would say that it had excess and give extra to the buyer. If it is bought in the next shop, he would weigh it perfectly. He wouldn't shake the hand that holds the scale. He would hold the scale at a perfect angle when you watch carefully.

Kavitha: We would check while they weigh it. Suppose we feel that there is shortage in the weight and ask them to weigh it again. They would weigh and show us, it would be correct. If there were any shortage in the weight, they would say that this package had a shortage and ask their staff to change it and give us the packet with correct weight. They would take back [the package with the shortage].

Understanding Maximum Retail Price

Interviewer: Now, you buy different items from the wholesale market like [store name], prepare pickles, and sell it. Do you know what MRP [maximum retail price] is?

Jamuna [a 34-year-old woman with a 10th-grade education, pickle seller]: MRP means the rate of the product. It is the production cost; that is why it is called MRP.

Interviewer: Do you buy soaps?

Jamuna: Sir, it is in that packet.

Interviewer: What is printed on it?

Jamuna: The rate of the soap is printed followed by MRP.

Interviewer: Do you know the meaning or expansion of MRP?

Jamuna: I know that they have printed the rate as MRP, that's all.

Treating Customers Similarly, Managing Customer to Customer

Interviewer: Do you make purchases in wholesale shops for cash or any credit? Do you avoid credit and costs associated with it?

Velamma [a 45-year-old woman with a 5th-grade education, utensils reseller]: No credit, only cash payment on hand.

Interviewer: Cash on hand purchase?

Velamma: Yes, cash on hand.

Interviewer: Have you bought anything on credit recently?

Velamma: I won't buy on credit. I have to pay back the credit. They may raise what is owed from Rs. 5 to Rs. 6. I am using this as an example. It is just for the sake of argument. Again, they may record what is owed as Rs. 8 instead of Rs. 6. I don't want these things and decided [to avoid credit].

Interviewer: When you give products, has any one complained that you are not giving a product worth the Rs. 300 they paid for it?

Velamma: Few people are like that…I would ask them to check the products that were given to others. I would tell them that I gave them the same products that I gave to others. Some may accept what I said and leave quietly; some may shout. I may have to adjust to both situations.

Interviewer: How are you managing such situations?

Velamma: I would invite them to check the quality of products supplied to other customers. The other customers would say that the product given was good and useful. This feedback would cool down their temper and they would leave quietly.

Interviewer: Suppose they say even after the explanation and feedback that the product is not good and that they don't want it?

Velamma: If they don't want, they can choose any other product available with me. But I won't return the money. At any cost, I won't give the money back.

Interviewer: Your principle is not to return the money.

Velamma: I won't give back money, only products.

Verbal Counting, Accounting

Rani: After arranging the products that I bought, I would calculate. We used to buy kerosene. I would buy it in bulk purchase. I would have bought LPG [gas] cylinder. I would add the cost of the kerosene and the LPG cylinder. Rs. 20 is the cost of this. By adding everything, it would have come to Rs. 100 or Rs. 120.

Interviewer: Do you write it down?

Rani: I couldn't write down all, sir.

Interviewer: All oral calculation?

Rani: Oral calculation.

Judging Customers

Velamma: I won't ask anyone [about creditworthiness of specific customers], any neighbors. I won't ask anyone. I would give [products]
based on my assessment and confidence.

They may tell me [if asked] but they may have quarreled [with the potential customers].

So they would tell me not to give products to their neighbors and say that they would move out of the area. Even the people paying me now would say that they don't know, when I am asking about their neighbors. They would respond without any seriousness.

Dealing with Customers

Rani: I won't talk much to them. It is our business. They should come again. I won't talk. This is because I want to run my business. I would get angry if they speak with anger. I would respond politely if they ask why something is like this. I would say that many people bought the same item earlier and never complained like this. "Only you complained."

Testing Products Through "Research"

Jamuna: First, we would taste it. Neighbors are using it. They told us that we had added excess tamarind in the garlic pickles prepared this year.

Summarizing the Vulnerabilities and Practices of Subsistence Consumers and Entrepreneurs

There are many examples of innovative practices along with many pitfalls where people are vulnerable and suffer negative consequences as buyers and as sellers. Vulnerabilities ranged from lack of awareness of rights to lack of confidence or lack of skills for day-to-day customer tasks. Tasks such as planning, creating shopping lists, checking prices, checking products, or requesting a bill were often not undertaken. As you can see from the interviews, consumers often do not fully consider the trade-offs of an exchange, such as travel time and other non-monetary or indirect monetary costs. Similarly, sellers do not analyze the marketplace or consider alternatives before starting enterprises. Lack of clear accounting is another issue, as is lack of a full understanding of the costs of doing business. People also had difficulty understanding return on investment.

The effective practices of buyers included bargaining, checking weights, checking prices, and checking product quality. Sellers were effective in dealing with customers in difficult situations, responding to demands from customers, managing word of mouth among customers, and researching the marketplace.

These innovative practices represent adaptation to the adverse conditions of subsistence marketplaces. Our research enabled us to develop a detailed list of issues that people face as buyers and as sellers, as well as a deeper understanding of life in the economic realm.

Development of Consumer Skills

Several factors affect the development of consumer skills—primarily formal education level, experience, and income. Using any of these three factors as a stepping-stone, people can develop their

- aptitude for maneuvering in the marketplace, capacity to be wise consumers,
- buying power, and
- ability to provide basic necessities.

However, when all three factors—education, experience, and income—are low, people usually have very limited consumer skills. We organize our understanding into the following topics.

Number Skills

Subsistence consumers develop verbal counting skills ("mouth arithmetic" is the transliteration of the native language term) through buying or selling experience; thus, they can usually compute totals and change received from transactions. However, they have difficulty with more complex computations of interest.

In turn, lenders and borrowers speak the simplified terminology of payments per day or month. Subsistence consumers often fixate on certain numbers, such as MRP (maximum retail price printed on packages); they are comfortable and familiar with the concrete use of such numbers. Similarly, low-literate customers may fixate on stores without much price comparison. Even on rare occasions when prices are lowered, low-literate customers may not check prices.

Adaptivity in Adversity

Adaptivity has been a central theme of the decision-making literature in psychology, economics, and related disciplines. Adaptivity in consumer behavior and elsewhere has been discussed in terms of using appropriate decision strategies in light of limited cognitive resources. However, in the context studied here, adaptivity is much more than finding the right decision strategy to fit a situation. Adaptivity involves making ends meet in various ways, including

- using homemade medicine,

- rationing medicine to save money or to trade off lost income due to illness,

- adjusting and reducing meal items,

- substituting lower-priced ingredients for some "less important" meals, and

- making, rather than buying, some food ingredients.

Customers often make rather than buy products or ingredients to save money, to customize to their tastes, and to consume fresh products.

Income and Consumer Skills

Severe income constraints can lead people to develop skills by necessity, such as planning their purchases and their food consumption. Some people must purchase items in installments. Setting an MRP (maximum retail price) is stipulated by the government. People commonly misunderstand the MRP to indicate the actual price or the cost of a product. Faced with the inability to read most package information except concrete numbers, such as price, low-literate consumers fixate on MRP. Noteworthy here is that having a reasonable meal at least once a day is a top priority; hence, considerable effort is expended toward making this possible.

Borrowing, having very low income, and the fear of humiliation in not being able to repay loans can lead to full cash purchases at affordable prices. With very low income, people tend to avoid high-interest loans, or avoid buying gifts due to peer and familial pressures or the demands of tradition. Thus, in a sense, extreme income constraints appear to lead to effective decision-making. Severe income constraints can engender an attitude of living within means and blocking out unnecessary expenses.

In fact, some customers report that they do not have any unnecessary expenses. Television advertisements and the like are not given much serious attention, but are viewed for entertainment value. A type of next-meal rationality leads to necessity-based skill development. Some people may stop borrowing, buying, or maintaining traditions.

The centrality of one-to-one interactions and people orientation may break down when income constraints are too severe and families have to isolate themselves from participating in any social activities that cost money. Some families reported being isolated from other relatives because they are unable to participate in traditional activities that involve monetary expenses (e.g., attending a wedding or a funeral).

Whereas very low incomes can engender in people the skills to plan and carefully purchase, very low income combined with laborious work schedules can lead to lack of product evaluation. When income constraints are severe, "filling one's stomach" is the bottom-line priority. In this situation, quality or taste is not important; simply eating is. There is rarely time for planned purchases and being discriminating on price. Thus, quality judgments and price comparisons are hampered.

Formal Literacy and Consumer Skills

We report many examples of ingenuity and resourcefulness that people display in the face of low literacy. However, we also found that low literacy can lead to fear of exploring the marketplace, particularly with respect to banks and other institutions. Experience is often at local retail stores; sometimes even buying wholesale is challenging. Over time, low literacy, lack of experience, and extreme income constraints combine to exacerbate the situation and thwart learning.

Low literacy can lead to fear of conversation, inability to ask or answer a question, fear of unknown prices, and hence avoidance of many products and feelings of futility in making enquiries or demands. An interesting parallel with low-literate consumers in the USA (Viswanathan et al., 2005) is avoidance of confusing price displays or of "% off" signs, due to computational problems.

With low literacy, there is a tendency to accept conditions as they are, without questioning. It also appears to lead to acceptance of products and their quality as is. "Quality is fine, that's all one can get," "Arguing is futile," "That's what you get for what you paid," or "Alternatives are few," are some of the refrains we heard from low-literate individuals. Low literacy leads to the assumption that available products are of the right price and the right quality for that price. Low-literate people rarely search for information or evaluate the quality of products; rather, product evaluation occurs through trial and error.

Low literacy leads to intuitive, rather than explicit, listing, planning, or budgeting, and concrete methods of accounting, such as placing money (say, investments versus profit for an entrepreneur) in different locations. Defensive rules employed include not carrying money to avoid unnecessary purchases and pattern-matching when unable to read the name of a medicine or a bus number.

Low literacy can lead to lack of awareness when cheating occurs. In fact, loyalty, a sense of obligation, and the lack of price and shop comparisons may compound these issues and lead to a conviction that cheating does not occur.

With low literacy, low income, reliance on credit from one store, and inability to plan and buy wholesale, customer-related experiences may not develop. Relationships with stores build loyalty, but can inhibit the development of skills to evaluate alternative shops and perform price and product comparisons. Such experiences as computing totals, evaluating products, or interacting with sellers lead to the development of consumer skills. Moreover, even if cheating is thought to occur, there is a sense of futility about argument or action as well as a lack of awareness of rights, the net result often being no change in behavior.

Low literacy lowers confidence in dealing with some large organizations, such as banks or English-oriented large stores. Low-literate customers may depend on literate children to read or compute or on a mother or mother-in-law to teach them some basic shopping skills. Dependence and word of mouth are both significant. Dependence occurs when dealing with institutions, such as completing forms at banks, for informational issues such as expiration dates on products, or for computations, such as totaling up a bill or preparing lists. Dependence is also inherent in some community-based services, such as savings plans. In a broader sense, a one-to-one interactional marketplace is really a dependence on everyone, somewhat reducing the need for dependence on specific individuals.

Literacy engenders confidence in dealing with shops and institutions. Here, the difference between no formal education and even a 5th-grade education can be stark. Literacy or experience can provide a foundation to build on, and, combined with income, lead to experiences, skills, quality judgments, and the like. As discussed earlier, adult education leads to exchange of information among customers and can be transformational for low-literate individuals with regard to their marketplace behaviors. Adult education can convey awareness of issues and rights and lead to concrete redressive actions, such as switching store loyalties and shopping elsewhere.

English language skills are an issue in India because of the use of English in many large organizations. India is characterized by having many different languages and numerous dialects. People speak Tamil in the state—Tamil

Nadu—in which this research was conducted. In poorer segments, parents often strive to educate their children in English, a way out economically and a source of pride.

Experience and Consumer Skills

In the rich context of one-to-one interactions and the need to evaluate generic products, experience can be a very effective teacher. The key in the Indian environment is to have a trigger that leads to experience, which in turn is very effective in teaching skills. Experience leads to knowledge about what works and what does not, whether with products or in money management. However, this trial-and-error learning by itself does not safeguard against making errors on single purchases that are information-oriented—for example, purchases based on price or weight.

Low literacy is often associated with perceptions of lack of ability in specific domains. Experience in a trade or through selling can provide a sense of dignity and confidence. In a sense, experience provides a specific form of functional literacy in the here and now, literacy in a trade or in a certain domain, which, in turn, broadens functional literacy. It enables individuals to overcome fears and, thus, triggers the process of learning.

People can gain proxy buying experiences through work experiences. For example, housemaids can be involved in purchases and learn through those experiences. Such experiences can lead to skills in counting and buying. Experience can accumulate through selling and buying. Whereas low literacy can lead to fear of exploring the marketplace and low income can inhibit experience, some form of experience can, in turn, alleviate the negative consequences of low literacy and low income and trigger learning. The interaction between education level, income level, and experience is central to the development of consumer skills, with learning perhaps being accelerated when certain threshold levels of these variables are reached.

Comparing and Contrasting Consumers in the US and in India

In the rest of this chapter, we move from understanding subsistence marketplace skills to comparing and contrasting low-literate, low-income consumers in the United States with subsistence consumers in India. Our understanding of consumer behavior stems largely from studying literate consumers in relatively resource-rich settings. Yet, a sizable proportion of people in the United States and even larger proportions around the world face resource and literacy barriers. In fact, some communities in the United States are comparable to the subsistence communities we have encountered elsewhere. As noted earlier, we describe the consumers in the United States that we focused on as low-literate, low-income rather than subsistence consumers, as their level of poverty was not as extreme.

Background on Literacy in the US

Literacy relates to reading and writing skills whereas numeracy relates to counting. Functional literacy relates to possessing the reading, writing, and counting skills to function in day-to-day life (Kirsch and Guthrie, 1997). Literacy and functional literacy will be used interchangeably in this chapter. Low literacy, of course, is associated with low income as well, and our discussion will emphasize low-literate, low-income consumers in the US, disentangling these two factors where possible.

Literacy rates in the US until a few decades ago were reported to be 99%! However, such statistics were based on a question in the Census whether an individual was literate. Subsequently, when grade-equivalent tasks were used (e.g., if you are in a certain grade, you should be able to write a check or read a package label), the estimates of low literacy have varied from 20% to considerably higher.

Statistics about literacy carry a sense of prestige with them and therefore, often reflect biases at individual and more aggregate state or country levels. The 2002 National Assessment of Adult Literacy (NAAL) showed that at least 22% of US consumers lack skills to perform retail tasks (e.g., calculating unit prices and price discounts, comparing product attributes), and between 34% and 55% lack skills to look up reference materials to identify foods containing a particular vitamin (Kutner, Greenberg, and Baer, 2005).

Method

In describing literate versus low-literate consumers, it is important to understand that this is a continuum and that there is no demarcation that makes someone non-literate; hence the preference here to use the term low-literate. Also relevant here is how we can study low-literate consumers. Experiments and surveys are not the most effective approaches, unless very carefully designed (Viswanathan, Gau, and Chaturvedi, 2008).

In our work, we used observations of classrooms at adult education centers, observations of shopping trips, and interviews of teachers and students. Typically, such centers have students divided by grade equivalent levels, such as 0-4, 5-8, and 9-12, based on reading and math tests administered periodically and that indicate ranges of literacy from low to moderate levels.

Although we offer a number of insights on these pages, please note that some apply more to those at the 0-4 level than, say, those at the 5-8 level. We observed both vulnerabilities and strengths in our work and that is important to acknowledge as well. Low-literate consumers overcome constraints borne out of their circumstances, sometimes in ingenious ways, and display extraordinary resilience in negotiating a marketplace that assumes a certain level of literacy.

Illustrative Findings

In our observations of low-literate consumers while shopping, most striking were the things that, we, the literate consumers, take for granted. A typical trip to the grocery store for a literate consumer may involve some trade-offs between price and attributes of products. If the intention is a cash purchase and one is short by a few dollars, it is usually not a big issue to leave behind some items and attribute things to one's forgetfulness. But this example, which happens frequently, does not begin to describe the kinds of issues that low-literate shoppers face, particularly those at the low end of the continuum.

Here are just a few of the challenges that low-literate people face while shopping:

- Locating a product can take considerable time when reading signs is difficult or just not possible.

- It is not always easy to ask store employees for directions, particularly when a person's lifetime with low literacy has caused many travails. Identifying the correct volume can be difficult—finding 150 candles, for example, involves finding two different packets of 100 and 50. With the many different price tags and sales signs, finding the bottom-line price can be confusing.

- Low-literate people may need to rely on written computations to find out the price of multiple units when the price of one is known. Percent-off sales signs can be another cause for concern; some may completely avoid them due to difficulty computing the final price or embarrassment with having to ask a store employee. (Others may use them partially when, say, an item is 50 percent off but not when 30 percent or 70 percent off(!), because computing half off may be relatively easier.)

- Computing the total on a shopping trip may be difficult, leading to solutions such as moving currency bills after each item is added to a cart or visually subtracting from an imagined set of currency bills.

- Similarly, allowing for taxes can be a significant concern leading to rules of thumb like buying one thing if one has five dollars. Unit prices are essentially abstractions that are difficult to understand and often ignored.

- Similarly, people may not pay attention to nutrient values and percent of daily allowances, serving sizes, and even expiration dates, because they don't understand them.

Adding to cognitive difficulties, issues such as being short of money at the checkout counter are cause for despair, as this is a result of one's low literacy rather than forgetfulness. Similarly, having enough money can be cause for celebration. Underlying their shopping interactions for low-literate consumers is the need to maintain self-esteem and avoid being exposed for their low-literacy. Thus, in addition to cognitive issues, emotional issues are also central, with anxiety being a common aspect of seemingly mundane shopping activities.

Cognitive Tendencies

A cognitive tendency that is most striking is one of concrete thinking, focusing on single pieces of information such as price, without abstracting across, say, price and size or price and other attributes (Viswanathan, Rosa, and Harris, 2005; Gau and Viswanathan, 2008). Buying the cheapest product without attention to size is an example of this tendency. It manifests in a number of ways, through seeking familiar stores, and learning to use expiration dates or other concrete information, such as numerical information, without understanding its meaning (Figure 4.1).

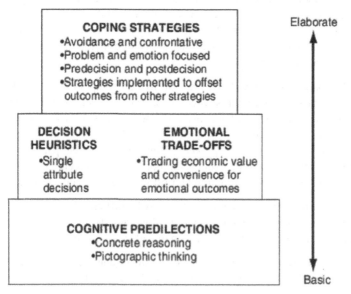

Figure 4.1: Thinking, Feeling, and Coping By Low-Literate Consumers.

Consumer and Entrepreneurial Strengths and Vulnerabilities

In a study of low-literate peasants in Central Asia in the early 1900s, a Russian psychologist asked participants to view tools (e.g., an axe, a hatchet, a log, and a saw) and asked them to group three of these objects that can be described by a word or that belong together (Luria, 1976). Participants responded in terms of how they could chop firewood to stay warm, i.e., how they could use what they saw in day-to-day life. Thus, low literacy and difficulty with abstractions tends to lead consumers to think in the immediate, visual, graphic, here-and-now world of how they can use things.

Another cognitive tendency is pictographic thinking (Viswanathan et al., 2005; Gau and Viswanathan, 2008). Although consumers in general depend on pictures, pictographic thinking is qualitatively different. It means viewing text such as brand names not as something to read but as an image, and thus remembering brands to buy through pictorial elements. Pictographic thinking also manifests in visualizing quantities to buy rather than using symbolic information. For instance, when buying an ingredient like sugar to bake a cake, low-literate consumers may visualize baking the cake and pouring sugar into it and buy the package of corresponding size.

Pictographic thinking may even involve "counting" by visualizing currency bills. Some low-literate consumers match patterns on prescriptions with medicine packages to find the right medicine. Whereas low-literate consumers may have poorer memory for textual information when compared to consumers with higher literacy, we have found that their memory for pictorial information, such as brand signatures, can be as good (Viswanathan et al., 2009). Such improvement in memory appears to arise from familiar pictorial elements.

Decision-making, Emotional Trade-offs, and Coping Strategies

Decision-making protocols may range from single-attribute decisions (buy the cheapest) to habitual decision-making to random decision-making (e.g., picking up the first item in a product category that you see, for a planned or unplanned purchase). Sometimes simply locating a product can lead to its purchase. Contrast this with conventional decision-making models, which cover a number of steps.

Also intertwined with decisions are emotional trade-offs. For instance, low-literate consumers may trade off utility to save embarrassment, as maintaining self-esteem is central as they negotiate the marketplace. Having sufficient money at the counter may be cause for celebration whereas being "caught" short may be cause for despair. The anxiety associated with negotiating a complex marketplace while lacking in literacy and trying to avoid being exposed on this account is the larger emotional context where day-to-day shopping occurs.

Along similar lines, Adkins and Ozanne (2005) identify types of low-literate consumers based on dimensions such as acceptance or rejection of stigma arising from low literacy. They find a number of coping strategies including avoidance, self-esteem maintenance, dependence on others, and social deception. Low-literate consumers cope in a number of ways—depending on others, coming up with rudimentary defensive rules like buying one item from the menu at a time to avoid being short of money, and even giving all the money they have at the checkout counter.

Some of the ways in which they cope are ingenious, such as in "counting" by visualizing currency bills. They often depend on others, sometimes even helpful store employees, to help them with shopping and avoid situations and stores that are likely to lead to embarrassment. They strive to maintain self-esteem in all their interactions.

Low-Literate Shopping Behavior

Here we present a model of low-literate shopping behavior to contrast low-literate consumer behavior with more conventional consumer behavior. Low-literate consumers may bypass or spend minimal effort in steps such as pre-purchase searches and evaluating alternatives. Or they might bypass the entire decision process altogether by mimicking others or by delegating responsibility to others.

A model of shopping behavior for functionally illiterate consumers is illustrated in the interview quotes provided earlier in the chapter. As indicated in the direct link from "need recognition" to "purchase," some consumers may completely delegate the decision-making to others, highlighting the theme of dependence on others (Figure 4.2).

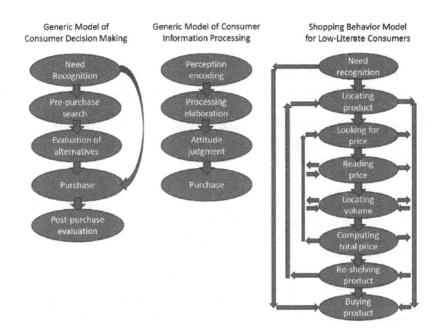

Generic Model of Consumer Decision Making	Generic Model of Consumer Information Processing	Shopping Behavior Model for Low-Literate Consumers
Need Recognition	Perception encoding	Need recognition
Pre-purchase search	Processing elaboration	Locating product
Evaluation of alternatives	Attitude judgment	Looking for price
Purchase	Purchase	Reading price
Post-purchase evaluation		Locating volume
		Computing total price
		Re-shelving product
		Buying product

Figure 4.2: An illustration of shopping behavior for low-literate consumers.

The first step in the decision-making process is locating a product. Due to the effort often expended in locating a product in the store, the low-literate consumer might simply purchase the product without further searching or comparison of other products.

After locating a product, the consumer may also need to ascertain the correct volume or number of units s/he needs. When a combination of package sizes is needed, the consumer might be significantly challenged. If the consumer locates the needed volume, s/he might immediately purchase the product—but most often would then search for the price.

S/he might need to expend effort in looking for the price, a distinct step in the process. S/he might run into problems identifying the price because of not knowing what the price tag says, or where it is, or finding multiple price stickers. So at this point, with the price confusion, s/he might either re-shelve the product, or buy it, hoping or believing s/he has enough money. S/he might try to compute a total price, with some iteration needed to perform the computations. S/he might also need to look again at the price, rereading it many times, or re-identify the correct volume. At this point, s/he will either re-shelve the item or purchase it, culminating the at times exhausting decision-making sequence.[12]

Contrasting Low-Literate Consumer Behavior in the US to Subsistence Consumers in India

Research regarding low-literate consumer behavior in the US versus India suggests some interesting differences. This discussion of these differences, however–even though it is based on years of field research–is speculative in nature.

Our research in India suggests that concrete thinking and pictographic thinking are also common in subsistence marketplaces, as are coping mechanisms to compensate for individual shortcomings in marketplace proficiency. In fact, very low income and a need to survive the immediate time frame can accentuate tendencies like concrete thinking. Self-esteem issues are also widespread, as documented earlier in this chapter, with low literacy leading to fear of interaction, inability to ask or answer questions, avoidance of unknown products and unfamiliar pricing schemes, and feelings of futility in making enquiries or demands.

Although subsistence customers in India struggle with many of the same challenges faced by low-literate customers in the US, the one-to-one interactional

---

[12] Although not strictly comparable to generic models of decision-making and information processing adapted from the literature (Bettman 1979), the shopping behavior model for functionally illiterate consumers highlights the importance of one or two stages in other models. In contrast to these typical decision-making and information-processing models, the emphasis here is on perception of information, leading to surface-level processing of primarily one or very few pieces of product information, (e.g., price information), often with error.

Whereas typical information processing models include perception, encoding of information, elaboration of information, evaluation, and then purchase (Bettman 1979), the emphasis for low-literate consumers is on perception with regard to location of product and identification of price. Encoding of information may be of a transient nature with a view toward completing the immediate purchase task, rather than leading to memory and integration with prior knowledge.

While this model may resemble low-involvement models of decision-making and models of repeat purchase, in terms of lack of active information seeking and lack of comparison of attributes (cf., Zaichkowsky 1985), fundamental processing differences are noteworthy. The decision-making process bypasses several steps when compared to traditional decision-making models. Rather than arising from a lack of motivation that characterizes low-involvement decision-making and repeat purchase models, this process can be quite challenging. Thus, striking differences between consumers who differ in levels of literacy are illustrated by contrasting decision-making processes.

marketplace affords some unique advantages that can enhance coping ability. Opportunities to develop consumer skills appear to be generally higher for a person with a low level of formal education in India when compared to the US.

A key factor here is the rich, one-to-one interactional experience base from which customers can learn. Dealing with vendors requires developing the ability to judge products and mentally count money. Frequent one-to-one interactions with sellers and other customers lead to developing skills such as what to buy, where to buy it, and how to get a bargain. Customers commonly seek advice from neighbors and people on the street, a sort of perceptual, off-line community.

Also, because many generic products are not packaged or presented with nutritional information, customers have to learn to judge the product for themselves. Contrast this with the typical context in the US where customers deal with large chain stores, products with package information about nutrition, and registers to compute transaction totals. Ironically, the US environment, rich in symbolic information and technology, is not necessarily conducive to the development of skills for low-literate customers.

Consumer skills also develop from learning skills as sellers, often the way out economically for many people in India. This is in contrast to working for a larger organization in a certain clearly defined capacity. Experience in India can be twofold, buying and selling; in the US, employment is often for a larger organization. Being a vendor in India requires developing skills such as bargaining, counting, and completing transactions that then transfer to the customer realm.

Another factor that may lead to higher consumer skills in India is the more severe income constraints that lead, out of necessity, to careful planning. Often, when the decision involves the next meal, careful purchase and consumption habits develop. Discounts and "free" promotions are carefully pursued when income constraints are severe and possessions are few.

Striking differences between the US and India among low-literate customers include the ability of customers in India to plan carefully, their level of numerical skills, and the lack of impulse purchases. Some factors, such as lack of impulse purchases and planning, may well be the result of extreme income constraints.

Numerical skills may necessarily develop from dealing with small vendors in small transactions. Compared to the US, experiences in a one-to-one interactional world may be richer and lead to faster development in subsistence contexts in India, with formal education enabling absorption of richer experience and exploration of the marketplace environment and leading to more advanced skills. In the US, experiences may not be as effective in developing skills; product information is symbolic, computations are mechanized, and one-to-one interactions may be lower in frequency and less involved in nature. Work experience and shopping experience may both be narrower in the US from the perspective of consumer skill development.

Low-literate customers in India may also be less dependent on others when compared to customers with similar formal educational levels in the US; they depend on word of mouth for some purchases, such as appliances. Generally speaking, Indian customers appear to be less passive, willing to exercise their rights and redress grievances. However, low literacy is certainly a significant factor in many situations, such as in making habitual purchases, with little searching unless told of a deal by someone, or in evaluating weight, price, date, and other symbolic information.

In fact, when having no formal education, little experience, and low income, the low-literate Indian customer resembles the low-literate US customer at the lowest level of literacy. There may also be less stigma attached with being low-literate or poor in India when compared to the US.

Conclusion

In summary, comparing the two consumer groups discussed here, although speculative and cognizant of the wide range of differences within low-literate consumer behavior in the US, say between urban and rural areas, and similarly in subsistence consumer behavior, a number of differences are noteworthy.

In advanced economies like the US, the marketplace context assumes a certain level of literacy. Large chain stores have technology needed to compute totals, and symbolic package and shelf information abound. Thus, low-literate consumers may be isolated from the marketplace and consumer skills development may be impeded when compared with the one-to-one interactional subsistence marketplaces we describe.

In the subsistence context, generic products are evaluated in face-to-face interactions with prices determined by enquiry and bargaining, and money and change counted out. Consumers learn skills by being vendors themselves and managing various aspects of a business, rather than being engaged in an occupation in a narrowly circumscribed role for a large business, as may often be the case in advanced economies. Extreme poverty leads to learning in order to somehow get the next meal. Thus, ironically, the low-literate subsistence consumer may develop functional skills needed to negotiate the one-to-one interactional marketplace, when compared to the low-literate consumer in the United States who has to negotiate a relatively impersonal marketplace that assumes a certain level of literacy.

References

Adkins, Natalie and Julie Ozanne (2005), "The low literate consumer," Journal of Consumer Research, 32(1), 93-105.

Bettman, J. R. (1979). Memory factors in consumer choice: A review. The Journal of Marketing, 37-53.

Gau, Roland, and Madhubalan Viswanathan (2008), "The Retail Shopping Experience for Low-Literate Consumers," Journal of Research for Consumers, Issue 15, Consumer Empowerment Special Issue.

Kirsch, Irwin S. and John T. Guthrie (1997), "The concept and measurement of functional literacy," Reading Research Quarterly 13 (4), 485-507.

Kutner, Mark, Elizabeth Greenberg, and Justin Baer (2005), "A First Look at the Literacy of America's Adults in the 21st Century," Department of Education, Washington, DC: National Center for Education Statistics.

Luria, A. (1976) Cognitive Development: Its Cultural and Social Foundations. Harvard University Press. Cambridge, MA.

Viswanathan, Madhubalan, Roland Gau, and Avinish Chaturvedi (2008), "Research Methods for Subsistence Marketplaces," in Sustainability Challenges and Solutions at the Base-of-the-Pyramid: Business, Technology and the Poor, Forthcoming, Editors Prabhu Khandachar and Minna Halme, Greenleaf Publishing.

Viswanathan, Madhubalan, Jose Antonio Rosa, and James Harris (2005), "Decision-Making and Coping by Functionally Illiterate Consumers and Some Implications for Marketing Management," Journal of Marketing, 69(1), 15-31.

Viswanathan, Madhubalan, Srinivas Sridharan, Roland Gau, and Robin Ritchie (2009) "Designing Marketplace Literacy Education in Resource-Constrained Contexts: Implications for Public Policy and Marketing," Journal of Public Policy and Marketing, forthcoming.

Viswanathan, Madhubalan, Lan Xia, Carlos Torelli, and Roland Gau, "Literacy and Consumer Memory," Journal of Consumer Psychology, forthcoming.

Zaichkowsky, J. L. (1985). Measuring the involvement construct. Journal of consumer research, 341-352.

Chapter 5
Drawing Macro-level Insights from Micro-level Understanding of Subsistence Marketplaces[13]

Image 5.01: Maasai tribesmen in Tanzania going back to their village from a weekly market. Photograph courtesy of students in the course "Product and Market Development for Subsistence Marketplaces."

Through our research, we have developed deep insights into a marketplace of one-to-one interactions and exchanges. This stands in contrast to the consumer-to-large-organization interaction that characterizes much of the marketplace exchange in the United States and Western Europe. Households and communities in subsistence marketplaces are characterized by severe resource constraints that encompass finances, informational resources, and

---

[13] This chapter includes material adapted from the following previously published work:

Viswanathan, Madhubalan, Anju Seth, Roland Gau, and Avinish Chaturvedi (2009), "Internalizing Social Good Into Business Processes in Subsistence Marketplaces: The Sustainable Market Orientation" *Journal of Macromarketing*, 29, 406-425.

basic infrastructure such as transportation and sanitation (Maranz 2001). Life in subsistence is characterized by the lack of control over many aspects of day-to-day life, such as the availability and quality of water and electricity, often taken for granted in relatively affluent settings.

Overlaying this issue is the level of complexity in a variety of realms of day-to-day life. Basic tasks, such as food preparation, may be dependent on unknown or uncontrollable factors, such as the availability of potable water and the quality of generic ingredients. Similarly, transportation may be unavailable or unreliable. In urban settings, the lack of resources can lead to a lack of mobility, leading to most purchases being made at the neighborhood retail shop. However, travel over some distances for purchases at different locations in urban settings is more viable than in geographically dispersed rural settings, which are generally characterized by much poorer infrastructure. The unique environment represented by the subsistence marketplace has important implications at three distinct levels:

- the nature of product and service needs at the individual and household levels;
- the interactions between and among buyers, sellers, and individuals at the relationship level; and
- the social milieu at the marketplace level.

These three levels of analysis are apt for subsistence marketplaces as their defining characteristic of severe resource constraints that lead to the lack of affordability at the product level, interdependence at the relationship level, and the lack of mobility and dependence on groups at the marketplace level. These levels capture the individual and household at the product level, the social-relationship level, and the marketplace level as different levels of aggregation of a bottom-up approach that are germane to understanding subsistence marketplaces in light of the defining characteristic of extreme resource constraints.

Our ensuing discussion is represented in Figure 5.1, with illustrative quotes presented in Illustrative Descriptions and Quotes, Section 5.1. As we discuss each of these dimensions below, we will elaborate on resource constraints and related factors that lead to key objectives at each level (left column of Figure 5.1), and in turn lead to central implications for enterprises discussed in the next section of the book (middle column of Figure 5.1).

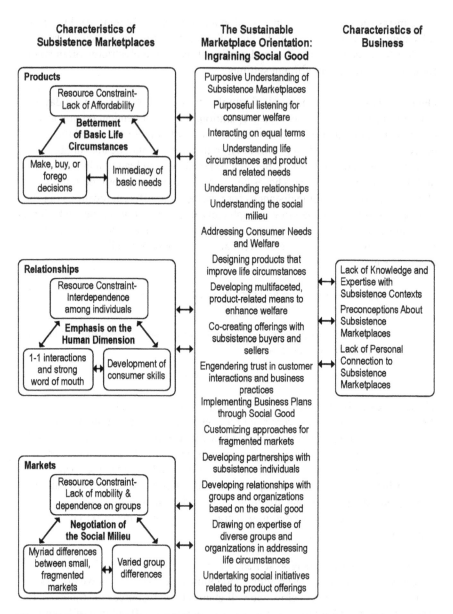

Figure 5.1: Characteristics of Subsistence Marketplaces and the Need for a Sustainable Market Orientation.

Products, Needs, and Betterment of Basic Life Circumstances

The typical low-income, low-literate person spends a high proportion of income on necessities (e.g., food and clothing) and unexpected expenses. Basic needs often go unmet. At the level of product needs, severe resource constraints for people and households lead to the inability to afford many products. A decision that consumers often confront is whether to make (if viable), buy, or forgo a product. Often, people may opt to make an item, such as an ingredient in a food preparation, allowing for customization while being affordable. Alternatively, they may forgo products because of resource constraints. Within narrow affordability limits, people are discriminating of quality and willing to pay for quality, particularly for fundamental products, such as staple foods, and consumption events.

Illustrative Descriptions and Quotes, Section 5.1

We begin with two examples that bring out the struggles and resilience of those living in subsistence as they strive to better the life circumstances of their children. Jayanthi is a 50-year-old woman who grew up in a village without education and overcame extraordinary adversity, losing one of her four children and her husband due to premature deaths.

> **Jayanthi:** So, I wanted to educate my children. ... We haven't studied. ... I had no one to support my school education. ... At the least we should give a good education to our children. I had such an interest, so I provided education to my children. I thought that although we face difficulties in our life, we should provide them with education. I felt that they should not face problems without education, like us. Hence, I provided education to all of my children.
>
> We had been struggling from our childhood. It should not be repeated to any others. Wherever we would be, everyone would come to us and live happily. We should have a good name and happy life as long as we are alive. Others would speak about it in the future. When my son died a year ago, the other children in the street cried for him for two days. They wondered and cried because it was rare to see such person like my son.
>
> The death of my father when I was eight years old was one of the reasons [why we struggled]. Then, I didn't have any brothers in my family to take care of me and fulfill my needs. It is a kind of good thinking I have that others should not face the same, though we are

facing problems and I feel that it should be ended with us. These kinds of problems should not be repeated to any others. There are people with problems worse than ours and we could not deny that. We should guide those who need help, to our level best to overcome from their problems, and it is good for us, too. We could not live on others' earnings or assets until the end. If we worked hard, we could get a little money for our balance. We could have a happy life from that hard-earned money. But, we could not see any progress in our life, if we depended on others and others giving us everything continuously. This is my thinking and principle.

Jayanthi's driving principle in life is to prevent others—and particularly her children—from going through the suffering she has endured. She has done everything humanly possible to better their basic life circumstances in the near and long term.

Rani, a 30-year-old woman with no formal education, illustrates the need to better life circumstances in the context of medical care for her children. She describes her motivation to seek a private medical practitioner when her children are ill, while settling for a government hospital when she is ill.

Rani: I always go to the government hospital. But I would take the children to private practitioners when they fell ill. The treatment in the government hospital is not very effective. When I take the children to the government hospital, they advise [the children] to take ¼ tablet or ½ tablet when we are supposed to take 1 tablet. So, it won't be cured.

But, I wouldn't prefer a [private practitioner] for myself; I would compromise and go to the government hospital.

… When we go for treatment for a cough and cold, [the private practitioner] gives cough medicine, tablets, everything. He prescribes medicine if we feel that the child is too ill and we ask him to prescribe. Otherwise, he won't prescribe. The drugs he provides are sufficient.

I would ask [the practitioner] to prescribe; I can't tolerate when the children are affected by cough and wheezing. Otherwise, there would be high shivering due to fever. They would be crying. I am struggling completely for the children. I should take care of them, so I ask the doctor to prescribe medicines and assure him that I will buy them outside.

At the product level, resource constraints and affordability, immediacy of basic needs, and making, buying or foregoing combine to create an emphasis on the betterment of basic life circumstances. This motivation is evident in near-term and longer-term goals.

Resource constraints also lead to interdependence, such as between the small neighborhood retailer and the buyer, with the former providing credit in times of need in return for regular patronage. Two brief examples illustrate the relationship level of our analysis. Chandra, a 28-year-old woman with no formal education, responds to a question about buying from a different shop than the one she regular buys at below.

> **Chandra:** Yes, we cannot buy there after buying here. We should buy in the same shop. We can get acquainted if we buy in the same shop. If we skip this shop without buying here and go to that shop, this shop owner would get angry. If I skip them and don't buy regularly, he would be upset. So, we buy in the same shop.

Bharathan is a 32-year-old man who has completed the 9th grade. He explains how he checks the medicine he buys by consulting with the doctor, another example of the one-on-one interactional marketplace.

> **Bharathan:** I will buy after inquiring. I will go to the doctor and ask. They themselves will say whether it is correct. [The medicine] is not that powerful. This company is different.
>
> If the company is different, the medicine may be the same with same power. If I have a doubt, I will go to the doctor and ask him whether I can take the medicine.
>
> If they give another brand of medicine, I will go to the doctor and ask whether it can be taken, since the children are going to use it. If it is used by us then it is ok to take it.

We cover more detailed examples of individuals who span our product- and relationship-level analysis. Velamma, discussed in Chapter 1, is a 45-year-old woman who reported that she studied up to 5th-grade education in a village. She ran her household for many years, often having nothing to eat and substituting meals with an inexpensive beverage rich in carbohydrates for herself, her husband, and children. Under these circumstances, she never borrowed, choosing to live within very limited means.

> **Velamma:** We didn't have even clothes to wear. No clothes, sir. When I came to Madras, all my relatives regretted it. The people

here have pity on me; I struggled that much. They would say, "Why are you being so innocent without experience?" Relatives won't help anybody. No one helped me. That is why there is stubbornness in me. I struggled to that extent. I should take continuous effort and retain the courage. I should not take any cowardly decision to die. You say, if I am coming to work in your house, and I work throughout the day, you may give Rs. 100. My husband never allowed me to work like that. He gave me the courage. He would take me to the temple with confidence. He would take me along with him to the shop, if we wanted to go. So, I learned and got experience.

Her life circumstances, as do many others', illustrate resource constraints, lack of affordability, and the immediacy of basic needs at the product level. Velamma's life illustrates many examples of making, buying, or foregoing (especially the latter) at the product level. About 15 years into running her household as described above, her husband became dysfunctional. To become the primary breadwinner, she started a business reselling utensils bought from stores located some miles away in her community. In running her business, she takes on the challenges associated with a marketplace characterized by frequent one-to-one interactions between and among consumers, sellers, friends, relatives, acquaintances, and even strangers. Below, she emphasizes the need to insist on a single price when consumers do not like a product.

> **Velamma:** Few people are like that. … I would ask them to check the products that were given to others. I would tell them that I gave them the same products that I gave to others. Some may accept what I said and leave quietly, some may shout. I may have to adjust to both situations.

> ….I would invite them to check the quality of products supplied to other customers. The other customers would say that the product given was good and useful. This feedback would cool down their temper and they would leave quietly.

> ….If they don't want [the original item], they can choose any other product available. But I won't return the money. At any cost, I won't give the money back.

> ….We can't encourage this, [or else] others may follow it. They may go and announce to others that they got the money back from [me]. So the others would follow suit. Hence, I give the product only. Whatever item, they can ask, but no money. I do not give the money back.

Velamma reflects a number of relationship elements as well, and, in particular, the one-to-one interactional marketplace and associated word of mouth. In this one-to-one interactional marketplace characterized by customers making constant demands based on personal preferences, she resists exchanging a returned item for a costlier item, fully aware that the consequences will be swift, with the word getting out and all buyers making similar demands. Similarly, when a consumer refuses to pay for a product that she has taken possession of, the seller insists on payment. Whether such payment is made or not, the seller cannot be seen as waiving payment and wavering on this issue.

> **Velamma:** Without any knowledge of the item, they would ask what the price is. Some didn't know the price, so they would ask their husbands. If they asked their husbands, what would they say? They would say that it does not have to be bought. So I would explain to those who don't know anything. I would tell them not to consult their husbands. If they consult the males, they cannot add a single article in their house.
>
> I would tell them: "See, you should save Rs. 3. When they give Rs. 10 for the family expenses, you could pay me Rs.1, and you save the balance of Rs. 2. You have children. Suppose they get married tomorrow. What would the others ask you? They should say: 'Okay, your talent has saved [the situation] though your husband is an alcoholic.'" When I talk in this manner, they get confidence and courage. They would decide that they should support me and encourage me, who counseled them and gave them the courage. I have the skill [to do this]. They would listen to my words and ask me to enroll them. They would appreciate me for encouraging them. They would support me in this manner.

Here, Velamma tries to explain and educate the consumer about the benefits of buying certain items that would be useful during important life-events such as marriage. In fact, the seller counters what husbands are likely to say, discusses a hypothetical situation such as the marriage of a child, and points out that others would commend the potential consumer for having saved despite having an alcoholic husband. She is willing to discuss to this length with individual consumers, but maintains confidentiality. She expects potential consumers who were encouraged to be courageous to then reciprocate and give her business for having counseled them. In a one-to-one world, how a consumer would look in the eyes of others is an important consideration in decision-making.

Reciprocation for counseling of this sort, where the consumer-person distinctions are blurred, is through purchasing from the seller and helping her out as well. Velamma relates the empathy that leads to purchases from her.

Velamma: They would pity me. They would say, "Not bad, you are working with such boldness."

Another example that spans the product and relationship levels of our analysis is provided by Kamala, a 44-year-old woman with an 8th-grade education, who discusses her decisions as a consumer.

> **Kamala:** Chili powder is sold ready-made. But I do not buy it. I buy Chili and Dhania and crush it to make chili powder in my house. I will crush and prepare even turmeric powder. Sometimes packet products may not be fully usable. I even crush wheat to make flour. Flour is sold in a packet. But there is no gain for me if I buy it.

> ....I gain. It will also be clean. When we do this, we will be satisfied because [the shops] may also adulterate the product. We will watch the process when chili powder is crushed in the machine. When chili and dhania are crushed in the shop, they add rice powder. I have seen this. What we make ourselves is good for our health. Seragam, pepper, and dhal [ingredients] are added to [my] crushed chili powder. They are not added in the [store-bought] chili powder.

Making instead of buying is illustrated by the quote above.

> **Kamala:** Monthly, when we allocate Rs.100 for the clothes shop and when such an amount is available to me, we will be able to have more clothes. But when there is less cash on hand at the end of the month, I will reduce the side dish. Sometimes when we prepare sambar (a liquid dish to mix with rice), we will prepare only one side dish (porial). But at the end of the month we will prepare only a sambar and no side dish will be prepared. At that time, we will stop the porial and prepare a pappad (cheaper snack/side item). This is how we reduce the items. We cannot eat all items always.

The mix of making, buying, and foregoing is also displayed in how Kamala adjusts meals. Foregoing is also the case when it comes to celebrating the most valued of religious festivals. Within a narrow range of affordability, individuals may be willing to pay a little more for central ingredients that address basic needs and consumption events such as one good meal a day. Kamala describes her willingness to pay a little more to buy the right kind of lentils (Dhal).

> **Kamala:** ... some dhal can be boiled easily and after boiling, it will be broad. When we prepare gravy, it will stretch it out. Some dhal will be small, but the rate is low. When we prepare gravy it will not have the same taste and the quantity will also be less. For us even

[if] it costs another Rs.2 or Rs.3, [it] does not matter; that product bought by us will be suitable for us. So we buy such products. [When] we get tamarind, in some there will be more nuts, in some only one or two nuts, but the latter will cost Rs.2 more than the former. I will buy the latter only. Even when it costs more, I will buy only that. If there are more nuts in the tamarind it cannot be dissolved. When we dissolve half of the nuts are gone. So we can buy tamarind with less nuts than the tamarind with more nuts. Just like that, I will see every time and buy.

Conclusion to Illustrative Descriptions and Quotes, Section 5.1

The interrelationship of three factors influences product decisions and the search for a small set of affordable products that meet basic necessities:

- severe resource constraints and lack of affordability,

- immediacy of satisfying certain basic needs when facing deprivation in several facets of life, and

- constant trade-offs between buying, making, and foregoing.

Intertwined with (and often blurring with) these factors related to product needs is the betterment of basic life circumstances. This betterment is a central driving motivation in day-to-day subsistence life. This motivation operates in the short term through a focus on immediate and basic needs—for example, providing healthy food and proper medical attention for children. It also operates in the long term, such as in the desire to educate children for a better future.

Given the deprivation associated with subsistence, products have the potential to transform lives. Such deprivation is multifaceted, and spans a wide range of dimensions and vulnerabilities, ranging from the material to the psychological (Hill 2001; Narayan 2000; Maranz 2001). Because of the level of deprivation in which people in subsistence survive, basic life circumstances can be bettered significantly in ways that do not translate to non-subsistence settings.

Such betterment is often immediate. Though similar to instant gratification in time frame, the betterment of basic life circumstances is for the most fundamental of needs, namely, for survival and subsistence. Consumption of specific foods to add vital nutrients to the diet, the use of soap for hand washing, and the use of cell phones for medical emergencies, such as in the middle of the night in a village, are examples where products in subsistence contexts can have immediate effects on basic life circumstances.

Relationships and the Human Dimension

At the relationship level, the severe resource constraints of subsistence marketplaces create interdependence, accentuated by barriers to physical mobility. Reflecting the interdependence between and among buyers and sellers, the environment is characterized by frequent face-to-face interactions (see Illustrative Descriptions and Quotes, Section 5.2). Therefore, intertwined with resource constraints and the consequent interdependence are relational marketplaces that we refer to as one-to-one interactional marketplaces. One-to-one interactional marketplaces are characterized by buyers and sellers interacting face-to-face and overcoming shortcomings such as their lack of literacy through social skills and personal connections with others.

This context leads to frequent communication, accountability, and service considerations on the part of sellers, who personally know buyer preferences. There are constant pressures from individual, group, community, and neighborhood influences to customize goods and services. Transactions are often fluid, with price and quantity negotiated, installments not paid for defective products, and prices adjusted for personal circumstances for both buyer and seller. However, sellers may need to adhere to consistent procedures and equitable treatment of customers, for fear of powerful word-of-mouth effects and preferential treatment being demanded by everyone.

The one-to-one interactional marketplace can engender the development of skills, awareness of rights, and self-confidence, for both consumers and vendors, with the latter often the route for economic survival. Buyers, sellers, friends, relatives, acquaintances and even strangers share information and advice in the one-to-one interactional marketplace characterized by lack of informational and other resources and interdependence (see Illustrative Descriptions and Quotes, Section 5.2). One-to-one interactions, in turn, lead to the development of consumer skills by providing a medium for low-literate, low-income people to participate in and learn about the marketplace. Extreme income constraints can also lead to skill development out of the need for short-term survival. Skills can combine with one-to-one interactions and strong word-of-mouth effects to counter unscrupulous practices or poor quality offerings.

Interdependence, the one-to-one interactional marketplace, strong word-of-mouth influences, and the development of consumer skills result in an emphasis on the human dimension in exchanges (see Figure 5.1 and Illustrative Descriptions and Quotes, Section 5.2).[14]

---

[14] We use the term human and the phrase emphasis on the human dimension to refer to the centrality and immediacy of basic life circumstances of people in economic and other relationships.

In terms of dependence, people cope with lopsided exchanges by appealing to empathy for basic life circumstances at a human level, rather than the purely economic dimension. Thus, shared adversity, such as the need to survive and make a bare living, is often used as a basis for appealing to the other side to negotiate exchanges. Blurring the economic with the social and with a human emphasis, a sense of fairness and trust plays a large role in day-to-day marketplace activities and relationships. This is not to paint a rosy picture of an intensely harsh reality, but to emphasize positive elements of the one-to-one interactional marketplace, which can be network-rich, although resource-poor. In fact, social networks can cut both ways: people who do not participate in traditional practices may be ostracized, and public humiliation may be used as the means for enforcing loan repayment.

Although research focusing directly on subsistence marketplaces is sparse, literature developed in other contexts provides relevant insights that support our findings on relationships. One example is the nature of exchanges that have been categorized into reciprocal and market exchanges. Reciprocal exchanges are based on "informally enforced agreements to give goods, services, information, or money in exchange for future compensation in kind" (Kranton 1996, 830) while market exchange "takes place among anonymous agents who use money as a medium of exchange" (Kranton 1996, 833).

Reciprocal exchanges in subsistence contexts occur for a variety of reasons, including the need to establish relationships to shield oneself from financial crises. Consistent with our observations, such relationships are characterized by the use of influence and the emergence of trust (Molm 1994). In an environment where there are myriad human interactions and a shared sense of adversity, relationships are central to business exchanges. Although resource-poor, subsistence marketplaces may be rich in social capital—that is, the institutions, relationships, attitudes, and values governing interactions among people and contributing to economic and social development (Coleman 1988, S100-01; Iyer, Kiston, and Toh 2005, 1016-17). When used for coping, social networks provide a range of support, including money, in-kind assistance, emotional guidance, and information (De Souza Briggs 1998, 178-9).

Illustrative Descriptions and Quotes, Section 5.2

Kamala also describes how she negotiates the marketplace with the help of her children.

Kamala: Now, if we buy medicines, I do not know much of it.

...That [expiration date] I don't know what. Whether the medicine written and given by the doctor is the same must be compared and seen, should it not? Mostly his handwriting cannot be understood; even the English is not known. So we send our children to the medical store to buy it. They sometimes even change the medicine and give. But when we ask, they will say that the company is the same and that is nothing. So I may buy also the changed items. But our children will see it first, when they come. After seeing, they will say it is not this, this item is not this. Hence, mostly I will give [the prescription] to them and ask them to buy it. In such cases, we are not able to do without them. Even when I go to the bank, I do not know how to write it. I don't know to fill up the form. I don't know to withdraw or to deposit money. They have given training for this. First, you write it like this, fill it, like this, if the cheque is given you should withdraw like this, this and that is taught by them. With that I was trained and I will do it by myself.

Resource constraints and interdependence, the one-to-one interactional marketplace and word of mouth, and development of consumer skills are all displayed in Kamala's description above.

Kamala: Business is related to their conscience. Some do business by giving good quality things, even if the profit is less, expecting more customers will buy. But some desiring more profit will only think of selling the things on hand at that time.

....When I buy vegetables in the market, the rate for 1/4kg will be Rs.2 but in the nearby shop it will be Rs.4. If we point out the difference to the next shopkeeper, he will say that the rate is high because he has to go and get vegetables from Koyembedu market spending money on transportation. Such and other reasons will be given by them. The weight of the vegetables will also be less. Not only in this shop, in all the nearby small shops, the weight will definitely be less. When we go to the ration shop, the weight will be even smaller. We cannot ask them. Even if I go and ask, what can one person be able to do by going against them? The common balance is, there you have the chain on one side, on the side of the weight stone, and the chain will be hanging in a bunch. We will be able to see it clearly in a ration shop. If we buy and check at home, the quantity will be less. From kerosene to all other items, it is less in the ration shop. Likewise, the weight is less when I buy vegetables in the nearby shop. At the same time, if I buy vegetables from the market and compare, there will be a difference. Once a week on Sunday, being a holiday for my children, I take them to the market to buy vegetables in bulk since I alone will not able to carry the weight. I will save more money by buying the vegetables from the market than buying from the next shop.

Kamala describes the emphasis on the human dimension in exchanges while displaying the development of consumer skills in a one-to-one interactional marketplace with resource constraints and interdependence. With the lack of informational and other resources and interdependence, myriad one-to-one interactions and development of consumer skills through the exchange of information and advice between and among buyers, sellers, and others, there is an emphasis on the human dimensions in exchanges. Empathy in terms of the need for people to make a living and survive is a prominent sentiment and a frequent basis for argument or appeal. Buyers and sellers interact and converse about a variety of topics. Buyers give weight to the hardships that sellers go through in deciding to buy. Sometimes, buyers distribute their purchases across shops selling similar items to provide patronage and help the livelihood of both shopkeepers. Long-term relationships between buyers and sellers often blur the economic with the personal realm. Empathy also extends to multiple members in different parts of the value chain and to government officials who interact with vendors.

Sumitra, a 46-year-old woman with no formal education introduced in Chapter 1, discusses issues that span our relationship and marketplace levels of analysis. As she could not read, she would match patterns to identify the numbers of buses to travel on, often travelling by the wrong bus or being treated rudely by strangers whom she asked for help.

> **Sumitra:** I would show [the number written on my hand] and ask whether this particular bus would stop here. … Whether the 37 would stop here or the 27 would stop here. I would show it and ask the people in the bus stand, and then I would catch the bus.
>
> I didn't want to ask anyone in the middle of the journey. … I wouldn't ask anyone who was standing in the bus stand. First, I would judge the people around, whether they were good, then I would ask them. I could identify the right people from their faces and appearances. … [The wrong people] wouldn't tell or guide, but criticize. So I would decide that we should not ask such people; instead I should catch whatever bus comes. I would catch the bus and enquire from the bus conductor in the middle of the travel. Suppose he was a good person, he would say that this bus wouldn't go on the route I asked and he would guide me to get down and show the proper stop to catch the right bus. Sometimes, the conductor was not in a good mood or was an irresponsible person, and he would shout at me in anger with filthy words and ask me to get down from the bus.

Her experience reflects interdependence as well as the one-to-one interactional marketplace we discussed. She relates above, how she would compare the bus number written on her hand by her husband. Sumitra reported being abused and controlled by her husband until his death. When he was alive, she reported having minimal skills as a consumer. After his death, she became the primary decision-maker. She took some adult literacy classes that have transformed her life as a consumer and led to the development of consumer skills.

Sumitra: Nowadays, I am asking with a commanding tone. [The shopkeeper] would tell me that a drumstick was Rs. 2. I would ask him whether he would be ready to sell it for Rs.1; otherwise, I would go to next shop. I would ask everything very assertively and in a high tone...

....He had exploited me [previously]. ... I wouldn't have calculated. I wouldn't know the price. It was just what he told me. I have just followed the same [pattern] for the past 36 years. I was 13 years old when I got married. Now, my age is 46 [sic]. I had been buying for the same price that he fixed and stated. I paid the same. ... I wouldn't ask the price.

... Now, it has been okay for the past month. I would check and verify as they coached me. I would verify the bill. I know all this. I would ask [the shopkeeper] why he cheated me. It happens in the wholesale shop too. [The local shopkeeper recently] asked why I am not like I used to be earlier. [The wholesale shopkeepers] realize that I have changed. [The local shopkeeper] asked like that. He sells soap for Rs. 11, which is sold for Rs. 10 at the wholesale stores. I would ask him how he could sell like that. I would ask him to justify. He would ask me to pay the wholesale price and not to shout there. He cheats well. It is the place for cheating. We earn hard money. Here, we could earn good money if we know [how to avoid] cheating.

... [The shopkeepers] are cheating. They cheat, even the weighing is not correct in the local shop. The person here has bought a new machine. I would check the weight, because sometimes it was wrong.

Sumitra describes below the humiliation she suffered when unable to repay a loan, which can be enforced through public humiliation.

Sumitra: We had borrowed Rs. 30,000 when my husband was ill. The moneylender came once and shouted with filthy words. We felt sad and worried much. My husband felt that the person who came up well [in life] with his support shouted at him because of the credit. So, he instructed that I should not go to [the moneylender], whatever the family situation in the future.

Marketplaces and the Larger Social Milieu

At the marketplace level, severe resource constraints are reflected in dependence on poor infrastructure (e.g., roads, buses, and utilities), which may limit physical mobility in urban neighborhoods and severely curtail it in geographically dispersed rural settings (see Illustrative Descriptions and Quotes, Section 5.3; Jacoby, Murgai, and Rehman 2004). Such constraints translate to dependence on the larger community. Each village or neighborhood is akin to a unique, small, fragmented market, with many differences between each market. Reflecting the resource-poor environment and community level interdependence, different types of organizations function in both urban and rural settings, including self-help groups, non-governmental organizations (NGOs), and local groups (see Illustrative Descriptions and Quotes, Section 5.3).

Together with groups borne out of tradition, such as castes and governing bodies, these groups form the sociopolitical structure, creating unique environments. For example, self-help groups of women in urban areas and villages often buy and sell products together, creating a powerful word-of-mouth effect (e.g., Rew 2003). Myriad group influences play a powerful role (see Illustrative Descriptions and Quotes, Section 5.3), combining with mistrust of outside organizations, who are often perceived to be uncaring or exploitative.

This creates influence at the grassroots level, which is diluted in relatively resource-rich settings where resources enable mobility among other things, and a significant degree of insulation from local influences. With mobility constraints and varied group influences, subsistence marketplaces are noteworthy for the many differences among villages, urban neighborhoods, and the otherwise fragmented markets they represent. Underlying these factors is the complex, larger social milieu that must be negotiated and is embedded with marketplace-level activities.

Illustrative Descriptions and Quotes, Section 5.3

As this quote reflects, group influences and negotiation of the social milieu is central in these one-to-one interactional settings. While her husband's death was liberating in many ways, Sumitra (introduced in Chapter 1) lives the way her husband "would have wanted" her to, apprehensive of what others would think of her even in such seemingly mundane events as eating at a hotel.

Sumitra: We visited, when my husband was alive. Supposing I go now, there is a chance that my neighbors would notice it. If someone noticed me in the restaurant, they would tell others that so-and-so's wife is eating in the restaurant. They wouldn't say that I was in the restaurant to have food because I was hungry. But, they would pass sarcastic comments like "Look at her, she goes to the restaurant instead of cooking at home."

I would get angry if I heard such comments. So, I won't even buy and have a snack from the shop nearby. You could check with others. Even when I am hungry, I prefer to prepare rice porridge and eat it. I don't have the habit of eating in hotels.

This is the negative side of the one-to-one interactional marketplaces, with myriad group influences in a world of extreme resource constraints, limited mobility and dependence on groups, and small, fragmented communities and markets, emphasizing the importance of negotiating the social milieu.

Another example that spans relationship and marketplace levels is provided by Kavitha, a 38-year-old woman with a 5th-grade education. She describes how she copes with the marketplace as a consumer, seeking information from buyers, sellers, relatives, friends, and acquaintances in the one-to-one interactional marketplace. In turn, development of consumer skills is a central characteristic associated with relationships in subsistence marketplaces.

Kavitha: .... The [shopkeepers at the corner retail store] also go out to buy from other places and do their sales here. Since we live close to the shop, we have to pay and buy. If we realize that the [shop owner] is cheating us, we ask him immediately why he supplied less when he charged more. He would say that this is what he can supply. I would tell him, "don't cheat us, I inquired in the nearest shops and you can check it up with other shops." But he would say that he gives us the wholesale rate. ... Sometimes, it would appear that he cheats us, but what can we do, we would buy and come.

...If it were the first time I wished to buy [something], I would ask the grandma living in the neighbor's house. She is very old; she would guide me to buy. Even If I buy a mat I would ask the neighbor's suggestion: "Grandma, they tell me this much is their final selling price, please come and see whether it is worthy and it is a genuine price". She would verify the material and suggest the legitimate price, then I would buy."

Kavitha also explains how groups form to administer financial schemes ("chits") that encourage savings and provide help in times of need, emphasizing the myriad group influences at the marketplace level.

> **Kavitha:** We would enroll ten members. A [chit conductor] would enroll ten members. If ten members joined and there were regular collections of chit amounts every month from all members, it would reach ten thousand at the end, and we could use it to repay any of our loans. Like savings in the bank, we should continue to pay [the conductor]. We would get cash in lump sum.
>
> ...They won't visit; they invite the neighbors and people known to them for the enrollment. They would tell us that [the conductor] is going to start chits and would ask us whether we are interested in joining. We should be present [at the scheme organizer's house/place] promptly on every tenth day [of the month]. We should be ready with the chit amount when the bidding starts. Collected chit money would be available for bidding. Those interested can join in the bidding. Whether you join the bid and take the money or not, you should remit your monthly chit dues immediately to the organizer.

In this setting, myriad group influences come from a variety of different groups ranging from local governmental bodies to non-governmental organizations and community based organizations, and self-help groups of women. Kavitha explains the role of an NGO in her urban community in providing a number of services including small business loans, adult literacy programs, and health related services. (Two of the members of our research team used to work for this NGO.)

> **Kavitha:** We never used to go out of our house. All women were within the four walls of their house. Ever since this office came here, [the NGO] often conducts meetings, and tells us many things which we didn't know. [The NGO representative] would give some assignment, like asking us to visit the neighborhood and do the collection [on savings plans], and we would do it. We were at home without any exposure; we didn't even have the confidence to speak like this. We have gained it all because of him.
>
> ...[He] would visit this office regularly and sit in his chair like [the interviewer], and we would help the needy families meet him. He would call five or six women members too [to join in the discussion]. [A woman would] call the families and members to have a discussion with him. ... We would bring [the families]

to this office and make an arrangement for a meeting with [the NGO officer]. He would counsel them. I think they haven't taken advantage of the programs due to a lack of information or knowledge. But, all people in this area have utilized it; you can inquire, check, and confirm this with anyone from this area. Everyone has benefited from the [NGO]. I was idle at home without any exposure or knowledge. First, they conducted a meeting and invited all of us to discuss the issues and problems that affect our life. [The NGO officer] advised me that I wouldn't know anything if I continued to be idle at home. Instead, I could attend any training. I attended sewing training. Now, I have a sewing machine in my home and use it to stitch even the old clothes or worn out ones, if I have any. I would not give [the work] to another tailor shop; we have that kind of talent, especially among the women, and it was brought out by the (NGO).

Conclusion

Unique characteristics of subsistence marketplaces relevant to our rationale are summarized in Figure 5.1, driven by extreme resource constraints at different levels. At a product or household level, resource-poor people must make careful purchases of a few affordable products that meet immediate basic needs, while considering making items or foregoing them altogether as alternatives. Given the level of deprivation that people face, betterment of basic life circumstances is a driving motivation in daily existence.

From a business perspective, these factors emphasize the importance of understanding life circumstances and designing affordable products that improve these conditions. It is noteworthy that there is a lack of a range of resources, such as informational resources, which can inform people about products that can improve basic life circumstances (e.g., the importance and need for hand washing). This emphasizes the importance of products that offer multifaceted solutions that address these needs, paralleling the need for integrative development strategies discussed in the literature on poverty alleviation (Fairley 1998).

At the relationship level, resource adversity leads to interdependence, a one-to-one interactional environment with strong word-of-mouth effects, and the development of consumer skills (see Section 5.1). Embedded with these issues at a relationship level is the human dimension in exchanges, i.e., the basic life circumstances of survival and subsistence. From a business perspective, these factors emphasize the importance of fairness and trustworthiness in relationships with customers and communities, as well as an emphasis on customer and community welfare.

At the marketplace level, resource constraints lead to interdependence among groups and organizations, and are coupled with constraints in physical mobility (see Figure 5.1). In effect, the larger market consists of small, fragmented markets (Jacoby, Murgai, and Rehman 2004), with myriad differences stemming from various group and organizational influences. Marketplace activity often blurs with the larger social milieu. From a business perspective, these factors emphasize the importance of finding the common denominator of social good that resonates with diverse groups, as well as the importance of working with, and drawing from, the expertise and influence of diverse individuals, organizations, and groups in implementing business plans (cf. Brugmann and Prahalad 2007). In summary, extreme resource constraints in subsistence marketplaces suggest unique characteristics at the product, relationship, and marketplace levels, with important implications for businesses that are explored in the next section of the book.

References

Brugmann, J. and Prahalad, C.K. Cocreating business's new social compact. Harvard Business Review 85 (2): 12-25.

Coleman, J. 1988. Social capital in the creation of human capital. American Journal of Sociology 94 (Supplement): S95-S120.

De Souza Briggs, X. 1998. Brown kids in white suburbs: Housing mobility and the many faces of social capital. Housing Policy Debate 9 (1): 177-221.

Fairley, J. 1998. New strategies for microenterprise development: innovation, integration and trickle up approach. Journal of International Affairs 52 (1): 339-346.

Hill, R.P. 2001. Surviving in a material world: Evidence from ethnographic consumer research on people in poverty. Journal of Contemporary Ethnography 30 (4): 364-391.

Iyer, S., Kiston, M., and Toh, B. 2005. Social capital economic growth and regional development. Regional Studies 39 (8): 1015-1040.

Jacoby, H., Murgai, R., and Rehman, S. 2004. Monopoly power and distribution in fragmented markets: The case of groundwater. Review of Economic Studies 71 (3): 783–808.

Kranton, R. 1996. Reciprocal exchange: A self-sustaining system. American Economic Review 86 (4): 830-851.

Maranz, D. 2001. African Friends and Money Matters. Dallas, TX: SIL International.

Molm, L. 1994. Dependence and risk: Transforming the structure of social exchange. Social Psychology Quarterly 57: 163-176.

Narayan, D. 2000. Voices of the Poor: Can Anyone Hear Us? New York: Oxford University Press.

Rew, A. 2003. Why has it ended up here? Development (and other) messages and social connectivity in Northern Orissa. Journal of International Development 15 (7): 925-938.

Chapter 6
Understanding Subsistence Marketplaces[15]

Image 6.01: Fresh produce for sale in Essaouira, Morocco. Photograph by Vince Millett; Creative Commons licensed image via Fotopedia: http://ja.fotopedia.com/items/flickr-833971009.

This chapter will help you develop broader insights about subsistence consumers, entrepreneurs, and marketplaces, aiming to provide you with a big-picture understanding. Seven themes characterize these marketplaces (see Figure 6.1). We categorize these themes according to the phenomena they describe.

Our study of the larger marketplace context, reflecting the backdrop of subsistence life in general, revealed two essential themes: "pervasive interdependence" and "pervasive orality." We also considered the relational marketing environment, reflecting the norms governing all interactions, and

[15] This chapter includes material adapted from the following previously published work:

Viswanathan, Madhubalan, Srinivas Sridharan, Robin Ritchie, Srinivas Venugopal, and Kiju Jung (2012), "Marketing Interactions in Subsistence Marketplaces: A Bottom-Up Approach to Designing Public Policy," *Journal of Public Policy and Marketing*, 31 (2), 159-177 (Lead Article). DOI: 10.1509/jppm.11.049

observed two themes, which we label "interactional empathy" and "enduring relationships." Finally, the essence of buyer-seller dealings—marketing exchange—was characterized by three themes: "buyer-seller responsiveness," "fluid transactions," and "constant customization."

In the following section, we elaborate on each of these themes, illustrating them with quotes drawn directly from our interviews with informants. (We use fictitious names to preserve anonymity.) Where necessary and possible, we also include the adjacent discussion to provide context for you.

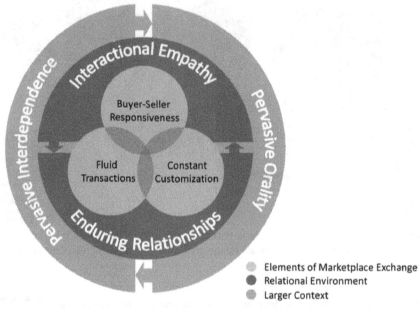

Figure 6.1: Marketplaces in Subsistence: Embedded Interactions and Exchange.

Larger Context

As noted, we discovered two themes within the larger context of the marketplace. The first of those is pervasive independence.

Pervasive Interdependence

Social interdependence is a condition that exists "when the outcomes of individuals are affected by each other's actions" (Johnson and Johnson 1989). Individuals exhibited an unusually high degree of social interdependence in both their economic and non-economic dealings. Interdependence was so widespread that it was the presumptive norm in virtually any situation, encompassing not

Understanding Subsistence Marketplaces

just buyers and sellers engaged in marketing exchange, but also family, friends, neighbors, and other members of the individual's social network. Individuals frequently relied on neighbors and family members for help in executing their roles as consumers and income earners. Read the words of Jayanthi, a 50-year-old woman with a 2nd-grade education:

> **Jayanthi:** Since our neighbors knew we were poor and struggling, they would take us to the field and coach us how to do these jobs.... If we went along with them, they would guide and demonstrate to us how to do a particular job.
>
> I was living with my mother-in-law and father-in-law for more than two years. They used to visit the shops. They would give me cash and ask me to buy the items from the shop. I practiced in the beginning as per their instruction and later I learned to go independently.

Sumitra, a 46-year-old woman with no formal education introduced in Chapter 1, spoke of relying on family members to calculate bills:

> **Sumitra:** [The shopkeeper] would give me the bill; I would show it to my children to check. My younger son doesn't know to calculate. My elder son would calculate the bill. If the total showed an extra Rs.2 or 3, he would ask me why I paid more. I would tell him, "What do I know?"

Conversely, the individual who relied on others in one situation often became the person counted upon by others in another. Says Jayanthi:

> **Jayanthi:** We didn't have the support of any male to maintain our family. So, my mother and I [went to work]; my brother and sister were small children... We provided education only to these children in our family. We both used to go for jobs.

Jayanthi spoke of the need to help others and work hard:

> **Jayanthi:** These kinds of problems should not be repeated to any others. There are people with problems worse than us and we could not deny that. We should coach and guide those who need help, to our level best to overcome their problems; and it is good for us, too. We could not live on other's earnings or assets till the end. If we worked hard, we could get few amounts as our balance. We could have a happy life from that hard-earned money. But, we could not see any progress in our life, if we depended on others and others gave us everything continuously. This is my thinking and principle.

Interdependence with Professionals

Interdependence also included trusted professionals who were clearly in a higher socioeconomic class but practitioners within the local community. Rani, a 30-year-old woman who has a 2nd-grade education and is a food shop owner, says this about medical help:

> **Rani:** I would ask [the practitioner] to prescribe; I can't tolerate when the children are affected by cough and wheezing. Otherwise, there would be high shivering due to fever. They would be crying. I am struggling completely for the children. I should take care of them, so I ask the doctor to prescribe medicines and assure him that I will buy them outside. He would prescribe within Rs.20 to Rs.30.

When asked where she would buy the medicines, she noted there was a medical shop nearby, and that she would ask the doctor there to check the prescription.

So, Rani depended on local professionals to not only prepare a prescription suited to her low income, but to verify its accuracy after purchase. This likely occurred because the doctor depends on the continued patronage of low-income patients in the community, despite being from a very different socioeconomic sphere. The pharmacist, too, is a member of the circle of interdependence, in that his professional legitimacy hinges on the doctor's approval of the medicines he dispensed. It is a cooperative system, which Deutsch (1962) likens to a relay race, where the doctor expends effort (by inspecting the pharmacist's dispensation of medicines) to ensure compliance by the pharmacist, because both depend on the patronage of low-income patients for their economic well-being.

Interdependence at the Same Socioeconomic Level

We also witnessed interdependence between marketplace actors of comparable socioeconomic standing. Local merchants were keenly aware of their interdependent status with their local clientele. They often employed tactics to maintain and leverage that interdependence. Some informants noted that while they would extend credit to specific customers in times of their need, they would also demand immediate repayment if a customer who owes money bought elsewhere. Twenty-eight-year-old Chandra, a woman with no formal education, explains:

> **Chandra:** Yes, we cannot buy [at the large reseller's] after buying [at the neighborhood retailer who offers her credit]. We should buy in the same shop. We can get acquainted if we buy in the same shop.

If we skip this shop without buying here and go to that shop, this shop owner would get angry. If I skip them and don't buy regularly, he would be upset. So, we buy in the same shop.

The consumer is not without power in this interdependent relationship. In the extreme, she has the option of covertly moving out of the neighborhood without making her repayment. More typically, she will engage in widespread word-of-mouth about the unfairness of credit terms of the seller, thereby influencing his reputation—perhaps his most valuable asset.

In sum, all parties seem to be aware of the need to channel individual efforts toward a common goal of economic survival. Thus, it is not dependence (i.e., the outcomes of one person are affected by the actions of a second, but not vice-versa) or independence (i.e., one person's outcomes are unaffected by the actions of others), but rather mutual interdependence (Johnson and Johnson 1989) that offers the best framework for marketing exchange in the subsistence context.

People have both the means and the motivation to influence those around them. In the end, vendors survive only if customers are able and willing to buy from them, while customers' daily lives rely on the presence of local vendors who can respond and adapt to their needs.

This is different from competitive situations in conventional marketing contexts, where retailers seek to extract maximum profit from customers (since doing so does not jeopardize most customers' financial viability), and customers seek to maximize benefits at minimum cost (since there is a broad choice of retailers, and a reasonable substitute is always available if one retailer fails).

Previous descriptions of the marketing exchange context in Indian subsistence marketplaces contain illustrations of interdependence: widespread sharing of information about the most useful products and the most trustworthy shops, community-based savings schemes where families pool their financial resources to garner marketing advantages (Anderson, Locker, and Nugent 2002), and self-help groups where groups of consumers and entrepreneurs collaborate to enhance each other's marketing potential (Narayan and Petesch 2002).

In the literature on conventional, advanced economies, too, marketing scholars have noted that interdependence is the key to a stable and mutually-oriented economic system (Achrol 1997). Common examples include service encounters (Czepiel 1990) and cross-cultural and agency relationships in marketing channels (Skarmeas and Katsikeas 2001). However, whereas interdependence in these contexts is often limited to the financial or knowledge dimensions, the interdependence in subsistence contexts is both intense and pervasive, as we have described above.

Pervasive Orality

Communication is a basic requirement of interpersonal exchange. Low levels of literacy mean that spoken language is the communication mode of choice to navigate marketplace exchanges. This is consistent with the concept of 'orality'—the predominance of oral-verbal literacy that exists in some cultures (Ong 2002).

The predominance of oral communication heavily influenced negotiation tactics in marketing exchanges engaged in by our informants. Because contracts between buyers and sellers were made without written agreement, and oral communication precluded the possibility of information storage, exchange partners were forced to rely on people's memories.

Accordingly, offers tended to be accepted or rejected on the spot, and sellers who extended credit tended to collect the receivable relatively quickly, to avoid problems arising from forgetting and inaccurate recall. Take, for example, the experience of Narayan, a 32-year-old man and neighborhood small-store owner with a diploma in electrical appliance maintenance:

> **Narayan:** They won't come with their notebook while coming for the purchases…we used to give them a small pocket notebook… sometimes they may not bring that book due to urgency or some other reason…. We would accept [their credit] and supply their needs after making entries on our book. They may not visit our shop for a few days. If we reminded them, they would ask "When did I buy this?" or "I bought this much only." They would agree when I showed them my notebook entries and reminded them of the situation when they visited our shop. So, I would strictly tell them that they would be given supplies only if they come with that small notebook. There are such problems we have faced in this transaction. Whatever the cautious approach we maintain, we have to face such problems.

Blurring the Distinctions

The reliance on oral communication tends to blur the distinctions between economic and personal spheres of life. This is especially important in the subsistence environment where not-for-profit social institutions tasked with funding charity-worthy projects are visible marketplace actors alongside profit-oriented small businesses. These social institutions offer much support for marketplace-related needs (e.g., seed money or in-kind support for entrepreneurship), but make decisions often based on considerations of life in general. Says 45-year-old Velamma, a woman with a 5th-grade education who resells utensils:

> **Velamma:** I asked for assistance. My daughter was studying through [a local NGO]. They had been helping us for the education. I told the lady that we didn't have a cycle for my husband to go for a job. They delayed for a little time...because...would anyone give suddenly? ... I would visit the office daily. I asked. Then they came to my house and inquired about my family details and our history. We told them that we did vessels business and we did cake business. It is our family situation. A son burnt his hand from the stove flame. I sent him to school up to the 10th [grade] and provided for the needs. ... He can't go for outside jobs. He used to do painting job with his right hand. So [the non-profit organization] gave me Rs. 4,000 immediately, when I asked them.

Literacy Shortcomings and Financial Challenges

Reliance on oral, rather than written, communication also created some challenges. Some people were constrained in their financial dealings because they were unable to perform complex calculations or keep extensive accounts. However, this did not necessarily translate to an inability to perform everyday calculations. People who lacked formal training in mathematics or writing used an oral system (commonly referred to in the local marketplace as "mouth-arithmetic") to perform calculations by talking their way through the process. Muthamma, a 37-year-old woman with no formal education, explains:

> **Muthamma:** As I can't write, I can say the income orally. I can make only oral calculations. I can say the income and expenses orally. I can say the income received, expenditure incurred, and balance to be paid or received, all through oral calculations. I can't keep it in writing. It is difficult for me. It is good to keep in writing, which could be useful to refer to at any time. Yes, it is one of the difficulties for me.

Some of our respondents appeared to be particularly fearful of situations where their literacy shortcomings could be exposed or leave them vulnerable. They talked about:

*   steering clear of conversations with unacquainted shopkeepers for fear of being asked questions they could not answer;

*   avoiding making demands because they did not know their rights; and

- sidestepping unfamiliar products because they did not understand their pricing or feared they would be unaffordable.

In other words, the visible stigma stemming from low literacy became temporarily concealable by limiting their scope of economic activities or giving up their rights, although this only perpetuated the stigma. The result was that many people tended to buy exclusively from known shopkeepers under familiar circumstances—such as Balaraman, a 31-year-old man with no formal education:

> **Balaraman:** Since I have not studied, when I speak to others I talk to [shopkeepers] with fear. Because I have not studied, I find it difficult to answer them when they ask any questions. Suddenly, if [the bank] gave [me] a paper and ask me to write, I don't know completely [what I would do].

Adds Gauthami, a 28-year-old woman with a 3rd-grade education:

> **Gauthami:** How to make the purchases if I go to a shop? How to ask the seller? How much would they say [the price costs]? Whether we should ask the rate first or we should ask the item, these are all problems. ... If I had studied well, at least up to 8th [grade]...you see, sometimes [larger shops] ask me what my education is. I feel bad. I wouldn't have such feeling if I had studied. I could state my education proudly.

The Strengths of Oral-Verbal Communication

Such communication apprehension appears to be a product of one's low literacy. However, it does not necessarily correlate with one's verbal abilities as a whole. In fact, strong oral-verbal abilities are acknowledged to flourish in some populations that are low-literate and socially marginalized.

For example, the thriving of oral-verbal traditions is seen as integral to African Americans and to the maintenance of cohesiveness in their communities (Harris, Kamhi, and Pollock 2001). In other words, it can be a useful lever in the marketplace context. Spoken language is generally simpler than writing in content, structure, and word choice, yet concurrently more complex in how it conveys meaning—aided by nonverbal cues such as gestures, intonation, volume, pitch, pauses, and visual cues such as appearance and movement (Liberman 1995). Oral communication also invites creativity in the sound, rhythm, and memorability of utterances (Goody 1987). The ability to use spoken language colorfully, persuasively, and even playfully, was a useful marketplace interaction tool in the context we studied.

Thus, the orality we observed could constitute a unique form of literacy that is neither correlated with nor subjugate to text-based literacy (Ong 2002). From a marketing perspective, it underscores the importance of "building dialogical foundations in marketing" (Varey 2003). In conventional marketing environments where the written word plays a more central role, marketing efforts by sellers have typically been one-way and information-driven.

However, our data suggests that subsistence people who excel most in oral-verbal literacy may experience the greatest discomfort when confronted by written communications. Their frustration arises from difficulty with reading, but is perhaps accentuated because their facility and flair with spoken language stands at odds with their struggles with the written word. The result, as seen in quotes above, is often a feeling of powerlessness and an enhanced sense of psychological distance from stores and people—typically from higher socioeconomic strata—who are more comfortable reading and writing.

Relational Environment

Embedded within the larger context are two themes that characterize how interactions play out in day-to-day commercial activities: interactional empathy and enduring relationships. We describe both of these, in turn, below.

Interactional Empathy

A central feature of interaction in the subsistence setting we observed was its strong emphasis on the human dimension, on the needs and circumstances of each individual. Read the words of Mythili, a 40-year-old woman with a 4th-grade education who sells flowers:

> **Mythili:** Business is not that important, but first, the human being is very important… "How are you now?", you should inquire about me. "What happened, you usually speak freely but appear dull now." You should ask me in this manner and I should ask you in return… This comes first, money comes next. Yes, first we should approach each other with love and care like our relatives.

The above quote reflects the high degree of consideration that sellers often give to their customers' daily life circumstances. Treating people with dignity first, and focusing on the abstract rules that typify formal marketplaces second, is a key component of the interdependence seen in the marketplace. In contrast with developed markets, informants in our study indicated that buyer-seller negotiations regularly included references to the need for each party to make a living and survive.

Among the buyers we interviewed, a common refrain was: "the seller needs to make a living as well"—a sentiment that contrasts sharply with the zero-sum-game perspective of conventional buyer-seller dealings (Dwyer, Schurr, and Oh 1987). Sellers, for their part, commonly varied prices in response to their acute understanding of the specific life circumstances of their customers. In the words of 32-year-old Preethi, a female tailor with a 6th-grade education:

> **Preethi:** If you ask me how we fix the rate...one of my customers is from a poor family and the other one is from a rich family.[16] I charge Rs.22 from the customers who belong to middle-income families, charge Rs.25 from those who come from rich families and charge Rs.20 from those poor people who are working at jobs like housemaids and other odds and getting low wages...

> **Interviewer:** Would any other customer come and ask you, "Why did you charge her Rs.25 when you had charged Rs.22 or Rs.20 from others?

> **Preethi:** One or two would question me... Hence, I would inform these people that I charge [the other customers] only Rs.20 since they are poor and struggle in life. I would caution [poor ladies who get a discounted rate] not to reveal it to others...because, [whichever customers have more] money, they won't accept it.

Working Together to Survive

Buyers told us that when a seller was charging prices that seemed unreasonably high, they would frequently remind him or her of the need for everyone to survive. Conversely, sellers reported that, when customers ask for additional quantities, they would often explain business costs and the problems involved in providing these "extras" in terms of their personal situation. One interesting instance was reported by the aforementioned Rani, who dealt with customers who failed to pay for already consumed products and services:

> **Rani:** Some people would order, and after having the food, they would say that they had no money and would pay it tomorrow or in the evening. It would frustrate me. I would tell them, "Don't come to eat on credit. I am not rich, I can't afford to extend credit. After all, I am solely depending on my business. Hereafter, don't come for credit." I would get angry because these people would tell me that they had no money only after ordering and eating.

---

[16] Preethi speaks in relative terms, as her clientele are all of low-income background.

Having uttered some angry statements to make her personal situation clear to her customers, this seller reported subsequently allowing them to continue in the economic relationship—in essence, forgiving them. In another instance, when asked if she checks prices before buying, one informant—a customer of a neighborhood retail store—explained that it would not be right to inquire about the price of a product with a seller who had helped her in times of need. She wondered aloud "how the seller would feel" about such behavior.

Empathy: A Common Denominator in the Marketplace

Such understanding, consideration, and forgiveness at a human level in marketing exchange is reflective of the concept of empathy. Empathy involves Person A viewing Person B's situation from the perspective of B, allowing A to feel as if the situation is personally affecting him rather than someone else (Basil, Ridgway, and Basil 2008).

Empathy has been extensively studied in the psychological literature (e.g., Toi and Batson 1982) and is ideally applicable to marketing exchange relationships. Whereas empathy in relationship marketing contexts (e.g. sales, B2B, and international trading or partnering situations) has been expected to improve cooperation and allow buyers to feel more participative in the exchange process (Evans and Laskin 1994), it is difficult to detect empirical evidence of empathetic exchanges in the context of formal marketing systems. Perhaps, for empathy to occur, there must be psychic and social proximity between actors (Basil, Ridgway, and Basil 2008; Conway and Swift 2000). In short, whereas social distance appears to enhance the need for empathy in securing better outcomes, it may also inhibit its emergence. Conversely, empathy may play a central role in subsistence environments where marketplace actors are heavily invested in their common futures and simultaneously socially isolated from other formal marketing systems.

The central role of empathy in subsistence marketplace dealings does not, in any way, take away from the harsh life circumstances. However, by explicitly acknowledging the individual's life circumstances in the process of navigating the marketplace, these circumstances become an overt part of the negotiation. In this sense, the human and the economic factors are blurred. This is very distinct from the discussion of empathy in formal marketplaces, where empathy has been argued to lead to altruism and helping behaviors within exchange—a benign connotation with clear power differentials.

Enduring Relationships

A second hallmark of the relational environment in the subsistence marketplaces of South India is the emphasis that buyers and sellers place on cultivating long-term relationships. This is grounded in sound economic logic, as the lifetime value of a loyal customer multiplies their economic importance to the seller (Jain and Singh 2002), and loyalty to a seller reduces choices, and thereby costs of choosing, for a consumer (Sheth and Parvatiyar 1995).

For many of our informants, the potential need for credit in times of hardship was a powerful motivator of customer loyalty to neighborhood retailers. Unless the buyer exhibited continued patronage, the seller would generally withdraw credit and press for repayment of loans, an untenable situation for consumers when navigating phases of extreme vulnerability.

Conversely, because sellers also required a stable source of income to subsist and survive, they would work hard to be responsive and maintain a loyal clientele. Narayan, a 32-year-old man with a diploma in electrical appliance maintenance, who owns a small neighborhood store, says:

> **Narayan:** Few good customers are among the families who are living in rented houses. They would pay cash, buy more quantity and buy good items regularly. Suddenly they may not have cash, they would ask credit for Rs.50 and assure that they would settle the bill on the first date of the coming month. Like that, first I would test a few customers by providing credit for Rs.100 or Rs.200. They, too, would settle the bill promptly as they assured. They would become our regular customers gradually and we would provide them on credit.

In conventional markets, economic considerations would normally only engender financial loyalty, as evidenced in the literature on relationship marketing (e.g., Berry 1995). In the context we observed, however, social interdependence of the actors appeared to motivate the cultivation of more multifaceted, longer-term relationships. Hence what develops is relationship marketing at a deeper, social level (see Berry 1995 for a discussion of financial, structural, and social levels of relationship marketing).

Advantages of Long-term Relationships

Aside from fostering trust and the economic value of individual customers, long-term relationships can also impart specific transactional advantages, including increased seller willingness to accept product returns, extend credit, and offer better service and higher quality goods. This creates both tangible (i.e., economic) and intangible (i.e., psychological) benefits to the parties involved. Read what Kamala, a 44-year-old woman with an 8th-grade education, reports about long-term relationships:

Kamala: We would not change the shop. We would buy in a single shop. If there were any differences in the shop, we would return it to them. We would boldly go and ask, as these things are not good and up to expectations. [The shopkeeper] would immediately change the item... For me, he would give the best goods after weighing. I would say, "I am buying it from you continuously, how could you give me this?"...I have not been cheated by anyone so far. If the shop owner desired that we should not leave his shop and that we should be regular customers, he would be very courteous to us.

You need to view these advantages in context to fully appreciate their significance. For example, it is a common practice to deliberately improperly weigh products—but not so, in the experience of Mythili, a 40-year-old woman with a 4th-grade education who delivers flowers. Mala buys regularly from the same shop. She says:

Mala: If you buy regularly, they give extra and won't miss the weight. If you do business with a single shop they would give extra and won't make any mistake in the weight.

Sometimes, the trust engendered by long-term relationships can be a strong driving factor, as it reduces the perceived need for consumers to carefully scrutinize product information, thus countering the potential negative effects of their low literacy. Says Kavitha, a 38-year-old woman with a 5th-grade education:

Kavitha: We visit the same doctor...we get cured when he administers the injections, and we get a quick remedy. Other doctors would ask us to visit again and again. He doesn't do this; he administers an injection and tells us that it will be cured in one visit. ... If we went to another doctor, he would prescribe costly medicines for one hundred rupees and ask us to visit him again and again for three days. He would administer three injections, too. The fees would cost around 60 rupees and the medicine cost around 100 rupees, so it would cost a total of 160 rupees. But, we visit the same doctor here and try to finish it within 100 rupees.

Relationships Not Always Benign

These same relationships can, of course, provide a basis for exploitation and abuse as well, illustrating how the effects of social networks are not necessarily benign. In the example below, public humiliation is regularly employed to enforce repayment of non-collateral loans. Sumitra reports:

Sumitra: We had borrowed Rs.30,000 when my husband was ill. The moneylender came once and shouted with filthy words. We felt sad and worried much. My husband felt that the person who came up well [in life] with his support shouted at him because of the credit. So, he instructed that I should not go to [the moneylender], whatever the family situation in the future.

Marketplace Exchange

Having described both the larger context and the relational environment that characterize the subsistence marketplace, we move on to three themes that describe the specific interactions through which marketplace exchange plays out: the responsiveness of buyers and sellers, the fluidity of transactions, and the constant demand for customization.

Buyer-Seller Responsiveness

In a marketplace of frequent one-to-one interactions, sellers are well-acquainted with their customers' preferences. Retailers are usually small, locally-owned shops serving a limited number of regular customers with whom they interact personally. As local residents, they also benefit from easy access to current word-of-mouth information about their customers. Their customer interactions are highly responsive to individual circumstances, which enables offering a product-and-service mix that is carefully tailored to local situations.

As Narayan, a 32-year-old man with a diploma in electrical appliance maintenance and the owner of a small neighborhood store, describes:

Narayan: Since they prefer that particular brand, I buy and keep it in stock. I would arrange it immediately. Suppose I noticed in the morning that it was not available in my shop, I would rush immediately and make arrangements to have the parcel ready within the evening. I would request [customers] to come in the evening if anything was not available or temporarily out of stock. So, customers won't go out of the area to buy; they would go only if we didn't have stock. I would clear even those problems within the evening. Hence, they would try to wait for me until the evening.

Such responsiveness—even if it involves stocking a product for just one consumer—is central in cultivating a trusting relationship befitting one's position as the consumer's primary retailer. Responsiveness, however, is not merely about proactive trust-building, but also reactive trust-restoring. Because product complaints can be raised immediately and directly, the seller faces significant pressure to manage and address them.

Read the words of Rani, the food shop owner, who responds to a question about checking the quality of food sold at local shops:

> **Rani:** We can't find out by looking. We would find out at the time of cooking. In the case of rice, the quality can be determined. While cooking, it may look very nice, but it may be something different after filtering the boiled water. In such a case, we would inform the shop owner that the rice was not good. We would question him about the quality he supplied. "Please change the rice." He would say that the rice bag was changed today, and that we could buy another variety of rice.

This is a different emphasis from formal market systems, where relationship marketing tends to focus largely on building trust (Sheth and Parvatiyar 1995). As earlier quotes about relationships and interdependence illustrate, such responsiveness is from both sides of the exchange as buyers strive to be responsive to sellers as well.

Fluid Transactions

A striking finding of our research was the fluidity of transaction terms, in the sense that they were neither standardized across individuals nor fixed over time. This was perhaps most aptly demonstrated in the frequent potential for the adjustment of product quantity (i.e., weight) by sellers on the spot unobserved by customers, in response to the price negotiated.

In the experience of two women:

> **Chandra:** If we go and ask [the shopkeepers about weighing], they would say, "No, no…it is the same price. I would have given [the other customers] a bit more quantity, that is why I had quoted them a slightly higher price. But, I would have given you a little less in weight, hence, I had given it to you for a lower price."

> **Mythili:** The weight depends on the weighing method. You can do tricks. The person who weighs the scale can keep the fingers open. If they push a finger to the right side it, [that side] would fall down. The innocent would think that they are getting more than the weight and the amount of supply is high and accept it. The experienced person should see the top of the scale.

Relative to individuals in more affluent societies, subsistence consumers buy a greater proportion of their food as raw materials rather than finished or packaged goods. This makes transaction fluidity even more important, because it applies to product quality as well as quantity. In times of high costs, for instance, sellers will often substitute a lower-quality generic item for their usual offering. Narayan reports:

> **Narayan:** Suppose the customers ask us to give them the lower rate, and question us as to why we sell [the item] for one rupee higher than the other place while it is sold for less price in the other place. Here, we keep the [product of the] second quality, too. We sell this just to show them the quality difference. We would explain to them that this is the quality they are selling there for this rate. For example, if the dhal is Rs.35 there, here it is Rs.40. If they asked why it is Rs.40 here, while the same is sold for Rs.35 there, I would tell them that I, too, could give them for Rs.35 and ask them to take this second quality for that rate.

Constant Customization

There is a fundamental tension between the demand for customization and the pressure to treat everyone the same. If the seller accedes to a buyer's request, the offer is accepted quietly—a nonverbal signal to the buyer to keep the discounted exchange confidential, lest it be withdrawn. This quote from Velamma, a 40-year-old utensils reseller, illustrates the nuances involved in agreeing to replace one item with another but not renegotiating the price or giving a refund:

> **Velamma:** Suppose they don't want a certain item, I would agree to exchange it with another item but the price wouldn't be costlier. The item could be a different one as they wished. But no difference in the price of the item. … I would give the product only. Whatever item, they can ask, but no money. I would not give the money back.

Sellers manage word-of-mouth by ensuring they are seen as adhering to a single price and not writing off loans. They also use the fluid nature of transactions to their advantage—charging higher prices for credit purchases, replacing a lower quality generic product for a higher quality one, and weighing differently. This reflects the idea of multiple realities in marketing exchange relationships rather than homogenizing the content of a marketing exchange.

Conclusion

In elaborating seven central themes at three different levels of analysis, our findings paint a rich picture of marketplace interactions in subsistence settings. At the broadest level, they underscore the importance of the distinction between direct and indirect exchange (Blau 1964). Direct exchange (Blau

1964) is especially suitable for small social systems, where interactions occur face-to-face, remain flexible and informal, and are guided by a shared general understanding of what is acceptable behavior (Blau 1964). In advanced economies, transactions are frequently conducted between social aggregates (e.g., organizations) rather than individuals, and governed by institutions whose guidelines make these transactions highly predictable—yielding indirect exchange.

The marketing exchange we observed in the subsistence marketplace follows a very different paradigm, with transactions conducted via direct social interaction between people, and market expectations informed mainly by the nature of the relationship between the market actors in question (direct exchange).

References

Achrol, Ravi S. (1997), "Changes in the Theory of Interorganizational Relations in Marketing: Toward a Network Paradigm," Journal of the Academy of Marketing, 25 (1), 56–71.

Anderson, Alistair R. and Sarah L. Jack (2002), "The Articulation of Social Capital in Entrepreneurial Networks: a Glue or a Lubricant?" Entrepreneurship and Regional Development, 14 (3), 193–210.

Basil, Debra Z., Nancy M. Ridgway, and Michael D. Basil (2008), "Guilt and Giving: A Process Model of Empathy and Efficacy," Psychology & Marketing, 25 (1), 1–23.

Berry, Leonard L. (1995), "Relationship Marketing of Services—Growing Interest, Emerging Perspectives," Journal of the Academy of Marketing Science, 23 (4), 236–45.

Blau, Peter M. (1964), Exchange and Power in Social Life. New York: Wiley.

Conway, Tony and Jonathan S. Swift (2000), "International Relationship Marketing: The Importance of Psychic Distance," European Journal of Marketing, 34 (11/12), 1391–1413.

Czepiel, J. A. (1990). Service encounters and service relationships: implications for research. Journal of Business Research, 20 (1), 13-21.

Deutsch, Morton (1962), "Cooperation and trust: Some theoretical notes," in Nebraska Symposium on Motivation, Marshall R. Jones ed. Lincoln NE: University of Nebraska Press, 275–320.

Dwyer, F. R., Schurr, P. H., & Oh, S. (1987). Developing buyer-seller relationships. The Journal of Marketing, 11-27.

Evans, Joel R. and Richard L. Laskin (1994), "The Relationship Marketing Process: A Conceptualization and Application," Industrial Marketing Management, 23 (5), 439–52.

Goody, Jack (1987), The Interface Between the Written and the Oral. Cambridge, UK: Cambridge University Press.

Harris, Joyce L., Alan G. Kamhi, and Karen E. Pollock (2001), Literacy in African American Communities. Mahwah, NJ: Lawrence Erlbaum.

Jain, Dipak C. and Siddhartha S. Singh (2002), "Customer Lifetime Value Research in Marketing: A Review and Future Directions," Journal of Interactive Marketing, 16 (2), 34–46.

Johnson, David W. and Roger T. Johnson (1989), Cooperation and Competition: Theory and Research. Edina, MN: Interaction Book Company.

Liberman, Alvin M. (1995), "The Relation of Speech to Reading and Writing," in Speech and Reading: A Comparative Approach, Beatrice de Gelder and José Morais, eds. Hove, UK: Erlbaum, 17–32.

Narayan, Deepa and Patti Petesch (2002), From Many Lands: Voices of The Poor. Washington, DC: World Bank and Oxford University Press.

Ong, Walter J. (2002), An Ong Reader: Challenges for Further Inquiry. Thomas J. Farrell and Paul A. Soukup, eds. Creskill, NJ: Hampton Press.

Sheth, Jagdish N. and Atul Parvatiyar (1995), "Relationship Marketing in Consumer Markets: Antecedents and Consequences," Journal of the Academy of Marketing Science, 23 (4), 255–71.

Skarmeas, D. A., & Katsikeas, C. S. (2001). Drivers of superior importer performance in cross-cultural supplier–reseller relationships. Industrial Marketing Management, 30 (2), 227-241.

Toi, Miho and C. Daniel Batson (1982), "More Evidence That Empathy Is a Source of Altruistic Motivation," Journal of Personality and Social Psychology, 43 (2), 281–92.

Varey, Richard J. (2003), "A Dialogical Foundation for Marketing," Marketing Review, 3 (3), 273–88.

Chapter 7
Subsistence and Sustainability[17]

Image 7.01: Dharavi pipe walk in Mumbai, India. Photograph by Meena Kadri; Creative Commons licensed image via Flickr: http://www.flickr.com/photos/meanestindian/5433295466/.

Environmental challenges are most pronounced in poverty contexts, where local environments are disproportionately at risk due to planetary destabilization. A majority of the poor in developing regions of Asia and Africa live in ecologically fragile areas (Leach and Mearns 1991). At a broad level, debates center on the need for eradicating poverty before addressing environmental problems and the role of environmental degradation in causing poverty.

The centrality of natural resources in poverty contexts have been studied in terms of deforestation, access to water and sanitation, health-related outcomes, and a variety of other topics. The relationship between poverty and the environment is very complex, with a range of moderating factors at different levels of society. In this chapter, we describe the material and psychological realities in subsistence contexts as they relate to the environment.

---

[17] This chapter includes material adapted from the forthcoming *Journal of Macro Marketing*. Permission not required as per other previous adaptations from the same journal. Titled: Subsistence and Sustainability: From Micro-Level Behavioral Insights to Macro-Level Implications on Consumption, Conservation, and the Environment.

Learning from the Subsistence Context

Why is the subsistence context an important source of learning about sustainability in all contexts? For one, at the human level, the resource constraints fast arriving on the shores of affluent societies have always been a fact of life in these contexts. As such, the inventiveness and adaptivity that subsistence consumers and entrepreneurs display in evolving and engaging informal systems of exchange, in doing more with less, and in having a minimal carbon footprint hold lessons for all societies.

Trade-offs between consuming to survive the immediate term and conserving for the longer term are common facets of day-to-day life. Moreover, subsistence contexts represent the most unsustainable of human conditions, and solutions created here may have far-reaching implications. For instance, distributed solar power options when there is a lack of infrastructure related to electricity may have applications in affluent contexts vested in specific infrastructure.

Finally, subsistence contexts are particularly informative about the interplay between the people and planet aspects of sustainability. Being, by definition, unsustainable from a people perspective, these extreme conditions provide a window into what sustainability really means and how the local environment affects day-to-day lives. In turn, it provides insights into how the people and planet elements are inextricably interlinked even in relatively affluent societies and the implications it holds for business practice in this regard.

Given our bottom-up orientation, a number of questions at the intersection of subsistence and sustainability are germane:

- What does sustainability mean from the perspective of consumers living in subsistence?

- What are the sub-domains of local sustainability as they relate to entrepreneurship (e.g., sociocultural, environmental, economic)? How are these sub-domains interrelated?

- How do subsistence entrepreneurs trade off between short-term and long-term conservation of scarce resources? What are the challenges and opportunities for sustainable business practices in subsistence marketplaces?

- How can business solutions in subsistence contexts create win-win-win scenarios with regard to their impact on people, planet, and profits?

Using these broad questions as a starting point, we examine the interconnections between subsistence marketplaces and the environment. The discussion covers the distinctive nature of environmental issues in subsistence contexts in terms of being immediate (household), near (local), moderate (society), or farthest (global) in distance, both physically and psychologically.

Several coping strategies emerge beyond reducing and reusing, such as making and foregoing. These strategies reflect how people sustain themselves through activities related to survival, relatedness, and growth. We develop propositions that link distances and coping to efficacy and motivation to act and derive implications for macro-level issues in marketing management, and public policy.

Observations

A few words about our research approach with this specific topic are appropriate as there are some unique aspects. We began interviews at a concrete level in terms of problems people face with their immediate environment, how their local environment affects them, and how they affect their own local environment. We then moved onto broader issues of how we affect nature and in turn are affected by nature. Terms such as global warming and climate change were reserved for the end of the interview, given their abstract nature and the need to discern individuals' perceptions. We begin by listing some unique insights.

All Ecology is Local

In subsistence marketplaces, environmental issues are not at some level of abstraction wherein people can compartmentalize them and move on. Rather, they hit home at a local level. If people use plastic bags to dispose of their defecation, sewages get blocked and diseases spread. Environmental issues are not distant, geographically or temporally, but are a day-to-day reality. The quote below illustrates neighborhood practices and how they affect quality of life:

> **Nandini:** Nobody disposes of their garbage properly. It is spread everywhere. The air passes through the garbage, bringing the bad effects and foul smell. It is inhaled by everyone, from children to adults. Then...the smoking of cigarettes...the smokers smoke the cigarettes in public places, which affects everyone.

The individuals quoted below relate ways in which they attempt to follow some sustainable practices in the face of daunting challenges:

> **Sharada:** Even today I saw a plastic bag containing garbage thrown on the street by someone. My own principle is not to use plastic. I used to go with a cloth bag while shopping. I used to advise others not to use plastic. But nobody listens...they pack their domestic waste and garbage in a plastic bag and simply throw it on the corner of the street while they go to work or shopping. People are too lazy

to use a broom and a box to keep separate the bio-degradable and plastic materials. Even the [educated] people going to work come out of their houses, keeping their handbag in one hand and a plastic bag filled with garbage in the other hand. They never bother about the dust bins; they simply throw the garbage on the corner of the street. There are many bachelors who have migrated from other cities; they, too, make the same mistakes. Due to the plastic covers, the heat is increased; it blocks the water flow also.

Venkatesan: We should try to keep our environment clean and protect our family members from diseases. It would help us to reduce medical expenses. ... As individuals, we can't do anything to control or contain the air pollution. The number of vehicles is increasing day by day; controlling this is not in my hands. We can grow plants and creepers, if we have a little space. We can prevent the breeding of mosquitos, which is a major hazard in the city, if we avoid the stagnation of water around our living places.

Erosion of Social Networks

Individuals also linked development to the erosion of social networks. They reminisce about a previous time when there was a thriving joint family system, and bemoan the lack of neighborhood support in current times. This is how one individual put it:

Bhuvaneswari: Nowadays, more flat systems (apartments) are flourishing and available than individual houses...there was attachment in the joint family system. We cannot expect such socialization and attachment among the families living in a flat system, whereas we can expect a kind of homogeneity among the families living in individual houses on a street. Families living in a flat system will not bother about their neighbours.

Individuals also talked about unsustainable development affecting local environments:

Nandini: Unnecessary buildings are mushrooming everywhere. In the past, the houses were made with thatches and used palm leaves or coconut leaves. We didn't find that much pollution when we were living in such houses, because those leaves or thatches controlled and filtered whatever dust passed through air. Now, we aren't safe because of the present types of buildings. If we resides in a flat where someone came and murdered us, no one would notice us or come forward to rescue us. The structure is not conducive to alert the neighbors. They can't hear what is happening in a nearby house.

Lack of Accountability

Due to the emergence of these types of buildings, poor people continue to be poor and rich people continue to be rich. Overlaying all these issues is the issue of governance and lack of accountability at the neighborhood level:

> **Nandini:** Irrespective of the people or organization, whether it is a company or government or service organization or politicians, they take care of hygiene in their own rooms and drinking water for their needs. They should give preference to providing clean water to the public. They use the official machinery to keep their compound and nearby areas free from sanitation problems. They wouldn't bother about the end of their own street or the next street where the public reside. ... Nobody understands that pollution would affect everyone. The air coming out from A/C machines, air coolers, electric cookers, microwave ovens, etc., is poisonous....

Unsustainable Material Expectations

Individuals also noted a central issue that underlies sustainability—unsustainable material expectations! Living at or near subsistence, they are able to recognize how central such expectations are to sustainability, perhaps something likely to be taken for granted in more affluent settings.

> **Nandini:** There is no truth; truth does not prevail in society. Mothers have no sincere affection for their children, children have no affection for their parents. It becomes like a mechanical life; all become like machines. ... The reason is because of expectations. People try to cheat when they have too high of expectations. For example, those who are riding bicycles wish to acquire motorbikes; those who have bikes wish to get their own car; those who have their own car wish to buy their own bungalow. Real affection is diluted while the level of expectations increases.

Intuitive Perceptions of Sustainability

Both in rural and urban settings, subsistence living entails close interaction and intimacy with the local environment. People have an intuitive sense of sustainability that can be attributed to the value placed on scarce resources and the direct dependence on nature. The subsistence farmer's direct reliance on rain for his or her livelihood illustrates this point. Again, this is in contrast to relatively affluent settings where people can shield themselves for the large part from the vagaries of nature, such as the weather. Depending on nature for a variety of needs also leads to this orientation:

> **Nandini:** Nature has changed. There is a change in the seasons. Ancestors classified the seasons in a year into four—winter, summer, etc. There is a proverb that says "Even the grinding stone will be moved by the winds/storm coming in the month of [16 July-15 August] ... But, we can't notice the wind at all in this month.

> **Anbazhagan:** We should not destroy the forests that are beneficial to humans. It will lead to lack of air, failure of rain, and destruction of nature. When the forest goes, even the plants and small trees will disappear automatically. Awareness should be created to join hands in protecting the forest. We should protect nature.

Economic Sustainability is Paramount

In subsistence, ultimately, economic sustainability is paramount. Without it, survival is in doubt. The following person expresses concerns about economic sustainability:

> **Pankajam:** Money is everything for human sustainability. ... I don't go to such an extent to make changes in my life or change practices for the sake of sustainability of the society, as I am living within the family level. My time is enough only to manage and fulfill the needs of my own family. How can I bother about society's needs? I can only be concerned about society if I am satisfied that I have fulfilled the needs of my own family. If we are unable to solve our own problems, then how can we solve others' problems?

Societal Sustainability

Social institutions are seen as being central to the issue of sustainability. Individuals assert that business institutions have a key role to play in the provisioning of essential goods and services. Social institutions are also seen as being important in the process of education regarding sustainability and sustainable practices. The following quotes illustrate these points:

> **Bhuvaneswari:** Business institutions should ensure that all products that address the basic needs of people are readily available in the market. These products should be of good quality and be given as

free samples or available at lower prices. Each of their products should create brand trust.

Society should enable its children to learn good habits and practices. Society should ensure that its children grow healthy and are protected from diseases and are provided with good education. They should be taught the importance of protecting their environment. Society should encourage the younger generation to grow with a social consciousness and plant trees, etc.

Climate Change and Global Warming

When individuals had heard of global warming or other larger phenomena, they responded as follows, drawing from an intuitive sense of the environment and nature:

> **Bhuvaneswari:** I have heard that the hole in the ozone layer caused global warming. I believe that the pollution and high smoke is the reason for the hole in the ozone layer. Erecting deep bore wells in too much depth and sucking enormous water is also one of the reasons for the earth warming. Now the number of trees and plants is decreasing. More forests and more trees will give rain. There is a possibility for the earth to get cooler if it receives more rain due to forestation.
>
> All the smoke and pollution is the reason for climate changes. Also, the overuse of electricity is one of the reasons for climate changes. It is good for each person to reduce their consumption of electricity by their level best. We should avoid burning more lights for more hours. Everyone should try to plant and grow trees as much as possible. Government and society should help us to achieve this through awareness.

Coping

Despite the lack of control in so many aspects of life, people find ways to cope and pass on sustainable practices to the next generation:

> **Bhuvaneswari:** I try to provide a good education and healthy food for our children. I dispose of the garbage carefully and maintain cleanliness. I try to encourage my children to walk instead of depending on vehicles. I encourage them to exercise to maintain their physical health. I stopped using plastic items. I collect the garbage from my house and dispose of it at the dustbin erected by

the corporation. I use the brinjal, tomato, and chili seeds, which otherwise would become waste while preparing the vegetables for the preparation of food, to plant at the corner and side wall by my house. Sometimes the seeds yield more... I try my level best to walk to the places where I want to go and avoid using vehicles.

They engage in many household-level sustainable practices to wrest back some control in what is essentially an uncontrollable environment:

Nandini: My own practice to prevent the pollution in the house is... to choose a light color or white cloth to stitch window curtains. I always use a variety of cloth containing minute holes to filter the dust from the air. The minute holes in the curtain cloth enable the free flow of air as well as filter the dust. You can look at the cloth after three or four days and find layers of dust.

We can boil the water and cool it before drinking it. Believe it or not, until today I used the earthen pots to cook rice with water and ate the boiled rice after filtering the rice water.

Although we have a pressure cooker, we don't use it. I purchased a pressure cooker and tried it, but as I found the method was not fit for my health, I stopped it. The benefit from the earthen pot is that the boiled rice doesn't become solid when it is cooked, whereas the rice cooked in the pressure cooker becomes like a rock.

People also find ways to cope by reducing, reusing, and cross-using.

Venkatesan: If you take food, for example, we can have non-vegetarian food as many as four days a week. But, we restrict it to have only one day a week to save money. I try to reduce my own expenses, such as fuel and travel costs. Earlier, I used a two-wheeler or hired an auto to attend all my tasks.

Selvi: I wouldn't hesitate to use the old saree that was used by my sister...I would use the clothes or dresses very gently so they would last for years.

We wouldn't waste even the water used to wash and clean the rice before cooking. We keep this rice-washed water for some time for dilution. We remove the sluggish and precipitated contents and use the diluted water for the preparation of gravy and side dishes. We use the remaining waste water for other purposes such as watering the plants, etc.

We sow the tomato and chili seeds from cooking at the terrace filled with sand. They grow and yield for our family to use.

We dig a pit in a corner of our compound and dump the garbage left in our houses. We leave it for some time to compost and become like manure. We use it as organic fertilizer for the plants. We also grow herbal plants, such as curry leaves, around our house. We use the leaves of these herbal plants to make hair oil, which help us to groom our hair.

We get fresh air around our house as we grow all these plants and trees. We can make simple dishes from these vegetables and herbal plants.

Sharada: I used to keep the garbage in a box and hand it over to the garbage collectors when they visited our street. I wouldn't throw it on the street like others. I try to keep my environment clean. I have made arrangements to ensure that the rainwater that falls on the roof enters the well through erected pipes. I wouldn't allow the rainwater to be wasted. When we have continuous rain we collect the rainwater and use it for domestic purposes.

Doing More with Less

Underlying these coping strategies is the issue of doing so much more with less. The following quotes from multiple respondents illustrate this point:

Selvi: For example, we used to prepare a kind of soup from the combination of rice-washed water, drumstick leaves, a few chiles, and onions. We wouldn't waste any materials. For example, we had a damaged and rusted iron cot. When we tried to dispose of it, we were offered only Rs.50 for the cost of the scrap iron. So, we converted it into a lid for the water tank and saved money. It protects the tank water from contamination through dust or birds' excreta.

We have coconut trees in our compound. We make broomsticks from the coconut leaves grown on our trees. We do this ourselves without hiring any external labor, whether it is cleaning of our sewage system or renovating the well.

We collect the waste fabric from the tailor shop and make pillow covers and mats. We used to make cloth bags from the old pants. We would dispose the old irons and plastic wastes for the exchange of a new plastic bucket.

Bhuvaneswari: If we prepared rice for all of our family members but one or a few do not return home on time to have the food and a little rice remains, ... we will make it as fried rice lace (vadagam/ vathal) or give it to needy people. If any dishes remain from the prepared vegetables from the afternoon lunch, we will use them while preparing the night's food. Nothing is wasted; it would be useful in any other way than it was prepared for.

Burning soap covers along with neem leaves will chase away the mosquitoes. We use the waste covers from the soap we used and collect a few dry leaves, including neem leaves, from the tree near the house to burn and chase out the mosquitoes in the late evening.

Sustaining the Next Generation

People understand that passing sustainable practices on to the next generation is at the heart of sustainability, whether they know it by this label or not. According to two parents:

Suseela: If every parent provides education to their children and has a little savings for the next generation, they can manage the future. Education is the basic need for the survival of all. If they get a good education, they can get jobs and earn enough to meet their needs.

Bhuvaneswari: I try to provide a good education and healthy food for our children. I dispose the garbage carefully and maintain cleanliness. I try to encourage my children to walk instead of depending on vehicles. I encourage them to exercise to maintain their physical health. I stopped using plastic items. I collect the garbage from my house and dispose of it at the dustbin erected by the corporation. I try my level best to walk to the places where I want to go and avoid using vehicles. Instead of using motorized two-wheelers, we should be encouraged to use bicycles. (But the roads are not conducive for riding.)

Challenges in Subsistence Marketplaces

Our individuals living in subsistence encountered environmental challenges at immediate (household), near (local), moderate (societal), or far (global) distances. Here is how we categorized those distances:

- Immediate (household) distance: Refers to people's homes and surroundings where most of their time is typically spent.

- Near (local) distance: This refers to the local environment in terms of issues outside the home, in the streets, and in the community, such as sewage, air, and water.

- Moderate (societal) distance: This represents larger society, such as cities, sets of villages, a province, or the country.

- Far (global) distance: This represents traditional global environmental issues in other settings, such as climate and global warming.

Challenges—Immediate and Near

In subsistence marketplaces, environmental issues are not abstract; they hit home at a local level. For example, local water supplies to households are contaminated, and sewages are often blocked by people using and disposing plastic bags, resulting in disease spreading. Three individuals describe the problems they face:

Chiranjeevi: Currently, the water is a problem [due to rain], the supply is mixed [contaminated], and the water is the main source of the spread of diseases. The water from drainages is mixed with drinking water supply, so it is contaminated.

Nandini: Nobody disposes of their garbage properly. It is spread everywhere. The air passes through the garbage, bringing the bad effects and foul smell. It is inhaled by everyone, from children to adults. Then...the smoking of cigarettes...the smokers smoke the cigarettes in public places, which affects everyone.

Sharada: Even today I saw a plastic bag containing garbage thrown on the street by someone. My own principle is not to use plastic. I used to go with a cloth bag while shopping. I used to advise others not to use plastic. But nobody listens...they pack their domestic waste and garbage in a plastic bag and simply throw it on the corner of the street while they go to work or shopping. People are too lazy to use a broom and a box to keep separate the bio-degradable and plastic materials. Even the [educated] people going to work come out of their houses, keeping their handbag in one hand and a plastic bag filled with garbage in the other hand. They never bother about the dust bins; they simply throw the garbage on the corner of the street. There are many bachelors who have migrated from other cities; they, too, make the same mistakes. Due to the plastic covers, the heat is increased; it blocks the water flow also.

One can see that environmental issues are a day-to-day reality. The quotes above illustrate how neighborhood practices affect local quality of life and survival. Another individual spoke of rain ruining a paddy, adversely affecting lives and livelihoods. Heavy rains have a disproportionately negative impact on poor urban neighborhoods because of bad roads, drainage, and sanitation problems that result in immediate economic implications.

By the same token, local environmental resources often act as safety nets during times of uncertainty, leading to a proximal relationship and, consequently, a very concrete view of the environment. There seems to be an orientation of nurturing, with the immediacy of survival not always leading to disregard of the environment. In a rural setting where the local environment is the source of livelihood, a farmer describes how land is nurtured, and reflects on how poor people relate to the land as they would to a person:

> **Anand:** We cannot compare farming with business, because we put our faith in the land—'bhoomi' [earth]—asking it to take care of us and we take care of it equally like our child.

Challenges—Moderate and Far

Both in rural and urban settings, subsistence living entails close interaction and intimacy with the near/local environment. People have an intuitive sense of sustainability because they value the scarce resources they have and are directly dependent on nature. Subsistence farmers' direct reliance on rain for their livelihood illustrates this point. Again, this is in contrast to relatively affluent settings where people can typically shield themselves from the vagaries of nature, such as the weather. Depending on nature for a variety of needs also leads to this orientation about the moderate/societal distance, as one individual noted. In a rural setting, another individual spoke of uncontrollable factors such as weather playing a major role.

> **Anbazhagan:** We should not destroy the forests that are beneficial to humans. It will lead to lack of air, failure of rain, and destruction of nature. When the forest goes, even the plants and small trees will disappear automatically. Awareness should be created to join hands in protecting the forest. We should protect nature.

> **Anand:** We grow ground nuts also, but at present they are not growing well; we feel frustrated when we think of ground nuts. Those are the the the easiest to grow, but because of the unseasonal rains and the change in climatic patterns, we are not able to make profits with that. Even those who sowed now face heavy losses.

Individuals discussed the negative impact of economic survival on common pool environmental resources, and noted a central issue that underlies sustainability at a societal level–unsustainable material expectations. Living at or near subsistence, they recognize how central such expectations are to sustainability, perhaps something likely to be taken for granted in more affluent settings.

> **Anand:** Earlier, there were forests, but now all that has been encroached and it has been brought under cultivation, and the way people work has also changed. Those days, they used to take the effort to mix the vegetation by stamping their feet with dung and prepare the manure, and only then did they start farming. But now, people don't even want to remove their shirts. Nowadays, the whole context has changed; nobody wants to work, everybody wants more money very quickly, and people want to become rich fast.

At the broadest level in terms of the distant/global environment, individuals expressed thoughts about nature itself. When individuals had heard of global warming or other global phenomena, they drew from an intuitive sense of the environment and nature.

> **Bhuvaneswari:** I have heard that the hole in the ozone layer caused global warming. I believe that the pollution and high smoke is the reason for the hole in the ozone layer. Erecting deep bore wells in too much depth and sucking enormous water is also one of the reasons for the earth warming. Now the number of trees and plants is decreasing. More forests and more trees will give rain. There is a possibility for the earth to get cooler if it receives more rain due to forestation.

All the smoke and pollution is the reason for climate changes. Also, the overuse of electricity is one of the reasons for climate changes. It is good for each person to reduce their consumption of electricity by their level best. We should avoid burning more lights for more hours. Everyone should try to plant and grow trees as much as possible. The government and society should help us to achieve this through awareness.

Summary of the Challenges

The actual distance from environmental issues in subsistence is a striking contrast to relatively resource-rich settings, where higher-resourced people and communities can create a distance between themselves and these environmental problems. The means to do so include choice of the environment to live in, environmental regulation, and mobilizing resources to transport out garbage to landfills, thereby creating a distance from the problem. The environmental justice literature underscores the power inequality faced by poor communities in proactively participating in decisions related to the environment (Capek 1993).

Whereas these distances are primarily spatial, they also have an impact on psychological distances. Distance itself has been differentiated along time, space, social ("happening to people like me"), and probabilistic (hypothetical, or how likely an event is) dimensions (Trope and Liberman 2010). In subsistence contexts, all these distances are small when compared to relatively resource-rich contexts. As noted in previous research, the ability to envision beyond the immediate is restricted by cognitive constraints as well. Immediate and near distances capture one's social context, whereas the societal and global represent greater social distances, with the latter two being further distinguished.

With the temporal dimension, the immediate and near spatial distance may be closely tied to the immediate term and the near term. Societal and global levels may seem temporally more distant and distinguished as well. Thus, what we describe originally as in terms of spatial distance may be associated with other dimensions of psychological distance, with the immediate and near distances representing relatively small psychological distance and the moderate and farther spatial distances representing greater psychological distances.

In contrast, in relatively resource-rich settings, environmental problems are often isolated at a physical distance. They intrude in some forms such as pollution in large cities and are often perceived as impacting dissimilar others (low-income communities, or inhabitants of poor nations). In addition, environmental problems are perceived in terms of the broader issues of rising sea levels and warming temperatures whose ill effects are temporally thought to be somewhat distant (years or decades away), and have levels of likelihood attached to them rather than absolute certainty. In this regard, research in relatively resource-rich settings using distances categorized as self, town, country, continent, and world has shown perceptions of more serious environmental problems at greater distances (Uzzell 2000).

Coping and Sustaining

The next area of discussion relates to the ways in which people cope. Despite the lack of control in so many aspects of life, people find ways to cope and strive to move to a sustainable future. The way they cope depends on the distance from environmental issues and roughly corresponds to the degree of control they can exert. The nearness of challenges is roughly associated with the degree of control that subsistence individuals can exert at least in a relative sense as they respond and cope in day-to-day life. There are many examples of coping at the immediate distance. Here is how one individual copes:

Nandini: My own practice to prevent the pollution in the house is... to choose a light color or white cloth to stitch window curtains. I always use a variety of cloth containing minute holes to filter the dust from the air. The minute holes in the curtain cloth enable the free flow of air as well as filter the dust. You can look at the cloth after three or four days and find layers of dust.

People also cope by reducing, reusing, recycling, cross-using and harvesting resources (Lehman and Geller 2004; USEPA 2012). Additionally, making and simply foregoing are other ways to cope as noted elsewhere in Chapter 5 (Viswanathan et al. 2009). For example, one person spoke of collecting waste fabric from a tailor shop to make pillow covers and mats, and making cloth bags from old pants.

Cross-using limited available resources is a recurring theme in the coping strategies displayed in both rural and urban contexts:

Selvi: We have coconut trees in our compound. We make broomsticks from the coconut leaves grown from our trees.

Sanjeevan: We use our cow for milk, and for getting manure for the farm. We get manure from the dung for the farm, and the milk we don't use at the house is sold at the society, and we make a little extra money for household expenses.

Reducing or sometimes even foregoing the use of resources is a strategy often adopted in subsistence to address the issue of resource constraints:

Venkatesan: If you take food, for example, we can have non-vegetarian food as many as four days a week. But, we restrict it to have only one day a week to save money. I try to reduce my own expenses, such as fuel and travel costs. Earlier, I used a two-wheeler or hired an auto to attend all my tasks.

Reusing resources such as clothes and water ensures that these limited resources are optimally used. For example, one person spoke of keeping rice-washed water to prepare gravy and side dishes, and using the remaining water to water the plants. Underlying these coping strategies is the issue of doing so much more with less. These coping strategies address various facets of life such as better health, reduced expenditure and better quality of life.

Even in urban settings, the environment is something to be nurtured, providing resources and benefits. Relating to the environment is a key element to coping; for example, planting trees and plants around the house enhances the quality of life by improving the quality of air and by providing fresh vegetables and herbs for cooking.

A central aspect of these coping strategies is that they involve the immediate environment, i.e., the household, perhaps the only arena where there is some degree of control. Individuals speak to the need to relate to the environment and nurture it at immediate and near distances. Collective action is another aspect of coping for issues at near (local) distance.

> **Selvi:** We can collect water from the well for domestic use. If we face any water scarcity, we will report it to the ruling party man. They will approach the authorities and arrange the potable water through water tankers. It will be stored in a common potable tank and shared by our neighbors.

Sustenance through Survival, Relatedness, and Growth

In enacting these coping strategies, people strive to sustain three key elements: survival, relatedness, and growth (see Figure 7.1). The first arena is physical survival, which includes basic needs such as food, water, shelter, sanitation, and clean air. The motivation here is simply survival, or having the basic necessities for subsistence, the foundation for sustenance. It relates to a variety of physiological needs, which, in turn, are dependent on the local environment. Environmental degradation has a direct impact on health, quality of life, and a host of other issues related to basic physical survival. A number of examples given earlier in this chapter relate to physical survival in terms of food and clean air and other such necessities.

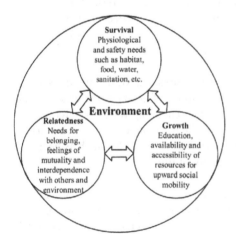

Figure 7.1: Bottom-Up Perspective on Sustainability.

Subsistence and Sustainability

Another theme is relatedness, starting with basic identity and extending to relationships with family, community, the environment, and other entities. Other chapters have emphasized the one-to-one interactional world of intensely personal interactions (Viswanathan et al. 2012), and the quotes earlier emphasize the erosion of social networks with unsustainable development. The realm of relatedness provides the bulwark against the next crises and a sense of identity in the face of the lack of basic resources. Relatedness is tied to the environment in many ways, such as through the erosion of relationships with development, or unsustainable material expectations that affect relationships, or the erosion of cultural beliefs in the face of materialism. In this regard, environmental degradation may be perceived as "shared" by the households of close-knit communities. Environmentally hazardous behaviors such as disposing of garbage on the streets may be weighed against the social cost of harming relationships.

Relatedness also extends to the local environment itself, as earlier quotes on nurturing natural resources highlight. For example, livestock is nurtured in rural settings, emphasizing the need for people to relate to their natural environment:

Selvarasan: When we start farming, we need to take care of the cows; they need straw. If we grow ground nuts, then the plants can be used as fodder for the cattle and the goats, so we consider that at least for the sake of the cattle we have grown this crop.

If we are spending the capital from our money alone, then we can wait until we get a good rate for the produce and then sell it. But supposing we have borrowed from others and used it, then we could not afford to wait. So, rather than wait for the three or four months and get that five rupees extra, we just sell it as soon as we get the harvest and settle the loans.

Relatedness plays a multifaceted role in subsistence. For example, neighboring farmers share information on farming and also collaborate to guard against pest attacks, which can have a disastrous impact on their income. Relatedness also provides a buffer in times of cash constraints, as financial assistance from friends and family becomes critical with limited access to formal financial services:

Sanjeevan: I get the money from my friend and return it when I get my money, sometimes taking money from someone who can give, and the rest we manage with our own funds. Even now, we spent 15,000 for the crop; I have borrowed 10,000 from my friend and I will return it to him in about two or three months. That is how we manage.

The final theme is growth, best captured by the quotes about striving for a better future for one's children through education. Closest to the conventional notion of sustainability in an intergenerational sense, the aspiration to move toward a better future is reflected in this theme. If survival is based on finding a footing in terms of basic physiological needs and relatedness is about identity, then growth is about building on this foundation to reach for a better future.

A better environment for children to live in is implicit in growth, although prominent in the quotes are the need for growth in terms of education and quality of life. The theme of growth refers to people passing sustainable practices on to the next generation and is at the heart of sustainability. In the following quotes, two parents discuss growth:

Bhuvaneswari: As far as education is concerned, the government is doing well and encourages female children to continue their education by providing educational materials, including free bicycles to travel to school. We should prepare our next generation with awareness on the importance of education, clean air, etc., to manage their future.

Narasimhan: My children are studying in the 4th grade. Computers is one of their subjects. If they feel that they need a computer, I would consider the purchase of a computer for them. Neither have I learned about computers nor had opportunities to operate them. But I shouldn't allow my children to face a lack of computer knowledge or opportunity. I would always consider my children's needs; they are my priority.

Although growth needs are an important facet of sustaining oneself, the present condition of subsistence often poses trade-offs between growth and survival needs. One parent noted that education is the basic need for survival of all. Jobs with higher incomes could be foregone for the sake of preserving the important safety net of livestock. Despite the lack of control in so many aspects of life, people find ways to pass on sustainable practices to the next generation–for example, planting trees and plants.

These elements interact with each other. For instance, the immediacy of survival has a potentially negative impact on relatedness, as cultural norms and traditions are more difficult to comply with–but it has a potentially positive impact as well, in terms of bringing social support closer:

Pankajam: Society is helpful in providing employment. If we approach society and seek employment opportunities after sharing our family problems, they will give priority to us among the ten or fifteen already searching for a job. We survive because of the cooperation from the society.

Relatedness and growth may also have a complex relationship, as certain aspects such as identity and belonging provide a foundation for growth, but norms and expectations may inhibit growth and the pursuit of opportunities.

Survival is of course necessary for growth, but the pursuit of survival often focuses on the immediate while sacrificing medium-term growth opportunities. Thus, the bottom-up view of what subsistence people strive to sustain is a complex interplay between the need to survive and subsist in terms of basic, physiological needs, the need to relate in terms of basic psychological needs, and the need to move from subsistence toward a more sustainable path through growth for oneself or the next generation.

Placing this discussion in the context of extensive past research (Maslow 1943; Kenrick et al. 2010), Maslow's classic work organizes the hierarchy in terms of immediate physiological, safety, love, esteem, and self-actualization needs. The notion of a hierarchy rather than primary and secondary drives is based on cognitive and developmental priorities. Many researchers have examined and modified the hierarchy, such as an updated hierarchy of fundamental human motives–immediate physiological, self-protection, affiliation, status/esteem, mate acquisition, mate retention, and parenting (Kenrick et al. 2010).

In this regard, we categorize what individuals strive to sustain in subsistence contexts. We argue that a key set of needs relates to basic physical survival, encompassing the physiological and safety aspects of the hierarchy. Survival is the basis or the necessary condition for thinking about what to sustain. Clearly, the issues in this category can be further divided and placed in established hierarchies of needs. The category of relatedness captures love and esteem needs in the classic Maslow hierarchy or affiliation and status/esteem in one of the modifications of the original hierarchy.

As research on subsistence marketplaces shows, there is constant interaction between the need to relate and the need to survive. Sometimes, the need to survive in terms of basic physiological and safety issues may mean an inability to participate in social relationships in terms of keeping up traditions that involve scarce resources. Often, relationships bolster the ability to survive. Included in the need to relate is how one's own identity and sense of dignity is closely tied to relatedness in this one-to-one interactional world and the motivation to survive.

Survival and relatedness provide the foundation to envision growth, whether for oneself or for the next generation, through such means as education and upward mobility. Growth places people on a sustainable path, made possible by first gaining some foothold through survival. Perhaps the parallel here is to self-actualization, but it is not so much one's full individual potential that is in focus with extreme constraints. Rather, the focus is on realizing some path that leads to growth for one's family in the immediate or medium term or for one's children in the longer term. Growth is fueled by the hope for a better future, if not for oneself, then certainly for one's children. It captures the essence of a sustainable path. Self-actualization, on the other hand, is a luxury that people living in subsistence environments often cannot afford.

Efficacy and Motivation to Sustain at Different Distances

The different distances discussed earlier may have a complex relationship with the themes of survival, relatedness, and growth. We focus specifically on two sets of concepts, one related to control, self-efficacy, and response efficacy (Ajzen 1991; Bandura 1977), and another related to motivation to act (Nicolaij and Hendrickx 2003; Pahl et al. 2005). Survival involves a minimal carbon footprint but the use of resources for the immediate term, sometimes without considering the medium term (e.g., firewood and deforestation). Survival-related issues arise at immediate and near distances. Whereas people exert some control over the immediate, they lack much control over the near distance, although perhaps having some collective efficacy in addressing local issues.

Relatedness also manifests at immediate and near distances and includes relating to the local environment and one's own community. Relatedness may lead to community-level action that may improve the local environment. Cultural beliefs and traditions that arise in a relational context may both enhance or potentially harm the environment as well. Survival and relatedness are also needed in the immediate and near distances to negotiate the present.

However, growth pertains to the longer term or the farther distance temporally and may involve envisioning moderate and sometimes farthest spatial and social distances as well. With an emphasis on a better life for children of the next generation, people may consider societal and global issues as well. With an overwhelming lack of control of near distances and the large local environmental challenges, survival and relatedness may take precedence here. However, growth may in fact focus on the moderate and farthest distance environmental issues. In the realm of growth, people may perceive some level of efficacy in engineering change at farther distances.

Our analysis is summarized in Figure 7.2. The immediate spatial distance is the arena where people possess relative control and efficacy. It relates to basic survival, punctuating the motivation to act. It also pertains to relatedness in terms of belonging and one's own family. Physical survival and relatedness go hand-in-hand in reinforcing their effects in this regard. Degree of control and efficacy falls off in moving to the near distance and the local environment despite the negative impacts on the immediate as the local environment permeates the household.

Nevertheless, there is room for collective efficacy and the motivation to act, while lower, is still at a moderate level. The immediate spatial distance is also one where social, hypothetical, and temporal distances are immediate, with the joint effects of different types of distances perhaps accentuating their effects. In this regard, the research on subsistence marketplaces reviewed earlier also points to the emphasis on the here and now, arising from the survival impetus as well as from cognitive constraints such as low literacy and consequent concrete thinking.

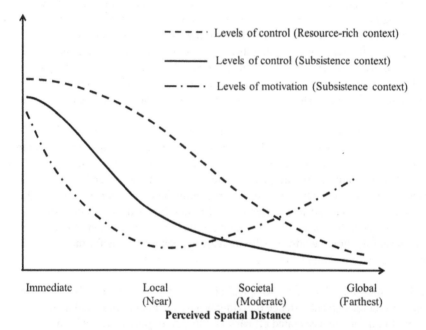

Figure 7.2: Levels of Control and Motivation as a Function of Perceived Spatial Distance.

In moving to greater spatial distances and considering the societal and global levels, social and temporal distances grow as well, with no control or efficacy. However, the growth imperative in striving to sustain may lead to a moderate level of motivation to act for challenges framed at societal and global levels. The discussion is summarized in Figure 7.2 where immediate, near, moderate, and farthest distant environments are represented in one axis along with degree of control or level of efficacy as well as degree of motivation on the other.

Subsistence and Sustainability   **153**

How does our analysis contrast subsistence with relatively resource-rich contexts? The biggest distinction in environmental issues between affluent versus subsistence contexts is one of distance–temporally, socially, spatially, and hypothetically. Past research suggests that as psychological distance from the perceiver increases, the importance of environmental problems is significantly discounted.

In general, environmental risks and their perceptions in affluent settings are psychologically distal, meaning that they are uncertain, alienated from the "here and now," and unlikely to affect selves and similar others. Therefore, environmental risks in affluent contexts are more likely to be mentally represented in abstract terms, and their negative consequences seem abstract and metaphoric, as a result not leading to appropriate action. In other words, when environmental risks and their negative consequences are psychologically distant, one's relevance and vulnerability to them would become weaker and less immediate, lowering risk aversion and motivation to act. In contrast, environmental risks and their perceptions in the subsistence contexts are psychologically near, meaning that they are certain, happen "here and now," and are likely to affect selves and similar others. As psychological distances are likely to be very small, people would make concrete representations of environmental events, which are deeply embedded in their daily lives.

Taken together, these considerations argue against findings in resource-rich settings that people have greater behavioral intentions for remedial actions when environmental risks are psychologically proximal. Rather, coping takes the form of small solutions in one's own home (i.e., the immediate environment), to try to minimize the harmful effects of the immediate and near (i.e., the local environment) in a small way. When feasibility dominates the evaluation of actions at a near distance with overwhelming lack of control, it may lower behavioral intentions, while actually increasing such intentions for more psychologically distant phenomena (e.g., global warming).

Farther rather than closer psychological distance of environmental risks may be central to increasing subsistence individuals' engagement in remedial actions. Level of control and associated efficacy is, thus, an important variable to consider for immediate, near and distant environments on the spatial dimension. The growth motivation for subsistence contexts and the overwhelming challenges with the local environment and the lack of control over it in immediate and near distances may lead to a greater motivation to act for farther distances then for those in resource-rich contexts.

Conclusion

Our micro-level research provides the foundation for macro-level implications that are firmly rooted in the material and psychological realities of subsistence marketplaces. Our delineation of different spatial and psychological distances, and associated motivation and control, explain the complex behaviors observed in subsistence marketplaces in connection to the environment. This contradicts broad generalizations that characterize this population as merely survival-focused and short-term oriented.

Whereas people in subsistence marketplaces are more likely to act on their immediate needs (Viswanathan, 2011), this does not suggest that only one simple dimension exists, or that people in subsistence marketplaces fail to see farther distances. In light of the complex relationship between different motivations at varying distances, and consequent actions, practitioners need to recognize and address each of the levels of spatial distance as well as the various dimensions of psychological distance and their interactions.

Despite imminent challenges to bare survival, people do not make decisions based solely on the immediate and the economically beneficial, but consider the influences from the different distances. Even under resource constraints, many are aware of and consider conflicting motivations at different spatial distances. But they are often only able to act at the immediate level due to bare survival necessities and lack of control over farther distances. However, in making impossible trade-offs, people still strive to not compromise in certain domains, such as children's education. Even while lacking resources, people are able to plan for the future through sacrifices and investments at an immediate distance.

Environmental sustainability does not necessarily come at the cost of immediate economic gains. Whereas growing population and scant material resources often lead people to consume in unsustainable ways for survival, they realize the value of environmental sustainability and are able to make decisions that create synergy between economic gains and sustainability at the immediate and, to a lesser extent, near distances.

This chapter focuses on understanding the notion of sustainability from the perspective of those living in subsistence to complement top-down notions. Through ongoing qualitative research, we discussed the spheres of life where subsistence individuals view a conflict between ecology and economic activity and the need for sustainable solutions. What is emerging from our research is a local notion of sustainability that at its heart is holistic—an interconnected web of issues such as deterioration of the physical environment, reinforcing a lack of civic values and social networks and the erosion of local culture, and the attenuation of human relationships.

Sustainability is interwoven into daily life and local ecology, as the impact of an unsustainable local environment is immediate and subsistence individuals do not have the resources to protect themselves. Reusing, reducing use, and using for multiple purposes come naturally in these resource-constrained settings.

Facets of life are not compartmentalized; the social, environmental, and economic realms of life blur, and unsustainable development and failing ecology lead to erosion of social relationships, unsafe physical environments, and threats to livelihoods.

The intersection of sustainability and subsistence presents a most challenging arena for research and practice. On the one hand, severe resource constraints make for a natural proclivity to conserve and do more with less. Subsistence is, of course, intertwined with under-consumption and a natural tendency to conserve precious basic necessities, such as water. On the other hand, the need to use available resources in unsustainable ways to survive the short-term is also central; for example, the use of firewood for cooking, adding to pollution and causing respiratory illnesses.

References

Bandura, Albert. (1977), "Self-Efficacy: Toward a Unifying Theory of Behavioral Change," Psychological Review, 84 (2), 191–215.

Capek, Stella.(1993), "The 'Environmental Justice' Frame: A Conceptual Discussion and Application," Social Problems, 40 (1),405-424.

Kenrick, Douglas T., Vladas Griskevicius, Steven L. Neuberg and Mark Schaller. (2010), "Renovating the Pyramid of Needs: Contemporary Extensions Built Upon Ancient Foundations," Perspectives on Psychological Science, 5 (3), 292–314.

Leach, Melissa and Robin Mearns. (1991), "Poverty and Environment in Developing Countries: An Overview Study," in Report to ESRC, Global Environmental Change Programme; and Overseas Development Administration , ESRC: Swindon.

Lehman, P. K., & Geller, E. S. (2004). Behavior analysis and environmental protection: Accomplishments and potential for more. Behavior and Social Issues, 13(1), 13-32.

Maslow, Abraham. (1943), "A Theory of Human Motivation," Psychological Review, 50, 370–396.

Nicolaij, Sietske and Laurie Hendrickx. (2003),"The Influence of Temporal Distance of Negative Consequences on the Evaluation of Environmental Risks," in Human Decision Making and Environmental Perception: Understanding and Assisting Human Decision Making in Real-life Situations. Groningen, The Netherlands: University of Groningen.

Pahl, Sabine, Peter Harris, Helen Todd, and Derek Rutter. (2005), "Comparative Optimism for Environmental Risks," Journal of Environmental Psychology, 25 (1), 1–11.

_____ (2010), "Construal-Level Theory of Psychological Distance," Psychological Review, 117 (2), 440–63.

U.S. Environmental Protection Agency. (2012),"Reduce, Reuse, Recycle: Resource Conservation," (accessed November 12, 2012), [available at http://www.epa.gov/epawaste/conserve/rrr/index.htm]

Uzzell, David. (2000), "The Psycho-Spatial Dimension of Global Environmental Problems," Journal of Environmental Psychology, 20 (4), 307-318.

Viswanathan, Madhubalan. (2011), "Consumer Behavior Across Literacy and Resource Barriers," in Wiley International Encyclopedia of Marketing, Volume 3–Consumer Behavior, 44-54.

Viswanathan, Madhubalan, Anju Seth, Roland Gau, and Avinish Chaturvedi. (2009), "Internalizing Social Good into Business Processes in Subsistence Marketplaces: The Sustainable Market Orientation," Journal of Macromarketing, 29 (4), 406-425.

Viswanathan, Madhubalan, SrinivasSridharan, Robin Ritchie, Srinivas Venugopal, and Kiju Jung.(2012), "Marketing Interactions in Subsistence Marketplaces: A Bottom-Up Approach to Designing Public Policy," Journal of Public Policy and Marketing, 31 (2), 159-177.

A Bottom-up Approach to Understanding Subsistence Marketplaces[18]

Image S1.01: Maasai women at a USAID literacy event. Photograph by the USAID Africa Bureau; Creative Commons licensed image via Flickr: http://www.flickr.com/photos/usaidafrica/6595765317/.

This chapter summarizes insights from earlier chapters about subsistence consumers, entrepreneurs, and marketplaces.[19] The summary is comprehensive if somewhat repetitive, to serve as a chapter to revisit to gain the gist of the earlier chapters, and is summarized in Figure S1.1.

---

[18] This chapter includes material adapted from the following previously published work:

Viswanathan, Madhubalan (2010), "A Micro-Level Approach to Understanding BoP Markets," *Next Generation Business Strategies for the Base of the Pyramid: New Approaches for Building Mutual Value*, Editors, Ted London and Stuart Hart, FT Press.

[19] See, for example, the summary of the Subsistence Marketplaces Initiative at http://www.business.illinois.edu/subsistence.

The "What" of Subsistence Marketplaces: Context and Characteristics at the Micro Level

On the following pages, we highlight some key aspects of the subsistence context, providing micro-level insights with particular emphasis on marketplace interactions among consumers and entrepreneurs (see Figure S1.1).

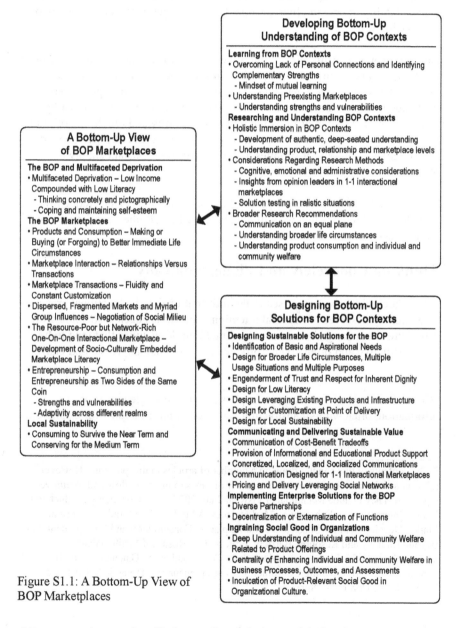

Figure S1.1: A Bottom-Up View of BOP Marketplaces

The Subsistence Marketplace and Multifaceted Deprivation

In the world of the subsistence consumer and entrepreneur, activities that are mundane and predictable in an affluent context can be rife with uncertainty. For example, cooking a staple such as rice for a central consumption event—in other words, the day's one square meal—may involve uncertainties associated with the availability of cooking fuel, the quality of the generic rice, or the quality of the cooking water.

Beyond a single consumption event, other uncertainties may include unreliable electricity supplies, intermittent public transportation, and uncertain seasonal income. These and other challenges create the ongoing need to plan from challenge to challenge, whether small or large. A shopping trip to a nearby town may be facilitated or thwarted by the availability and timeliness of public transportation. The successful operation of an enterprise is likely to depend on the reliable delivery of supplies and a more or less constant supply of electricity.

Poverty touches almost every aspect of life—a point that is made eloquently elsewhere, and upon which we will not elaborate here. Rather, our focus is on marketplace-relevant aspects of poverty.[20]

Thinking Concretely and Pictographically

A key facet of deprivation arises in the informational and educational arena. Low literacy deserves our special attention, since it has been associated with difficulties in making abstractions, leading to thinking styles that tend to be both distinctive and often counterproductive (Viswanathan, Rosa, and Harris, 2005).

"Concrete thinking," for example, implies a focus on single pieces of information, often without abstracting across other information—for example,

---

[20] The contents of this chapter draw on a number of articles in this program. However, relevant articles are cited a minimum number of times to maintain flow and minimize repetition. They include Madhubalan Viswanathan (2007), "Understanding Product and Market Interactions in Subsistence Marketplaces: A Study in South India," in Product and Market Development for Subsistence Marketplaces: Consumption and Entrepreneurship Beyond Literacy and Resource Barriers, Editors, Jose Rosa and Madhubalan Viswanathan, 21-57, Elsevier and Madhubalan Viswanathan, S. Gajendiran, and R. Venkatesan (2008), Enabling Consumer and Entrepreneurial Literacy in Subsistence Marketplaces, Dordrecht: Springer.

choosing to buy based on lowest price, without adequately factoring in size. Concrete thinking manifests itself in a variety of ways, such as:

- getting overly focused on isolated pieces of information such as price or expiration date without understanding the full meaning (e.g., what exactly the expiration date means, or what "maximum retail price" refers to);
- seeking familiar contexts (the same store);
- accounting by storing money in different places; or
- focusing on the immediate term, due to the difficulty abstracting across time (e.g., agreeing to pay exorbitant interest rates because they are presented in terms of seemingly modest daily payments, such as "Rs 10 per day").

Another thinking style is pictographic thinking: i.e., in the face of symbols that require a certain degree of literacy to read, falling back upon a rudimentary form of processing information that depends on a one-to-one visual correspondence with reality. Such thinking goes well beyond simply "depending on pictures" (which, in fact, individuals at all levels of literacy do). Typically, it involves viewing text such as brand names as images; "adding" or "subtracting" by manipulating imaginary currency bills; matching patterns to identify the right bus to board or medicine to buy; and buying goods by visualizing their potential uses and picking package sizes that match (e.g., the amount of sugar needed for a particular dessert).

Finding Ways to Compensate

Compounding low literacy is low income, which can require a focus on day-to-day necessities—that is, securing the next meal. This lack of resources, combined with the concrete thinking that arises out of low literacy, means both subsistence consumers and entrepreneurs do not consider much beyond the immediate term. Envisioning the future—whether in the form of searching for better products, or dreaming up new ideas for enterprises—ranges from difficult to impossible in the subsistence context.

And yet, even within these limitations, people find ingenious ways to negotiate around their lack of literacy and their low income. For example, they resort to oral counting skills (referred to in the local South Indian language as "mouth arithmetic"), pattern-matching (to match prescriptions with the names of medicines), or "concrete accounting" (that is, physically partitioning money).

Consumers and entrepreneurs also adapt to new technologies, such as cell phones, often finding innovative ways to use "missed" calls to communicate based on a predetermined code. For example, phone users who are not charged for missed calls sometimes use them to signal their arrival at a destination. Others close deals based on the number of rings they allow before "hanging up."

Reusing products, and using products for multiple purposes, are part and parcel of the resourcefulness that arises from necessity—e.g., using detergents to kill ants, and reusing newspapers and plastic bags in myriad creative ways. Similarly, entrepreneurs find ingenious ways to serve customer needs and engage in innovative business practices under extreme resource constraints—for example, developing installment payment plans for big-ticket items, managing communications to customers, and maintaining general business procedures and prices in the face of constant demands for customization.

Self-Esteem and Relationship Issues

The low literacy often associated with poverty is closely related to issues of self-esteem. Even in a context of widespread low literacy, people who are low-literate may feel apprehensive about starting or sustaining a conversation—say, with an unfamiliar shopkeeper—for fear of being asked a question they cannot answer. In fact, low literacy may create a more acute stigma than low income, given that low literacy can be seen as the cause of one's poverty.

"Literacy" serves as a special trap for subsistence consumers. They may be fully conversant in their native language, and yet be strangers in their own land when having to deal with banks or stores that require knowledge of, say, English. Subsistence consumers may navigate a potentially hostile marketplace— and defend their self-esteem—by avoiding unknown products or unfamiliar stores, or by seeking help from their children, friends, acquaintances, and even strangers.

Low-literate subsistence consumers may conclude that it is futile to question product price or quality, assuming, first, that they will not be able to express themselves convincingly; and second, that the available products and prices are the best that can be expected in light of their condition in life and their limited purchasing power.

Although the superimposition of Maslow's hierarchy of needs on subsistence contexts might seem to point toward the predominance of basic needs— survival needs—the truth is often far different. In a setting characterized by scant material resources, human relationships tend to trump other considerations. The upper tiers of Maslow's pyramid, including psychological needs, may actually become paramount. When one has little else, a strong sense of self-worth motivates subsistence and survival in the face of long odds, and sustains one's role in the social network. Thus, people truly have "everything to lose" when their good name is tarnished.

For the same reason, the nuclear and extended family, social groupings, tradition, and religious beliefs take on great significance in the subsistence context. People who have desperately little in a material sense lean all the more heavily on their families, traditions, and social surroundings—and in turn, support them as well.

The Reality of Trade-offs in the Subsistence Marketplace

People living in poverty regularly face stark and difficult—even impossible— trade-offs in the marketplace. For example, poor people might be forced to choose between buying something, making it on their own, or foregoing it altogether. When they make something on their own, it is both cheaper and more customizable than buying—e.g., packaged soaps, spices, and medicines are more expensive than their homegrown or homemade equivalents (Viswanathan, Seth, Gau, and Chaturvedi, 2009).

A second basic and sometimes agonizing challenge is to choose between two equally compelling types of consumption. Is it more important to get health care for a family member or pay for a child's education? There is no "right" answer; there is just an implacable question.

The drive to better one's immediate life circumstances, however, can have significant implications for products and consumption. In the subsistence marketplace, consumers are sometimes willing to pay a little more for better products, particularly for central consumption events that take on greater significance due to the chronic inability to consume.

This may mean, for example, purchasing higher-quality rice for the day's one square meal. It may mean purchasing symbolic products or brands that the consumer is proud to own (e.g., a silk sari, or a brand of cell phone with certain features). Even beyond what is experienced in more affluent settings, goods and services can take on immense importance in contexts of deprivation. For instance, a cell phone can be a lifeline when a parent in an isolated village seeks advice on treating a sick child in the middle of the night. A food that includes an important nutrient can be more than "nice to have"; it can be life-saving.[21]

Beyond the press of immediate circumstances, people living in poverty also aspire to a better life, which again may take the form of owning certain products. Many also share the basic motivations that drive wealthier consumers,

---

[21] We should note, however, that many subsistence consumers either don't know or may not be able to envision some of their needs, particularly as they relate to health-related essentials or longer-term considerations.

including—most powerfully—wanting a better future for their children, above all in the realms of education and healthcare.

Marketplace Interactions: Relationships Versus Transactions

When it comes to marketplace interactions in the subsistence context, people often have a primary economic relationship with one store—say, the neighborhood retail store in an urban area, or the large reseller farther away.

There are compelling reasons to develop these kinds of relationships. The neighborhood store may offer credit in times of need, and keep records (and of course, charge more) for credit purchases. The store owner may also offer vital peripheral services, such as holding money safely (again, for a fee). With uncertainty in so many aspects of their lives, and with the next crisis always just over the horizon, people tend to forge strong ties with vendors. "Solutions" that would otherwise seem rational—such as stocking up at the beginning of the month through purchases from large resellers—actually entail pitfalls, such as reducing liquidity that may be needed to deal with medical and other emergencies.[22]

Additionally, overcoming the next crisis may require maintaining a relationship with the neighborhood retailer, who extends invaluable credit in times of need. Thus, the relationship, rather than the transaction, often takes precedence for people who negotiate the marketplace under extremely uncertain conditions.

For subsistence consumers and entrepreneurs alike, coping with and riding out uncertainty requires developing trusting relationships through a medium-to long-term perspective, which multiplies their economic value as buyers or sellers. Ironically, survival in the immediate term requires investment in relationships in the medium term. When the immediate and near terms are not at risk—that is, in more affluent contexts—a short-term perspective on marketplace transactions becomes affordable.

Marketplace Exchanges: Fluidity, Constant Customization, and Buyer-Seller Responsiveness

In the one-to-one interactional marketplace described above, transactions can be fluid, as price and payment plan are negotiated face-to-face between buyer and seller. Weighings may be "adjusted" based on the price negotiated ("That's

---

[22] And for those living in rural settings, travel to larger resellers that offer lower prices may simply be impractical.

the weighing you get for the price you bargained" being a common refrain). Installments may not be paid when products are faulty (e.g., when the color on clothing fades). A central feature of such fluid transactions is customization, whether in price or product configurations. Sellers constantly have to navigate the tensions between adhering to general procedures and making exceptions.

Exceptions make for sales, but when word gets out about a special deal or the waiver of a payment, other customers are likely to make similar demands, on a scale that is detrimental to the business. Hence, sellers have to manage word of mouth. Sometimes, for example, they must insist on a "symbolic" payment to prevent news of differential treatment spreading out across the customer base. Given a reasonable rationale, however—e.g., regular patronage, extremely poor or elderly consumers—certain kinds of differential treatment may justifiable, and even essential.

Sellers are also knowledgeable about their customers' preferences; as they serve a limited number of regular customers and interact with them personally. As residents of the same community, they also have a unique vantage point and benefit from favorable word of mouth. Their interactions with customers are typically responsive to individual circumstances, tailoring offerings to local situations. Such responsiveness cultivates a trusting relationship–both building trust and restoring it as well when complaints are raised.

Marketplace Relationships: An Emphasis on the Human Dimension

In a marketplace characterized by minimal resources, buyers and sellers place a special emphasis on relationships. In a sense, this multiplies the economic value of small transactions, and committed relationships serve as the basis for credits and discounts. Thus, as noted above, the long-term relationship— rather than the short-term transaction—is often the relevant unit of analysis in gauging value to exchange partners.

Due to these complex dynamics in the one-to-one interactional marketplace, the line between the "human" and the "economic" is inevitably blurred. Personal judgments are central in negotiating the marketplace, such as in finding trustworthy buyers and sellers, or in gauging creditworthiness. Appeals to empathy are often made in a larger context of shared adversity, with pleas for mutual benefit and fairness being common.

This presents a sharp contrast to the arms-length transactions that characterize more affluent settings. In the subsistence marketplace—in which skills develop, and word-of-mouth influences are strong—the human dimension and issues of fairness and trust overwhelm abstract notions of markets and competition. Intuitive and interdependent relationships that are viewed as fair and trustworthy—and therefore likely to lead to personal and community welfare—prevail.

Although an intensely relational environment can lead to many benefits— making many subsistence contexts network-rich, though resource-poor— substantial downsides to these relationships exist as well. Inevitably, parties take advantage of trust, and engage in cheating and abusive behaviors. Fluid transactions are exploited to the benefit of one party and the detriment of the other. Consumers make unreasonable demands for customization. Thus, the one-to-one interactional marketplace has unique and double-edged characteristics, and often comprises some harsh realities.

We should reiterate that these rich social networks can cut both ways. People can be hurt, as well as helped. Pleas for help in the marketplace from strangers or acquaintances may be rejected. Public humiliation may be used as the means for enforcing payment of non-collateral loans. Consumers may unfairly target entrepreneurs to settle personal differences. People may be ostracized from social circles for not maintaining traditions surrounding birth, marriage, and death that involve unaffordable monetary expenses.

Our intent here is not to put a gloss on what can be an extremely harsh reality, but rather, to emphasize that certain aspects of this reality are beneficial to consumers and entrepreneurs alike. Yes, social networks hold the potential for abuse and exploitation, but in many cases, they also can be leveraged for positive outcomes.

Fragmented Markets and Group Influences: Negotiating the Social Milieu

Also noteworthy in many poverty contexts are the highly fragmented, geographically dispersed markets. This certainly applies to many rural villages, but it can also extend to "isolated" urban areas. Poor infrastructure and limited resources, for example, restrict physical mobility. Thus, rather than finding the huge and relatively homogeneous markets that characterize the world's advanced economies, in the subsistence context we find heterogeneity and fragmentation. Languages, dialects, and social structures vary by state, region, district, and even neighborhood. Compounding the challenge of these fragmented markets are myriad and diverse group influences, including local governing bodies, social strata, non-governmental organizations and community-based organizations (e.g., self-help groups buying and selling goods and services), and many others.

Many such markets are characterized by a widespread mistrust of outside entities. Thus, negotiating the social milieu involves understanding differences across contexts, and working with diverse organizations and groups. Again, this state of affairs is markedly different from wealthier contexts, where greater resources, state-of-the-art infrastructure, pervasive communications channels, and other factors combine to inoculate affluent communities against strong local influences.

Developing Socio-culturally Embedded Marketplace Literacy

As noted, resource-poor poverty contexts can be network-rich, characterized by complex (and both satisfying and disappointing) face-to-face interactions. It is ironic that such a personal and idiosyncratic marketplace in widespread poverty helps people learn about economic and marketplace fundamentals, both as consumers and entrepreneurs.

Constant interaction with sellers and other consumers leads to the development of highly valuable skills, including negotiating tactics, and such orally-based interactions allow consumers of different literacy levels to participate and benefit. As they develop confidence, consumers may seek advice from other consumers, sellers, friends, acquaintances, and even strangers. Consumers may attain numeracy and acquire other skills as a result of being entrepreneurs themselves.

What emerges is a socio-culturally embedded form of what might be called "marketplace literacy," which should be distinguished from the "literal literacy" of reading and writing skills Viswanathan, Gajendiran, and Venkatesan, 2008). Marketplace literacy brings together consumer and entrepreneurial skills, an awareness of rights, and a measure of self-confidence. It enables low-literate consumers to negotiate the marketplace through verbal counting, bargaining, and switching stores, and low-literate entrepreneurs to manage consumer interactions and maintain rudimentary accounts. Finally, marketplace literacy in a context of one-to-one interactions and strong word-of-mouth provides a counterweight against unfair selling practices.[23]

---

[23] Discussed in research which includes the study of low-literate, low-income consumers in the United States is the contrast between the US marketplace with large chain stores, technology that computes for the consumer, and a plethora of symbolic labels that assume a certain level of literacy, and the subsistence contexts in South India with direct bargaining and counting in dealing with vendors, experience as vendors, and the one-to-one interactional marketplace (Viswanathan, Gajendiran, and Venkatesan, 2008). Speculating on this comparison in research settings, the subsistence consumers studied in India may possess relatively higher marketplace literacy than the low-literate, low-income consumers studied in the US, although lack of basic literacy is widespread in subsistence contexts.

Subsistence Consumption and Entrepreneurship: Two Sides of the Same Coin

In the one-to-one interactional marketplace, consumption and entrepreneurship are two sides of the same coin. To a far greater extent than in wealthier economies, they are interwoven phenomena.

Why is this so? The two roles of consumer and entrepreneur reinforce each other. Negotiating, counting, and closing a sale as a seller, for example, improve one's skills as a consumer. Many consumers themselves possess and run micro-businesses. People learn about the marketplace by sharing knowledge with others as consumers or sellers, and engage in face-to-face interactions with both buyers and sellers. The intertwined roles of consumer-entrepreneur form a symbiotic relationship, with the two parties sharing adversity and empathizing with each other. In day-to-day life, the two roles can be blurred, as entrepreneurs juggle supplies and resources between their enterprises and their families.

At a more macro level, these two roles feed off each other in fostering economic progress. A case in point is the cell phone market, as consumers' needs for communication are served by entrepreneurs selling cell phones or cell-phone minutes, who, in turn, are consumers with enhanced buying power. In the best of worlds—again, not always attained!—it is a virtual circle.

Strengths and Vulnerabilities

Subsistence consumers and entrepreneurs possess both strengths and vulnerabilities—an assertion that is surprising only because some of the literature has emphasized the latter over the former. Consumers and entrepreneurs are experts in navigating through and surviving in poverty contexts. At the same time, with low literacy and low income compounding the effects of concrete thinking, people are constrained in their ability to envision solutions.

As a case in point, a poor woman—having learned how to cook in the family context—starts a food shop near her home. Her goal is to survive and subsist, and perhaps improve the lot of her family. She begins with a concrete reality: her own. But this may be the wrong business to be in, it may be the wrong location, or it may not be the best part of the value chain in which for her to operate (e.g., there may be opportunities to sell specific food ingredients, like dough, to commercial establishments).

Adaptivity Across Different Realms

Entrepreneurs start businesses as a way to subsist and survive, or—depending on their luck and pluck—to escape from poverty. They operate in an environment of fluid transactions and constant customization, managing communications and customizing products and prices for different customers. Not surprisingly, the human and the economic tend to become blurred in these contexts. Entrepreneurs juggle a range of different roles: as buyers from suppliers, sellers to consumers, and breadwinners for their families. Again, this is in contrast to the arm's-length transactions and compartmentalized functions that characterize more affluent contexts.

Given this reality, analyzing any single element of their marketplace interactions—such as their selling or buying behavior—without understanding its interconnections with their family and larger life circumstances is incomplete, and potentially misleading. For instance, entrepreneurs may support their families in part by allowing them to consume unsold perishables—or, they may demand that their family forego consumption to help the business survive (Viswanathan, Rosa, and Ruth, 2010).

Local Sustainability: Near-Term Consumption, Medium-Term Conservation

The micro-level perspective also provides a window into what "sustainability" means for people in subsistence contexts. What do low-literate, low-income individuals strive to sustain, beyond themselves and their families? Do their priorities extend to comprise the local culture, the local environment, or the local economy?

The answers can be surprising. For people living in poverty, ecological issues are not distant, but immediate, with disease and death resulting from miscalculations and misdeeds. Whatever form the pollution takes—be it noise, dust, garbage, soil contamination, or water pollution—there is very little that people in the subsistence marketplace can do to protect themselves. Degradation of the local environment tends to have harmful effects on health, quality of life, relationships, and social networks—for example, the high-rise building erected in a crowded urban setting isolates parts of a community from each other, cuts off their sunlight, reduces their access to cooling breezes, and so on.

So for subsistence consumers and entrepreneurs alike, "sustainability" extends into several realms. There is, first and foremost, subsistence, in terms of basic physical needs such as food, water, air, health, and sanitation. There is also connectedness, in terms of community and local ecology, and growth or progress in terms of education, livelihood, and poverty alleviation. Additionally, there is conservation, albeit in a somewhat narrow definition of the term. Poverty almost always involves trade-offs between consuming and conserving. The family needs firewood to cook its next meal (the immediate term), but it also needs forests (versus deforestation) in the medium term.

Subsistence consumers and entrepreneurs respond to these trade-offs. They adapt by under-using, reusing, recycling, making, and foregoing. Through inventiveness and coping, they maintain a semblance of control over their immediate environment. So they cope. They invent makeshift solutions aimed at conserving resources: reusing plastic containers for storage, using clothes to screen against pollution at home or during travel, using public transportation, making rather than buying to save money and enhance nutrition, harvesting rainwater, producing products locally, using innovative cooking methods to retain nutritive ingredients, and many more.

We categorize challenges surrounding subsistence and environmental sustainability at four levels of distance—immediate, near, moderate, and far. In turn, coping is influenced by the distances of challenges and the associated degree of control. We also categorize sustenance in terms of surviving, relating, and growing.

This micro-level understanding of subsistence contexts underscores how poverty and the environment are deeply intertwined issues that cannot be compartmentalized, as may be assumed in affluent settings. Thus, solutions have to be socially, environmentally, and economically sustainable to address the many facets of deprivation, as well as their interconnected nature.

Conclusion

This chapter is a comprehensive summary of earlier chapters. We summarize the unique micro-level insights regarding subsistence consumers, entrepreneurs and marketplaces. We also delineate the underlying bottom-up orientation employed to generate these insights. We re-emphasize the need to learn from subsistence consumers and entrepreneurs and understand their behaviors at a micro-level. We contend that such nuanced understanding would be foundational to devising solutions that both reflect realities on the ground and positively impact individual and community welfare. Designing solutions is the focus of the next section of the book.

References

Madhubalan Viswanathan, Jose Antonio Rosa, and James Harris (2005), "Decision-Making and Coping by Functionally Illiterate Consumers and Some Implications for Marketing Management," Journal of Marketing, 69 (1): 15-31.

Madhubalan Viswanathan, Anju Seth, Roland Gau, and Avinish Chaturvedi (2009), "Ingraining Product-Relevant Social Good into Business Processes in

Subsistence Marketplaces: The Sustainable Market Orientation," Journal of Macromarketing, 29: 406-425.

Madhubalan Viswanathan, S. Gajendiran, and R. Venkatesan (2008), Enabling Consumer and Entrepreneurial Literacy in Subsistence Marketplaces, Dordrecht: Springer.

Chapter 8
Product Development for Subsistence Marketplaces[24]

Image 8.01: A woman pumping water by hand. Photograph by Oxfam International; Creative Commons licensed image via Fotopedia: http://www.fotopedia.com/items/ flickr-4642418846.

This chapter focuses on developing products for subsistence marketplaces. To do so, we examine yearlong projects conducted in courses we have taught as well as examples from practice. In this section, we draw from case studies of business practices, our direct experiences with class projects and a social enterprise, and other examples to glean insights about substantive issues in product development for subsistence marketplaces.

The platform for the class projects is an interdisciplinary, year-long graduate course taught to business, engineering, and industrial design students whose

[24] This chapter includes material adapted from the following previously published work:

Viswanathan, Madhubalan, and Srinivas Sridharan (2012), "Product Development for the BoP: Insights on Concept and Prototype Development from University-Based Student Projects in India," Journal of Product Innovation Management, 29 (1), 52-69. DOI: 10.1111/j.1540-5885.2011.00878.x

end-of-term deliverables are product prototypes and business plans. The projects span categories such as information and communication technologies, food and beverage, and health and medicine, with specific applications ranging from cellular phones and Internet access to nutritional foods and beverages, health education software, solar appliances, and educational tutorial software.

Our insights are organized around three issues:

- understanding subsistence marketplaces,
- designing products, and
- developing products.

Within each issue, we discuss insights relating to the "what" and the "how" that emerged from analyzing the course projects and real-world examples. A summary of real-world examples and selected pedagogical projects is presented in Table 8.1 at the end of the chapter, organized around the three issues listed above, and Table 8.2 presents details on some class projects as well as real-world examples for illustrative purposes. A subsequent discussion focuses broadly on steps in the process of product development.

Understanding Subsistence Marketplaces for Product Development

Understanding subsistence marketplaces is critical for product development, given the lack of familiarity and personal relevance that product managers and designers typically have with these contexts.

Identifying Critical Basic Consumer Needs

An understanding of subsistence marketplaces helps people identify critical consumer needs for product development. Critical needs are those that occupy the highest consumer priorities and, therefore, ones consumers are most willing to spend scarce resources on. As an example, a student team focused on healthy beverages found through their field research that mothers were willing to pay a premium for the availability of healthier beverage and food alternatives for their children.

This, however, does not suggest a narrow consumer focus merely on survival necessities like food and shelter. Consumer interest also extends to arenas such as communication, as revealed by the student projects that involved communication solutions, and also borne out by the recent market reality of widespread penetration of cell phones in developing countries and subsistence contexts. Cell phones serve vital communication needs, and in isolated rural communities can be a lifeline in the event of illness or other crises.

Aside from such considerations in the product domain, it is also critical to consider innovation in services that can serve critical needs. In healthcare, for example, many subsistence contexts lack good quality, affordable healthcare systems that could help avoid or overcome the tremendous loss caused by disease and ill-health. Innovative services have been tested in the market. For example, two companies in India—Mobile Medics and DISHA—have used a profit-based mobile healthcare concept, delivering health services to rural consumers in India through a van (see Table 8.1). Although both companies have ceased to be in operation, their initiatives offer an example of the possibilities in healthcare services innovation in subsistence contexts.

A sound conceptual basis of product development can lead to satisfying physiological and psychological needs through well-designed products. In subsistence marketplaces, it is not uncommon for even fundamental, survivalist life needs of people to remain unfulfilled. These basic needs tend to occupy the highest priorities of consumers (Viswanathan et al., 2009) and, therefore, are ones whose satisfaction consumers would most value. Hence, focusing on identifying such critical basic life needs may be an important success factor in subsistence marketplaces. The following sampling of projects illustrates this.

- **Faulty vision** (Project 1) is a commonly occurring problem in rural subsistence marketplaces in India and has severe adverse consequences for the economic fortunes of people (lost productivity, wages). It is also one that consumers cannot rectify by themselves; they depend primarily on larger public or private forces to provide a solution.

- **Solar heating for mobile vending carts** (Project 3) solves a critically felt ongoing need by street vendors—it enhances entrepreneurial productivity, a critical ingredient of daily cash flow, and it improves hygiene conditions, thus potentially attracting new customer segments and yielding more profitable pricing opportunities. The product in Project 3 is also one whose development is generally beyond the capability of the subsistence entrepreneur.

- **Projects 4, 5 and 8** all focus on nutritive additives or beverages. As such, these projects tap into the critical need for nutrition and the inability of subsistence families to pursue homemade solutions (which would have been common in previous generations of Indians) because of busy lifestyles and intergenerational loss of knowledge.

- **Project 10** focuses on a holistic approach to address basic sanitation and related education in rural areas, a compelling and widespread critical need.

The subsistence marketplace literature has suggested that consumers actively trade off the choice between buying and self-producing because of low and uncertain incomes (Viswanathan et al. 2009). This very rational and cognitive behavioral response demonstrates the archetype of "prosumer" (Toffler, 1980), i.e., a person who produces many of the items he consumes, rather than being a pure consumer. Its prevalence in subsistence marketplaces is consistent with its attribution in the literature to preindustrial marketplace traditions (Toffler, 1980).

When the findings from the above case studies are compared with this suggestion in the literature, it seems that products that both cannot be easily self-made and are critical in everyday life, are more likely to be considered for purchase in subsistence marketplaces. The choices made in the case studies suggest that the most critically felt product needs in subsistence marketplaces are often also very basic ones essential for survival (e.g., health, nutrition, sanitation). This is consistent with the portrayals of life circumstances in the literature. This is not to say that non-critical products will not be purchased in subsistence markets, but to establish an important distinction between critical and non-critical product utility in consumer willingness to pay.

Identifying Critical Aspirational Consumer Needs

The recent subsistence literature is replete with examples of subsistence consumers going beyond the Maslowian basic needs to aspire for products that satisfy higher needs. These aspirational needs of subsistence consumers include well-known brands that give them a choice set (often a situation not experienced before), and high quality products that enable newer lifestyles (Prahalad, 2005). These brand-related aspirations apply to both routine consumer products (salt, soap, furniture) and life-enhancing products and services (artificial limbs, eye surgery, bank accounts, micro-credit, etc.).

Cell phones are also an example of subsistence consumers aspiring for new generation products (Prahalad, 2005). Nokia, by understanding this critical aspirational need, developed a focused emerging market and subsistence market strategy, resulting in a whole line of ultra low-cost handsets that transcended the affordability barrier of subsistence populations.

In addition to short-term aspirations, transformational aspirations also play an important part in subsistence product psychology. Subsistence consumers aspire for a better life in a number of ways beyond specific brands or products, in the longer term and the immediate term. A powerful motivation, for example, is to enable a better future for one's children through good health and education. Three of the student projects analyzed in this chapter relate to this aspirational need of education; one relating to parental aspiration for their children to be able to speak English, seen as a way of opening up an entirely new set of economic opportunities, and others relating to health education for children.

In each case, participants found that parents were willing to make sacrifices in basic needs to enable their children to attain higher education and, thus, a better life. For example, in many low-income countries, formal and informal user-payment models exist for basic education (Hillman and Jenkner, 2002). When unable to pay cash, parents may make in-kind payments such as providing food for teachers, or doing manual labor for school construction projects.

In place of formal education, low-literate adults also aspire for education through other means for themselves. Gaining marketplace literacy through non-formal education, learning a trade, or gaining basic literacy through adult education are all means of improving life circumstances and are sources of pride as well.

Nokia also addresses the aspirational need of upward mobility through literacy and job prospects through its Nokia Life Tools service. This service, aimed at small town and rural youth, includes language lessons, assistance for education such as exam preparation, and career guidance. Similarly, an education venture supported by the Rural Technology Business Incubator in India (see Table 8.1) seeks to impart skills for rural youth through education using a distance education format and information and communication technologies.

One project on an e-training interface for teachers (Project 7) was based on a widespread aspiration on the part of people wanting to transcend social class by entering the 'teaching' occupation—a career perceived to be traditionally the preserve of higher social classes. Thus this solution offered benefits that covered not just functional but social aspects as well. Another team made the surprising discovery in their field research that impoverished mothers were willing to pay a substantial premium over existing alternatives for the availability of a healthier beverage for their children (Project 8). The team made sense of what was originally surprising when they understood the larger context of a lack of nutritional alternatives and the extraordinary importance placed on children's futures.

Satisfying Innate Human Needs

This emphasis on aspirational needs contrasts with some anthropological literature, which suggests that prolonged life in poverty stifles the achievement of dreams and aspirations and may deprive consumers of "aspirational resources necessary to contest and alter the conditions of their poverty" (Appadurai, 2004, p. 59). However, as found in the case studies, aspirations do exist among subsistence consumers. Consistent with psychological literature on "intrinsic aspirations" (Kasser and Ryan, 1996), subsistence consumers strive, like any other consumers, to achieve the satisfaction of innate psychological human needs (such as the need for autonomy, competence, and social connectedness—Deci and Ryan, 2000).

Aspirational needs underscore the complexity of subsistence marketplaces in that consumers do not remain at the bottom of Maslow's hierarchy of needs but traverse multiple steps, often skipping a few intermediate ones (Viswanathan, 2007). Being used to sharp contours in customer segments and guided by traditional segmentation and targeting models, product developers face fundamental complexity in subsistence contexts when encountering the juxtaposition of seeking products that critically aid immediate survival with seeking those that are aspirational and transformative in the long run. In this sense, the efforts of the student teams in perceiving the dimension of aspirational needs offer insight for means to achieve subsistence innovation.

From a product development standpoint, the case studies reveal that dynamic aspirations among the poor can be unlocked through life-altering products and services. Further, the teams discovered that subsistence consumer aspirations for a better life could go far beyond specific brands or products; although tied to specific choices made in the immediate term, they could be held active over a very long term (e.g., over a decade of a child's schooling). From a market research standpoint, the cases demonstrate that attempting to discover subsistence consumers' intrinsic aspirations and life goals can yield rich market data otherwise not available. In contrast, there is virtually no precedent in the literature to "ask and discover poor people's values and long-term aspirations" (Copestake and Camfield, 2010).

Envisioning Needs and Usage Situations

An important challenge for product development in subsistence marketplaces is to envision unfamiliar consumer needs and anticipate unconventional product usage situations. Developers accustomed to creating the most efficient product design for a predictable set of usage conditions need to understand that a product may be used by subsistence consumers in different and unanticipated ways, depending on situation and need (Sridharan and Viswanathan, 2008). For example, in Africa, Procter & Gamble learned that its detergents were sometimes being used in $20 washing machines made out of old barrels (Mahajan, 2008).

In our course projects, a broad understanding of household activities and spatial arrangements of consumer homes, and of the fluid point-of-sale conditions confronting vendors (e.g., vendors often rely on bicycles and carts and often have to change locations) has led participants to understand the variable nature of product usage situations. The need for design flexibility to account for this variability may be pertinent in many product categories. For example, food and beverage products may need to withstand a wide range of temperatures and cooking processes.

In the context of communications technology, Nokia has recently launched its Nokia Life Tools service that enables rural farmers to receive regular updates on their cell phones on weather patterns and crop prices (see Table 8.1). This reflects Nokia's discovery that rural farmers used cell phones primarily to obtain agriculture-related information.

Further, discovering that rural consumers in India and China often used cell phones on a shared basis among families, Nokia designed its 1200 and 1208 phones to contain shared use features (e.g. shared address book, call tracker). Developers accustomed to the goals of creating the most efficient product design for a predictable set of usage conditions need to understand that a product may be used by subsistence consumers in many different, unanticipated ways depending on situation and need (Sridharan and Viswanathan, 2008).

In Project 3, the product team realized after months of work that a conventional solar cooking appliance would not overcome cultural barriers that would prevent it from being adopted in Indian family conditions. The timing of cooking permissible by solar energy (only after daybreak), the lengthy duration it took to cook in a solar appliance (causing sanitation fears), and the constraints on opening and closing the appliance during the cooking process (hampering the gradual addition of spices and flavor), were all found to be at odds with local cooking traditions.

There were spatial and physical considerations, too—women in Indian kitchens would sit near the appliance to cook, placing specific demands on the size and dimensions of the product. From a design perspective, the team discovered the importance of achieving a broad understanding of subsistence household/ business activities and the spatial arrangements of consumer homes/entrepreneur selling spaces and the artifacts in them.

In Project 2, whose product solution was an audiovisual educational service focused on spoken English for children in urban subsistence contexts, the product team observed that students of existing English language services suffered from a lack of active use of skills acquired (e.g., they did not have opportunities to converse outside class as their parents did not know enough English to practice with them, teachers lacked the motivation to do so, and students' lack of confidence hampered speech).

In response, the team developed an integrated solution specifically designed to address the usage situation: a family literacy program rather than an individual one; bilingual service to enable easier comparative learning between native language and English; game-like content programming to reduce anxiety and enhance fun; emphasis on conversational skills rather than building blocks like grammar; vocabulary; and multi-stakeholder involvement among teachers, parents, and children.

In other case studies, students observed product usage situations such as cooking and food consumption, communication, education, and health. In these studies, the product teams envisioned the situational context in which the product would be deployed and incorporated it into product design (examples include students in Project 1 envisioning the eye-testing situation, and students in Projects 4 and 5 envisioning the cooking and consumption situations).

The key issue here is understanding the market for which the product is being designed. Although this market aspect has long been acknowledged to be a key success factor in product development (Marquis, 1972, Baker and Sinkula, 2005), it has not addressed the weighting of consumer needs (critical versus discretionary) or the time horizon value of those needs (long-term aspirations versus short-term needs).

Similarly, there is implicit assumption of complete usage context knowledge, i.e., that developers will have a good cultural understanding of the context in which the product will actually be used. The case studies in this research, however, reveal that in subsistence marketplaces, needs are weighted and traded off constantly; short and long-term needs are invoked simultaneously; and products are used in unique ways reflecting consumer adaptation to spatial and cultural contexts. Hence, the above propositions can impart additional layers of analysis to the literature on assessing market needs in product development.

Product Design for Subsistence Contexts

Image 8.02: Class project prototype of nutritional additive—ActivEdge. Photograph courtesy of Subsistence Marketplaces Initiative.

This section covers a variety of key topics in product design—designing products for harsh usage conditions, for multiple purposes, for customization, for low-literate users, and for local sustainability.

Designing Products for Harsh Usage Conditions

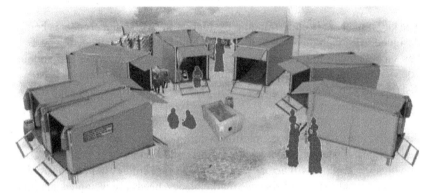

Image 8.03: Product prototype of the Almost Home, disaster shelter, designed as long-term temporary housing during recovery periods from disasters. Photograph courtesy of Subsistence Marketplaces Initiative.

In keeping with the broader point about envisioning different product usage conditions, our experience and business practice suggest that the nature of usage in terms of harsh or hostile conditions needs to be understood (also see Prahalad, 2005). For example, dusty, high-temperature environments on the African continent and in countries like India make for challenging settings where cell phones are used. Nokia's 1100 model cell phone sold in Africa is designed to be dust-proof to withstand dusty conditions. Its 1200 and 1208 model phones, sold in India, are designed with special grip areas to make them easy to hold in hot conditions, and also contain a built-in flashlight to contend with situations of power outages, common in India.

Cooking and washing often occur in harsh conditions in subsistence contexts. The Aga Khan Planning and Building Services undertakes structural improvement in homes in subsistence settings in Pakistan (see Table 8.1) to alleviate the effect of harsh conditions for everyday home-based tasks like cooking (e.g., solar cookers, water-warming facilities). In our class projects, we learned that nutritious beverages and foods need to be developed to retain nutritious additives in a wide range of temperatures of storage and cooking conditions (see Table 8.1) and packaging designed to transport and store products in a variety of conditions.

Designing Products for Multiple Purposes

Image 8.04: Product prototype for SoyChoyce, which combines the nutritional power of soy flour with an easy-to-use container. The accompanying pamphlet acts as an educational component, focusing on the importance of proteins and calories in the daily diet. Photograph courtesy of Subsistence Marketplaces Initiative.

Project teams focusing on healthy foods or beverages (Projects 4, 5, and 8) similarly encountered considerable diversity of needs, influencing how their proposed additive was to be mixed. They could either decide to design the additive for specific foods or beverages or design it for versatility in usage. For example, a soy additive (Project 4) had to be designed in the form of an unflavored, soluble powder which could be ground to different solubility standards, thus creating versatility in its use (as an additive in meals, as a drink based in water or milk). Another team that developed a multi-nutrient additive (Project 5) to be used in wheat flour had to avoid developing an enriched flour product because consumers wanted a separate additive packet that they could use as they saw fit.

Similarly, a solar application for mobile entrepreneurs ideally needed to address heating of foods and other beverages in addition to its original stated purpose of heating water, something that the prototype was only partially successful in achieving (see Table 8.2). Market research identified that subsistence mobile cart vendors needed a solar heater to address several practical uses. Vendors needed to heat utensils to freshly prepare food, periodically warm food prepared earlier in the day, and wash plates, cutlery, and utensils after use. However, as it turned out, the prototype developed in Project 3 was only partially successful in achieving this objective, as heating food remained a challenge with the eventual design.

These situations highlight the design considerations that products in subsistence contexts undergo. In such contexts, products have multiple purposes beyond their original intent, reflecting the inventiveness and adaptability of subsistence consumers and entrepreneurs as well as their affordability constraints. For example, detergent may be used to wash clothes as well as to kill ants. Even with cleaning, there could be unconventional use—for example, heavy-duty detergents used for hand-washing.

The implication for product development is to anticipate such multiple usage situations and design to account for them. Thus, specialized products designed for circumscribed usage situations (hand-washing soap) are less likely to be successful. Flexible products, on the other hand, can be quite successful. In one of our course projects, for example, soy additive could either be designed for specific beverages or made versatile in usage. Extrapolating from the solar application example, distributed energy sources for marketplaces lacking reliable energy infrastructure can be designed to be versatile in working with a range of household applications, such as lighting, water-heating, cooking, etc.

In response, it seems that products for subsistence marketplaces will also need to be innovative by being multifunctional and contextually malleable. However, the discussion on product innovativeness in the extant literature is generally dominated by technical newness, newness of product to the producing firm, and more recently, design newness (Talke et al., 2009). Generally speaking, the literature seems to implicitly assume usage context invariance, i.e. the context for which the product is designed will be the same as the context in which the product is actually used. This may not be a viable assumption in product development for subsistence marketplaces.

Designing Products for Customization

In the course projects and real-world examples, the need for customization has been a central theme. Student teams incorporated customization at a somewhat macro level through such means as different local language and dialect interfaces for communication solutions. However, at a more local level, projects have emphasized "assembly" by local entrepreneurs with the possibility of customizing (e.g., adding different nutritive ingredients for different segments, such as the elderly versus children, at the point of purchase; or manual versus software-based administration to cater to local variations with the spoken English application; see Table 8.1 and Table 8.2).

Customizing manufacturing and materials, Sun Oven International, Inc. allows local entrepreneurs to manufacture and assemble solar ovens locally. It, thus, lowers transportation costs and product price and provides local jobs, and also enables last-mile customization. In this regard, the one-to-one interactional relational marketplace in subsistence contexts is characterized by constant demands for customization (Viswanathan, 2007).

The decisions made in the course projects and by Sun Oven suggest that product design should anticipate this need for customization where possible by allowing for different configurations and the ability for final product configuration to be determined by local entrepreneurs. Product design should anticipate this where possible by allowing for different configurations and the ability for final product configuration to be determined by local entrepreneurs.

Designing Products for Low-literate Users

Our experience with creating a marketplace literacy educational program has highlighted a number of issues with communication and education for low-literate users (see Table 8.1 and Table 8.2). Although essentially an educational program, these issues are nevertheless instructive for product development. Three key issues highlighted in this regard are the need to concretize, localize, and socialize the educational program. These elements have immediate application for products as well. Product packaging and related communication and education should be conveyed concretely, in light of constraints due to low literacy. In course projects, challenges in this regard relate to conveying health and nutritional information in concrete terms or creating digital interfaces that are user-friendly with software-related products.

One class project involved a nutritional/medical supplement dispenser and health education solution (see Table 8.1). This project resulted in innovative design of the container, educating the user about savings, healthy practices, and medical supplements, and an enhanced electronic version for children in schools to key in answers to questions in a test format. Localizing content is very important in enabling low-literate users to relate to the communication, reflected in local icons and local language in designing product interfaces in our class projects.

Finally, given low literacy and the one-to-one interactional relational marketplace, socializing communication and education is another important consideration, thus leveraging the inherent social and oral language skills that subsistence consumers and entrepreneurs possess and grow up with. This can take several forms, including the inherent design of the product, reflected in a project leveraging parent-child and community-level interaction into the design of a spoken-language solution (see Table 8.1 and Table 8.2); through final "assembly" for a nutritional additive by a local entrepreneur who can communicate the value and benefits to low-literate consumers; or through packaging with socially relevant information spreadable through word of mouth.

As discussed, research suggests that low-literate people engage in concrete thinking and pictographic thinking (Viswanathan et al., 2005). Product interfaces and packages should similarly be designed with these constraints in mind. For example, text-free user interfaces for computers and cell phones are a promising and essential direction, as is local language adaptation. Microsoft researchers in Bangalore, India, have developed a text-free computer user interface with applications like Kelesa Konnection (Medhi, Pitti, and Toyama, 2005), which allows low-literate, subsistence individuals to seek jobs as domestic help and also provides a platform for prospective employers to connect with them. In our projects, packaging and educational software emphasize such elements as text-free visual interfaces and audio instructions.

Related to interfaces is the need to visualize benefits. Rather than consider these elements as separate communication and educational issues, they can be integrated into the product design and reflected in the design of the core product as well as in its packaging and other aspects.

In all the projects, designing for low-literate users was a central concern, given the widespread incidence of low literacy in subsistence marketplaces. A soy-based nutritional supplement was designed with a reusable container, which had a visual indicator of the amount to be consumed per person per day and a portion-control-metering device (Project 4). An enriched flour product had to undergo changes in its marketing communications program after its original promotional tagline, "A Doctor in a Bottle," caused consumers to perceive the product as mainly medicinal (Project 5).

Yet another nutrition product in the form of a nutritional candy for children was designed to have selling channels that could double as education avenues (Project 9). Because the point of sale of the product involved both homes and primary schools, the team opted for village-based local agents to communicate with parents as well as provide entertaining, interactive dispensers in primary school classrooms.

The innovative design of the dispenser meant that it could educate children about nutrition by adopting a test format—a child would come to class in the morning, approach the dispenser, and key in her personal identification number; the dispenser would ask her a series of nutrition questions on an LCD display and speaker audio in the local language; upon getting all answers right, the child would be rewarded with a vitamin gummy.

A collapsible kiosk and inventory bag in Project 1 emphasized ease of use and user-friendly instructions for rural vision entrepreneurs. Several projects pursued the localizing of content (e.g., use of local icons and local language), presumably because it enabled low-literate users to relate to their communications (e.g., Project 6 on cellphone interface).

As mentioned earlier, socializing product-related communication—i.e., allowing it to occur embedded in the local relational and social context—is another important consideration. For example, such a strategy resulted in the design of a spoken language solution that embedded parent-child and community-level interaction into the "product" and allowed them to learn together. Leaving the final mixing of a nutritional additive to the local retailer, as mentioned earlier, is an example (Projects 4 and 5).

The team members reported that aside from product customization, the strategy also allowed them to leverage the local "radius of trust" (interpersonal trust would only extend to known people within the community and who are similarly low-literate). Also, the inherent social and oral language skills that subsistence marketplace exchanges often involve in order to compensate for the lack of literal literacy, could come to the fore in a socialized product.

Designing Locally Sustainable Products

Both the course projects and real-world examples highlight the need for designing locally sustainable products. For instance, for food and beverage products, participants envision the role of a local entrepreneur in adding value to the product and selling it (see Table 8.1 and Table 8.2). Packaging, local production, and other issues that relate to the local ecology are emphasized as well as the local economy. The real-world example of Sun Oven illustrates this issue (Table 8.1); the company offers the Micro-Sun-Bakery program in subsistence contexts around the world as a form of sustainable livelihood enterprise, equipping and training local entrepreneurs.

Also emerging in class projects is cultural sensitivity, through sustaining local culture while providing solutions that enable adaptation to changing conditions. In projects involving healthy beverages and foods, many concepts needed to be understood, including those of health and healthy cooking, the cultural nuances of cooking, energy usage and heating capacity for solar heating for mobile entrepreneurs, and the stigma attached to lack of knowledge of English for a spoken English solution (see Table 8.2). For solar cooking appliances, Sun Oven needed to understand the timing of the night meal in some countries in Africa (Table 8.1). Food cooked with solar ovens that lost warmth in the evening reportedly led to spousal abuse, emphasizing the primacy of culture over technology and the need for innovations to stem from deep understanding of the cultural context.

ROPE, a business-social enterprise supported by RTBI in India, uses production centers in rural villages to make high quality crafts-based products using local materials and craftsperson skills, and sells them to global clientele (see Table 8.1).

On the ecological dimension, the company focuses on products made from natural fibers, which ensures that the raw materials come from the villages where the products are made, and maintains a balance between what is taken out versus what is preserved. On the economic dimension, it provides stable livelihoods to local artisans. On the social and human dimension, it sustains individual and community welfare by emphasizing entrepreneurship at every possible step in the value chain, enabling communities to leverage evolving market trends while being non-intrusive of local culture.

All projects incorporated an element of designing locally sustainable products, although what constitutes local sustainability appeared varied and broad in scope. As alluded to already, several projects involved local entrepreneurs to add value to the product. Again, in addition to enabling customization of the product itself, this strategy had an economic impact (e.g., job creation), enhancing economic sustainability of subsistence marketplaces. As a strategy, this was represented in the projects through local assembly (see Table 8.2—vision kiosk) and local manufacturing capacity (see Table 8.2—components of solar heater).

Research indicates that indicators of local sustainability are "socially constructed" (Astleithner and Hamedinger, 2003), i.e., they center on the interaction of various local actors, all seeking to define jointly what sustainable development is. Whereas notions of sustainability that are top-down emphasize profits, people, and planet, our micro-level approach explicitly introduces elements of sustainability from the local perspective into our course-based product development projects.

For instance, for food and beverage products, participants envision the role of a local entrepreneur in adding value to the product and selling it. We emphasize packaging, local production, and other issues that relate to the local ecology as well as the local economy. The design of products should aim to improve personal and community welfare, sustaining the all-important social dimension of sustainability as well as the ecological dimension.

Socioeconomic projects that do not help to sustain or maintain local cultural stability have readily failed (Kottak, 1990). The case studies demonstrate that this argument extends to the product domain as well. It was particularly telling in the case studies involving health beverages, foods, and cooking, where the concepts of "health" and "healthy cooking" carried unique local, cultural meanings. Although the originally proposed home-use solar cooker reflected healthy cooking from the designer's perspective, its liability of yielding a cooked product after several hours caused consumers to interpret the cooking process as "unhealthful."

In a similar vein, the severe stigma that the lack of English language knowledge imparts in a low-literate population in India meant that the spoken English service had to be designed to minimize such barriers (e.g., "collective learning" philosophy reduced anxiety; "we wait until you get it right" approaches by the software-based tutor enhanced encouragement; "parent-child learning" design enabled low-literate parents to become more confident in participating).

These strategies are consistent with research perspectives suggesting that indicators of local sustainability are socially constructed (Astleithner and Hamedinger, 2003)—i.e., through the interaction of various local actors, all seeking to define jointly what sustainable development is. Whereas the treatment of sustainability in the organizational literature emphasizes profits, people, and planet in a macro sense (Elkington, 1997), the case studies hint at the consideration of sustainability from the local perspective, which might be at the level of individual, family, and community welfare, as discussed in Chapter 7.

A more direct aspect related to environmental sustainability is the design of product composition and packaging using locally sourced raw materials. This is motivated by the need to avoid unfavorable impact on local environments by foreign materials (an example would be the reference in the trade press to a countryside littered with plastic in the otherwise popular subsistence product innovation of shampoo sachets).

What we learn from these illustrations, then, is that the design of products for subsistence contexts should aim to improve individual and community welfare, achieving the all-important social dimension of sustainability as well as the ecological dimension.

Product Development Within Existing Infrastructure

All product development needs to take into account the infrastructure within which it exists. Of course, at times, little or no infrastructure will be in place, and products will need to be developed with this in mind. When infrastructure does exist, developers will want to leverage that infrastructure. In the following sections, we'll look at a variety of infrastructure issues that product developers will need to consider.

Leapfrogging Lack of Infrastructure

Observation of business examples suggests that, from the point of view of product development, innovations that leapfrog currently lacking infrastructure are important to effectively reach subsistence consumers. Subsistence consumers live in highly uncertain environments in arenas relating to basic human needs. With absent or failing infrastructure, even completion of the most mundane of daily activities such as cooking is contingent on availability of water, staples, and other ingredients. Lack of electricity and power cuts in areas with electricity are both common.

The distributed energy solutions in the examples of solar-powered appliances (e.g., sun ovens) leapfrog failing or unavailable (off-grid) energy infrastructure, and cell phones leapfrog nonexistent landline infrastructure. Student projects reflected this understanding as well. A class project on solar water heating solution for mobile carts essentially provides a distributed energy solution (see Table 8.2). The product need was essentially for a distributed energy source in a market context lacking reliable energy infrastructure.

In the overall marketplace, numerous entrepreneurs helped close the gap in distributing food and beverages produced to cater to a subsistence clientele. However, they operated in conditions lacking energy infrastructure. In a project whose core product was an automated pharmaceutical dispensing machine, the solution represented a leapfrogging of the lacking human infrastructure of pharmacists at each site (in this case, villages).

The idea was similar in vision testing (see Table 8.2), where remote villages lacked a physical infrastructure of vision-testing laboratories, along with a lack of telecommunication services. In this case study, the target segment had to take time off work, pay for transport to a neighboring town (often for a companion as well), and wait several days for delivery of glasses. Hence the periodic visit of a vision entrepreneur, armed with vision-related knowledge and a collection of eyeglasses, and a deployable-on-demand vision kiosk to screen for vision problems, amounted to bypassing the lack of medical infrastructure in the village. Similarly, an electronic teacher-training interface leapfrogged the need for brick and mortar infrastructure and logistical infrastructure to access clients in remote villages (project 7).

From the point of view of product development, innovations that leapfrog the lack of infrastructure are important. Such is the case with cell phones that leapfrog the need for landline infrastructure. The TeNet group pioneered a "last mile" solution called corDECT that enabled individual homes in remote rural areas of India to be wirelessly connected to the nearest telephone exchanges, leapfrogging the need for the conventional copper wire network, which was nonexistent in such areas.

Several times cheaper than the prospect of creating conventional infrastructure, it also provided more advanced technological usage possibilities with its capability to carry voice and Internet traffic simultaneously and to split them at the user end. The RTBI educational venture discussed earlier leapfrogs nonexistent physical schooling infrastructure and problems of teacher absenteeism by delivering services through interactive online formats, as do the mobile healthcare solutions by leapfrogging an entire layer of infrastructure for alleviating basic healthcare problems (see Table 8.1).

Leveraging Existing Infrastructure

Image 8.05: A low-cost ATM machine for rural settings, India. Image by Vortex Engineering India.

A related issue brought out in class projects is the need to leverage existing infrastructure in developing products. Creating a device and a micro-financing plan for every consumer or entrepreneur need is not realistic. Working with existing infrastructure is a key necessity.

Rather than think in terms of a separate device, Project 2 on spoken English software involved using cell phones (used to call toll-free numbers) and televisions (through which the educational program was hosted), both products increasingly common in low-income households. Solar heaters needed to fit on mobile carts—a ubiquitous cultural phenomenon—rather than be designed on an unrelated platform (Project 3). Nutrients needed to be integrated with already common food products such as wheat and rice, rather than be presented on their own as "important new products" (Projects 4 and 5).

Applications dependent on unreliable Internet connections needed to be designed to "refresh" periodically to download updates, taking advantage of times when connections were working (e.g., Project 7 on e-training interface). The cell phone provides a unique platform in this regard and the development of user-friendly interfaces and video-friendly screens will only hasten the breadth of possible applications.

With software-based education, the need to use a network of existing computer kiosks or the use of cell phone platforms is another example. Desicrew, a provider of rurally-sourced business process outsourcing services in India, leverages existing Internet kiosks for use by its employees, and provides the kiosk entrepreneurs with an additional and stable revenue source, similar in some ways to the RTBI education venture described earlier.

In the corDECT platform described earlier, the original version of the product was capable of serving only those areas and homes that had an existing telephone exchange within a 10-kilometer radius (or at best a 25-kilometer radius when used in conjunction with a solar-powered relay station). However, its developers later produced versions that served homes with no telephone exchanges nearby. corDECT effectively leveraged existing infrastructure by transporting signals through spare copper wires running alongside tracks that are used for voice communication in India's vast railway network.

Another example of leveraging existing infrastructure is the telemicroscopy innovation spearheaded by researchers at the University of California, Berkley. This innovation leverages the existing infrastructure of ubiquitous cell phones by upgrading the camera of a standard cell phone into that of a clinical-quality microscope. This innovation allows rural health workers to use their cell phones fitted with these 5-50x magnification cameras to take images of patient blood samples and send them quickly and directly to doctors or labs in nearby cities. Cell phone cameras and Internet-related applications include providing advice and consulting from a centralized site on agriculture and health.

Designing Product-Related Infrastructure

Observations of class projects and real-world examples suggest that, instead of viewing a product as a standalone, companies developing subsistence products should consider supporting elements that address multifaceted deprivation. In the project related to nutritional foods and beverages, monthly supply, storage, proper measurement, and mixing in cooking procedures were all incorporated into the package design (see Table 8.2).

As noted, a nutritional/medical supplement dispenser and health education solution educated the user about savings, healthy practices, and medical supplements through package design, and an enhanced electronic version allowed children in schools to key in answers to questions in a test format (see Table 8.1). This is not to suggest that each product be supported by elaborate infrastructure investment, but rather to consider a range of resources.

For example, in settings where informational resources are severely lacking, educational aspects may need to be built into the design, such as through packaging (e.g., education about benefits of hand washing, with Unilever's promotional campaign for soap (Prahalad, 2005)). Central to the design of the product is the need to consider how the educational component can be incorporated as a core element of the product. Nokia's Life Tools service is another business example of building informative and educational aspects into the design of a product-service mix (see Table 8.1).

In our class experience, we found that a nutritional/medical supplement dispenser and health education solution requires innovative design of the container—one that educates the user about savings, healthy practices, and medical supplements, and incorporates an electronic component in an enhanced version for schoolchildren to key in answers to questions in a test format. The final product took on a comprehensive role—it included one month's supply, an appropriate container for storage, and instructions for dosage and to mix in with cooked food (Project 5). This comprehensive product and package design suggests a departure from conventional notions of a product as a standalone entity serving a particular utility.

To counter multidimensional deprivation in subsistence contexts (literacy, low income, social stigma), each product may have to represent critical elements of infrastructure. The type of educational elements that were built in to the medical supplement dispenser were evident also in the projects relating to vision testing, sanitation, and e-training (Projects 1, 7, and 10).

Although it may be impractical for each product to be supported by elaborate infrastructure investment, on the evidence of some of the case study projects, developing cost-effective, product-related infrastructure is crucial in subsistence product development. The medicine dispenser project, in fact, provided an illustration that infrastructure does not have to be confined to what is "given to" the consumer through the product, and that it can also pertain to what is "learned from" consumer behavior.

Aside from its main purpose of dispensing medicine, the prototype in this project also acts as an information-gathering device by feeding user input about rural medicine consumption and health patterns back to manufacturers and medical practitioners (Project 11).

Using Existing Products as Vehicles for Addressing Critical Needs

The student-based data also points to the role of existing products in serving as vehicles for important add-ons. Projects with food and beverage products invariably chose the route of adding important supplements to currently used foods and beverages. Similarly, the solar energy solution for mobile entrepreneurs was designed as an add-on to existing carts, rather than as a stand-alone park-and-charge type of solution.

Even a mundane commodity product such as table salt served as an important vehicle to deliver vital daily doses of iodine in subsistence consumer diets, and as a result, addressed iodine deficiency disorder, a major health concern (Prahalad, 2005). In addition to adding important supplements to currently used foods and beverages, the central ingredients can be reconstituted to provide important protein and other nutritional value. Similarly, cell phones appear to offer a versatile platform for educational and informational products, as illustrated both with student experience in the course and with businesses like Nokia.

Consumer product habits in subsistence marketplaces tend to be deeply ingrained due to a combination of beliefs and circumstances. The nutrition additive project groups, for example, had to design their products as supplements to particular foods and beverages currently used by the population rather than introduce new ways of consumption (Projects 4, 5, and 8). Thus, from a consumer acceptance point of view, the usage of already existing products as a medium for new innovations can be an important success factor. This runs counter to the design newness considerations often applicable in advanced economy contexts.

Product delivery to subsistence consumers commanded significant attention in the case studies. Whereas in the literature, design and delivery are implicitly treated as two distinct stages of the product development process, the case studies indicate that in subsistence marketplace contexts, the two have to be intertwined. Aspects relating to the point of sale or the point of use often have to become incorporated into the product design rather than kept separate (e.g., an educational program designed for use with mobile phones and TV, or eyeglasses stacked neatly in a bag and presented in the form of a display).

In summary, several substantive insights emerged from the product development projects data. Collectively, these insights, comprising market immersion, market research, identifying critical needs, and designing and developing products, carry substantial nuances that are unique to subsistence contexts. Applying these nuances will enable product developers to begin to address the complexity-based uncertainty inherent in subsistence marketplace contexts.

Building on this discussion of the "what" of subsistence innovation, the next sections discuss the "how," addressing a sequence of steps in the product development process, potentially capable of yielding subsistence innovations.

Sustainable Product Development Processes for Subsistence Marketplaces

With each offering of our course, learning associated with it, and subsequent modifications, a product development process and rationale have emerged from the multi-year experimentation. We focus on variations from recommended steps in a traditional product development process (e.g., Ulrich and Eppinger, 2008) to minimize repetition.

Virtual Immersion in Subsistence Marketplaces

The product development process begins with virtual immersion—simulated exposure to sensitize participants to subsistence contexts. This classroom-based immersion uses textual and audiovisual aids, and helps participants gain an initial understanding of life circumstances of poverty, sensitizes them to cultural issues, and gives them an understanding of the possibility of a range of product usage conditions.

Virtual immersion is an important first step in the product development process for subsistence marketplaces, ideally suited for the complexities of such contexts (see Figure 8.1). Virtual immersion is likely to be most productive when conducted with interdisciplinary teams who view the experience from different perspectives.

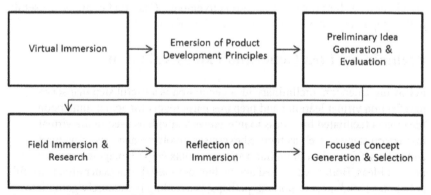

Figure 8.1: A Concept and Prototype Development Process for Subsistence marketplace/Subsistence marketplaces.

We employed several methods in virtually immersing our students. One example is a "poverty simulation," where participants simulated a 4-week period (in a 1.5-hour session) in the lives of poor people trying to make ends meet through financial decisions and interactions with banks, lenders, and other entities. In this phase, participants also analyzed transcripts of interviews conducted with subsistence respondents, completed slide and video-based exercises aimed at understanding the larger context, needs, and product usage situations, and developed cause-effect or organic conceptual models of poverty, of local-ecological issues, and of needs, products, and markets. Day-in-the-life videos and even a movie based on research provided additional stimuli for virtual immersion.

Emersion of New or Modified Product Development Principles

Aided by this exposure, teams then executed a phase of emersion (defined as "an act of emerging" or "reappearance"). Following virtual immersion, we recommend a step of emersion, where the team regroups and delineates some unique principles for product development at the intersection of business, engineering, design, and related functions.

Emersion involves comparing and contrasting generic product development and related concepts from different perspectives (marketing, management, design, and engineering) that have been developed in relatively resource-rich settings with the unique circumstances of subsistence, a step that loosens preconceptions of possessing solutions for unfamiliar contexts and reflects on learning from virtual immersion. For example, an optimal design perspective can be tempered by the need to envision a wide range of usage situations. Again, such emersion needs to involve participants from different functional perspectives for related principles as well as potential trade-offs to emerge. Case studies are very useful in this step in enabling analysis and emersion of principles.

Preliminary Idea Generation and Evaluation

Following emersion, preliminary idea generation is a useful step that serves to reflect on virtual learning and prepares participants for actual immersion. Ideation is facilitated by access to interviews and videos used in the virtual immersion stage as well as focused exercises involving analysis of pictures and videos. Given the unfamiliar settings, visuals help to imagine possible product ideas. Both needs-based and technology-based idea generation is useful at this stage, and most important, perhaps, is avoiding prematurely going into evaluation mode or adopting a mindset of knowing "what the poor need or don't need." Participants develop sets of needs, their drivers, and the larger contextual factors in which the needs and their drivers manifest, as a basis for idea generation. They also engage in bottom-up deconstruction of needs/problems and develop ideas that address the elements that are generated from this process. Premature closure, even by people who are relatively familiar with the context, sidesteps the discovery and consequent out-of-the-box thinking processes that open-minded people unfamiliar with subsistence contexts can engage in.

Through idea generation, one first develops and then assesses a manageable family of ideas in preparation for field research. The aim of this assessment is not to eliminate any ideas prematurely (given the lack of direct market research up to this point), but to narrow down to a related set of ideas. Sometimes, the output from this process may be two or three categories of ideas that form the basis for upcoming field research. During this phase, one should also develop an exhaustive list of criteria to evaluate the ideas, which are customized to subsistence marketplace contexts (e.g., affordability and criticality of need).

Immersion and Field Research

At about four months into the course, teams participate in an 11-day field immersion experience in one subsistence market context (in this case, India). During this phase, students traveled to Indian subsistence contexts and visited retail shops, marketplaces, and consumer dwellings. Using both extended observations and in-depth interviews with multiple stakeholders, teams aim to understand broader life circumstances and conduct market research relating to focal product categories. Ideally, broader immersion includes observations of retail outlets, marketplaces, dwellings, and urban and rural areas in subsistence contexts. Focused market research includes observations of focal or related products in usage, and in-depth interviews with potential customers.

Such actual immersion is transformational in a number of ways. Actual experience of the context brings a dimension that cannot be captured through any virtual means. It enables participants to experience the environment and connect the dots in powerful and unpredictable ways. For example, project teams focusing on healthy foods and beverages (see Table 8.2) found that an effective nutritional product would need to cause minimal change to the traditional food preparation process in homes, counter to the US market where a range of nutritional foods exist that either alter significantly or entirely substitute for home-based cooking processes.

Similarly, understanding of spatial issues in urban areas was instrumental in the eventual focus and design of the solar application toward mobile entrepreneurs, rather than, say, household usage (see Table 8.2). The lack of a personal connection can also be advantageous in other ways, as participants can bring fresh perspective and potential ideas that people familiar with the context may be prematurely dismissive of and may not be able to anticipate. Interactions with people enable compelling understanding of their point of view.

The nature of in-depth interviews at this stage should cover broader life circumstances as well as specific issues about product categories. In this regard, a progression from broader issues to narrower topics and even solutions was typical of the experience from our projects. In a sense, each day of the immersion experience is rich in stimuli and learning, and participants need to regroup and refocus their research method at the end of each day to take into consideration new learning. It is extraordinarily valuable to experience such immersion with teams with diverse perspectives, where individual members "see" different parts of reality and interpret them differently.

Actual experience of the context invariably brought a dimension to the process not replicable through virtual means. For example, many teams realized for the first time that it was critical to bring multiple stakeholders to the table to overcome the many social layers and hierarchies that impinge upon product use and market choices in subsistence contexts. Teams often reported, also for the first time, after returning from this field immersion, developing a deep personal commitment to the success of their projects.

This is not unlike the theme consistently emphasized in ethnographic literature to "engage personally with the fieldwork" one is doing, which produces emotional consequences over and above dispassionate research learning (Coffey, 1999). For example, one team spoke of being "inspired by" an unexpected optimism among the poor. A quote from one of the team members provides some perspective:

> "However, we discovered upon visiting...that most of these ideas were not practical for a variety of reasons. We were really only able to find useful ideas from having a chance to listen to individuals who live in the rural subsistence marketplaces...and from seeing their life context first-hand."

We acknowledge that field immersions are not insignificant efforts. In the course, the ability to conduct such immersion experiences considerably stemmed from having core members of the overall research team on the ground and actually originating from the very subsistence contexts that are the subjects of study, and also having vast experience in community development efforts.

The broader engagement with specific communities in India that envelops the context of the course and this particular study has also involved social initiatives over a number of years, such as the provision of marketplace literacy education to low-literate adults (see Table 8.2). Thus, the long-term experiences and relationships forged on the ground substantially enabled the support of communities, and more importantly, facilitated interaction directly with people at the lowest strata of society.

Viable alternatives in other situations may include working with NGOs that are credible and well-respected in the community. It is important here to avoid depending on information filtered through layers of information channels. Direct access to people living at the lowest strata of society is critical. Translators need to be trained to allow a direct interaction and not edit questions and responses.

Similarly, it is also useful to train translators who may themselves be from slightly higher strata to not be prematurely dismissive of ideas and begin to respond on the behalf of participants. Finally, it is also useful in the immersion exercise, especially in emerging economies, to observe the entire spectrum of society, such as high-end malls and high-tech companies, to understand how subsistence is intertwined with other strata in emerging economies.

Reflection About Immersion Experience

This step serves to summarize learning from the immersion experience with emphasis on how preconceptions have changed. Such reflection is vital in setting the tone for the rest of the product development process. In a debrief of the immersion trip, topics such as cultural nuances are addressed. Given the hectic and stimulus-rich nature of the immersion, this step helps participants to put their learning in perspective and correct misperceptions. Participants reflect on observations and interviews conducted during the trip using a show-and-tell format.

This is also an important step to compare and contrast learning from virtual versus real immersion and reassess emersion of principles for product development. Again, the need for interdisciplinary perspectives is important, as is the need to include team members who did not participate in the actual immersion.

Focused Concept Generation and Selection

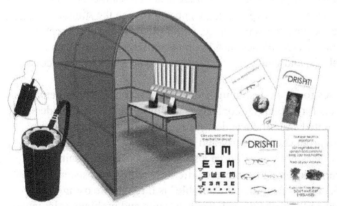

Image 8.06: Product prototype depicting a deployable kiosk for vision testing, from a class project. Photograph courtesy of Subsistence Marketplaces Initiative.

Image 8.7: Product prototype from a class project depicting a solar heating device to warm water for mobile cart vendors selling tea and food. Photograph courtesy of Subsistence Marketplaces Initiative.

Actual immersion is followed with focused concept generation that is not as expansive or all-inclusive as the previous phase that occurs before the field trip. Rather, the aim here is to avoid premature closure on one or two concepts that may have emerged from the immersion experience. Participants are pushed to generate three to five concepts rather than fixate on one.

This was done to ensure that balance would be maintained, by allowing the focus to be on neither an unmanageably large set of ideas nor premature fixation on any one specific concept that may have gained prominence in the stimulus-rich immersion. Unlike the idea generation stage, participants detail the concepts to a greater extent. Through techniques such as brainstorming, function diagrams, morphological analysis, and voting, participants eventually choose a final concept.

Facilitative exercises focus on designing solutions for subsistence marketplaces. Analysis of products for unfamiliar contexts is useful in this phase to understand how needs were elicited and products designed (e.g., products for extreme situations, assistive products for elderly and disabled customers, products for emergencies or disasters, and children's toys). For concept screening and selection, participants developed extensive criteria specific to subsistence marketplace needs (e.g., is the product re-usable? is it replicable using local talent?). Bottom-up and top-down need deconstruction and problem articulation in various stages keeps the focus on the unique orientation of our approach.

In the last phases, teams worked on integrating all of their work into an overall set of deliverables due at the end of the year. These deliverables demanded both technological analysis—involving the design of product prototypes and manufacturing plans—and commercial analysis—involving preparation of detailed financial and marketing plans. The iterative experience in delivering the course over many years has allowed an emergent view of this process of subsistence marketplace product development up to the commercialization stage (see Figure 8.2).

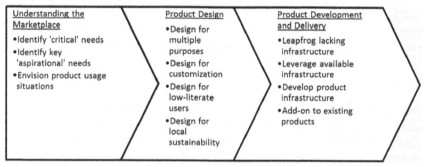

Figure 8.2: Key Factors of Concept and Prototype Development for Subsistence Marketplace/Subsistence Marketplaces.

Discussion

This chapter addresses two questions:

- What factors determine effectiveness of market-based product development in and for subsistence marketplaces?

- How and why are these factors uniquely important in subsistence marketplaces (when compared to non-subsistence marketplaces)?

We discuss the following factors: the ability to

- identify product needs that are either critical to survival in the current term or critical to transformational progress in the long term or both;

- envision unfamiliar usage situations;

- design products with a high degree of local usability, flexibility, and sustainability; and

- look beyond infrastructural deficiencies and take advantage of even meager alternative resources in developing products.

As for the second question—understanding factors that are uniquely important to subsistence marketplaces—these factors are important because of the unique characteristics of subsistence, such as deprivation along multiple facets and the preponderance of consumer decisions rooted in seemingly impossible trade-offs among essentials. Broadly speaking, because livelihood strategies in subsistence markets are executed from a position of severe constraints, often the resulting choices and trade-offs are unconventional in comparison to middle-class consumer behavior, thereby making the factors cited in this research uniquely relevant to subsistence contexts.

Further, the poor economic conditions faced by subsistence consumers (and producers) are often underpinned by systematic social deprivations, which often deny them freedom to participate in economic interchange (Sen, 1999), a condition less salient among consumers in industrial, democratic economies. This difference underscores the relevance of factors such as seeking local sustainability or sidestepping decrepit public infrastructure.

Two key themes that stand out from our analysis and extant knowledge about subsistence marketplaces are the uncertainty that pervades many consumption events and the ingenious adaptivity shown by consumers and entrepreneurs in many product-use situations. Parallels in developed market contexts point to product development best practices to address these phenomena.

For example, although of a very different kind, consumption uncertainty is a central feature in high technology environments as well, owing to rapid changes in technological standards. In such conditions, cross-functional teams and lead user teams have been shown to stimulate more creative product development (Sethi, et al. 2001). Deploying cross-functional teams to immerse themselves in the marketplace and co-develop product concepts with key participants from the subsistence population could impart out-of-the-box creativity to the product development process that results in meaningful solutions to critical needs.

Finally, in contrast to relatively affluent settings, there is a crucial need to assess products and every aspect of the development process (design, engineering, testing, and production) in actual usage settings rather than in labs and factories.

Conclusion

This chapter suggests a number of useful insights for managers. The first is the potential of using lead user feedback in market research for subsistence marketplace product development, as outlined earlier. In developed markets, lead users typically enjoy greater privilege and access to technology than typical users, and thus develop insights into usage conditions which lie in the future for most people (von Hippel, 1986).

In contrast, in subsistence contexts, some consumers acquire lead user capabilities not through any advantages over typical subsistence consumers (indeed they suffer the same market constraints), but through a superior ability to draw practical insights from unfamiliar domains, purely through imagination, aspiration, and creativity. Learning to identify such people and including them in the market research process can prove a key subsistence marketplace new product development (NPD) capability for product development teams.

A second important managerial implication relates to the strategic approach that firms use for subsistence marketplace product development and innovation. In high-tech product markets in advanced economies, the development of new technology or sophisticated products is underpinned by the "breakthrough" approach (Garud and Karnoe, 2003)—one where new opportunities are spotted by creative entrepreneurs, funding is provided by visionary capitalists to "design and build the best" product, and policy assistance is provided by regulators to spawn associated industries supplying advanced components.

In contrast, the NPD approach for subsistence marketplaces suggested by the experimentations of the projects analyzed in this study is best described as a "bricolage" approach (Garud and Karnoe, 2003)—one where the development curve may start with a relatively low-tech but locally suitable design, and subsequent progress is made through inputs from participants who possess local knowledge. A key feature of the bricolage approach is that, because of the involvement and interaction of multiple actors, micro-learning and co-shaping occurs to a great extent.

When looking to deploy people to subsistence marketplaces, some personal characteristics become important. These people should be completely open to learning from unfamiliar settings; they should be empathetic, so they can discern transformational consumer needs and aspirations; and they should be culturally sensitive, so they can examine contexts outside of their own cultural comfort zone.

Taken as a whole, this framework contrasts with traditional recommendations for product innovation, which, aside from obtaining customer inputs within a staged market research/test marketing paradigm, follows a development process where the products are developed in relative isolation from the market, and where a specific set of usage conditions and supporting infrastructure are assumed as givens.

Although this chapter focused on subsistence marketplaces, the implications may hold true for product design in other contexts experiencing moderate to extreme constraints and with which managers are equally unfamiliar (e.g., disaster relief contexts). In a time of escalating environmental degradations and resource shortages, the deeper understanding of unpredictable product usage scenarios, the focus on local sustainability (local materials, local skills, local culture), and the leveraging of any available infrastructure that have been discussed here, may become critically important non-subsistence marketplace contexts as well.

Appendix 1

Project 1

This project involved the development of a solution for vision care needs in rural subsistence marketplaces in India. Market research revealed to this project team that failing or faulty vision critically affects livelihoods in rural India. However, existing literature seemed to suggest that the subsistence consumer was either too busy to care or too resigned to life circumstances (e.g. cannot afford eyeglasses). In contrast, the team subsequently learned from first-hand interactions that rural Indians in subsistence marketplaces actually placed great importance on vision—they had strong dietary beliefs relating to vision and a high willingness to pay a small premium for high-quality glasses even from very meager cash resources. It also found that villagers mainly trusted eye doctors while not placing much value on vision care services provided by intermediaries—technicians, NGOs (especially when offered free of charge). Similarly, the team discovered that product delivery approaches that often worked for consumable products like soap (e.g. door-to-door sales) were not readily transferable to the category of eyeglasses. A different dynamic of trust was required, one that established the credibility of expertise, signaled high quality, and communicated compassion but without necessarily giving things away for free.

Addressing these imperatives in concert with the needs outlined by the project sponsor, the team designed a vision care solution comprising a 'vision bag' to be taken into the market door to door by 'vision entrepreneurs.' The bag was designed to hold all necessary product components in appropriate quantities (72 frames and 660 lenses) as well as to transform itself, when needed, into a rotating point-of-purchase display of glasses. Essentially, it offered the credibility of a vision 'expert' as well as urban-style 'retail atmospherics.' The door-to-door process also performed multiple functions depending on the situation, alternating between actually providing glasses and being an initial screening clinic to recommending hospital visits. The solution also included a deployable vision kiosk that could be carried in collapsed form and set up in villages at short notice, where high-quality personalized service and expert assessments would be provided. Glasses were priced at an average of $3, with complete business plans for financial sustainability. The key component of delivery was designing the process to benefit from the limited radius of trust and social goodwill by recruiting vision entrepreneurs and kiosk personnel from the local regions.

Project 2

This project involved developing an educational service to teach children ages 5-12 conversational skills in the English language. In an early phase, the team learned about the major emphasis on ability to converse in English in India. With roots in the country's colonial and post-colonial experiences, this is seen as a lever to achieving social and economic progress, particularly in subsistence contexts. Hence, the team discovered significant aspiration among parents to educate their children in English. Formal education appeared to focus on 'building blocks' (grammar, vocabulary) rather than build conversational skills. A pertinent fact here is that social stigma, lack of confidence, and nervousness often led to 'production blocking'—i.e., inability to generate relevant words for the context. The team recognized that there was unmet demand in subsistence marketplace segments for generating adequate English conversation opportunities, which children lacked because of their low social status.

To develop an appropriate solution, however, the team found it had to meet families, school teachers, education entrepreneurs, self-help groups, youth, and many other interested parties. Such liaison with a diverse set of stakeholders revealed many surprising nuances. Children, for example, were found to get annoyed with their parents for trying to converse with them in English, as their responses were slower and inaccurate. Parents, on the other hand, felt that their children only learned 'bookish' English and were unable to hold actual conversations of practical value. Teachers admitted to a lack of motivation but were also quick to point out that the children too lacked incentive to speak in English. Such learning proved very useful to the team, as it helped crystallize the design goal of making the service a joyful experience (which would then alleviate the considerable stress and anxiety seen to be associated with learning to speak English). Further, although parents and children had mismatched attitudes, they nevertheless were bound in an interdependent relationship; this prompted the team to arrive at the eventual design of a 'family literacy' program.

A separate design decision that could be viewed as counter-intuitive for subsistence marketplaces was to make the service software-based. It was reasoned that to achieve scale in serving what was such a large need, the training of personnel for physical delivery would not be adequate. Developing a software-driven education service also allowed for the integration of multiple media. The service was designed as a television show in which children would participate by calling in to the program by dialing a 1-800-type number using mobile phones. The design leveraged the fact that these technologies were already in heavy use in subsistence marketplaces. India has been experiencing one of the fastest growth rates in mobile phone subscriptions in the world (about 8 million new subscribers a month), and [at the time of the project] had more than 100 million households with television. The use of technologies that were already established was expected to minimize technology anxiety in the target segment. In the TV program, an animated teacher with an animated parrot would conduct the show, asking questions to which several children would call in and offer a response. For example, in a lesson on pronunciation of the word 'Apple,' the responses would be collected and matched against the accurate pronunciation of 'Apple.' Upon finding the best match, the teacher would identify the name of the child who got it right—as the child's name was communicated to everyone watching the show, it would help instill confidence. The program was also designed to be bilingual to help overcome confidence barriers. If no response matched the expected standard, then the teacher would continue until a majority got it right.

The design offered much flexibility in execution, and the program could be set to follow locally appropriate rules as determined by local stakeholders (e.g. teachers). For instance, children with similar skill levels (assessed through screening calls) could be assigned to the same time slot; alternatively, a small network/group from one school or one village could be allowed to participate together in order to emphasize social learning. Thus, although mediated by software and technology, the actual learning process was designed to be conducted in consonance with local social and human capital and was customizable.

Project 3

This project involved developing a thermo-siphoning, solar-powered, water heating system for mobile beverage vendors. Vending beverages is one of the most commonly pursued entrepreneurial activities in subsistence marketplaces. However, the activity lacks adequate energy sources and is very inefficient with what is available. Typical results are severe mobility constraints for entrepreneurs and unhygienic consumption conditions for customers.

After going through several potential product concepts that evolved continually as the team went through iterative immersion and emersion processes, the team eventually developed a solution of a thermo-siphoning solar liquid heater built onto a push cart. The sun's rays would help heat copper coils containing cold water through a pane of glass, creating a greenhouse effect. The heated water would flow up to a storage container, which could be tapped for hot water to make tea and other beverages. The hot water thus generated would be amenable to multiple uses—for example, in the local context where hygiene is a critical issue and a potential competitive advantage, applications like pure drinking water, sterilizing utensils, and warming food trays are very useful to the vendor.

This adaptability extended to being compatible with alternative fuel sources as they became available.

Although the eventual product was designed to be a solution for entrepreneurs, the team originally started with the relatively conventional idea of developing a solar cooking solution for the home. After discarding the original idea for various reasons, when trying to adapt a home solar oven idea to be used outside the home by a mobile entrepreneur, immersion experiences allowed the team to understand that a solution designed to "produce volume and aid in wealth creation" would be a very different design proposition from one "designed to make life easier for household cooking." A second aspect was that, whereas the home-use solar oven was designed to 'bake' by heating the air around food, the mobile vendor's needs demanded an appliance that could 'heat liquid.' Further, when the proposition of heating oil presented many practical design problems, the team came to understand the significant market potential of heating water. India produces 1/3rd of the world's tea and consumes 1/6th of it, with a significant proportion consumed through exactly the type of mobile vending cart the team eventually targeted. As such, not only the technology but the use it is subjected to and the usage situation itself were shaped by iterative exposure to the subsistence marketplace context—something that would be unachievable through merely logical processes conducted in labs.

Project 4

Please refer to the case titled Soy Choice on the web portal.

Project 5

Please refer to the case titled ActiveEdge on the web portal. A brief summary is provided here:

This project entails the design and development of a nutritive powder additive to be mixed in wheat flour for consumption among subsistence consumers in India. As a first observation, the product team zeroed in on a critical basic need of subsistence marketplaces—nutrition; in India alone, there are 60 million malnourished children—the highest in the world. Thus the product choice reflects addressing a critical need in the market. For example, they learned that Indian women put children's health, family's health, and their own health in a descending order of importance, allowing the students to eventually position the product as primarily a child nutrition solution. An interesting challenge encountered in this project is that whereas the target market considered nutrition to be a vital issue, it was not willing to tolerate more than minimal change in food preparation methods. Understanding this enabled the team to adopt a powder form, which could be mixed in with wheat flour as part of the common practice of preparing wheat dough to make chapattis. The product thus achieved the ability to address a critical need using existing products (chapattis) as vehicles. The product was designed to be entirely produced locally in India, offering entrepreneurial opportunities ensuring sustainability of the local economy. Even at a consumer level, the selling of additives separately rather than pre-mixed in some form of 'enriched' wheat flour enables consumers to participate in the product creation process. In subsistence settings, this highlights the futility of pre-conceived notions such as "being low-literate, they cannot read and follow mixing instructions carefully." Instead, there is an aspirational factor in consumers wanting to be active participants. However, as proportions are important, the team ensured some infrastructural help was available along with the product by developing an innovative container that would help the consumer perform the mixing. Monthly supply, storage, proper measurement and mixing in cooking procedures were all incorporated into the package design, providing product-related support through information.

Project 6

The details of this project are not available for dissemination through this medium.

Project 7

Please refer to the case titled TownSchool on the web portal.

Project 8

Please refer to the case titled Health Beverage on the web portal.

Project 9

Please refer to the case titled Vita Jeevan on the web portal.

Project 10

The details of this project are not available for dissemination through this medium

Project 11

The details of this project are not available for dissemination through this medium.

Project 12

The details of this project are not available for dissemination through this medium

Project 13

The details of this project are not available for dissemination through this medium

Table 8.1: Analysis of Case Studies of Product Design and Development in Subsistence Marketplaces

Table 8.1 lists critical needs for people living in subsistence, the organizations that are addressing those needs, understanding and research regarding those needs, along with designs and developments ot address those needs.

Critical Need	Organization	Understanding	Design	Development
Access to basic healthcare services	Mobile Medics [India] Sources: Primary research "Mobile Medics – A Genius is Born?" *Sandpaper,* *BITS Pilani Alumni Magazine,* Fall 2006 similar innovations DISHA [India – rural] ACWP [Vietnam – rural] Project Renewal [US – urban]	Lack of immediate access to basic healthcare in rural areas in India. Student team immersion in villages in Rajasthan, India, in 2005 to learn about healthcare-related infrastructure, needs, and consumer behavior. Face-to-face market research to discover that 30% of villagers willing to pay (at least minimally) for quality healthcare if made accessible in their villages. Envision need for service based on understanding. Design of healthcare-in-a-van concept to administer basic health services.	Choice of rugged vans for optimal performance in hot, dusty conditions of Rajasthan, India. Design of van to be manned by a team of three professionals – a senior doctor, a junior doctor, and a nurse. Entrepreneurial role for each team running their own customized business as an independent profit center. Marketing communications designed to be understandable by low-literate audience, with posters on walls and pamphlets rich with symbols.	Absent infrastructure of hospitals and clinics in rural villages, the mobile concept to serve a need and enable bypassing normal costs and challenges. Leveraging existing human capital of small-town doctors and nurses willing to take on additional roving duties for augmenting income.

Product Development for Subsistence Marketplaces

Access to affordable communication technology, and livelihood-relevant information	Nokia [Global] **Sources:** Nokia website http://www.nokia.com/A4136001?_newsid=1266168 **Similar innovations** Microsoft [Global] Grameen Technology Center [Bangladesh]	Many rural subsistence communities unable to achieve socio-economic progress, untouched by communications. Immersive market research to understand both a critical basic need for families and an aspirational need for farmers and entrepreneurs seeking productivity and business progress.	Ultra-low-cost handsets to address affordability concerns and reflect realities experienced in subsistence marketplaces. Design of phones for use by low-literate users; features such as a speaking clock, audio messaging, and icon-oriented interfaces and address books.	Product development not confined to the actual phone - imminent introduction of Nokia Life Tools service in India along with its 2323 phone model reflecting need to supplement core product. Access to vital livelihood-related information such as crop prices and weather patterns for rural farmers.
Access to new skills and market opportunities	1. **Desicrew** [India] **Sources:** Primary research Desicrew website http://www.desicrew.in/ **Similar innovations** PilaniBPO [India] Drishtee [India] Byrraju Foundation [India]	For rural youth in India, dwindling opportunities in traditional profession of agriculture - need for new, market-oriented skills and jobs. Business premise around training and employment of rural youth in the new economy sector of business process outsourcing (BPO). Immersion in small towns to grasp specific nuances regarding skill sets, gaps, and the infrastructural context to refine its "BPO at SUBSISTENCE MARKETPLACE" product concept. (The rural BPO	Local sustainability through creating enduring opportunity in the local rural economy rather than pave a migratory path to urban areas – creation of local skills and wealth that empower and enrich the local economy. Collaboration with local organizations to ensure customization to local needs. In Palladam (rural Indian town), took the role of training provider for a government program jointly designed by	To meet complex infrastructural challenge of training and housing dozens of employees in geographically disparate locations, piggy-backing on Internet kiosk infrastructure created by other organizations. Despite small size of kiosks (about three to five computers), multiple shifts to ensure optimal use and continuous customer service.

business model has thus far mainly only been demonstrated in India.)	itself, a local women's NGO and the local administration to provide skills and livelihood to women in families below the poverty line.	In exchange for using kiosks as vehicles for its business, addition of aspect of jobs and livelihoods to the kiosk model, addressing a pressing need in rural contexts previously dependent on agriculture for income.	
2. Rural Opportunities Production Enterprise [ROPE] [India] **Sources:** Primary research ROPE website http://ropeinternational.com/	Complementary business model of transforming traditional, low-paying skills of artisanship to a globally-oriented, market-focused enterprise underlined by new capabilities in design, production, logistics, and marketing. Model emergence from immersive understanding leading to removal of inconsistency quality and the exploitation of middlemen from the traditional rural artisan business model and outcome of a new, market-oriented sustainable enterprise.	Local sustainability through nature of use of manpower and materials - rural artisans using, honing, and sustaining their traditional skills; incomes enhanced and markets expanded for products. Production managers overseeing the work of artisans locally employed, thus leveraging indigenous knowledge and social capital. Materials used from local, naturally growing plants or agricultural by-products, spurring market forces toward promoting ecological sustainability.	Handicraft skills and products already existent in the rural marketplace. Product-related infrastructure provided by ROPE-workshops, supervision, training, marketing, logistics, and quality control.

| Access to education and literacy | 1. Marketplace Literacy Project [MLP] [India]

Sources:

Primary research MLP website
http://www.marketplaceliteracy.org/

Similar innovations

Consumer Financial Literacy Program, University of Georgia [USA]
http://www.fcs.uga.edu/ext/econ/financial_literacy.php | Marketplace literacy education critical for effective marketplace participation - complementing market access and micro-finance.

MLP founded based on immersive research.

Recognition of critical basic need of subsistence buyers and sellers to acquire skills and overcome vulnerabilities stemming from lack of literacy.

Recognition of higher level aspirational need for consumers to transition from novices to experts and even to become entrepreneurs, and for entrepreneurs to run successful businesses. | Harsh realities of a strenuous daily schedule of domestic or business duties constrained prospective learners' ability to participate.

Different configurations of consumer and entrepreneurial literacy – individual modules offered over 1-day or 2-days, extended, complete version over 5-days.

Course design involved low-literate participants in a non-intimidating and fully participative manner, using visual stimuli and myriad group and role-playing tasks.

Concretized, localized, "social"ized content to leverage inherent social and oral communication skills of participants. | Design of materials assuming classroom and other pedagogically-related infrastructure non-existent.

Design of course materials relatively independent of such infrastructure, often using rudimentary, replenishable, and easily transportable materials.

Incorporation of local livelihood opportunities as examples in educational program.

Use of existing infrastructure (televisions, computer kiosks) for multi-media learning (in progress). |

2. RTBI [India] Sources: Primary research RTBI website: http://www.rtbi.in/education.html	Critical need in rural subsistence contexts, to learn basic formal literacy elements suitable for easier employability. Education program targeting rural youth, teaching spoken English, basic computer usage, and tutorials and tests using an online curriculum.	Design of curriculum and delivery customized to fit local cultural needs, mindful of cultural barriers.	Infrastructure for education often non-existent in remote rural areas. Teacher absenteeism rampant when physical infrastructure available. RTBI leapfrogging problems through ICT-enabled service.
3. Course project on educational solution [India]	Critical need felt by parents for spoken English capabilities for children to achieve economic and social mobility. Virtual and actual immersions and market research to understand specific opportunities and constraints operative in the social context	Room for customization in implementation to accommodate local variation in costs and constraints [e.g. tasks can be automated by software or done manually]. Local sustainability of the product through community-oriented features helpful in removing social stigma.	Significant penetration of cell phones and televisions despite lack of infrastructure. Design of educational service leveraging infrastructure; calling specific telephone numbers to get English lessons and tutorials through interactive television program.

| Access to robust housing and improvement in living conditions to counter harsh context | 1. Aga Khan Building and Planning Services [Pakistan, India, and Central Asia]

Sources:

Website http://www.akdn.org/akpbs | Need for improvement in living conditions.

Focus over 20 years on assisting construction of durable, low-cost homes, refurbishing older homes for durability, and improvements in living conditions at home. | Numerous applications (seismic resistant homes, insulation techniques, in-home smoke reduction), reflecting design for hostile user conditions.

Local sustainability through involvement of local entrepreneurs, architects, and artisans in design, manufacture, and installation of products. | Refurbishment program reflects need to build on existing infrastructure.

Development of self-sustainable hygienic, low-cost latrines not dependent on municipal water and sewer systems to bypass absence of infrastructure. |
| | 2. SunOven [Africa]

Sources:

Primary research

SunOven website: http://www.sunoven.com/ | Sustainability dilemma in subsistence between conservation of resources and necessity to survive [e.g. use of firewood in cooking].

Solar cookers to reduce firewood use and serve need for low-cost cooking appliances. | Well-insulated design of solar oven to prevent food from getting cold quickly.

Demonstrates need for local customization; in many contexts, culture of working while sun is out and eating meals after sundown not conducive to low insulation designs. | Import model not cost-effective; non-existent infrastructure for local production; Sunoven approach to leverage local manpower and materials and provide training for local assembly; creating jobs and building incomes to buy product. |

Access to nutritional supplements to counter malnutrition	**Course project on nutritional product, ActivEdge** [India] **Similar innovations** Plumpy' Nut [Africa] Solae soy foods [Global]	Virtual and actual immersions in Indian subsistence marketplace context for deep understanding of cultural significance of cooking, and associated design demands and constraints on nutritional product. Market research with insights from potential users, vendors, local doctors, and self-help group leaders to understand usage patterns.	Design of packaging for low-literate audience – pictures and visual representation of nutrients and benefits. Micro-nutrients and bulking agents to be locally procured and blending locally outsourced to stimulate local economy. Additive designed to be unobtrusive to local cooking practices.	nutrients not enough to promote use; Infrastructure around the product in the form of holistic packaging to enable storing nutrient as well as mixing in correct proportion with other ingredients for consumption.

Table 8.2: Summary of Class Projects

Table 8.2 lists each semester the course has been offered, which needs have been addressed by them, the products that students have developed to address those needs, the majors of students within the project teams, and the type of sponsors that have helped with each project.

S.No.	Need Addressed	Product Category/Product/Service Prototype Form	Team Composition*	Sponsor
1	Low cost eye testing and prescription eyeglasses in rural areas sold by vision entrepreneurs	Deployable kiosk and inventory bag for vision entrepreneurs	Business, Industrial design (UG), engineering (chemical, mechanical), architecture	Large social enterprise
2	Spoken English education for children (and their parents) to address problems with regular school education focusing on written English	Spoken English service for children	Business, industrial design, engineering (aeronautical, UG - computer science)	Large multinational

Product Development for Subsistence Marketplaces

3	Local energy source for mobile entrepreneurs to heat water and keep prepared food warm	Solar water siphon heater to fit carts for mobile entrepreneurs	Business, Industrial design (UG), engineering (civil, computer)	Small company making solar ovens
4	Protein enrichment diet that could be blended into existing dietary and cooking habits	Nutritional additive - Powder plus one-time educational, sustainable, and metering container	Business, Industrial design (UG), Industrial engineering, Communication, Plant biology	Research center at university
5	Nutrition in diet that could be blended into existing dietary and cooking habits	Nutritional additive - Powder plus metered mixer-container	Business (UG and GRAD), industrial design (UG), engineering biomolecular engineering (Ph.D)	Entrepreneur exploring small startup
6	Low-cost access to Internet in households	Internet access for households	Business, Industrial design, engineering (electrical/computer, systems and entrepreneurial)	Large multinational
7	Usable cell phone interface and information for low literate users with native language skills	Customized cell phone interface and support software	Business (UG), Industrial design, economics (UG), systems and entrepreneurial engineering (PhD)	Large multinational
8	Education for children in rural areas about health	Online health education for children through rural kiosks	Business (UG and GRAD), industrial design, engineering (systems and entrepreneurial, electrical/computer)	Large multinational
9	Training for teachers in remote and geographically dispersed rural settings	E-training interface for distance training for teachers in rural areas	Business, Industrial design (UG), Education administration (PhD), Human resources education (PhD), Human resource development	Large social enterprise

10	Important nutrients in beverages	Healthy beverage	Business (UG), Industrial design, Engineering (chemical and bio-molecular (PhD), industrial)	Large multinational
11	Vitamin deficiencies and education about health for children	Health education and vitamins	Business, Industrial design, Engineering	Large social enterprise
12	Sanitation in rural areas	Sanitation solution	Business, Industrial design (UG)**	Large multinational
13	Provision of pharmaceuticals as part of health care	Pharmaceutical dispensing	Business, Industrial design (UG), Engineering (computer, electrical, civil, mechanical)	Small enterprise

*Current majors specified, previous degrees not listed, Masters level unless otherwise specified and Business Masters refers to MBA, UG—undergraduate, Doctoral students specified

**Previous degrees included relevant technical expertise

References

Appadurai, A. (2001). Deep Democracy, Urban Governmentality, and the Horizon of Politics. Environment and Urbanization 13 (2):23-43.

Appadurai, A. (2004). The Capacity to Aspire: Culture and the Term of Recognition. In: Culture and Public Action: A Cross-Disciplinary Dialogue on Development Policy, Vijayendra Rao and Michael Walton (eds.). CA: Stanford University Press, 59-84.

Astleithner, F. and Hamedinger, A. (2003). The Analysis of Sustainability Indicators as Socially Constructed Policy Instruments: Benefits and Challenges of 'Interactive Research.' In: Local Environment, ICLEI, 8 (6):591–614.

Atolagbe, S.O. (1989). Product Design and Development: A Developing Country's Experience. In: Proceedings of International Conference on Engineering Design, Harrogate.

Bailetti, A. and Litva, P. (1995). Integrating Customer Requirements into Product Designs. Journal of Product Innovation Management 12 (1):3-15.

Baker, W. and Sinkula, J. (2005). Market Orientation and the New Product Paradox. Journal of Product Innovation Management 22 (November):483-502.

Berg, B. (2006). Qualitative Research Methods for the Social Sciences. Toronto, ON: Allyn and Bacon.

Chakravarti, D. (2006). Voices Unheard: The Psychology of Consumption in Poverty and Development. Journal of Consumer Psychology 16(4):363-376.

Coffey, A. (1999). The Ethnographic Self: Fieldwork and the Representation of Identity. London: Sage Publications.

Copestake, J. and Camfield, L. (2010). Measuring Multidimensional Aspiration Gaps: A Means to Understanding Cultural Aspects of Poverty. Development Policy Review 28(5): 617-633.

Crul, M. and Diehl, J.C. (2006). Design for Sustainability: A Practical Approach for Developing Economies. UNEP Division of Technology, Industry, and Economics.

Day, G.S. (1994). The Capabilities of Market-Driven Organizations. Journal of Marketing 58(4):37-52.

Deci, E. L., and Richard M. (2000). The "What" and "Why" of Goal Pursuits: Human Needs and the Self-Determination of Behavior. Psychological Inquiry, 11), 227-268.

Donaldson, K. (2006). Product Design in Less Industrialized Economies: Constraints and Opportunities in Kenya. Research in Engineering Design 17(3):135-155.

Eisenhardt, K.M. (1989). Building Theories from Case Study Research. Academy of Management Review 14(4):532-550.

Eisenhardt, K.M. and Graebner, M.E. (2007). Theory Building from Cases: Opportunities and Challenges. Academy of Management Journal 50(1):25-32.

Elkington, J. (1997). Cannibals with Forks: The Triple Bottom Line of 21st Century Business. Oxford: Capstone Publishing.

Garud and Karnie (2003). Bricolage Versus Breakthrough: Distributed and Embedded Agency in Technology Entrepreneurship, Research Policy, 32, 277–300

Gassmann, O. Opening up the Innovation Process Towards an Agenda, R&D Management, 36, 3, 223-228.

Griffin, A. (1997). PDMA Research on New Product Development Practices: Updating Trends and Benchmarking Best Practices. Journal of Product Innovation Management 14(6):429-458.

Gundersen, C., Weinreb, L., Wehler, C., and Hosmer, D. (2003). Homelessness and Food Insecurity. Journal of Housing Economics 12(2):250-272.

Hammond, A. and Prahalad, C.K. (2004). Selling to the Poor. Foreign Policy 142:30-37 (May-June).

Hill, R.P. and Stamey, M. (1990). The Homeless in America: An Examination of Possessions and Consumption Behaviors. Journal of Consumer Research 17(3):303-321.

Kandachar, P. and Halme. M. (2007). An Exploratory Journey towards the Research and Practice of the 'Base of the Pyramid'. Greener Management International 51:3-17 (June).

Karlsson, C. (1997). Product Development, Innovation Networks, Infrastructure and Agglomeration Economies, Annals of Regional Science, 31, 235–258

Kasser, T., & Ryan, R. M. (1996). Further Examining the American dream: Differential Correlates of Intrinsic and Extrinsic Goals. Personality and Social Psychology Bulletin 22, 80-87.

Kottak, C. (1990). Culture and "Economic Development". American Anthropologist 92(3):723-731.

Leonardo-Barton, D. (1992). The Factory as a Learning Laboratory. Sloan Management Review 34: 23-38.

Mahajan, V. and Banga, K. (2005). The 86% Solution: How to Succeed in the Biggest Market Opportunity of the Next 50 Years. Upper Saddle River, NJ: Wharton School Publishing.

Marquis, D. (1972). The Anatomy of Successful Innovations. Innovation 1(1):35-48.

Perks, H., Cooper, R., and Jones, C. (2005). Characterizing the Role of Design in New Product Development: An Empirically Derived Taxonomy. Journal of Product Innovation Management 22(2):111-127.

Prahalad, C.K. (2009). The Fortune at the Bottom of the Pyramid: Eradicating Poverty through Profits. Revised and Updated 5TH Anniversary Edition. Upper Saddle River, NJ: Wharton School Publishing.

Rangan, V.K., Quelch, J.A., Herrero, G., and Barton, B. (2007). Business Solutions for the Global Poor: Creating Social and Economic Value. San Francisco: Jossey-Bass.

Stake, R.E. (1994). Case Studies. In: Handbook of Qualitative Research, N. K. Denzin and Y. S. Lincoln (eds.). Thousand Oaks, CA: Sage, 236–247.

Talke, K., Salomo, S., Wieringa, J.E., and Luts, A. (2009). What about Design Newness? Investigating the Relevance of a Neglected Dimension of Product Innovativeness. Journal of Product Innovation Management 26(6):601-615.

Toffler, A. (1980). The Third Wave. London, UK: Collins Books.

Tybout, J.R. (2000). Manufacturing Firms in Developing Countries: How Well Do They Do, and Why? Journal of Economic Literature 38(1):11-44.

Ulrich, K.T. and Eppinger, S.D. (2008). Product Design and Development, (4th ed.). NY: Irvin/McGraw-Hill.

Veryzer, R.W. (1998). Discontinous Innovation and the New Product Development Process. Journal of Product Innovation Management 15(4):304-321.

Veryzer, R.W. and Barja de Mozota, B. (2005). The Impact of User-oriented Design on New Product Development: An Examination of Fundamental Relationships. Journal of Product Innovation Management 22(2):128-143.

Viswanathan, M. (2007). Understanding Product and Market Interactions in Subsistence Marketplaces: A Study in South India. In: Product and Market Development for Subsistence Marketplaces: Consumption and Entrepreneurship Beyond Literacy and Resource Barriers, (Advances in International Management Series), Joseph Cheng and Michael Hitt (eds.), NY: Elsevier, 21-57.

Viswanathan, M. and Rosa, J.A. (2007). Product and Market Development for Subsistence Marketplaces: Consumption and Entrepreneurship beyond Literacy and Resource Barriers. In: Advances in International Management Series, Joseph Cheng and Michael Hitt (eds.). NY: Elsevier, 1-17.

Viswanathan, M., Seth, A., Gau, R. and Chaturvedi A. (2009). Internalizing Social Good into Business Processes in Subsistence Marketplaces: The Sustainable Market Orientation. Journal of Macromarketing 29(4):406-425.

Von Hippel, E. (1986). Lead Users: A Source of Novel Product Concepts. Management Science, 32 (7), 791-805.

Von Hippel, E. (2001). User Toolkits for Innovation, Journal of Product Innovation Management, 18, 247-257.

Wind, J. and Mahajan, V. (1997). Issues and Opportunities in New Product Development: An Introduction to the Special Issue. Journal of Marketing Research, 34 (1), 1-12.

Yin, R.K. (1994). Case Study Research: Design and Methods. Thousand Oaks, CA: Sage Publishing.

Zirger, B. and Maidique, M. (1990). A Model of New Product Development: An Empirical Test. Management Science 37(7), 867-883.

Chapter 9
Marketing for Subsistence Marketplaces[25]

We have deepened our understanding of subsistence marketplaces in earlier chapters (see Figure 9.1). Now it's time to examine the implications of that understanding for marketing.

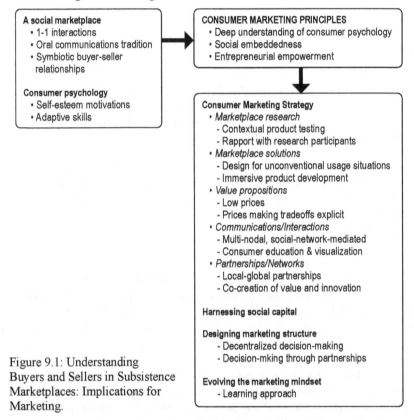

A social marketplace
• 1-1 interactions
• Oral communications tradition
• Symbiotic buyer-seller relationships

Consumer psychology
• Self-esteem motivations
• Adaptive skills

CONSUMER MARKETING PRINCIPLES
• Deep understanding of consumer psychology
• Social embeddedness
• Entrepreneurial empowerment

Consumer Marketing Strategy
• *Marketplace research*
   - Contextual product testing
   - Rapport with research participants
• *Marketplace solutions*
   - Design for unconventional usage situations
   - Immersive product development
• *Value propositions*
   - Low prices
   - Prices making tradeoffs explicit
• *Communications/Interactions*
   - Multi-nodal, social-network-mediated
   - Consumer education & visualization
• *Partnerships/Networks*
   - Local-global partnerships
   - Co-creation of value and innovation

Harnessing social capital

Designing marketing structure
   - Decentralized decision-making
   - Decision-mking through partnerships

Evolving the marketing mindset
   - Learning approach

Figure 9.1: Understanding Buyers and Sellers in Subsistence Marketplaces: Implications for Marketing.

---

[25] This chapter includes material adapted from the following previously published works:

Viswanathan, Madhubalan, Srinivas Sridharan, and Robin Ritchie (2008), "Marketing in Subsistence Marketplaces," in *Alleviating Poverty Through Business Strategy*, Editor, Charles Wankel, Palgrave Macmillan, 209-231. Reproduced with permission of Palgrave Macmillan. The full published work is available from: http://www.palgrave.com/products/title.aspx? pid=412803

Sridharan, Srinivas, and Madhubalan Viswanathan (2008), "Marketing in Subsistence Marketplaces: Consumption and Entrepreneurship in a South Indian Context," *Journal of Consumer Marketing*, Special Issue on Base of the Pyramid Research, 25 (7), 455-62.

In addition to economic constraints and uncertainty, the previous chapters outlined the one-to-one interactions that occur in subsistence marketplaces. These personal interactions result largely from the interdependence that characterizes life in resource-poor settings. Since incomes are modest and unstable, and low literacy is commonplace, people are frequently compelled to rely on others for help in times of need. Buyers and sellers often come from similar economic strata and thus experience similar adversities. In addition, buyers may have at least some experience as vendors. Owing to these factors, marketplace dealings are characterized by considerable empathy.

This has many consequences. For one, offerings are regularly customized, with price, quality, and quantity adjusted to account for the personal circumstances of both buyer and seller. In addition, word-of-mouth is heavily relied on by buyer and seller alike. This serves to limit unscrupulous practices and to condition people to be guarded about their transactions (e.g., keeping price discounts discreet). This stands in stark contrast to interactions in developed markets, where consumers often rely on detached exchanges with anonymous employees of chain stores.

For businesses seeking to serve subsistence contexts, the importance of these differences is this: the relationship between buyers and sellers in these environments extends well beyond their marketplace roles. As a result, economic exchange may be treated as an extension of everyday personal interaction, rather than being divorced from it.

This important insight can provide a basis for new marketing approaches, because it recognizes social relationships as a community-owned resource that might be harnessed to add value for that community through market exchanges. Such an approach has considerable appeal, as its underlying philosophy is one of leveraging the strengths of subsistence markets rather than of overcoming perceived weaknesses.

At the individual consumer level, our research has revealed that although consumers in subsistence marketplaces face severe material and psychological limitations, they employ several coping mechanisms in their consumption rituals, often successfully. Whereas marketplace-level phenomena are important considerations when serving subsistence contexts, it is also helpful to consider characteristics of individual consumers.

Particularly relevant are the rates of low literacy, low income, and the consequences that arise from their joint occurrence (see Figure 9.1). These marketplace-level and individual-level characteristics are important in that they differentiate subsistence environments substantially from relatively resource-rich markets that most formal businesses are used to dealing with.

This understanding of buyer, seller, and marketplace behavior has important implications for business practices in general and marketing practices in particular.

In summary, from our understanding of buyer, seller, and marketplace behavior, we derive three key principles for consumer marketers engaging in subsistence marketplaces:

- deep understanding of consumer psychology,

- social embedding, and

- entrepreneurial empowerment.

We will illustrate these principles with a brief analysis of three case studies of enterprises working in subsistence marketplaces in India, and end with a broader discussion of implications for consumer marketing in such contexts (see Figure 9.1).

Case Studies

To maintain consistency and comparability across these case studies, we concentrate on enterprises engaged broadly in the health sector, all focused on serving the rural poor as a market segment. We present an analysis of three healthcare services organizations, all engaged in delivering affordable healthcare to the rural poor in India.

Distance Health and Advancement

DISHA (Distance Health and Advancement) is a social enterprise that was operated on a pilot basis in 2005 as a for-profit business model to deliver affordable healthcare to the rural poor in South India (Business Line, 2005). Targeting people earning between $2 and $5 a day, the DISHA service aimed to bring mobile health care to the rural poor through a van equipped with state-of-the-art medical and satellite technology through which doctors in the city could be contacted for remote consultation.

DISHA functioned as a public-private consortium between Philips India, DHAN Foundation, Indian Space Research Organization (ISRO), and Apollo Hospitals Group, pooling resources and specific expertise. A partnership approach is often essential to business models for subsistence marketplaces. For instance, the consumer psychology in such settings can be such that villagers may not seek medical attention until it becomes absolutely necessary. The DHAN foundation, possessing social capital with local villages accumulated from years of operating amidst them, was thus a crucial partner in helping communicate with, educate, and persuade consumers. However, despite the lack of access to quality healthcare, consumers are still only willing to pay for high-quality services, and thus the well-known brand of Apollo Hospitals was a critical partner. Finally, for the mobile van concept to work well, technological inputs came from Philips (medical equipment technology) and ISRO (remote satellite technology).

However, the DISHA project did little by way of entrepreneurial empowerment, and eventually its centrally-planned character may have played a role in the venture not progressing beyond the pilot phase.

Mobile Medics

In contrast, Mobile Medics, a newly-started mobile health services provider in the North Indian state of Rajasthan, deploys medical vans to villages, similar to the DISHA concept, but with a key difference. It appoints the three-member medical team of each van (comprising of two doctors and a nurse) as a stand-alone, profit-oriented entrepreneurial team. Each team is free to customize its business approach and initiatives to the local needs of their specific clientele and its own entrepreneurial drive.

Lacking the high-powered collaborative capital available to DISHA, the reliance on the entrepreneurial spirit of its medical teams is crucial to the business model of Mobile Medics. In this venture, however, a key challenge is to gain consumer trust without a well-known brand and to understand consumer psychology and accordingly achieve workable and profitable price points.

Gram Mooligai

Finally, another critical dimension of being socially embedded is an alignment of products and services with existing socio-cultural traditions. For example, Gram Mooligai, an offshoot of an NGO in South India, launched the Village Herbs brand of herbal medicine to provide affordable healthcare to the rural poor in South India, but based entirely on a traditional heritage of using herbal remedies, a notion familiar to the target consumer households.

Due to such close alignment with the local socio-cultural and historical context, the organization is able to generate consumer trust and loyalty. Gram Mooligai pursues the promotion of entrepreneurial propensity, as it sources herbs from self-help groups of rurally based growers of medicinal plants and herbs and pays them 70% of their selling price (World Resources Institute, 2006). These self-help groups hold the majority of the shares in this public company, essentially also acting as the board of directors.

Case Study Summary

These case studies illustrate the three key principles of consumer marketing in subsistence marketplaces: a deep understanding of consumer psychology, social embedding, and entrepreneurial empowerment. The insights uncovered in our research and the results of these business case studies have significant implications for marketing practice, which we describe in the following section. These issues are adapted from Viswanathan et al. (2008), and are intended to add to the nascent literature on the implications of impoverished contexts for sustainable marketing practice.

Implications for Marketing and Management

We now derive implications for specific areas of marketing and management. This section discusses the following:

- marketplace research,
- development of marketplace solutions for the poor,
- designing, communicating, and delivering value propositions, and establishing partnerships with subsistence populations to co-create value.

Marketplace Research

To achieve a deep understanding of subsistence consumer psychology, researchers need to focus on meaningful market research. Similar to its centrality in any field of marketing activity (Malhotra, 2001), market research is critical to developing market solutions for subsistence marketplaces. Market research should account for the psychological uniqueness of low-literate and poor consumers, as well as their lack of experience as participants in market research.

There is, thus, a need for more realistic product testing situations, using concrete, visual stimuli rather than abstract tasks. Because low-literate consumers may focus primarily on experiential attributes, product testing should represent the product in as close to real form as possible. Issues of self-esteem emphasize the need for in-person administration of data-gathering exercises, aimed to build personal rapport and engender trust. The length and language of procedures should be reasonable, using tasks with which participants can relate.

The interdependent network of marketplace actors suggests the need to study collectives (i.e., groups, communities, etc.) in test marketing efforts, and monitoring word of mouth with special attention to the views of local opinion leaders such as retailers, community organizers, and leaders of local self-help groups. Researchers can also use focus groups to mimic the social interactions that occur naturally in the marketplace. Finally, given their likely lack of familiarity and personal connection with these contexts, market researchers need to develop a deep understanding of subsistence marketplaces.

Development of Marketplace Solutions

In subsistence contexts, the problem of survival suggests a need to develop solutions for consumers, not products per se. As illustrated in the health sector case studies, a creative solution that effectively serves basic needs is central to the marketing endeavor in subsistence contexts, as it warrants the expenditure of very scarce resources.

Marketplace solutions have the potential to transform lives, given the extreme deprivation that characterizes these contexts and the comparatively uneconomic social solutions thus far designed and delivered by governmental and civic agencies. For example, cell phones have already proven to be lifelines for seeking medical help in the middle of the night in a village, and nutritional additives have shown effectiveness in preventing life-threatening illnesses.

Marketplace solutions must pass muster in the context of symbiotic relationships between buyer and seller, and must be driven by a deep understanding of consumer needs and usage situations. For example, the conventional product development approach of designing efficient solutions for specific usage scenarios may not work well; instead, developers may need to anticipate considerable uncertainty and variability in usage situations as outlined in Chapter 8.

This suggests a grounded approach with all steps in the product and solution development process involving immersion in the field, and also using a collaborative approach as illustrated by some of the case studies, building and sharing insights from non-profit organizations, small vendors and retailers, and self-help group leaders.

Designing the Value Proposition

For managers involved in setting and managing prices for products marketed to subsistence markets, several important implications arise from careful consideration of the nature of these markets. In light of the monetary constraints faced by subsistence consumers, the preceding discussion suggests that firms must carefully consider the value proposition of their offering when setting pricing strategies.

For example, by recognizing instances where quality is highly valued, even though consumers are able to afford only products within a very narrow price range, firms can create a win-win outcome by offering higher-quality options and pricing them at an appropriate, affordable premium.

On the other hand, subsistence consumers often focus heavily on monetary cost when assessing the "give" component (what they give up) of product value, while ignoring potential savings of time and effort. For example, they may go to great lengths to pay less for product purchases, even at great risk to their health, or seek to reduce family expenses by skimping on important medical services. In the United States, consumers often consider savings of time and effort in the "give" component when considering a product's value (Zeithaml, 1988), such as in buying at a convenience store and saving travel time.

In contrast, the lack of monetary resources in subsistence markets makes it difficult for consumers in those environments to think beyond price. This is compounded by low literacy and a tendency toward concrete thinking, arising from difficulties with abstractions. The result is that subsistence consumers tend to consider price as the sole determinant of the "give" component when determining good product value.

However, even within these narrow price levels, consumers do demonstrate a discerning ability (Prahalad, 2005; Viswanathan, 2007) and are willing to pay higher prices for solutions that deliver higher value to their life needs (e.g., healthy foods, reliable cell phones that help enhance livelihoods). This is likely because some specific consumption events may be central to daily life (e.g., rice), and also because, to begin with, consumers may consider only a very narrow set of absolutely necessary products. For instance, since paying a slightly higher price often enables a person to obtain better quality rice (a staple food in South India), the importance of what may be the only square meal of the day can prompt consumers to pay more for an upgraded product. Thus, the notion of 'value' is a far more salient consumer issue than the notion of price.

Pricing managers should recognize that this tendency may exist across a variety of product categories, including expensive, high-technology products that have traditionally been seen as out-of-reach for subsistence consumers. For instance, an interesting consequence of the recent boom in the telecommunications industry in India is that rural fishermen, even those who are extremely poor, have come to rely on mobile telephones. They use these devices while working at sea to communicate estimated catch sizes and negotiate prices with fish buyers and wholesalers back on land. Such communication demands a reliable phone capable of supporting the fisherman's livelihood-generating activity; as a result, many are willing to pay more for better quality.

These issues must be considered when creating pricing strategies and structures, and the relationship between costs and benefits–including long-term benefits and benefits that may outweigh costs–must be carefully communicated to consumers. This communication should be done in a way that respects the value judgments of consumers, but also educates them and encourages them to form new value judgments.

Communicating the Value Proposition

Our understanding of how subsistence consumers think in terms of concrete thinking and pictographic thinking emphasizes the need to concretize, localize, and socialize communications, a theme we illustrate further in Chapter 13. As discussed earlier, communicating the value proposition (the give and get) in concrete terms is a central example. No matter what one's level of literacy and formal education, individuals can typically relate socially to others and understand their local context and native language. These strengths need to be built on in designing communications. Typically, this involves rethinking common approaches that take certain levels of education for granted. Designing product instructions and interfaces for a low-literate audience offers opportunities to provide education about the product and the need served to customers deprived on multiple fronts.

Life in subsistence conditions imposes not only material resource constraints, but also informational constraints, which is an important consideration in the design of marketing communications. For example, Hindustan Lever Limited's (HLL) campaign to promote hand washing has seen the company go to extraordinary lengths to explain the need for hand washing by encouraging consumers to 'visualize' the problem of germs (Prahalad, 2005; discussed in Chapter 10). In this case, the consumer benefit was communicated in a manner that utilized the pictographic thinking style of subsistence consumers.

Facets of the overall marketplace and buyer-seller exchanges are also important considerations in developing strategies for marketing communications. The heavy social quotient of subsistence environments suggests that the use of spokespersons or characters to personify the brand will be more effective than abstract information. Spokespersons can create "interactions" rather than just one-way communications. This is perhaps the most important paradigmatic difference in a model of marketing communications in subsistence contexts.

The tradition of intense oral communication suggests that marketing communications that can build on the heavy influence of word of mouth and the free-flowing information exchange through social networks will be effective. Rather than creating ads for mass communication, for instance, subsistence marketers may find it more effective to create branded content that can be circulated orally (such as jokes, jingles, or clever vernacular phrases).

An extension of this is to employ people who are a part of local social networks as brand communicators. Firms also need to reinforce the notion that it is indeed a partnership, rather than a conventional employer-employee relationship, by including subsistence consumers as genuine stakeholders when designing their marketing goals and strategies.

Often, such social systems can facilitate reverse flow of communication back to the company, thereby functioning as a feedback loop. Product trial and adoption as well as personal consumer feedback are made easier through social networks. To maintain the long-term effectiveness of such marketing communication systems, the social capital that makes the local representative a partner in the first place should be safeguarded, through such means as ensuring that products are of high quality and affordable, and information provided is accurate.

Understanding market-level aspects is also extremely important when developing strategies for marketing communications. Marketers are wise to leverage cultural knowledge, such as popular folklore, since this provides a rich repository of shared meaning that the marketer can draw upon without needing to explain.

As has been widely acknowledged, the effectiveness of word-of-mouth marketing depends heavily on a firm's ability to identify and influence the right people–i.e., the opinion leaders or "market mavens" (Feick and Price, 1987). To be able to exert such influence, a person–for example, the owner of a retail store or the leader of a self-help group–must possess both the respect of others and a sufficient number of social connections to allow the influence of their opinion to spread. Marketers who seek to leverage these individuals must thus be sufficiently embedded in the community so that they are not only able to identify them, but build a sound and trusting reputation with them, emphasizing the importance of market research approaches discussed earlier.

Perhaps most importantly, effective marketing communications in subsistence contexts requires "out-of-the-box" thinking. Marketing communications need to be built from the ground up, rather than administered from a preconceived perspective. Rather than using one-size-fits-all top-down approaches, our findings emphasize the need for marketers to work from the ground up and customize their approaches for what are invariably widely dispersed fragmented markets.

For example, village fairs, advertisements on vehicles, and other locally-suited media outlets are often extremely useful. Moreover, the nature of these communications must accommodate the constraints imposed by low literacy as well as the differences in local languages across various subsistence markets. Marketing communications must also expand beyond informational to educational approaches, and take on the challenge of conveying product benefits to a low-literate audience.

Delivering the Value Proposition

In developed markets, the norm is to make products available to end consumers by moving them through formal, centralized distribution channels. In subsistence markets, delivery to market is usually accomplished in a less formal manner, with small merchants obtaining their products from a diverse set of wholesalers, large retailers, and manufacturer representatives. This represents both a challenge for firms, as well as an opportunity to create value through innovation in go-to-market strategies.

For example, as Prahalad (2005) noted, consumers in many subsistence contexts–urban and rural–are often forced to pay a large premium to local intermediaries for services such as money loans. This is the result of a system in which intermediaries often must be used to obtain a particular product or service, and puts intermediaries in a position of power that can lead to unscrupulous practices.

An interesting implication, according to Prahalad, is that firms adopting certain types of direct distribution models have an opportunity to alleviate this "poverty penalty." In India, for instance, ICICI Bank now offers rural consumers direct access to financial services through micro-financing institutions and self-help groups, demonstrating this potential to innovate through marketing channels.

In Bangladesh, too, one of the key ingredients of Nobel Prize-winning Grameen Bank's micro-credit programs is the facilitation of direct access for subsistence consumers to credit and loans. ITC's e-choupal represents an approach where the supply chain has been streamlined to enable direct interaction between farmers and the company (Prahalad, 2005).

Interestingly, the direct-distribution model that this implies does not always need to be specifically designed to overcome the predicament caused by intermediaries. In many instances, the one-to-one interactional marketplace discussed earlier creates an environment where small, local retailers or service providers enjoy the trust and patronage of local customers.

In these instances, a direct distribution model can benefit significantly by securing the cooperation of local people rather than bypassing them. As illustrated with the Unilever example to be discussed in more detail in Chapter

10, people from specific communities can work as resellers, giving the company access to previously neglected markets.

This is also evident in the distribution of cellular phone services through local entrepreneurial women, a phenomenon increasingly employed by firms in subsistence markets around the world (e.g., Grameen Telecom in Bangladesh, Roshan in Afghanistan). As with marketing communications, approaches to distribution need to incorporate a willingness to work from the ground up and customize approaches, rather than adopt a one-size-fits-all approach.

As noted earlier, one of the key characteristics of the one-to-one interactional marketplace is the willingness of vendors to extend credit and adjust terms of trade when consumers find themselves in times of need–two practices that create a form of customer lock-in that is not easily disregarded. In a similar fashion, retailers form relationships with suppliers, creating mutual obligations that influence the future actions of both parties. This can be profitably leveraged by firms operating in such markets.

By adopting pricing and distribution practices that make it easier for retailers to extend credit, adjust prices, and vary product quality to accommodate the changing circumstances of their customers, manufacturers are likely to be more successful themselves. Part of the solution lies in offering products whose final stage of manufacture occurs at the retail level, allowing at least part of the cost to be incurred only when revenue is realized, and making it easier for size, quality, and so on to be adjusted to accommodate varied and changing customer needs. For example, a nutritional additive could be customized at the retail level to cater to the needs of different customers and different family members (elderly versus children).

Another way that firms can align their distribution systems to the needs of subsistence markets is through the use of information and communication technologies (ICTs) that leverage the strengths of the one-to-one interactional marketplace. A good example is the Inter-City Marketing Network, an initiative of the Chennai-based Foundation of Occupational Development (FOOD). This program gave mobile phones to some 100 community-based women's organizations as a means of encouraging the creation of social networks between artisans/skilled workers and people who could provide sales and promotion for their products in neighboring markets.

While created to encourage the small-scale manufacture and marketing of locally manufactured products, the program is a good example of a system that takes advantage of connections between people to identify and respond to commercial opportunities. Similar approaches could be used for a broad range of products and services.

Co-creating Value through Partnerships and Networks

The personalized marketplace in subsistence contexts involves small, local businesses or civic organizations that enjoy the trust and patronage of local consumers. As illustrated with the case study examples, establishing partnerships with them can give large businesses access to previously neglected markets, or small businesses access to new markets. However, the emphasis on the word "partnerships" is critical. As mentioned earlier, the traditional emphasis in the literature, on channels, distribution, and the "place" element of the 4Ps (Kotler, 1999) has always connoted a cost structure that must be borne by a local firm as the price to pay for connecting one's supply with the demand in the market.

This connotation is inadequate for accurately describing creative partnerships that can be constructed in subsistence marketplaces, as illustrated in the few case study examples we have discussed. In emerging subsistence marketplace partnerships, there tends to be significant knowledge sharing and learning and co-created innovation, which warrants an egalitarian description and a shared rather than unipolar focus on a focal business. When the scope of such partnerships expands, they can evolve to form broader networks (e.g., the DISHA collaboration) capable of producing socio-market innovations aimed at empowering subsistence marketplaces.

Organizational Implications

In addition to elements of marketing strategy, there are aspects of organizational structure and culture related to the role of marketing that businesses must address to approach subsistence marketplaces holistically. We outline these notions below.

Decentralizing and Externalizing Marketing Activities

As we have suggested throughout this chapter, a critical difference between developed and subsistence markets is the extent to which one-to-one interactions and interpersonal relationships play a role in facilitating economic exchange. This suggests that marketing activities in a firm must be mindful of the relational aspect of subsistence markets. To achieve the marketing principles outlined earlier, it is critical to decentralize decision processes and practices. Local managers need to understand consumer psychology in markets that are geographically dispersed and highly fragmented. To do so, they must be given a high degree of latitude in designing marketing activities and executing research programs.

Similarly, firms must socially embed products and services. These products and services must be conceived locally, with the intensely relational nature of subsistence marketplaces in mind. If businesses are to empower entrepreneurial activity among subsistence populations, the marketing processes must be decentralized to lower hierarchical levels within the organization, and devolved beyond the organizational boundary to local entrepreneurs (Kirchgeorg and Winn, 2006; Ritchie and Sridharan, 2007).

Decentralized marketing entails shifting responsibility and power to boundary-spanning employees who are close to the customers and can thus respond more nimbly to their needs and feedback. This is critical in subsistence markets, where social capital endows local individuals with superior access to knowledge about customer needs, preferences, and ability to pay.

Externalized marketing goes one step further, and sees the formation of marketing partnerships with local entities that are external to the firm—empowering these local partners to make marketing decisions independently on the firm's behalf (Ritchie and Sridharan, 2007). This "external" locus of marketing activity is critical from a social capital perspective because the rich social capital that facilitates effective marketing exchanges in subsistence markets is often available only within a specific "radius of trust" (Fukuyama 2001)–i.e., among a given community's members who know each other and are somewhat interdependent. In fact, a firm's attempts to internalize this asset by hiring community individuals as employees would likely fail, because it would undermine the social credibility of the person in his or her community, thereby nullifying the benefits of the social capital.

Decentralizing and externalizing marketing activities in subsistence contexts benefits a firm in at least three ways:

- First, it systematically increases the firm's access to detailed and nuanced knowledge about the customers and communities it aims to serve. Such market knowledge allows firms to be highly responsive to subsistence market needs, and helps them to offer tailored products and services. Externalization, in particular, makes the marketing system highly flexible and adaptable to changing local market conditions.

- Second, when these principles are pursued at a basic level, such that even the design and manufacture of products and services is decentralized and externalized, local marketing partners benefit from engaging in these value-adding activities and profit from them. This new stream of income creates wealth in the community, which in turn makes it more attractive as a market for the firm.

- A final benefit of decentralizing and externalizing the marketing organization is that it facilitates a symbiotic relationship between the firm and subsistence consumers. This stands in stark contrast to the unidirectional or independent relationships prevalent in traditional markets. This symbiotic potential can be most clearly seen in the forms of social capital that each party contributes to the marketing relationship. Close-knit subsistence communities can provide firms with access to a unique network of trusted relationships formed as a result of dense, strong links between people within the community–bonding social capital (Iyer et al. 2005).

In turn, firms can use their coordination and communication skills to facilitate relationships between disparate communities–bridging social capital. The form of social capital contributed by each entity is important to the other. For example, while strong bonds within a group are valuable from the firm's perspective–for successful product diffusion within the community, for instance–they may actually hinder the ability of group members to trust and work effectively with members of other groups (Fukuyama 2001).

Seen from a macro level, this has been argued to hinder economic growth. However, firms with experience interacting with several disparate local communities can facilitate sharing of information and technology across communities, enable the flow of new ideas for innovation, and even reduce conflict between communities. All of this can contribute to economic growth by encouraging the formation of business relationships that cross normal social and community boundaries.

Evolving the Marketing and Management Mindset

The marketing mindset is particularly germane for subsistence contexts that managers and researchers may not relate to personally, in terms of low income or low literacy. The dominant managerial assumption of "extensions of markets we know" will not work for these contexts (Prahalad, 2005), as they may need a new set of assumptions.

It is important to view subsistence environments as more than mere markets, and more appropriately as people and communities from which to learn about ways to co-create socio-market innovations. An approach that is open to learning from buyers and sellers in subsistence can lead to many advantages, including opportunities to co-create successful product designs.

Assumptions of "knowing what the poor need" are also problematic. An example is the dominant logic of product functionality mentioned earlier, which can obscure the reality that subsistence consumers may value very different features from those imagined by outsiders–product aesthetics, for example. It is instructive to note, for instance, that some of the world's finest art, handicrafts, and ornamentation are made by people living in subsistence conditions–a testament to their traditionally honed skills and appreciation of aesthetics.

In developed markets, the implicit assumption is that certain business-oriented institutions (e.g., retail stores) are necessary to facilitate buyer-seller exchange. It would be misleading, however, to engage subsistence contexts with the same assumption. Although businesses do play a role, the identities of various types of institutions that facilitate exchange are often not as clear-cut as those of developed markets. For example, the "family" is a social institution that routinely facilitates several very business-like exchanges between people with complementary motivations in India (e.g., exchange money with food, effort, childcare, medical care, and so on). Similarly, the "neighborhood" is an institution that facilitates numerous barter-type exchanges (e.g., childcare and friendship, handyman services and food), and economic exchanges (e.g., personalized service, loyalty to the neighborhood store). In rural settings, the "village" is an institution that facilitates complex exchanges that the marketing literature refers to as "heterogeneous exchanges" (Hirschman, 1987).

As discussed, a more effective approach may be to treat subsistence environments as places where firms can learn from the people and communities. Research has shown that such a learning perspective can facilitate "innovation blowback," the transfer of innovative practices to resource-rich contexts (Hagel and Brown, 2005). The Village Herbs brand of herbal remedies and products offers a case in point. As discussed earlier, launched by Gram Mooligai, an entrepreneurial venture in South India, this line of products was developed using the traditional medicine and knowledge of rural subsistence communities, and is now being successfully marketed to urban, non-subsistence markets as well.

Our intent here is not to dismiss the applicability of core marketing principles and ideas that have worked successfully in developed economies. Indeed, marketing has been useful, for instance, in the experiences of the World Bank, to represent the interests of the poor in market-based ventures in developing countries (Talukdar, Gulyani, and Salmen, 2005). Rather, we emphasize the need for a mindset that allows for learning from subsistence contexts.

We suggest such a learning approach because contexts with extreme resource constraints require new and creative notions of theory and practice. Conventional theoretical lenses and notions of "rationality" need to be adapted and enriched by the study of unique circumstances where resource constraints may render seemingly irrational behavior as perfectly rational, when viewed from the perspective of those who must live life under those constraints. An orientation that suspends preconceptions and enables learning from the dynamics of living and consuming at the level of mere subsistence can help marketers better understand and engage marketplaces in these contexts.

The importance of a firm's marketing culture to its business performance has been well documented. Marketing culture refers to the unwritten policies and guidelines that provide employees with behavioral norms, and more generally to the manner in which marketing activities are executed. Marketing culture at a broad level would translate to how subsistence contexts are viewed by marketing managers. Regarding such contexts as mere variations on traditional markets can easily lead to certain counterproductive tendencies, such as believing that solutions for such markets can and should be found by the firm or "exported" from non-subsistence contexts.

There is also considerable innovation in subsistence marketplaces, at both the entrepreneurial and consumer level, arising from a basic need to survive. Such insights arising from "doing more with less" reflect ingenuity in surviving under extreme resource constraints, using available products in innovative ways that cannot be easily anticipated by market researchers not exposed to life in these conditions.

Conclusion

Marketing in subsistence marketplaces involves a unique set of issues such as the need for deep understanding of consumer psychology, social embedding, and entrepreneurial empowerment. In turn, these issues have implications for marketplace research, development of marketplace solutions for the poor, designing, communicating, and delivering value propositions, and establishing partnerships with subsistence populations to co-create value. Implications extend to organizational issues of decentralization and externalization as well as evolution of the marketing and management mindset for the unique circumstances of subsistence marketplaces.

References

Business Line (2005), "Tele-medicine Project Disha: Taking the road less travelled," http://www.thehindubusinessline.com/2005/07/05/stories/2005070502950300.htm

Feick, L. F., & Price, L. L. (1987). The market maven: A diffuser of marketplace information. Journal of Marketing, 83-97.

Fukuyama, F. (2001). Social capital, civil society and development. Third World Quarterly, 22(1), 7-20.

Hagel, John III and John Seely Brown (2005), "Productive Friction: How Difficult Business Partnerships Can Accelerate Innovation," Harvard Business Review, (February), 82-91.

Hirschman, Elizabeth .C. (1987), "People as Products: Analysis of a Complex Marketing Exchange," Journal of Marketing, 51 (1), 98-108.

Iyer, Sriya, Michael Kitson, and Bernard Toh (2005), "Social Capital, Economic Growth and Regional Development," Regional Studies, 39 (November), 1015-40.

Kirchgeorg, Manfred, and Monika I. Winn (2006), "Sustainability Marketing for the Poorest of the Poor," Business Strategy and the Environment, 15, 171-184.

Kotler, Philip (1999), Kotler on Marketing: How to Create, Win, and Dominate Markets, New York: Free Press.

Malhotra, Naresh K. (2001), "Cross-Cultural Marketing Research in the Twenty-First Century," International Marketing Review, 18(3), 230-234.

Prahalad, C. K. (2005), The Fortune at the Bottom of the Pyramid: Eradicating Poverty through Profits, Upper Saddle River, NJ: Wharton School Publishing.

Ritchie, Robin, and Srinivas Sridharan (2007), Marketing in Subsistence Markets: Innovation through Decentralization and Externalization, in Product and Market Development for Subsistence Marketplaces: Consumption and Entrepreneurship Beyond Literacy and Resource Barriers, ed. Jose Rosa and Madhu Viswanathan, Elsevier.

Talukdar, Debabrata, Sumila Gulyani, and Lawrence F. Salmen (2005), "Customer Orientation in the Context of Development Projects: Insights from the World Bank," Journal of Public Policy and Marketing, 24 (1), 100-111.

Viswanathan, Madhubalan (2007), "Understanding Product and Market Interactions in Subsistence Marketplaces: A Study in South India," in Product and Market Development for Subsistence Marketplaces, Elsevier.

Viswanathan, Madhubalan and José Antonio Rosa (2007), Product and Market Development for Subsistence Marketplaces: Consumption and Entrepreneurship beyond Literacy and Resource Barriers, Elsevier.

Viswanathan, Madhubalan, S. Gajendiran and R. Venkatesan (2008), Enabling Consumer and Entrepreneurial Literacy in Subsistence Marketplaces, The Netherlands: Springer.

World Resources Institute (2006), "Rising Ventures: Gram Mooligai Brings Healthcare to India's Rural Poor," http://www.nextbillion.net/blogs/2006/11/21/ rising-ventures-gram-mooligai-brings-healthcare-to-indias-rural-poor

Zeithaml, Valarie A. (1988), Consumer Perceptions of Price, Quality, and Value: A Means-End Model and Synthesis of Evidence, Journal of Marketing, 52 (3), 2-22.

Chapter 10
Designing Enterprise Models for Subsistence Marketplaces: Doing Well by Doing Good[26]

This chapter uses insights gained from the unique context of subsistence marketplaces to consider enterprise models for organizations. We do so by discussing a sustainable market orientation for businesses, although the implications extend to other types of enterprises as well.

In Chapter 5, we discussed unique characteristics of subsistence marketplaces, driven by extreme resource constraints, at product, relationship, and marketplace levels. This line of reasoning is used to develop macro-level insights at the level of business models. Examples from practice are used to then present a framework representing a sustainable market orientation.

To recap the characteristics of subsistence marketplaces (Figure 10.1), at the product level, resource-poor people must make careful purchases of a few affordable products that meet immediate basic needs, while considering making items or forgoing them altogether as alternatives. From a business perspective, these factors emphasize the importance of understanding life circumstances and designing affordable products that improve these conditions.

At the relationship level, resource adversity leads to interdependence, a one-to-one interactional environment with strong word-of-mouth effects, and the development of consumer skills. From a business perspective, these factors emphasize the importance of fairness and trustworthiness in relationships with customers and communities, as well as an emphasis on customer and community welfare.

At the marketplace level, resource constraints lead to interdependence among groups and organizations, and are coupled with constraints in physical mobility (see Figure 10.1). In effect, the larger market consists of small, fragmented markets (Jacoby, Murgai, and Rehman 2004), with myriad differences stemming from various group and organizational influences. From a business perspective, these factors emphasize the importance of finding the common denominator

---

[26] This chapter includes material adapted from the following previously published work:

Viswanathan, Madhubalan, Anju Seth, Roland Gau, and Avinish Chaturvedi (2009), "Internalizing Social Good Into Business Processes in Subsistence Marketplaces: The Sustainable Market Orientation" Journal of Macromarketing, 29, 406–425.

of social good that resonates with diverse groups, as well as the importance of working with, and drawing from, the expertise and influence of diverse individuals, organizations, and groups in implementing business plans (cf. Brugmann and Prahalad 2007).

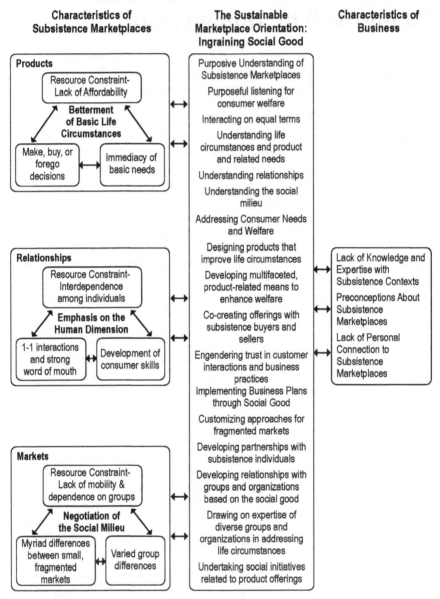

Figure 10.1: Characteristics of Subsistence Marketplaces and the Need for a Sustainable Market Orientation.

Designing Enterprise Models for Subsistence Marketplaces

Businesses in Subsistence Marketplaces

In this section, we discuss business practice in general and summarize case studies of businesses, two of which are from India, and one from the US. Businesses in arenas ranging from communication to health and hygiene are engaged in subsistence marketplaces. For example, Nokia is at the heart of the story of success of cellphones in these marketplaces. Nokia developed a line of affordable cellphones for use in a wide variety of environmental conditions around the world. Nokia's models in Africa are designed to be dust-proof, and its models sold in India have special grip areas for holding in hot conditions, and built-in flashlights for use during power outages. As rural consumers in India and China primarily share cell phones among families, Nokia phones contain shared use features such as address books. Additionally, Nokia Life Tools service enables rural farmers to receive updates on important information on their cell phones as well as provide small town and rural youth with education to enable upward mobility.

To sell its health and hygiene products to remote parts of India, Hindusthan Unilever Limited's (HUL) Project Shakti is a unique distribution network

consisting of poor women in villages acting as resellers who communicate with consumers about the benefits of HUL's brands (Prahalad, 2005). Working with governments, NGOs, and communities, HUL addresses informational needs in subsistence marketplaces, such as through a promotional campaign for its soap that was combined with an educational campaign about the importance of washing hands with soap to kill bacteria.

In addition to increasing access to health and hygiene products, its social initiatives are organized around health and hygiene, with educational and health camps in villages. The predominant outcome of HUL's efforts is a unique distribution system that enables it to reach subsistence marketplaces.

ITC limited is an Indian business conglomerate. The company is a major player in the agri-business and relies heavily on procurement of agricultural produce. Recognizing the constraints faced by subsistence farmers with regard to infrastructure and market information, ITC set up a large number of village-level internet centers called eChoupal. The eChoupals are operated by local farmers who are trusted within the village. The center provides information to farmers regarding market prices for produce and agricultural best practices. Access to such information significantly reduces the risks faced by farmers and ITC's transparent procurement system enables them to circumvent the mandi system where small farmers are often treated in an undignified manner.

In the financial sector, ICICI Bank developed a direct access model using microfinance institutions and self-help groups in villages in India (Prahalad, 2005). They trained groups of women to save and engage in banking and lending. Central issues confronted by ICICI include the need to raise the confidence and skill level of participating women, while also establishing trust in formal banks. ICICI Bank supports many activities that celebrate the achievements of participants. In addition to financial issues, self-help group meetings often focus on the needs of the village, given their larger role in the community. This direct model of banking has positively impacted women's self-confidence and self-worth, and prompted behavioral changes in saving habits.

In the health sector, Novartis' Arogya Parivar Initiative has the goal of delivering medicine to 50 million rural Indian patients who have little access to medicine. Arogya Parivar, which means "A Healthy Family," begins with an understanding of critical issues, such as the prevalence of easily treatable medical conditions, lack of access to health professionals in rural areas, and lack of knowledge and consequent neglect of medical conditions.

Novartis aims to increase the reach of its products into rural areas, partner with local health practitioners, and use a personalized approach to relate to patients. Novartis works with local pharmacists and builds relationships with local doctors and alternative health practitioners. It has created an organization consisting of smaller units responsible for covering geographic areas.

As these examples of business practice illustrate, subsistence marketplaces represent exciting arenas for responsible business to engage in, potentially enhancing individual and community welfare while being profitable as well. However, such engagement requires a deep understanding of the unique characteristics of these marketplaces and challenges in areas such as product design, distribution, and promotion.

Analysis of Three Case Studies

We combine an analysis of three case studies from available literature with our direct interactions with managers and resellers of the companies, and summarize the key points that directly relate to our arguments in Table 10.1. We then analyze these cases using our framework and rationale.

Table 10.1: Analysis of Business Cases

Table 10.1 lists business cases, the product needs they address for subsistence individuals, how they address relationships and the human dimension, and how they address marketplaces and the larger social milieu. Business cases include Unilever in India, ITC e-Choupal, and Sun Ovens International.

Case	Product Needs and Betterment of Basic Life Circumstances	Relationships and the Human Dimension	Marketplaces and the Larger Social Milieu
Unilever in India	Health and hygiene improvements	Use of women's self-help groups as sales channel	Increased market access for health and hygiene products
	Livelihood opportunities for entrepreneurs	Personal interaction and trust between entrepreneur and consumer	Health camps for communities
	Consumer education as a central element of promotional campaign		Partnerships with local and international organizations
ITC e-Choupal	Increased income and reduced risk for farmers	Alleviation of humiliation and enhancement of dignity for farmers	Improved access to information for farmers
	Reduction of cheating and abuse from interactions with middlemen	Community buy-in for selection of office bearers	Improved efficiency for agricultural markets
	Information for farmers through internet portals	Trust and fairness in designing transactions	Partnerships with disparate organizations
Sun Ovens International	Improvement in quality of life by avoiding indoor smoke and minimizing time costs of cooking for women	Trust-based relationships with consumers and households	Reduced costs for cooking energy
	Affordable cooking fuel source	Partnerships with local entrepreneurs	Alleviation of smoke-related ailments
	Education sessions in solar cooking	Education and outreach for communities	Partnerships with local NGOs, local entrepreneurs, and Rotary members
			Livelihood opportunities for entrepreneurs

Analyzing Hindustan-Lever, Ltd.

Our analysis of Hindustan-Lever, Ltd. (HLL), the subsidiary of Unilever in India, was based on the available literature (Rangan and Rajan 2005; Prahalad 2005), as well as our interactions with HLL managers and resellers. We focused on Project Shakti, a unique distribution system that HLL has developed in India for its health and hygiene products, which uses women's self-help groups as entrepreneurs to operate as a "rural direct-to-home" sales force.

At the level of product needs, success is dependent on resource-poor consumers being sufficiently satisfied with a product to be willing to spare scarce resources to buy it. This setting accentuates the importance of understanding and bettering basic life circumstances through high-quality, affordable products that address central needs. Moreover, a multifaceted solution that addresses product-related needs is essential, given the lack of a wide range of resources—particularly literacy and informational resources. For example, product benefits, such as disease prevention via hand washing, must often be explained through educational programs.

At a relationship level, success depends on distributors at the local level. Resellers function in a one-to-one interactional environment where people develop consumer skills, constantly obtaining feedback by interacting with customers. This emphasizes the need for trust in the resellers, the company and its product offerings, fair treatment of consumers, and improvement of individual and community welfare.

Additionally, at the marketplace level, this company must be able to operate with the continuous feedback and one-to-one environment that characterize these small marketplaces, as well as negotiate the complex social milieu in each village. The company accomplishes this by working with different groups, with individual and community welfare serving as a common denominator in interorganizational linkages. These issues emphasize the product, relationship, and marketplace level characteristics discussed earlier.

Analyzing ITC Limited's e-Choupal

ITC's e-Choupal presents a unique model of reengineering the supply chain (Jauhari 2005; Prahalad 2005; Vijaybhaskar and Gayathri 2003). Previous methods of buying crops from farmers involved exploitative middlemen and a system fraught with asymmetry of information, abuse of power, market inefficiencies, lack of timely price information, inaccurate weighing, delayed payments, and humiliating experiences.

ITC created new methods of weighing, quality control, and payment that solved many of the inefficiencies and exploitation that characterized the previous system (Jauhari 2005; Prahalad 2005; Vijaybhaskar and Gayathri 2003). The company provided computer portals in villages for access to timely information and also served a number of social functions for villagers. Further, it created a position in each village for a farmer to run computer portals and be the point of communication.

At the product level, the processes put in place reflected understanding of the farmer's basic life circumstances and the need to better them, as well as the need to provide product- or business-relevant support, such as information, that is critical with multifaceted deprivation. ITC's solution addressed the entire set of activities that the farmers went through, from purchasing inputs to selling crops.

At the relationship level, this approach highlights the importance of understanding the social environment by earning and maintaining the trust of the community. ITC engaged in a number of practices to create buy-in to the process. It established trust at the individual and village levels (e.g., it holds public oath-taking ceremonies, requiring that an active farmer actually runs the computer portal). It reengineered the roles of the middlemen in the previous system to create buy-in from this group. ITC's processes were characterized by transparency and attention to the welfare of the farmers.

At the marketplace level, the entire reengineering process entailed a number of interorganizational linkages with different governmental organizations and NGOs that emphasized individual and community welfare. These practices reflect the implications of product, relationship, and marketplace level characteristics of subsistence marketplaces. Outcomes include positive social impact in agriculture and in the lives of people, as well as positive business outcomes through an intimate knowledge of the customers (Murphy 2008).

Analyzing Sun Ovens International

Sun Ovens International Inc., in contrast to the other two examples, is a small company that makes solar ovens. It has been operating in subsistence contexts for over a decade, with a deep understanding of unique life circumstances. Our analysis is based on interviews with its CEO, a search of its website (www. sunoven.com), and related news stories.

At the product level, solar ovens serve a central need due to the lack of cooking fuels. Specifically, they alleviate constraints from high fuel prices, the overuse of a dwindling supply of firewood associated with deforestation, and respiratory ailments arising from smoke-filled living conditions. The company aims to provide an ecologically-friendly alternative that also improves the quality of life of its consumers, particularly women who must travel large distances to collect wood for cooking. Due to lack of awareness about solar appliances, Sun Ovens emphasizes educational programs such as classes on solar cooking. The product is priced carefully, with affordability being a primary concern, which results in the use of innovative financing schemes.

At the relationship level, Sun Ovens develops trust with members of the community and enhances individual and community welfare in a variety of ways (e.g., supplying solar cooking classes in Haiti; enabling people to set up self-sustaining micro-sun bakeries; and offering outreach programs). Additionally, in some markets, local entrepreneurs produce portable solar ovens, with only a key component being supplied from company headquarters.

At the marketplace level, the company works with diverse organizations (e.g., local NGOs, the Rotary) and local entrepreneurs to reach their customers, emphasizing individual and community welfare.

Summary of Case Studies

Such innovative practices offer many insights that relate to our central argument. As summarized in Figure 10.1, these cases demonstrate the need to focus on central, unmet needs and severe affordability constraints. The nature of the solutions reflects a deep understanding of life circumstances in subsistence. The cases illustrate understanding of life circumstances in subsistence and provide solutions for the betterment of basic life circumstances as well as product-relevant support, such as education to address the multifaceted needs of subsistence marketplaces.

The cases also demonstrate that the companies understand social relationships by establishing trust in complex, social environments and enhancing individual and community welfare. In pursuing business goals, they manage diverse group influences and unique environments by working with various organizations toward a common good, negotiating the larger social milieu in these markets (cf., Brugmann and Prahalad 2007).

Further, these case studies illustrate that businesses are responding to the needs of subsistence marketplaces in unique ways that blur social and commercial purposes. They also suggest that businesses are incorporating product-relevant social good at a variety of levels, starting at the highest strategic level, percolating down to day-to-day activities.

Rather than suggest that these businesses have ingrained product-relevant social good at an optimal level, our goal is to highlight the approaches that these businesses have adopted, and lessons to be learned from their innovative practices as they relate to our central argument. Such examples have been reported in the literature in several continents and aptly summarized by the following quote from Steve Fitzgerald of Conservation Corporation Africa: "We are doing well by doing good...We make more money by thinking differently, through community-based tourism" (Mahajan 2008, 196).

In considering individual and community welfare, issues such as the local ecology, the local economy, and local culture are also important considerations. In this regard, the cases described reflect the significant challenges in developing sustainable businesses in subsistence contexts. For example, agribusiness initiatives pursued by firms such as Mahindra & Mahindra, Tata Chemicals, EID Parry, and Rallis have been argued to be based on models that depended on intermediaries, who in turn may not be trusted by the individual farmer (Jauhari 2005).

Fundamentally, the approaches may not have addressed the vicious circle that farmers are in, characterized by low levels of productivity, investments, margins, and risk-taking ability (Jauhari 2005). Successful interventions require that businesses design product offerings and offer support that enhances individual and community welfare. In a sense, this is a magnified form of value creation in which revenue generation is based on not only the product, but on addressing the entire context in which it is sold and used.

Ingraining Social Good into Business Processes: A Sustainable Market Orientation

The unique characteristics of subsistence marketplaces have implications for businesses. Our discussion has built toward the case for ingraining social good into business processes in subsistence marketplaces. This section synthesizes the discussion and elaborates on how businesses can address the unique characteristics of subsistence marketplaces via a "sustainable market orientation," i.e., a simultaneous orientation to the market and to individual and community welfare (see Figure 10.2). In this section, we examine various elements, including purposive understanding of subsistence marketplaces, addressing customer needs and welfare, and implementing business plans for social good.

Figure 10.2: The Sustainable Market Orientation.

Ingraining Product-Relevant Social Good in Businesses

Our analysis of the product, the relationship, and the marketplace levels of the subsistence marketplace points to the need for businesses to ingrain product-relevant social good in businesses to succeed. That success will come when businesses do the following:

- At the product level, businesses need to understand, and better, basic life circumstances and improve individual and community welfare through product offerings and related support.

- At the relationship level, businesses should emphasize the human dimension in exchanges, engendering fairness and trust and enhancing individual and community welfare.

- At the marketplace level, businesses need to negotiate the complex social milieu and work with diverse organizations by emphasizing individual and community welfare as the common denominator.

Each of these levels of analysis points to the centrality of improving individual and community welfare for businesses to succeed in subsistence marketplaces. Our brief review of innovative business practices in subsistence marketplaces highlights elements of individual and community welfare that can be explicitly incorporated into different levels of businesses. Thus, we argue for the need for ingraining social good, in a product-relevant sense, in businesses as the means for successful engagement in subsistence marketplaces.

Successful engagement depends on three issues:

- developing a deep-seated organizational understanding of individual and community welfare as it relates to product offerings,

- incorporating the goal of enhancing such welfare into business processes, outcomes, and assessments, and

- inculcating product-relevant social good into the organizational culture.

We thus argue for a fundamental orientation that impacts the knowledge acquired by the organization, the processes, the outcomes, and the performance metrics and culture of the organization.

Our notion of ingraining product-relevant social good is evolving as we learn from emerging, bottom-up research about subsistence consumers and entrepreneurs and from the innovative practices of businesses. We elaborate on this notion with respect to three aspects—purposive understanding, addressing customer needs and welfare, and implementing business plans infused with social good.

These three aspects address the development of relevant knowledge about marketplaces, including issues relating to individual and community welfare, the design of offerings that address needs and welfare, and the implementation of business plans that make these offerings available—i.e., knowledge development and market research, and design of solutions and their implementation.

Social-Good Ingrained Organizational Knowledge: Purposive Understanding of Subsistence Marketplaces

The ingraining process for businesses begins with understanding subsistence marketplaces. Crossing the literacy barrier requires literate decision-makers and managers to undertake a fundamental shift in thinking, because business research and practice have been developed predominantly in relatively resource-rich contexts (see Figure 10.1).

Managerial and organizational experiences are severely limited for envisioning needs in subsistence marketplaces. Managers in resource-rich situations likely lack the knowledge, expertise, and personal connections to the subsistence context. Misconceptions about subsistence marketplaces and the "exporting" of solutions from non-subsistence marketplaces represent additional stumbling blocks. Prior notions of rationality and efficient problem solving may not generalize to subsistence contexts.

Crossing the resource barrier requires immersion in the daily lives of people in subsistence marketplaces. Such holistic immersion to garner insights about larger life circumstances should be contrasted with narrower approaches to understand product-related preferences or even with superficial immersion that does not provide the depth and breadth needed to understand life circumstances.

Coupled with the need to learn about radically different marketplaces is the need to develop a deep-seated understanding of individual and community welfare and product-relevant social good through the market research process. The immersion and authentic, deep-seated understanding called for from a sustainable market orientation intertwine with issues of personal welfare and social good arising out of the need to improve the life conditions of people living in subsistence.

Also underlying the approach to understanding subsistence marketplaces is the willingness to learn from subsistence marketplaces about consumption and entrepreneurship. An orientation to an equal plane with the subsistence marketplace is essential for purposive listening and can lead to innovative solutions from people with expertise regarding subsistence living. Our recommendations are consistent with calls for complex interactions and empathy in engaging fringe stakeholders, as well as immersion in the context (Base of the Pyramid Protocol 2007; Hart and Sharma 2004).

At a product level, understanding how products fit into consumers' lives is important in general, but is crucial in subsistence marketplaces, where the betterment of immediate circumstances through a small set of products can be critical. Understanding the consequences of product usage for individual and community welfare, such as in terms of local ecology, is also critical. At the relationship level, to engender trust and develop a reputation for social good also requires complete understanding of the nature of one-to-one interactions, word-of-mouth effects, and consumer skills development. At a marketplace level, businesses need to understand the socio-political structure of each village or neighborhood and the varied group influences.

It's important to understand such issues as livelihood opportunities that sustain the local economy and create wealth in the communities that businesses engage in. Such purposive understanding is also important for implementing business plans by working with diverse groups.

Social-Good Ingrained Design of Solutions: Addressing Customer Needs and Welfare

Designing products for subsistence customers requires a complete understanding of the role that specific products play in daily life. Products must satisfy immediate and basic needs and better people's lives while remaining affordable (Anderson and Billou 2007; Dawar and Chattopadhyay 2002). Thus, products have the potential to transform lives, and repurchase and long-term loyalty is likely to accrue for quality products that improve lives. The lack of a variety of resources across different spheres emphasizes the need for addressing product-related needs.

For example, a lack of informational and educational resources suggests that the entire set of basic needs, both informational and material, need to be taken into account. The need to address livelihood opportunities and enable buying power is also central in exploring potential partnerships to co-create products through business relationships. Companies need to design solutions that sustain elements such as the local ecology and the local culture.

In addressing customer needs, the willingness to look for solutions from people most experienced in these settings, i.e., those who live in subsistence, is central. Additionally, companies face many product design issues regarding performance in challenging environments. Wide differences across villages and locations may require customization. As noted, there is constant pressure for businesses to customize in the one-to-one environment.

It's critical to understand how products will be used in context before designing them (Green et al. 2006). An approach that does not anticipate the challenging and ever-varying conditions in which products are used is not likely to be successful. While it's important for companies to understand usage contexts for product design in non-subsistence contexts, it's imperative for them to do so in subsistence contexts, because of their unfamiliarity with the context and the varied and challenging usage conditions.

As the case studies indicate, physical attributes of processes and products are just one part of the solution. At the relationship level, establishing trust is critical, as is respect for the people involved. Maslow's Hierarchy of Needs (1943) suggests that, "If all the needs are unsatisfied, and the organism is then dominated by the physiological needs, all other needs may become simply nonexistent or be pushed into the background (373)." In relation to people living in subsistence, this model suggests an exclusive emphasis on physical needs.

However, in a material-poor environment where human relationships and needs trump other considerations, dignity, identity, and confidence are central to people's existence. Trust and credibility are also central because of the human level at which people relate to each other, as well as the tendency to mistrust organizations or outsiders. Trust is engendered by an emphasis on social good and individual and community welfare. Processes that respect basic dignity and emphasize both physiological and psychological needs are central.

Social-Good Ingrained Implementation: Implementing Business Plans Through Social Good

Implementing business plans for subsistence marketplaces requires bridging physical distances, as well as bridging the diverse socio-dynamic environments unique to these markets. As illustrated with the HLL example, physical access to small, fragmented markets with poor infrastructure requires innovative distribution channels (Dawar and Chattopadhyay 2002). The very nature of these means of reaching marketplaces has to be decentralized, involving individuals living in subsistence and engendering trust.

One-size-fits-all approaches are likely to be ineffective, given the myriad differences among small, fragmented markets. An underlying theme in the cases presented is the participatory business model in which people living in subsistence have a significant stake. Central to implementing a sustainable market orientation is the need to develop partnerships with people living in subsistence, and to provide livelihood opportunities across the value chain, essentially enhancing individual and community welfare in the process.

The actual implementation of various aspects of a business plan, such as building distribution networks in one-to-one environments, must negotiate the unique socio-political environment in each market, as well as the strong sociological influences. For instance, the retail store owner is often a gatekeeper who has the trust of the community. In addition to understanding and abiding by governmental regulations, businesses need to negotiate the local sociopolitical environment. This may vary not only by state within a country, but also by area within a state, or even by individual village.

Group influences, such as the powerful effects of word of mouth and the socio-political environment of these small markets can combine to increase transparency and accountability. Additionally, group-level dynamics, in terms of self-help groups and NGOs, provide a balance between diverse concerns and an opportunity and need for interorganizational linkages. The need to work with a variety of organizations in gaining access to, and functioning in, subsistence contexts also results in accountability to diverse groups with different goals ranging from women's rights to ecological concerns.

Such a context reiterates the importance of emphasizing individual and community welfare and social good as a common denominator that resonates at the group level. Rather than implementation from the top down, a bottom-up orientation is critical in understanding the concerns of individuals and the community, and balancing such considerations with purely economic considerations. Also, central to implementation is the need to measure outcomes in terms of the traditional bottom line as well as individual and community welfare, and use this information to make appropriate adjustments.

Holistic Versus Compartmentalized Approaches

Traditional distinctions are blurred in subsistence marketplaces. This occurs in the face of severe resource constraints: product needs and betterment of basic life circumstances, economic and human relationships, and the larger social milieu and marketplace activities. When needs are basic and immediate, and deprivation encompasses many facets of life, the social and the commercial are blurred. What remains central is the human—the basic life circumstances for survival and subsistence.

We argue for a corresponding blurring of social good and commercial purpose for businesses in these marketplaces, from the highest strategic levels, percolating down to day-to-day marketplace activities, and, simultaneously, percolating up as well. We contend that subsistence marketplaces require businesses to adopt a holistic approach that ingrains social good by purposive understanding of subsistence marketplaces, addressing customer needs and welfare, and implementing business plans.

This contrasts with the compartmentalization that may occur between a company's social responsibilities and its product offerings in relatively resource-rich settings (e.g., Elms 2006). The intertwining of needs, products, markets, and lives, along with difficulties accessing these markets, necessitates a blurring between the types of organizations that a business has to work with to implement goals as it negotiates the social milieu. Creating buy-in from diverse groups requires an emphasis on the common denominator of social good.

Conclusion

We see a convergence between research and successful business practice, pointing to a distinctly different business model for the subsistence context, which we dub a "sustainable market orientation." At the broadest level, we argue that the starkly different conditions of severe resource constraints in subsistence marketplaces warrant revisiting traditional beliefs and philosophies that work to different degrees in relatively resource-rich settings. We argue for a sustainable, market-oriented philosophy where social good and customer satisfaction build off each other, and are emphasized in parallel in business functions, product-relevant attributes, and product-related initiatives.

Whereas companies improve individual and community welfare through their products in all contexts, we demonstrate that the unique characteristics of subsistence marketplaces (i.e., the need to better basic life circumstances, the blurring of human and economic considerations, and the complex social milieu) require social good to be ingrained in businesses. In a relatively resource-rich context, purchases are typically discretionary and range from the essential to the peripheral, human and economic facets are relatively compartmentalized, and the marketplace is often relatively impersonalized and insulated from the immediate social milieu.

Our work also has implications for the literature on market orientation. Although we dub our approach as a sustainable market orientation, we maintain that it is market orientation in subsistence contexts. The sustainable market orientation captures customer focus, coordinated marketing, and profitability; the three fundamental elements of market orientation (Kohli and Jaworski, 1990).

Central to our approach are intelligence gathering, intelligence dissemination, and responsiveness, all aspects of a market orientation (Kohli and Jaworski, 1990). Whereas theorizing on market orientation has occurred in the context of relatively resource-rich markets, the sustainable market orientation was developed in light of the extreme resource constraints that characterize subsistence marketplaces. We similarly envision other markets where internalizing social good is central to a market orientation. A case in point relates to ecological sustainability and sharper resource constraints in the foreseeable future, wherein a viable market orientation may require internalizing social good.

In addition to the rationale we developed for our central argument, our approach is also appropriate in light of the plethora of ecological and social problems that beset the globe. Movement up the income pyramid that mimics advanced economies and higher income consumers in emerging economies spells a multifold increase in the severity of environmental consequences already predicted for the planet.

We envision a movement from subsistence marketplaces to economically, ecologically, and socially sustainable marketplaces, creating win-win-win scenarios for businesses, communities, and the society and ecology at large. As noted earlier, rather than view subsistence contexts exclusively as parallel markets to sell to, we view them as marketplaces to learn from and then create solutions for them, enabling sustainability in the broadest sense of the word. We view the notion of businesses ingraining social good as it relates to their offerings as an ideal to work toward, despite formidable challenges in achieving this ideal. We believe that pursuit of this goal is critical for both the success of businesses and for sustainable development.

Our bottom-up orientation is ideally suited to understanding life circumstances and for ingraining social good into businesses—through developing knowledge, designing solutions, and implementing business plans. Such a bottom-up orientation is particularly germane, given the ills of globalization that can be attributed to imposing top-down approaches. From our perspective, as illustrated in an earlier chapter, even notions of sustainability need to be examined from a bottom-up perspective to understand what they mean for those living in subsistence marketplaces and for elements such as the local ecology, the local culture, and the local economy that need to be sustained, as illustrated in Chapter 7.

Much of what we learned provides a starting point to consider extreme resource constraints and the consequences of these constraints. We also note that subsistence marketplaces are among the most difficult contexts for effective business practice.

Yet, investment for the long term can provide businesses with unique, competitive advantages, and create win-win scenarios of profit in addition to the alleviation of poverty and related issues of subsistence life. Our emphasis on social good also highlights the need to measure actual impact in enhancing individual and community welfare as well as the related need to understand what social good is in these contexts. In other words, we need to measure the product-relevant social good to which we allude.

In one sense, our focus on the unique characteristics of subsistence marketplaces demonstrates conditions where ingraining social good is essential to success. However, our conclusion should be tempered by various contingencies. Subsistence contexts vary greatly, including conditions of enduring war and even genocide to ecological disasters. Thus, it is important to begin to delineate the boundary conditions for the effectiveness of our approach.

At the product level, we emphasize products of the nature and quality necessary to better life circumstances. As noted, subsistence consumers have the resourcefulness to make products and the resilience to forego them. When such alternatives are not feasible, such as with critical healthcare needs, subsistence consumers are at the mercy of an extremely limited set of available products and exploitative practices.

Even here, a visionary business can create alternatives that enhance social good and build trust. Vibrant social networks, such as women's self-help groups, lie at the heart of relationships in the subsistence marketplaces we studied. These networks emphasize the human dimension and the importance of fairness and trust. Such networks may be weakened for reasons ranging from communal conflict to governing bodies preventing the assembly of people.

At the marketplace level, negotiation of the social milieu through social good as a common denominator can run counter to corrupt practices or political upheaval at the community level and beyond, overriding such efforts. Thus, there is no magic wand to wave away the extraordinarily complex problems that surround subsistence contexts, and it is not our intent to understate these problems or overstate the efficacy of our approach. Nevertheless, we contend that companies can find win-win-win solutions by leveraging some of the unique characteristics of these same marketplaces as they work to overcome the significant challenges that lie along the way.

In closing, we argue for a holistic approach to business that ingrains the notion of social good, in contrast to the largely compartmentalized treatment of alternative economic and social goals in the literature. The lessons learned may reach well beyond subsistence marketplaces—such as in learning to do more with less, and in developing win-win-win solutions that are profitable, while being socially and ecologically sustainable. And the lessons learned may well be necessary to collectively confront the unique problems of the 21st century.

Table 10.2: Comparison of Alternative Perspectives

Table 10.2 lists the philosophies associated with alternative perspectives and their basic propositions, their level of analysis / vantage point of research, illustrative rationales, and illustrative aspects of execution.

Philosophy	Basic Proposition	Level of Analysis/ Vantage Point of Research	Illustrative Rationale	Illustrative Aspects of Execution
Sustainable Market Orientation	Bottom-up orientation suggesting that product-relevant social good must be ingrained in businesses in order to be successful in subsistence marketplaces. Ingraining product relevant social good in businesses, refers to the development of a deep-seated organizational understanding of individual and community welfare as it relates to product offerings, the incorporation of the goal of enhancing such welfare into business processes, outcomes, and assessments, and the inculcation of product relevant social good into the organizational culture.	Micro-level–Subsistence Consumers, Entrepreneurs and Communities	Unique product, relationship and marketplace level characteristics arising in subsistence marketplaces from severe resource constraints and associated limits to affordability, interdependence, and lack of mobility and dependence on groups. These characteristics require central foci on betterment of basic life circumstances through product offerings, engenderment of trust in relationships, and negotiation of the social milieu at the marketplace level.	Social-good-ingrained organizational knowledge-- Purposive understanding of subsistence marketplaces Social-good ingrained design of solutions-- Addressing customer needs and welfare Social-good ingrained implementation-- Implementing business plans through social good
Base of the Pyramid (BOP) Protocol 1.0 [2]	"Selling to the Poor"--Multinational companies should leverage their vast resources to engage the vast market represented by the BOP.	Mid-level-- Outside Businesses	"Stop thinking of the poor as victims…start recognizing them as resilient and creative entrepreneurs and value-conscious consumers" [2]	Selling to the poor Deep listening Reduce price points Redesign packaging Extend distribution Arm's length relationships mediated by NGOs [3]

Designing Enterprise Models for Subsistence Marketplaces

BOP Protocol 2.01	"Business Co-Venturing"--Multinational companies should use their vast resources to co-create relationships with individuals and organizations in the BOP.	Mid-level--Outside Businesses	Working in partnership for the co-creation of mutual value is the key for building relationships in the BOP.	Business co-creation Deep dialogue Build local capacity Embedded processes Direct, personal relationships [3]
Inclusive Capitalism [4]	Companies have the responsibility to address poverty and sustainability in the emerging markets that they serve. [5]	Macro-level--Businesses and Society	Businesses can increase the poor's access to products, services, information, and infrastructure, and in turn, improve their lives.	Reconsidering the bottom line to improve the lives of vulnerable consumers as well as the empowerment of vulnerable consumers. [6]
Corporate Social Responsibility (CSR) [5]	Companies should do good for stakeholders (including the society as a whole) and the environment, while attempting to make profits. [7]	Macro-level--Businesses and Society	Businesses can increase the poor's access to products, services, information, and infrastructure, and in turn, improve their lives. [8]	Built around doing good for people or the environment, with the added incentive of improving a firm's reputation.[9] These initiatives are often independent of a firm's overall strategy. [10]

Table 10.2 Notes:

1. Simanis, E. and Hart, S. 2008. The Base of the Pyramid Protocol: Toward next generation BoP strategy," Cited Jan. 12, 2009. Available from: http://www.bop-protocol.org/docs/BoPProtocol2ndEdition2008.pdf.

2. Prahalad, C.K. 2005. The Fortune at the Bottom of the Pyramid. University of Pennsylvania: Wharton School Publishing, p. 1.[27]

---

[27] Though business approaches such as Project Shakti and e-Choupal are often lauded for their potential benefits, critics have emerged on several fronts. Karnani (2007) and others suggest that aspects of the BoP perspective are a "mirage" and may lead to as many problems as solutions. Karnani's critiques encompass issues with people (e.g., a focus on consumption rather than employment, facilitation of impulse buying rather than saving, taking advantage of consumer tendencies of the poor), planet (e.g., environmental concerns over single-serving products, particularly relevant to poor areas with inadequate trash collection), and profits (e.g., prohibitive transaction costs, overestimated purchasing power of the market, unrealistic cost-reduction strategies). Our approach and the ideal of ingraining social good addresses a number of the issues raised here. We do not view the companies we analyzed as having achieved the ideal level of ingraining, but rather

3. Hart, S. 2007. BoP: State of the Field. Cited Jan. 26, 2009. Available from http://www.wdi.umich.edu/files/Conferences/2007/BoP/Speaker%20Presentations/PDF/State%20of%20the%20field%20(Hart).pdf

4. In reference to "the belief that companies should take a more holistic approach to business—one that takes into account the needs of shareholders, employees, customers, society, and the environment," C.K. Prahalad notes "The best way to describe it is inclusive capitalism… It's the idea that corporations can simultaneously create value and social justice." Business week (2006), "Karma Capitalism," Business week, Oct. 30, 2006. Cited Feb. 16, 2009. Available from http://www.businessweek.com/magazine/content/06_44/b4007091.htm

5. "Global firms and institutions are [therefore] increasingly being expected to consider the societal and environmental impacts of their activities (p. 353)" from London, T. and Hart, S. 2004. Reinventing strategies for emerging markets: Beyond the transnational model. Journal of International Business Studies, 35 (5), 350-370.

6. "…a crucial aspect of this effort is the development of human capabilities that build economic and political freedom (p. 353)." Ibid.

7. "…corporate social responsibility can become a source of tremendous social progress, as the business applies its considerable resources, expertise, and insights to activities that benefit society (p.80)." from Porter, M. and Kramer, M. 2006. Strategy & society: The link between competitive advantage and corporate social responsibility. Harvard Business Review, 84 (12), 78-92.

8. "If, instead, corporations were to analyze their prospects for social responsibility using the same frameworks that guide their business choices, they would discover that CSR… can be a source of opportunity, innovation, and competitive advantage (p. 80)." Ibid.

9. "…proponents of CSR have used four arguments to make their case: moral obligation, sustainability, license to operate, and reputation (p. 81)." Ibid.

10. "All four [arguments]… creates a generic rationale that is not tied to the strategy and operations of any specific company or the places in which it operates (p. 83)." Ibid.

---

as providing interesting lessons that inform us through some innovative practices. For instance, Unilever's Fair and Lovely skin-whitening product has been criticized for the promises it makes and stereotypes it plays off (Karnani, 2007). Based on our framework, ingraining product-relevant social good entails making products that better basic life circumstances, engaging in customer relationships based on trust, and negotiating the larger social milieu with social good as the common denominator. Moreover, our bottom-up marketplace as distinct from a market orientation emphasizes engagement that leads to ecologically, socially, and economically sustainable marketplaces.

References

Anderson, J. and Billou, N. 2007. Serving the world's poor: Innovation at the base of the economic pyramid. The Journal of Business Strategy 28 (2): 14-21.

Base of the Pyramid Protocol 2007. Protocol Principles. http://bop-protocol.org/docs/principles.html. Accessed October 27, 2007.

Brugmann, J. and Prahalad, C.K. Cocreating business's new social compact. Harvard Business Review 85 (2): 12-25.

Coleman, J. 1988. Social capital in the creation of human capital. American Journal of Sociology 94 (Supplement): S95-S120.

Dawar, N. and Chattopadhyay, A. 2002. Rethinking marketing programs for emerging markets. Long Range Planning, 355: 457-474.

Elms, H. 2006. Corporate and stakeholder responsibility in Central and Eastern Europe. International Journal of Emerging Markets 1 (3): 203-211.

Ghere, R.K. 1996. Aligning the ethics of public-private partnership: The issue of local economic development. Journal of Public Administration Research & Theory 6 (4):599-621.

Green M.G., Linsey, J.S., Seepersad, C.C., Wood, K.L., and Jensen, D.J. 2006. Frontier design: a product usage context method. Proceedings of International Design Engineering Technical Conferences & Computers and Information in Engineering Conference. 10-13 September, 2006, Philadelphia, USA: 1-15

Hart, O. 2003. Incomplete contracts and public ownership: Remarks, and an application to public-private partnerships. The Economic Journal 113 (March): C69-C76.

_____ and Sharma, S. 2004. Engaging fringe stakeholders for competitive imagination. Academy of Management Executive 181: 7-18.

Jacoby, H., Murgai, R., and Rehman, S. 2004. Monopoly power and distribution in fragmented markets: The case of groundwater. Review of Economic Studies 71 (3): 783–808.

Jauhari, V. 2005. Information technology, corporate business firms and sustainable development: Lessons from cases of success from India. Journal of Services Research 5 (2): 37-76.

Karnani, A. 2007. The mirage of marketing to the bottom of the pyramid: How the private sector can help alleviate poverty. California Management Review 49 (4): 90-111.

Kohli, A. and Jaworski, B. 1990. Market orientation: The construct, research propositions, and managerial implications. Journal of Marketing, 54 (2): 1-18.

London, T., & Hart, S. L. (2004). Reinventing strategies for emerging markets: beyond the transnational model. Journal of International Business Studies, 35 (5), 350-370.

London, T. 2007. A base-of-the-pyramid perspective on poverty alleviation. Working paper William Davidson Institute/United Nations Development Programme.

Mahajan, V. 2008. Africa Rising, Upper Saddle River, NJ: Wharton School Publishing. Maslow, A.H. 1943. A theory of human motivation. Psychological Review 50 (4): 370-396.

Murphy, C. 2008. Report from India: In the villages, a tantalizing morsel of broadband. The InformationWeek Blog, Feb. 20, 2008. Cited on Feb. 16, 2009. Available from: http://www.informationweek.com/blog/main/archives/2008/02/report_from_ind_5.html

Nicholls, J.A.F., Lyn-Cook, M., and Roslow, S. 1990. A framework for effective export marketing: The Jamaican partnership of public policy and private enterprise. Journal of Public Policy & Marketing 9 (1): 195-210.

Prahalad, C.K. 2005. The Fortune at the Bottom of the Pyramid. University of Pennsylvania: Wharton School Publishing.

Rangan, K.V. and Rajan, R. 2005. Unilever in India: Hindustan Lever's Project Shakti—marketing FMCG to the rural consumer. Harvard Business School Case #505056.

Reich, M.R. 2002. Public-Private Partnerships for Public Health. Cambridge, MA: Harvard University Press.

Vijaybhaskar, M. and Gayathri, V. 2003. ICT and Indian development, EPW commentary. Economic and Political Weekly June 14, 2003.

Chapter 11
Research Methods for Subsistence Marketplaces[28]

Image 11.01: Conversations with Maasai women and author, Tanzania. Photograph courtesy of Subsistence Marketplaces Initiative.

In this chapter, we share our insights on research methods from our over 15-year-long experience working with low-literate, low-income people and communities in India and the US. We provide a semi-autobiographical account of our micro-level approach to behavioral aspects of buyer, seller, and marketplace interactions of people living in subsistence. We discuss our experiences and then place our insights in a broader context by discussing implications for research methods in subsistence marketplaces.

[28] This chapter includes material adapted from the following previously published work:

Viswanathan, Madhubalan, Roland Gau, and Avinish Chaturvedi (2008), "Research Methods for Subsistence Marketplaces," in Sustainability Challenges and Solutions at the Base-of-the-Pyramid: Business, Technology and the Poor, Editors Prabhu Khandachar and Minna Halme, Greenleaf Publishing, Sheffield, UK, 242-260. DOI: http://dx.doi.org/10.9774/GLEAF.978-1-909493-77-3_16

Previous Approaches to Research Methods

Several disciplines, such as anthropology and sociology, have traditions of researching impoverished settings. Our intention is not to provide a detailed review of existing methods; we will only mention literature of immediate relevance. Rather, our goal is to provide a semi-autobiographical account of our learning in this area over the last decade. Still, a brief background on other research methods should prove useful.

Some research on poverty and literacy has involved quantitative approaches, such as research conducted by economic institutions (e.g., World Bank), encompassing psychological constructs such as experiences of powerlessness, feelings of vulnerability and risk exposure, and experiences of ill- and well-being (Narayan et al. 2000). Sociological and anthropological research has examined some of the qualitative aspects of poverty, providing valuable insights into its causes. Critical ethnography is an example of this style of research (Denzin and Lincoln 2005), which views poverty as a qualitative, social experience, not as an absolute, measurable variable (Green 2006).

Another noteworthy approach is the participatory action research paradigm, "a participatory, democratic process concerned with developing practical knowing in the pursuit of worthwhile human purposes" (Reason and Bradbury 2001: 1; see also Ozanne and Saatcioglu 2008). This approach is oriented toward creating knowledge that informs action for social welfare (Fals-Borda and Rahman 1991), characterized by the intention of improving the conditions of those being researched. The solutions-focused aspect of this paradigm is an efficient way for researchers to influence the world around them.

In the business realm, the BoP protocol[29] adopts a more holistic view of poverty research, attempting to account for all stakeholders aiming to serve the poor (London 2007), examining the capabilities of the poor and leveraging them for poverty reduction. The BoP protocol is based on patience, mutual learning, mutual value creation, and the recognition of consumers' abilities. An objective here is to better understand the communities at a personal level to co-create business opportunities.

Studying Low-Literate, Low-Income People in the US

In our micro-level approach to behavioral aspects of buyer, seller, and marketplace interactions of people living in subsistence, we use a variety

---

[29] bop-protocol.org/docs/principles.html (accessed 27 October 2007).

of existing methods, customizing some for our purposes. Our research methodology evolved over time, typically with qualitative research providing big-picture understanding, and quantitative research providing in-depth understanding of specific phenomena. Although we only briefly mention the research methods from literature used in subsistence contexts, many aspects of our approach are consistent with previously used methods.

Overview

Research in the social sciences has often focused on relatively resource-rich, literate people and societies. Our goal was to cross literacy and resource barriers by examining resource-poor, low-literate contexts. However, the specific methods to use were far from obvious. Given the difficulties that low-literate people face with typical quantitative methods, we began with qualitative methods. Administering typical quantitative studies with low-income, low-literate individuals pose several difficulties. In addition, use of questions requiring abstraction on the part of the participant could pose difficulties for low-literate participants as highlighted in previous chapters. Further administering questionnaires in large groups becomes problematic since the participants could experience difficulties in reading, comprehending and responding to the questions in the scales by themselves. Low-literate participants could also feel test anxiety while responding to questions, which compounds the difficulties in administering studies. In light of some of these challenges, we began with qualitative methods.

The difficulty of accessing literacy levels, which are highly correlated with income, led us to contact adult education centers. Most of our low-literate participants in the US belong to lower income categories.

Our participants included students and teachers at adult education centers in Illinois. Students were categorized into grade equivalent levels from 0–12, based on reading and math scores administered at entry and at intervals thereafter, and assigned to classes based on three levels: 0–4; 5–8; and 9–12. We were trained as volunteer tutors to learn about a group of people whose problems and perspectives were unfamiliar to us.

This training uncovered many myths and misperceptions about low-literate people, highlighting the complex backgrounds of adult education students. Trainers made a number of key points, including the need to treat low-literate individuals as people with considerable "street knowledge" developed from the "school of life." A mindset of mutual learning and the importance of interacting with our participants on an equal plane were central to our research methodology.

Prior to conducting in-depth interviews with the 0–4 level students, we developed a rapport with this group through volunteer tutoring and group shopping observations as a part of our research. We also began interviews with teachers and at the 5–8 and 9–12 levels. Over time, we have been able to conduct in-depth interviews, one-to-one shopping observations with follow-up interviews, and experiments with students at all levels through our volunteer tutoring.

Our approach was to examine interview and observational data collected over a number of years, with a view to understanding the problems low-literate consumers face in the marketplace. We drew from guidelines for designing qualitative research (McCracken 1988; Strauss and Corbin 1990) and used unstructured interviews about shopping in general. Several of these interviews were preceded by individual observations at a grocery or department store, where students were recruited and observed from a distance while shopping, with occasional questions being directed to them. We also conducted group observations where students were given an assignment to choose a specific set of items while staying within a budget.

Interviews

We conducted a number of open-ended, relatively unstructured interviews intended to capture the person's perspective (Spradley 1979), ranging from 15 minutes to 2.5 hours in length, and averaging approximately 45 minutes. We asked broad questions about preferences for brands and retail outlets; price-value relationships; use of nutrition labels; the influence of ads, television, and other people on buying decisions; budgeting; and attitudes toward businesses. These questions were used to begin a conversation or to refocus it on consumer experiences. Participants were encouraged to talk about the things they considered important. A combination of personal views and desires, life histories, social values, and both positive and negative experiences as consumers emerged in the interviews.

To facilitate discussion, we often showed examples of packages, ads, and coupons to the 0–4 grade level consumers to enhance comprehension, leading to rich conversation and discussion. These concrete stimuli, rather than abstract discussion, enabled our participants to relate back to their day-to-day experiences. We also conducted interviews immediately after one-to-one shopping observations with questions organized around items purchased. In addition to adult education students, we also interviewed several teachers, asking them to provide insights about students' shopping behaviors. We tape-recorded all unstructured interviews and transcribed them for analysis.

In analyzing our data, we drew from the vast literature on qualitative research (e.g., Strauss and Corbin 1990). We examined transcripts and field notes to derive insights about the low-literate consumer experience, often reading and re-reading interview transcripts. We aimed to develop a deep understanding of the low-literate consumer experience in terms of challenges and coping strategies.

Observations

We conducted observations of adult education students on shopping trips. These shopping observations were regularly scheduled field activities that students anticipated enthusiastically. Teachers used shopping tasks as a part of the 0–4 grade-level shopping field trips. We asked students to find a set of items, list item prices, compute totals, and determine whether they stayed within the pre-specified budget.[30]

In addition, we conducted one-to-one shopping observations where participants completed their typical shopping trip. To supplement their personal funds, participants were each given a gift card worth $10 and coupons for commonly used items. During these sessions, we would initially observe students from a distance and occasionally ask questions, while still in the store, about the products they chose and the products they usually buy. This approach enabled students to follow their usual routine without interruption. We followed up these observations with interviews, where we sought additional clarification of shopping behaviors. We recorded field notes after the session and used them in our analysis.

Experiments

We conducted a number of experiments with students from adult education centers involving brand-related memory tasks, judgment tasks, evaluation of nutritional labels and educational materials, and evaluation of hypothetical new products. Illustrative examples of our experimental materials are shown in Figures 11.1–11.4, depicting the pictorial elements we incorporated and the tasks we asked participants to complete.

---

[30] Though assigned tasks can potentially change natural shopping behaviors, the running conversation among the students and between students and tutors during the shopping trips suggested that the students generally approached their regular shopping trips in a similar manner. Moreover, the students voted on which outlets to visit; this increased their sense of confidence and ownership of the task.

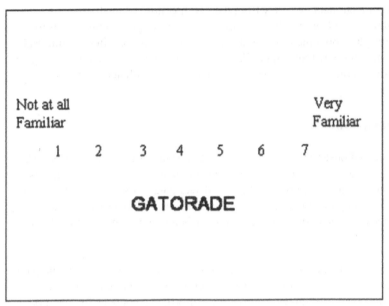

Figure 11.1: Stimuli from a simple task.

Figure 11.2: Stimuli from a simple task with pictorial elements (brand signature).

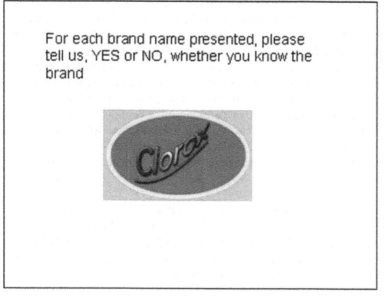

Figure 11.3: Stimuli from a simple task with pictorial elements (fictitious brand signature).

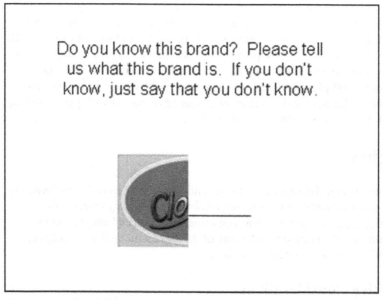

Figure 11.4: Stimuli for a memory task (fictitious brand signature).

We designed the studies to keep the participants engaged in simple tasks. Each task was brief, typically 10 minutes in length, and often conducted with other studies to fill out a half-hour session. In experiments, we verbally administered questions and recorded responses, so as to minimize the participant's need to read and write. Examples include rating items on a 1–7 scale for a variety of attributes, choosing the better value of two items, and picking two out of a set of three items that have more in common with each other. Each session was conducted one-to-one in a private area, ensuring confidentiality and alleviating potential embarrassment or discomfort associated with reading and writing. Participants were given a $5 incentive for each half-hour session. Our experiences suggest that students have generally been pleased to participate in our studies.

As noted, we divided students into 0–4, 5–8, and 9–12 grade levels for our experiments, providing us with a range of low- to medium-literacy abilities. To expand our range of ability, we sometimes used samples of undergraduate university students to represent higher literacy. Though we attempted to obtain sample sizes from adult education centers that were as large as practically possible, the final sample sizes were often smaller than ideal. When studying differences between conditions, our rule of thumb was to collect data from at least 12 participants in each condition.

However, even achieving this small sample size proved difficult, given the three levels of literacy that form a separate factor in the design. For example, for a 2 x 3 (levels of low to medium literacy) between-subjects factorial experimental design, we aimed for 72 participants, which was approximately the total number of willing participants in the adult education centres in our area. When we had studies with multiple conditions, we had to choose between waiting until the next semester for new students to enroll, using fewer participants per condition, or traveling to nearby counties to collect data.

Insights

Conducting successful research in these settings requires special considerations. Our experiences reveal some common threads in conducting research in these environments, categorized as cognitive, affective, and administrative considerations. We discuss below some of the successful (and unsuccessful) characteristics of our research endeavors.

Cognitive Considerations

This section covers the cognitive considerations of our research on subsistence consumers in the US. A central issue is the difficulty experienced by low-literate consumers when faced with abstractions discussed in earlier chapters; this difficulty discussed first in Chapter 4 is labeled concrete thinking (Viswanathan et al. 2005). A related predilection is pictographic thinking—the tendency to view brand names and prices as images rather than symbols, and to think about product quantities by picturing them rather than using available symbolic information. Low-literate people develop several coping mechanisms to deal with their literacy limitations, including dependence on others or buying items one at a time.

Central here is a need to maintain self-esteem by avoiding settings that could potentially expose their low literacy. Thus, the characteristics of individual consumers (e.g., low literacy, low income, and joint effects) are particularly relevant when designing research methods (see Figure 11.5). Coupled with these characteristics is their unfamiliarity in participating in research studies. Figure 11.5: Task that was not understood by a 0–4 grade level participant (use of pictorial stimuli may have been helpful).

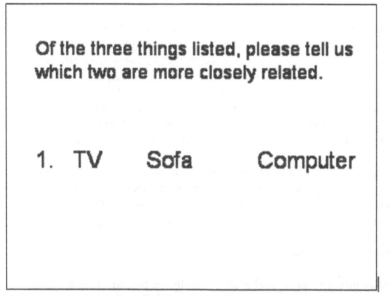

Of the three things listed, please tell us which two are more closely related.

1. TV   Sofa   Computer

Figure 11.5: Task that was not understood by a 0–4 grade level participant (use of pictorial stimuli may have been helpful).

In our qualitative methods, we focused on having conversations that our informants felt comfortable with at a cognitive level. We used straightforward questions that let participants focus on the ideas behind the question, rather than the wording of the question. We emphasized that we were not looking for right or wrong answers, but that we were studying how different people behaved in different ways.

We avoided interactions that could cause anxiety through the cognitive challenges placed on participants. This was often a matter of being sensitive to the reactions of our informants, and not pursuing a line of questioning when it caused discomfort. Cognitive challenges may stem from abstract terminology or the way literate interviewers pose questions. Such issues can cause something akin to test anxiety. The same questions posed in ways that enable informants to tap into their experiences are more effective.

Another way we responded to the needs of our sample was by using plain, everyday language. A challenging issue was in adjusting the word choice for the questionnaires we used, where commonly-used terms did not seem particularly complex. However, our perception of the level of difficulty was based on our understanding of the world, which differed greatly from that of our participants. Instead of asking participants to rate their level of "brand awareness" or "brand preference," we used phrases such as, "How well do you know this brand?" or "How much do you like this brand?" This allowed for low-literate participants to respond with more confidence.

We found that minimizing reading and writing tasks was important in our studies. This improved the likelihood that our participants really understood our questions. Virtually all of our participants could communicate effectively verbally, but varied in reading levels. Regardless of a participant's grade level, we verbally explained our consent forms. We administered our questionnaires verbally, by asking every question and requesting every answer verbally, and recording their responses. This was very important, but administratively time-consuming and expensive, requiring data collection in a one-to-one setting.

We also showed our questions to participants, so that they had access to visual cues that could aid processing, by administering studies with a series of slides on individual pieces of paper or in PowerPoint presentations on a laptop computer. We used large fonts, typically with one question per page. We read the same script to all participants, asked questions in the same fashion, and recorded participants' verbal answers.

Thus, every question was available to be read by the participant, and was also read aloud by the experimenter. Some participants believed that they were being tested on their reading ability. We reassured them that this was not the case and helped our respondents to refocus on our questions. Again, we emphasized that we were not looking for right or wrong answers, but rather at how different people behaved in different ways, and how literacy and income played a role in behavior.

The actual tasks we used were simple. Commonly used tasks in social research (e.g., assigning points to choices, ranking choices, or otherwise comparing a number of choices) can be too abstract and artificial for low-literate consumers. We asked participants to perform tasks such as making a single choice between two options, rating various attributes of an item (one attribute at a time) and answering simple "yes/no" questions.

We were sensitive to participants trying to please the researcher. Overall, our approaches have been helpful in our data collection with the 0–4 grade level. However, participants in the higher grade levels were often able to read and process the materials faster and they often tried to move quickly through the tasks. We maintained consistency by setting the pace of the presentation, slowing down participants to enable them to think about the questions asked, rather than anticipating answers.

Despite our conscious efforts to use manageable tasks, on some occasions we removed data from our sample when a participant did not understand the task. In one instance, a student in the 0–4 grade level was asked to choose two items out of three that were most similar to each other. The participant did not respond verbally and, after a long pause, pointed at two items on the page. Pausing to think about a problem was not unusual with our participants, nor was simply pointing at choices. However, after the next few questions, the participant quickly pointed to the first two choices. After being asked if the instructions were clear, the participant stated, "No, not really." (A sample slide from this study is shown in Figure 11.5 above.) There is also the likelihood that, on a few occasions, we were unable to detect when participants did not understand the task.

Affective Considerations

As discussed in earlier chapters, emotional research considerations, such as the management of stigma and self-esteem, are very salient for low-literate individuals (Adkins and Ozanne 2005; Viswanathan et al. 2005). Fundamental to our approach was the trust that we engendered in our interactions, the respect we displayed for our participants, and the sincerity and empathy with which we conducted our research. More than anything, central to our research method was our ability to carry on a sincere, well-intentioned conversation. We did not exploit participants' vulnerabilities for some perceived benefit for the research, but instead strived to understand their unique worlds.

To ensure that we did no harm with our research, we avoided making judgments on participants' answers, which was difficult, given the verbal interaction inherent in our method. We often asked participants questions such as, "Do you know this brand?" We reacted to their answer, whether affirmative or negative, in consistent ways. Our typical response was simply, "Good. How about this one?" as we continued with the task.

On one occasion, we noticed that we were only replying, "Good. How about this one?" to a participant's affirmative answers, whereas negative responses were answered with "Okay. How about this one?" The participant then encountered three consecutive brands that he did not know, the last of which resulted in a verbal expression of frustration.

Although it is not clear that our response was the cause of this frustration, we took extra care to be consistent in our procedures, to ensure that our responses did not influence participants' answers. We tried not to make salient a person's lack of reading, writing, or math ability. In qualitative interviews, this issue arose when participants expected us to react to their responses, particularly their consumption habits. It was important to keep a positive tone, but not endorse or discourage specific practices.

At the end of an interview, if asked, we attempted to explain the facts of an issue, such as an information display or the meaning of serving sizes. In one instance, a participant was misusing nutritional facts labels, due to a conceptual misunderstanding of the % daily value. After we completed the interview, we answered questions about how nutritional facts labels should be used.

Overall, we aimed to balance the need for consistency required for structured research methods with the need to do no harm. We attempted to minimize the levels of frustration that our participants experienced by designing tasks to focus on abilities, not deficiencies. We attempted to be nonjudgmental in our interactions, and we debriefed participants, responding to any questions they had.

Administrative Considerations

In our research, the need to maintain consistency in structured data collection was crucial, given the one-to-one interactions involved. We accomplished this in several ways. We used a private room to minimize outside interruptions and potential feelings of embarrassment associated with having peers watch participants' responses. We used consistent procedures in obtaining informed consent, explaining instructions and responding to questions during a structured data collection process. When using undergraduate student samples as comparison groups, we administered studies in small groups where they wrote down their responses. However, we strived to keep all other aspects of the procedures identical.

To gain access to participants, we sought to build trust and support with the adult education centers and social work programs that we visited. It was crucial that we had buy-in from all parties involved, including the program administrators. It was important to have more than just tacit approval to carry out the research; we sought active support. We attempted to learn from many people working in these programs in different capacities. We showed the administrators our experimental materials, obtaining feedback from them.

Having program directors vouch for our research gave us credibility with the classroom teachers. In turn, having the approval of the teachers gave us credibility with our student participants. We conducted interviews with teachers and learned from their vast experience. The teachers were invaluable in helping us recruit individual students.

Collecting data in the adult education centers can lead to interruptions of classes and add to the complexity of the class activities. To maintain the support of the teachers, we were conscious of how each class worked. We tried to understand the instructional methods and the flow of daily activities in order to minimize disruption. We did not interrupt group instruction times, but instead waited for individual study times to carry out interviews.

Our research used observations of social workers in the field. Our experience with social workers was relatively structured, as we simply observed them on their scheduled visits (Viswanathan and Gau 2005). We learned about conducting field research in these observations and were able to observe real-life interactions, away from the relatively controlled setting of the adult education centers.

The social workers were remarkable, facing uncertain environments in every interaction. They taught a specific curriculum, but their clients had questions about real-life situations. The setting was never ideal, with distractions, such as televisions turned on and children playing and crying. The social workers constantly adapted, and satisfied the planned and unplanned needs of their sessions. We tried to incorporate some of these skills into our own research.

The in-store observations we conducted were with the permission and cooperation of store managers. We encouraged our participants to shop as they normally would, observing them from a discrete distance. We did not take notes while they shopped, but rather interviewed them after they had finished shopping. Additionally, we sometimes requested participants go back to a certain part of the store to ask questions about how and why they purchased specific items. Our aim here was to alleviate anxiety during the actual observation, preventing feelings of being judged and avoiding influencing actual purchases.

Overall, our planning of data collection required a long timeframe. As described earlier, our data was collected one participant at a time (in contrast to data collection with undergraduate students, which was often conducted in a group). One-to-one administration greatly increased the time spent on data collection.

For our research, data collection took place over the course of several months, rather than a few days. This constraint amplified the need to create effective questionnaires administered correctly the first time. The option to rerun a study was a very expensive one. We often ran into problems with sample size, as we were only able to obtain data from 10 or 12 participants per condition, making the need for well-designed studies even more important.

For in-store observations, we generally drove out to a participant's home, drove them to the store, and drove them back home, because many of our participants did not own cars. We had a relatively high no-show rate when we planned to meet directly at the store, with only one out of five, or sometimes even one out of ten scheduled participants turning up.

In short, collecting data was very time-consuming. We adopted a long-term perspective and tried not to be discouraged when an entire morning was spent on only two individual surveys, or if another observation fell through. It was helpful to understand that we were building a research program in this setting, and not simply completing a study.

In designing studies, willingness to respond was a central issue. There is stigma attached to low-literacy and low-income levels, which means that people in this group tend to be reluctant to give their opinions or participate in this sort of research study. However, and somewhat surprisingly, we had great success with regard to the willingness of our participants. As would be expected in any research endeavor, we encountered people who were not comfortable speaking with us. However, we often found ourselves in the middle of fascinating conversations with remarkable people willing to speak freely about personal issues. The one area where we were not successful was with scheduled appointments to meet people at grocery stores for observation.

Summary

To summarize, our experience has centered on conducting successful research among low-literate, low-income individuals in the US. In this vein, it was critical to incorporate specific cognitive, affective, and administrative considerations. For instance, we avoided making salient participants' deficits in knowledge or ability, but instead encouraged them to express what they knew. They often surprised us with the ingenious ways in which they not only coped, but thrived. Much of this was a result of simply assuming a role of observing and knowing the participants.

This was not only true in a physical sense, in that we entered our participants' environments (e.g., their homes, the adult education centers, etc.), but also in a human sense. Our prevailing attitude in conducting research took the perspective of our participants. Perhaps this was a natural outcome of conducting research in a one-to-one setting, and being able to genuinely empathize with our participants. Our ongoing relationship with the different adult education centers and social work programs has enabled us to take a more holistic view. We knew that we could go back to talk again to participants.

When carrying out research with efficiency as the focus, we may obtain an extra response in a given data collection session, but often at the expense of something greater. We acknowledge the difficulty in designing research in this setting and the considerable amount of time and effort required to complete the simplest study. We also propose that a key to effective data collection is to be patient, to slow down to hear what people are saying, even when we are not asking anything specific. The spontaneous conversations that arise often become key sources of ideas for future research.

In many cases, we found out more during the conversation in a 15-minute filler task than we did in the actual study. In this sense, we suggest that, even with structured data collection, there is room to explore, to spend a few minutes talking with participants about a study, to find out whether or not it made sense to them and what they thought about it.

Though we may have lost the chance to conduct one more survey, we gained by the additional things we learned in these conversations. Many participants enjoy the conversation, and are appreciative of the notion that we can learn from them. We have had many conversations where our participants have spoken frankly about their lives in ways that transcended our study. The people that we encountered often have insufficient interactions with others. We were able to fill a social role, if only briefly. The benefits that we obtained were well worth the few extra minutes of our time.

Researching Subsistence Marketplaces in India

Paralleling our experience in the US is our research in India, where there is a range of low-literacy and extreme poverty. In the next sections, we describe our experiences and discuss insights.

Overview

The collection of data in subsistence contexts in India represented another discovery process over many years. Data was collected in Chennai, Tamil Nadu (formerly Madras, the fourth largest city in India) and nearby rural areas. To begin the project and gain access to participants, we interacted with a community-based, non-governmental organization (NGO) that works to integrate family and community development in low-income areas, providing a variety of services to these communities. This NGO works towards having its target beneficiaries form neighborhood-based organizations, helping them by implementing programs and activities in a variety of areas, including health, literacy, and finance.

Initially, we hired two part-time employees from the NGO who, between them, had over two decades of experience in development work and were themselves from subsistence backgrounds. They later became full-time associates of our research program, assisting with recruitment and interviewing of participants, and transcribing and translating interviews. The team has evolved, with all members of our research team having experienced subsistence livelihoods firsthand, giving a unique characteristic to our research.

Approach to Data Collection and Analysis

Our data collection sites range from urban low-income neighborhoods to agrarian villages in developing nations and adult literacy centers to soup kitchens in developed nations. In all of these sites, prior to or concurrent with collecting data, we have spent significant time understanding the context, building relationships with the local community, and building general goodwill within the community. Building such enduring relationships is crucial in accessing informants, gathering rich data, and following the development of the community over time in a holistic manner. Central to this enterprise are our field workers, many of whom hail from the communities in which we work.

Our general understanding of the community enables us to identify and access interviewees who are best placed to inform the specific research questions. Interviews are generally conducted in locations within the community and participants are debriefed on their rights as research participants in the local language. Interviews are conducted on a one-to-one basis in the local language.

The average duration of the interviews is 45 minutes to an hour. The interviews are typically open-ended, starting with questions regarding the broad life circumstances of the individual and subsequently turning to more focused questions related to the area of research. Such an interviewing strategy enables us to understand the specific behaviors of the individual in light of his/her broad life circumstances. The interviews are audio-taped and subsequently transcribed and translated into English.

In the translation process, we exercise enormous care to capture the individual's voice faithfully without any interpretation of our own. After the transcripts are generated, the researchers read them individually and identify emergent themes. In case there are doubts regarding cultural meanings of objects, member checks are performed with our field colleagues to ascertain accurateness of understanding. Having individually analyzed the transcripts, the researchers discuss the findings and attempt to evolve theoretical insights through a process of discussion and consensus building.

Interviews

We began with qualitative interviews that allowed individuals to freely provide information. We covered topics in an unstructured, conversational fashion, beginning with life circumstances, then moving to the economic realm, asking about recent shopping trips. We then covered a variety of issues, such as decision-making for different products, attitudes toward businesses, instances of being cheated, and budgeting.

Rather than cover a "shopping list" of questions, we allowed the interview to develop, enabling participants to relate their life stories with a particular emphasis on marketplace interactions. Our own research journey was to move away from specific questions on marketplace interactions to broader conversations, mostly driven by individuals' narratives (sample interview information is available at the web portal).

We recruited people from different communities to cover a range of literacy levels and incomes. We audio-taped interviews, reviewed them on an ongoing basis, and made adjustments (e.g., adding questions) as the data collection ensued. Participants were typically given monetary, and sometimes, non-monetary compensation, e.g., a utensil in return for their participation—a plastic bucket useful for storage and transportation of water during times of shortage.

We conducted the interviews in Tamil, the language spoken in the state of Tamil Nadu, and also the native language of the interviewers. Interviews were first transcribed into Tamil, then translated and typed in English. Research associates who were fluent in Tamil and moderately fluent in English performed the transcriptions. This worked well, as the translation remained close to the original text.

Using qualitative analyses, we explored themes about the lives that low-literate, low-income people lead. In our in-depth interviews, we received valuable feedback from our associates who had considerable experience in subsistence contexts. In addition to listening to interviews, immersion in the environment was central in developing field notes, modifying our interview questions, and developing surveys and experiments based on a rich, contextualized understanding of the local subsistence marketplace. For example, in studies where participants performed a categorization task requiring them to group together similar items from a list of items, we used familiar visual cues from local contexts to enable comprehension and familiarity.

Experiments and Surveys

We have conducted a number of surveys and experiments in subsistence contexts in India, paying participants for their efforts. Our measures have involved translated scales relating to well-being, happiness, and individualism, as well as scales on confidence and skills, relating to consumer and entrepreneurial issues (Viswanathan, Gajendiran and Venkatesan 2008b). We have successfully used cognitive tasks involving visual perception, picture matching, and line drawings to gauge size perceptions.

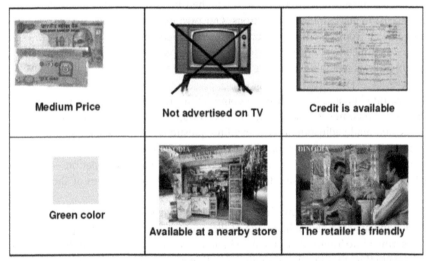

| Medium Price | Not advertised on TV | Credit is available |
| Green color | Available at a nearby store | The retailer is friendly |

Figure 11.6: Stimuli featuring pictorial information used as experimental stimuli in India.

One example is a task in which participants sort sheets of paper containing pictorial representations of a product. The various versions differed on several attributes—appearance, cost, convenience, vendor familiarity, availability of credit, and whether the product was advertised on television. The sorting task provided a means of eliciting responses without overburdening the participant with a relatively abstract task, such as rating different attributes. An example of these experimental stimuli is shown in Figure 11.6.

Insights

A number of insights from our experiences are discussed below, again organized in terms of cognitive, affective, and administrative issues (Figure 11.7)

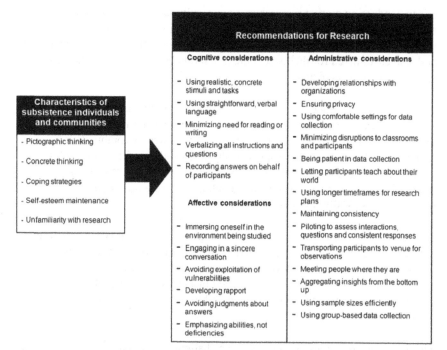

Figure 11.7: Recommendations for Research in Subsistence Marketplaces.

Cognitive Issues

Concrete reasoning and pictographic thinking also apply in subsistence contexts in India. For example, questionnaires are likely to produce more valid findings if they feature images of actual product packages, rather than lists of brand names. However, there are a number of differences from our experiences in the US. As noted in earlier chapters, the subsistence context of India is characterized by pervasive one-to-one interactions (Viswanathan 2007). Some level of literacy, income, or experience enables people to learn from this environment and improve their marketplace skills, as evidenced by the ease of handling counting tasks due to experience in buying and selling.

In contrast, the US is characterized by an environment with chain stores, symbolic information, and relatively impersonal transactions, potentially hindering the development of marketplace skills. Also pertinent is the constant verbal communication that characterizes the Indian subsistence context. Nevertheless, the issues discussed for US samples also apply in the Indian context—using straightforward tasks, employing simple language, and reading instructions out loud. We emphasize the unique cognitive considerations below.

When conducting market research in a cross-cultural setting, effective translation of survey instruments into the local language is critical. In subsistence marketplaces, translation should be done at the level of language, and also customized for the local context in terms of content (e.g., choice of stimuli, situations depicted).

For a study in which we explored thematic and taxonomic categorization schemes, we designed easy-to-understand, locally relevant items. Participants were asked to pair two out of three objects, with particular combinations indicating either usage relationships or physical similarity. The choice of actual items used in the task was influenced by the local context. Not surprisingly, unfamiliar items, such as "panda" or "hamburger," were not as effective for our participants as locally familiar items.

Given the cognitive challenges and unfamiliarity with typical tasks, structured approaches can raise participants' anxiety. An example of this was rating products from memory on abstract attributes and assigning them points on a seven-point response scale. We had several instances where people provided the same response to a series of items, possibly due to not understanding the questions asked.

This led to our sensitivity to the cognitive challenges that may lead to such responses. Subsequently, we gathered data using numerical scales in a two-stage process. We first asked participants whether they were neutral, in agreement with, or disagreed with particular statements (or were positively or negatively inclined to an object or felt neutral about it). We then asked for further discrimination within the agreement or disagreement (positive/negative) side of the scale.

Other considerations include the length and language of procedures. Tasks employed should be ones to which participants could relate, as abstract tasks can lead to inaccurate responses. Participants should also understand the purpose of the research. Language and procedures should be straightforward to avoid unreasonable cognitive demands.

Surveys should be of reasonable length. Long interviews can be conducted if they employ interesting tasks to which participants relate. Such procedures should include planned breaks and be administered by empathetic interviewers who develop genuine rapport with participants. We have had success with visual tasks and, overall, these tasks appear to transfer well to subsistence settings by being less cognitively challenging, particularly with appropriately translated instructions.

Affective Considerations

As with the US samples, the central role of negative emotions and self-esteem suggests the importance of using personal administration that emphasizes rapport and trust. Accentuating issues of self-esteem is the high status that researchers are perceived to have, combined with the low status that participants view themselves as being at, as they often worry about their ability to contribute or the value of their contribution.

A personally administered, relatively unstructured approach results in less anxiety for participants. It is important to create trust and avoid deception, as distrust can lead to bias—for example, giving a response to please the researcher. To maintain trust, researchers should clearly communicate the purpose and potential benefits of the research to informants. Quantitative techniques should be customized for realism and relevance, perhaps by using actual product packages or pictorial representations as stimuli. Language and procedures should be straightforward. The tasks and administration procedures should not threaten participants' self-esteem, and should not place high cognitive demands on them.

Research design should recognize that self-esteem plays a central role in the decision-making of subsistence consumers, compounding problems of low literacy and unfamiliarity with research protocols. One-to-one administration of surveys is effective in building personal rapport. Eliciting trust from participants may help alleviate the test-taking anxiety triggered by low literacy. At the confluence of culture, poverty, and low literacy, caution is necessary in translating certain instruments that apply in a Western context to global subsistence contexts.

This is particularly the case when using instruments requiring emotional responses on controversial topics, such as romance. When faced with this issue, we were careful to modify items to emphasize affectionate (rather than romantic) relationships, given the cultural issues in this regard, which were accentuated by having male interviewers and female participants.

Administrative Considerations

In light of the cognitive and affective issues discussed, the need to maintain consistency in administration is central. Pilot testing is critical in gauging issues that arise in administrating surveys and developing consistent responses to questions raised by participants. As with the US context, administrative issues posed significant problems. A key factor in our success was our network of NGOs and community-based organizations. We built these relationships through our research team, which consisted of members from these communities. Finding appropriate people to serve as research associates was extremely important. Our team benefits from deeper access to participants through relationships carefully developed over several years.

Implications for Market Research by Organizations

Market research is crucial for organizations to better understand the life circumstances and economic realities of people in subsistence marketplaces. Our discussion suggests a number of implications for business research at cognitive, affective, and administrative levels.

Cognitive Issues

Approaches to market research for relatively resource-rich, literate settings are often based on attribute-based approaches that aim to identify an optimal combination of product attributes. However, for low-literate consumers, ratings along attributes may be relatively abstract, resulting in more holistic and experiential judgments of products (Viswanathan, Sridharan and Ritchie 2008).

Therefore, market researchers should use realistic stimuli in their approaches. Our approach—sorting pictures representing products and related attributes—is an example of making tasks realistic. Field-testing and observations of product usage may be highly effective in these settings. Previously discussed issues (e.g., using simple language, simplifying responses, administering procedures to facilitate reading or comprehension, avoiding lengthy procedures or providing breaks to minimize fatigue, enabling a comfortable environment to avoid anxiety) apply to market research.

Affective Issues

Self-esteem, coupled with unfamiliarity with market research, plays a central role in investigating subsistence consumers (Viswanathan, Sridharan and Ritchie 2008). Personal administration with an emphasis on developing rapport is particularly relevant here. The key is to enable a sincere, empathic conversation. We have found that the challenge is to overcome participants' preconceptions of researchers, specifically their perceived higher status.

Thus, it is important for researchers to develop a mindset of learning from participants. The lack of personal connection and familiarity that many researchers have with subsistence marketplaces makes it imperative that they suspend preconceptions, at least for the purposes of data collection (Viswanathan, Gajendiran and 2008b). Market researchers should develop a deeper understanding of subsistence contexts to gather valuable information that leads to useful products.

Administrative Issues

A number of administrative issues are noteworthy. In both India and the US, we developed relationships with a number of organizations that work with low-literate, low-income people. These organizations have enabled our work and have been instrumental in our efforts. In India, our team consisted of people from the contexts studied. They have been integral to our research by providing key insights and offering in-depth knowledge of the communities in which we conducted our field research.

It is interesting to view our insights in terms of a conventional, top-down approach toward survey design—defining a universe, developing a frame, picking a probability-based sample, and administering a survey. In subsistence contexts such as India, a bottom-up approach, where insights are stitched together one community at a time, may be more practical and effective (Viswanathan, Sridharan and Ritchie 2008). The one-to-one interactions that we observe in subsistence marketplaces suggest the need to pick deliberative samples of people, groups, and communities, and the need to aggregate insights from key people.

Test marketing in selected communities may be an effective approach for monitoring word of mouth, particularly if special attention is given to the views of local opinion leaders (e.g., retailers, community organizers, leaders of local self-help groups). Additionally, group-based data collection, such as focus groups, may be particularly effective, given the importance of word-of-mouth communication in subsistence communities.

Given the nature of issues associated with conducting research in these settings, aggregation may often not be of specific, quantitative data, but rather of qualitative insights gleaned from methods such as focus groups. Even in the US context, where participants can be conveniently sampled based on geographic considerations, such as housing units, our experiences suggest that a variety of difficulties could lead to a high rate of non-response. Therefore, sampling procedures that are sound or optimal on paper may break down in practice with the unique challenges of collecting extensive data.

Conclusion

We describe our experiences with research methods in the US and India, place our insights into the larger context of the literature on research methods, and highlight implications for market research for organizations in subsistence marketplaces. In all contexts, we adopt the mindset that our participants provide unique and interesting insights into their worlds, regardless of literacy or income levels. Our discussion focuses on the cognitive, affective, and administrative issues that were salient to our research experiences (see Figure 11.7):

- With regard to cognitive considerations, we try to reduce the potential for discomfort in our studies by minimizing the levels of reading and writing that are required and using stimuli that are pictorial and familiar.

- To address affective issues, we emphasise the need to build a rapport with participants. We communicate to our participants that we are sincerely interested in their experiences, and that we have much to learn from them.

- To address administrative issues, we attempt to build strong relationships with the organizations that we work with, enabling us to conduct research more effectively, while gaining added insights from the teachers and administrators of these programs.

- These issues take on different meanings in the different contexts of the US and India, given the social considerations of the intensely one-to-one nature of the Indian marketplace.

In conclusion, we demonstrate that the unique characteristics of low-literate, low-income people in the US and subsistence marketplaces in India provide interesting similarities and differences, with important implications for research methods.

References

Adkins, N., and J. Ozanne (2005) 'The Low Literate Consumer', Journal of Consumer Research 32.1: 93-105.

Denzin, N., and Y. Lincoln (2005) The Handbook of Qualitative Research (Thousand Oaks, CA: Sage).

Fals-Borda, O., and A. Rahman (1991) Action and Knowledge: Breaking the Monopoly with Participatory Action Research (New York: Apex Press).

Green, M. (2006) 'Representing Poverty and Attacking Representations: Perspectives on Poverty from Social Anthropology', Journal of Development Studies 42.7: 1,108-129.

London, T. (2007) 'A Base-of-the-Pyramid Perspective on Poverty Alleviation', Working Paper, William Davidson Institute/United Nations Development Programme.

McCracken, G. (1988) The Long Interview (Newbury Park, CA: Sage).

Narayan, D., R. Patel, K. Schafft, A. Rademacher and S. Koch-Schulte (2000) Voices of the Poor: Can Anyone Hear Us? (New York: Oxford University Press).

Ozanne, J., and B. Saatcioglu (2008) 'Participatory Action Research', Journal of Consumer Research (in press).

Reason, P., and H. Bradbury (2001) 'Introduction: Inquiry and Participation in Search of a World Worthy of Human Aspiration', in P. Reason and H. Bradbury (eds.), Handbook of Action Research (Thousand Oaks, CA: Sage): 1-14.

Spradley, J.P. (1979) The Ethnographic Interview (New York: Holt, Rinehart & Winston).

Strauss, A., and J. Corbin (1990) Basics of Qualitative Research: Grounded Theory Procedures and Techniques (Newbury Park, CA: Sage).

Viswanathan, M. (2007) 'Understanding Product and Market Interactions in Subsistence Marketplaces: A Study in South India', in J. Rosa and M. Viswanathan (eds.), Product and Market Development for Subsistence Marketplaces: Consumption and Entrepreneurship Beyond Literacy and Resource Barriers (Oxon, U.K.: Elsevier): 21-57.

Viswanathan, M., S. Gajendiran and R. Venkatesan (2008a) 'Understanding and Enabling Marketplace Literacy in Subsistence Contexts: The Development of a Consumer and Entrepreneurial Literacy Educational Programme in South India', International Journal of Educational Development 28.3: 300-319.

Viswanathan, M., S. Gajendiran and R. Venkatesan (2008b) Enabling Consumer and Entrepreneurial Literacy in Subsistence Marketplaces: A Research-based Approach to Educational Programmes (London: Springer).

Viswanathan, M., and R. Gau (2005) 'Functional Illiteracy and Nutritional Education in the United States: A Research-Based Approach to the Development of Nutritional Education Materials for Functionally Illiterate Consumers', Journal of Macromarketing 25.2: 187-201.

Viswanathan, M., J.A. Rosa and J.E. Harris (2005) 'Decision-making and Coping of Functionally Illiterate Consumers and Some Implications for Marketing Management', Journal of Marketing 69 (January 2005): 15-31.

Viswanathan, M., S. Sridharan and R. Ritchie (2008) 'Marketing in Subsistence Marketplaces', in C. Wankel (ed.), Alleviating Poverty Through Business Strategy (New York: Palgrave Macmillan).

Chapter 12
Creating Educational Initiatives on Radically Different Contexts[31]

Image 12.01: Students and peer mentors discuss issues relating to a virtual immersion exercise at the University of Illinois Urbana-Champaign, United States. Photograph courtesy of students in the course "Product and Market Development for Subsistence Marketplaces."

In this chapter, we describe a variety of educational initiatives that we have developed about subsistence marketplaces. These initiatives cover courses at undergraduate, graduate, and executive levels in business; graduate level across

[31] This chapter includes material adapted from the following previously published works:

Viswanathan, Madhubalan, "Curricular Innovations on Sustainability and Subsistence Marketplaces: Philosophical, Substantive and Methodological Orientations," Journal of Management Education, Forthcoming. DOI: 10.1177/1052562911432256

Viswanathan, Madhubalan, Ali Yassine, and John Clarke (2011), "Sustainable Product and Market Development for Subsistence Marketplaces: Creating Educational Initiatives in Radically Challenging Contexts," Journal of Product Innovation Management, 28, 558–569.

disciplines such as business, design, and engineering; and undergraduate level in engineering.

Our marketplace orientation described earlier leads to a number of central elements in the learning experience we describe in this chapter (e.g., understanding life circumstances and existing marketplace dynamics as a starting point, and creating solutions that are locally sustainable in terms of economy, culture, and environment). Efforts to enable the large proportion of people living in subsistence to participate in the marketplace have to also be guided by the need to find sustainable solutions that preserve natural resources for future generations.

Sustainable Product and Market Development for Subsistence Marketplaces

We begin with our experience teaching a unique course on sustainable product and market development for subsistence marketplaces.

A year-long inter-disciplinary graduate-level course on subsistence marketplaces with an international immersion experience, Sustainable Product and Market Development for Subsistence Marketplaces, has been offered now for 7 years. This course was recently rated one of the top entrepreneurship courses by Inc. magazine. New product development lab courses are not new; however, what is new here is the pioneering attempt to design a course that focuses on developing products and services to serve the needs of those living in subsistence marketplaces. Students in business, engineering, industrial design and other areas spend the Fall semester understanding subsistence marketplaces through immersion in this context and through emersion of business principles. Five weeks of virtual immersion in subsistence contexts in Fall include a poverty simulation, analysis of interviews of subsistence individuals, analysis of life circumstances in subsistence, development of conceptual models of poverty, low literacy, and consequences, and development of conceptual models of needs, products, and market interactions of subsistence individuals.

The next six weeks are spent in emersion of principles using a rich set of cases, and guest speakers ranging from social workers to technologists and entrepreneurs. In parallel, student groups are formed to balance technical and business skills and match interests with our company sponsors. Student groups generate and evaluate a long list of possible ideas, and narrow them down to a smaller set. The final weeks of the semester are spent on designing market research to be conducted during a field trip.

The class travels for immersion in the context and to conduct market research during part of the winter break. The field trip has been conducted in urban areas including Chennai, Bangalore, Hyderabad, Delhi, Agra, and Jabalpur, as well as rural areas of India. Students observe households in urban and rural subsistence contexts, as well as retail and wholesale outlets. Students interview low-literate, low-income individuals in urban and rural settings regarding product ideas for group projects. Students also visit educational institutions, non-profit organizations, and corporations engaged in the development of innovative programs and technologies for subsistence contexts. The field trip geared to visiting the environment of the urban and rural poor requires considerable planning and rehearsal, and has been a transformative learning experience for the students. The Spring semester is spent developing and testing concepts, developing workable prototypes, and developing manufacturing, marketing and business plans. To date, 27 projects with a variety of small startups, social enterprises, and large corporations have been completed.

Our two-semester course sequence on sustainable product and market development for subsistence marketplaces combines in-class teaching with experiential learning, and results in useful and marketable product concepts, prototypes, and detailed business plans. Graduate students in various business and engineering disciplines and industrial design, as well as other areas, learn and use principles of business planning, marketing, cost accounting, project finance, engineering design, and manufacturing to develop new products for subsistence marketplaces that are economically, socially, and environmentally sustainable.

Interdisciplinary student teams work over two semesters to identify an opportunity of general need in important domains such as education, health, and agriculture. The students, subsequently, conduct field market research to better understand subsistence consumer needs and contexts through an international immersion experience, develop a product concept, convert the concept to a workable prototype, and develop a manufacturing plan, marketing strategy, and overall business plan for the product. In the first four years of executing this class, we have partnered with a variety of multinational companies, startups, and social enterprises. Projects have focused on a variety of product categories ranging from information technology to food and beverages.

Overlaying the content found in a typical new product development lab course, we develop a contextual understanding of subsistence marketplaces. This type of immersion in the consumer context sets the stage for new product development. Travel to subsistence markets (our initial focus has been on India, the location of our research) for actual immersion in the context and to gather specific market information is a central aspect of the learning experience.

The course addresses a number of issues, a few of which are listed as exemplars: What are the characteristics of successful and unsuccessful products for subsistence marketplaces? How should products be designed for such marketplaces? How should market research be conducted throughout the new product development process? Detailed description of course elements is provided below and the full course schedule can be found on the course website (http://www.business.illinois.edu/subsistence).

Course Design and Class Enrollment

In our pilot effort we used an application process to build a class of diverse students, with a broad range of technical and business knowledge, skills, and backgrounds. We held several information sessions on campus and sought faculty assistance to build a class consisting of business, engineering, and industrial design students. We primarily targeted our information to graduate students, although we considered outstanding senior undergraduates. Key enrollment challenges were the commitment for the two-semester course and the international immersion experience and associated expenses. In addition to the students representing a variety of disciplines and experiences, we were also able to create a cohort that contained a rich and international diversity of cultures and socio-economic backgrounds.

Student expenses for the course were held to a minimum ($1,000 to $1,500 for the immersion experience), and there were no textbook costs. We applied for grants and sought company funding to support the course and reduce student costs. We needed the two-course commitment to develop a product prototype and a detailed business plan, to allow for the international immersion experience between the two semesters, and to enable students to develop specific deliverables for partnering companies.

We strongly encouraged students to make a two-course commitment, although we did allow for some flexibility. In our second execution of the course, the two-course commitment was a strict requirement, but caused reluctance among students, as well as difficulties in enforcing verbal commitments. Therefore, in the third execution, we had asked students to decide by mid-semester in the Fall before we finalize group compositions.

Virtual Immersion in Subsistence

Five weeks of virtual immersion in subsistence contexts in the Fall semester includes a poverty simulation, analysis of interviews of subsistence people and videos, development of conceptual models of poverty, low literacy, and consequences, and of needs, products, and market interactions. We use many assignments to learn about poverty in different cultures and contexts, such as the US and India, and understand the commonalities and differences through comparison and contrast. Students begin to learn about poverty in a context they are familiar with, i.e., the US, before moving to unfamiliar contexts of subsistence, such as developing economies with widespread and extreme poverty.

Before the first meeting, we ask students to read a book providing rich biographical accounts of living in poverty in the US (e.g., Nickel and Dimed by Barbara Ehrenreich or The Blue Sweater by Jacqueline Novogratz). The first meeting includes a poverty simulation conducted by the Cooperative Extension program at the University of Illinois or the local United Way staff. Each organization is experienced in serving the poor; for example, the Cooperative Extension program serves a large population in the state living in poverty through nutrition education and other programs. In this simulation in a face-to-face setting, students are assigned to specific roles in families and asked to make financial decisions with limited amounts of money over a four-week period.

Each week is simulated in about 15 minutes, where students play their characters and interact with shops and government offices staffed by the organizers of the simulation. A number of needs, such as food, medicine, and rent have to be met while paying for transportation and other services. Often, students find that they need to forego basic necessities to make ends meet. The simulation concludes with the organizers asking students to relate their experiences and then providing a summary of poverty in the state. Students are asked to complete an assignment where they describe their experience in the poverty simulation, their emotions and behaviors when participating in it, and broader lessons learned about living in poverty.

This simulation enables students to think about poverty as well as the constraints that arise as a result. Often, students relate how they assumed that people chose in some way to live in poverty but in fact, it is very difficult to get out of the vicious cycle of poverty. They develop an appreciation for the economic, psychological, and other factors that need to be overcome by those living in poverty.

The following quotes, which have been kept anonymous, illustrate student reflections on the poverty simulation experience:

> As the activity progressed, I was getting more and more anxious. Our family was not making ends meet and my mother was rarely home. Communicating with my mother was becoming difficult because she was always out looking to get us money. This just made me desperate to find a way to make money.

> Desperation was probably the first emotion that came up during the simulation. I felt desperate once I learned that there was no cash

available and I started panicking since I did not know what to do and knew that my family was depending on me for food. Later I became increasing frustrated because I was not able to find a way to obtain any cash while a string of misfortunes crashed down on us, including our house getting robbed, our car breaking down, a member of the family being sent to jail, and the family getting evicted from our house. I also felt a huge amount of pressure on my shoulders as my wife and kids were very much dependant on me to make decisions for the family and obtain food and essential needs as well.

I did feel the pressure of my circumstances, such as having to pay my mortgage for fear of being evicted. My decision making was based exclusively on the idea of getting out of poverty.

For the second week, we ask students to read rich, in-depth interviews of buyers and sellers living in subsistence in India and then write first-person narratives of the lives of people interviewed. The class discussion in the second week, partially organized around specific interviewees, is wide-ranging and touches on various aspects of poverty as well as issues of literacy and culture.

The discussion is not restricted to poverty in one country, but rather, students from different cultures and backgrounds are asked to make observations about poverty in their respective cultures. Such an approach enables a bottom-up, data-driven discussion of insights based on students' analysis of interviews as well as broad-based coverage of poverty in different contexts.

In preparation for the third week, we ask students to read more interviews of buyers and sellers and then develop a model of poverty covering antecedents and outcomes. The model can take a number of forms, such as a conventional causal diagram or a collage. Students from engineering, industrial design, business, as well as other areas, are very creative in this open-ended approach to understanding poverty. We organize class discussion in Week 3 around presentations of poverty models by students. We also introduce videos of life circumstances in subsistence to generate class discussion.

Noteworthy in the first three weeks is the focus on a deep understanding of subsistence contexts, which provides a basis to understand the marketplace realm in the following weeks and is central to our marketplace orientation. In the last two iterations of this offering, we have introduced an assignment where students develop models that capture local environmental issues.

In Week 4, students analyze additional interviews and videos to derive models of the set of needs, products, and markets for people living in subsistence—

thus moving the focus to the marketplace realm. We organize the class around presentations by students about needs, products, and markets. In Week 5, students develop models of the local environment in poverty.

We also use Week 5 to summarize key issues about low literacy and poverty, using research in the US and in India. As preparation, we ask students to summarize and critique two papers on low literacy and poverty in the US and in India (Viswanathan et al. 2005; Viswanathan 2007). As noted, we cover poverty in a variety of contexts and even eras, using comparison and contrast to gain insights.

In recent iterations, we also invite organizational sponsors to speak to the class about possible topics for projects in the first three weeks of the semester.

Emersion of Business, Design, and Engineering Principles for Subsistence Marketplaces

In this part of the course, our aim is to help students understand the emersion of principles for product development, marketing, management, and engineering, through comparison and contrast with principles for non-subsistence contexts. We accomplish this partly through cases that cover a range of issues including product development, technology, engineering, distribution, promotion, and pricing. Groups of students analyze cases, with some charged with leading discussions and others with submitting write-ups.

We have used three to five cases in our previous experiences, including ITC e-Choupal, Annapurna Salt, and Jaipur Foot Company (Prahalad 2005); the aim being to cover different topics and subsistence contexts, although there is an over-representation of cases about India in the literature. The analysis of each case focuses on the following issues:

- needs and consumer behavior (specific needs being served, relevant consumer behaviors, product and market context, larger context of life circumstances);

- market research (examples of methods used, suggestions for methodological improvements);

- management and engineering issues;

- technology, products, distribution, promotion, and pricing issues;

- recommendations for product and market development for subsistence marketplaces; and

- specific lessons learned for group projects.

.

We also invite guest speakers, ranging from technologists to commercial and social entrepreneurs, to discuss their experiences in subsistence marketplaces.

Group Project

We form student groups, in earlier iterations in the middle of the semester, but in more recent iterations by the third week or so, based on background, skills, and interests. These groups work with partnering organizations on potential projects. Our organizational partners have ranged from a small startup to several large multinationals in the arenas of information, communication and computer technology, food and beverage, and health and hygiene.

Students interact directly with executives to better understand existing marketplace challenges, issues, and experiences and to determine the focus for the project. For example, some organizations may request a focus on a narrow product category, such as a beverage market, whereas others may encourage consideration of a wide range of product categories.

Groups then generate a range of ideas and approaches, erring on the side of inclusion. This ideation stage can be facilitated by reviewing video and interview material to consider needs and ways to address them through a market-based approach. Alternatively, students can consider technologies that could lead to innovative product ideas. In the next stage, they carefully narrow their list of ideas; the aim is not to reduce to a single idea but to have a manageable set of ideas as a basis for designing qualitative research. Qualitative market research instruments are readied for use during the immersion experience. We encourage students to develop visual material representing product ideas that will facilitate the data collection process. Throughout this process, groups summarize their progress to the rest of the class, thus sharing and learning from all the projects addressed in the class.

International Immersion Experience

The class travels for immersion in the context and to conduct market research during part of the winter break. We have visited Chennai, Delhi, and Agra each year as well as Bangalore, Hyderabad, Jabalpur, and Pondicherry, as well as semi-urban and rural areas, in December-January, with other destinations being tentatively planned. Students observe households in urban and rural subsistence contexts, as well as retail and wholesale outlets. They interview low-literate, low-income people in urban and rural settings to conduct market research for their group projects. Targeted interviews are also arranged based on each team's requirements. For example, project-specific interviews have been arranged in the past with farmers, tsunami victims, and individuals with disabilities. In addition, students also visit educational institutions and companies engaged in developing innovative technologies for subsistence contexts, and social enterprises providing services.

The immersion experience has been a central and transformative experience in the larger context of the course. A number of immersion aspects of the trip are central to the learning experience. Students spend long days with many interactions with subsistence people and contexts. These interactions are not scripted and allow students to engage in a discovery process in a radically different context. They are encouraged to reflect on what they are observing by maintaining diaries and through debriefing and facilitated discussion sessions.

The trip takes many months of careful planning and preparation and is preceded by detailed orientation sessions for students. The nature of the experience— interacting with people and communities in urban and rural areas—requires careful planning and rehearsal and the cooperation of many organizations and people. Many of the amenities and facilities that are taken for granted in field visits to corporations or in other field trips in middle-class settings cannot be assumed here.

For instance, careful planning is required to select villages to visit, to ensure that people are willing to be interviewed, to ensure that facilities are available to conduct interviews, and so on. Our ability to organize the field trip is greatly aided by a core team of people from the contexts we study—the people who are central to our research, teaching, and social initiatives. We draw on the cooperation of community-based organizations and self-help groups as well as educational institutions and companies. The relationships we have developed over many years through research and social initiatives (Viswanathan et al. 2008) are central to implementing the immersion experience.

Topics in Product Design and Development

The Spring semester builds on the learning and data gathered in the field to convert concepts to workable prototypes, and to develop manufacturing, marketing, and business plans. Product design and development is a well-researched and documented subject within the context of resource-rich and formal economies (Pugh 1991; Ulrich and Eppinger 2007). However, in subsistence contexts, it remains a highly unexplored and unstructured area of research and practice (Donaldson 2006).

Accordingly, in the spring semester we teach a systematic and structured approach for developing products and services for subsistence marketplaces. This includes conceptual design, system (architectural) design, detailed design, financial modeling, and prototyping methods. In addition, it includes writing project mission statements, business plans, and other related topics at the intersection of business and engineering. Our main objective is to educate students on product development topics while focusing on relevant issues for subsistence marketplaces, such as:

- design functionality and its fit to social and cultural needs or norms,
- design affordability and cost-effectiveness,
- design robustness and its ability to withstand harsh operating conditions, and
- design manufacturability and local sourcing of materials, parts, and expertise.

This part of the course commences with debriefing sessions, which usually take a "show and tell" format. Each team prepares a set of slides that often includes photographs and videos taken during the immersion experience and presents their observations and experiences. Students describe qualitative interviews and observations and broader impressions based on their overall trip experience. The team concludes the brief by presenting a few concepts.

We cover a number of topics during the semester to support the development of the project. We discuss the characteristics of an effective business plan, using several documented cases (Horan 2004; Sahlman 1997). We also discuss project and team management issues in class, focusing on project scheduling techniques, and a laundry list of dos and don'ts for effective team communication, workload sharing, and distribution.

We cover topics such as the state of design practices in developing countries, the importance of proper needs assessment in subsistence contexts, and appropriate technologies. We discuss the various design strategies and processes observed in developing countries to identify design opportunities and constraints (Donaldson 2006; Tybout 2000). We emphasize that design practices and processes must be consistent with local conditions in order to support sustainable economic development, emphasizing our marketplace orientation and the need to enable sustainable marketplaces.

We discuss the importance of deep contextual understanding as a necessary precursor to any engineering design endeavor, particularly in a subsistence context. We describe, in detail, a contextual needs assessment method to discover and document the "how," "where," and "who" factors of the design context (Green et al. 2006, Rodriguez et al. 2006). We use bottom-up and top-down need and problem deconstruction to further understand the focus of the projects.

We cover intermediate or appropriate technology (Schumacher 1973), providing an effective yardstick for the student groups to evaluate whether technologies are suitable for subsistence marketplaces (Prahalad and Hammond 2002). We emphasize that appropriate technology does not necessarily mean primitive or less advanced. On the contrary, a quantum leap in technology may be required in subsistence contexts when compared to advanced economies (e.g., use of cell phones and wireless technology due to lack of infrastructure for landlines).

We ask students to read articles concerning the quality function deployment method, innovation processes, and design decomposition approaches (Hauser and Clausing 1988; Hargadon and Sutton 2000, Stone et al. 2000). Our objective is to teach students a way of mapping customer requirements that were developed during the fall semester and the immersion experience into meaningful and measurable engineering criteria or specifications.

Once these quantifiable and measurable attributes are defined, students have a documented list of measurable attributes that their designs should adhere to in preparation for the next stage of development that concerns concept generation and selection. During concept generation, brainstorming techniques, design decomposition (function diagrams), morphological analysis, and voting techniques are covered. We then ask students to go through two or three rounds of exercises focused on finding design solutions for subsistence marketplaces (usually, we choose arenas where a product that the students are not likely to be aware of already exists). Sources of design examples for subsistence marketplaces are available on the Internet (e.g., http://designthatmatters.com).

We enable modular concept generation by deconstructing a black-box model of the overall desired product functionality into sub-problems and sub-functions that collectively deliver the intended or desired overall product functionality. We accomplish this by identifying subsistence functions that can be grouped together and implemented through a single subsystem or module (Stone et al. 2000).

By identifying the modules that cater most effectively to critical subsistence needs, we can generate solution concepts for modules that simultaneously encapsulate subsistence-specific requirements and allow for product adjustability (and upgradeability) by consumers. This approach allows the development team to address important sub-functions that require special attention in subsistence marketplaces.

In concept generation, we found it helpful to ask student teams to search the Internet for products designed for unfamiliar contexts. These types of products are helpful in at least two respects: to study how customer needs were elicited in such contexts (Hannukainen and Holtta-Otto 2006), and as a source of innovation to use in subsistence marketplaces (Geschka 1986, Herstatt and von Hippel 1992). Such design contexts include products for extreme situations, such as assistive products for elderly and disabled customers, or for emergencies or disasters.

For example, the freeplay radio, originally designed and marketed for emergency applications, offers a solution to educate and broadcast information to entire villages that lack electrical power and cannot afford to buy batteries (Chick 1997). Children's toys are another useful source of innovation, with their ruggedness, simple and intuitive user interfaces (relevant for low-literate consumers), simplistic designs, and inexpensive materials (e.g., Kinkajou projectors; see http://designthatmatters.org).

During concept screening and selection, we propose a rating matrix to choose a single concept for further development based on a Pugh rating chart (Pugh 1991). A subsistence Pugh chart is similar to a traditional Pugh chart, where the alternative solution concepts are listed in the columns of the selection matrix and selection criteria are listed in the rows of the matrix. However, special attention is devoted to the selection criteria used in the chart (see Table 12.1 for a sample selection matrix). In this task, we develop a set of subsistence-specific selection criteria based on the type of product developed and the subsistence context addressed. Students also learn about the various prototyping techniques, including a thorough discussion of strengths and weakness of each technique for subsistence contexts (Ulrich and Eppinger 2007).

We introduce students to the world of materials and their general properties (Ashby and Johnson 2003), and learn various traditional material removal and forming processes, and particularly, plastics injection molding, using short instructional videos (SME 2003; SME 2004). Our main focus here is on manufacturing strategies and material-sourcing decisions as they relate to a particular subsistence context.

Local manufacturing is beneficial to both the enterprise and local community as it is cost effective and imparts new skills to local people. In addition to product design, it is also essential to consider servicing and maintenance issues that could potentially arise from new products. Issues in providing reliable maintenance for the products that become an integral part of subsistence individuals' lives include localized provision of service and supply of specific parts.

Table 12.1: Sample Selection Matrix

Table 12.1 lists selection criteria by category: marketplace fit, needs fit, constraints fit, and behavioral fit. Each criteria is rated according to bar code, automated voice with paper, paper-based with oral interactions, and mobile QR codes.

S.no	Category	Criteria	Bar Code	Automated Voice with Paper	Paper-Based with Oral Iterations	Mobile QR Codes
1		In line with existing norms, practices, and relationships	2	2	5	2
2	Marketplace Fit	Harnessing existing marketplace strengths	2	3	5	2
3		Addressing gaps in existing marketplace	2	3	5	3
4		Captures all business-relevant information	5	5	5	5
5	Needs Fit	Transmission of information along the chain	4	5	5	4
6		Positive impact on bottom line	5	5	5	5
7		Infrastructural constraints	4	4	5	4
8	Constraints Fit	Technological constraints	4	2	5	2
9		Human resource constraints	5	5	5	5
10		Investment constraints	2	4	5	2
11		Ease of adoption	2	4	5	3
12	Behavioral Fit	Ease of use	3	4	5	3
13		Incentive for adoption	3	3	4	3
		Total	43	49	64	43

We also cover the financial side of product development and production economics. We use a hands-on example of an Excel-based model for performing financial analysis and determining the financial and social return on investment for the project. Students learn about the notion of robustness using Taguchi's robust design methodology (Taguchi and Clausing 1990). At the concept development stage, students evaluate the robustness of their concept, and whether it will work in a variety of environments, for a variety of customers, and under conditions with variation anticipated in a particular subsistence context.

Throughout the semester, we aim to equip students with various required competencies and tools that they can apply to their projects. The rest of the semester focuses on analyzing case studies on design for subsistence marketplaces in more detail, as mentioned earlier.

Product Development Deliverables and Evaluation

The final deliverables of the group projects include a detailed business plan, a prototype, and an oral presentation. Intermediate deliverables are:

- Preliminary mission statements and project schedules (includes identifying major stakeholders, target markets, and major project milestones)

- Conceptual design (developing sketches of the most promising alternative solution concepts)

- Detailed design (detailed drawings, engineering specifications, material selection, and preliminary cost analysis, along with a written report and a midterm oral presentation)

- Financial modeling and manufacturing plan (break-even analysis and project financial feasibility analysis, including make/buy recommendations and local content decisions)

Intermediate deliverables are about two to three weeks apart to allow students time to apply the concepts discussed in class, obtain feedback, and make revisions. Members of the research team in India are also able to conduct additional market research at the detailed design stage to support the projects through preliminary concept testing.

Depending on the complexity of the product, and time and cost constraints, prototypes vary in comprehensiveness from a computer-aided design or a simulation model to a physical prototype. Physical prototypes range from a look-like or work-like prototype to a beta prototype. Final presentations are made in front of a diverse audience including corporate partners, other faculty, staff, and students. We evaluate the final presentation and written report based on multiple criteria: fulfillment of subsistence marketplace need(s), innovativeness and sustainability of the solution, attention to details and execution of the design, thoroughness of the manufacturing plan, comprehensiveness of the prototype, and coherence of the business plan.

Outcomes

In terms of the impact of the learning experience, in addition to prototypes and business plans that have met the criteria described above, student feedback has been extremely positive, with descriptions of the experience as being transformative or life-changing. Student recruitment has become easier as past students promote the course and speak to the value of the experience.

Organizational partners have also provided very positive feedback on the quality of the prototypes and business plans and our sponsors have been very engaged. One sponsor, a senior vice president at a large global food company, in the course of a trip to India, traveled to meet with the students at the end of their immersion experience to better understand the learning outcomes and to participate in the reflection process. Another sponsor, from a large global software company, was very appreciative of the interactions with students and the quality of the output and keen to learn about the insights gained from the course. Prototypes have also been taken to the next stage by some of our organizational partners, and elements of the business plan put in practice.

We are beginning to see organizational sponsors considering working models or using aspects of the business plan. In fact, we are increasingly seeking organizational sponsors who are likely to take the outcomes to the field. We have developed prospective case studies based on a number of the project reports for use in future classroom instruction, available through our web portal. These cases are unique in taking the marketplace orientation we described earlier and, rather than being retrospective, reflecting business solutions that could be carried out in the future.

Discussion

The pioneering nature of this course lends itself to some unique learning opportunities for students. Students have a full and firsthand experience of applying principles of new product development in a radically different context. They learn innovative ways of conducting market research to learn the needs of a unique customer segment and then apply this knowledge and information to develop new products that can function in a radically different context. It provides an opportunity to compare, contrast, and, therefore sharpen product development, marketing, management, and engineering skill sets for traditional marketplaces.

Therefore, this course is of great benefit to students who intend to work in any context as lessons learned for subsistence marketplaces, which can, in turn, be applied in other marketplaces. The course provides an opportunity to broaden one's perspective across cultural as well as literacy and resource barriers. Our ability to provide such a course is based on extensive experience in research, teaching, and social initiatives and a team composed of people from the subsistence contexts we study.

Our experience also speaks to the nature of product development in subsistence marketplaces. Our course is organized around understanding life circumstances of people living in poverty. In fact, we do not bring focus to the marketplace realm until about four weeks into the course. This is deliberate, emphasizing the need for students (and managers and researchers) to immerse themselves into a context that they usually cannot personally relate to and are not familiar with, that of subsistence. Most students (and managers and researchers) have not experienced the kind of poverty we focus on and are also very literate.

Thus, virtual immersion in subsistence contexts is the foundation of the course with actual immersion occurring during the international immersion experience. Most important perhaps, when compared to product development in relatively resource-rich contexts that managers can relate to, is the need for deep listening and understanding of customer needs. In resource-rich contexts, product designers are themselves customers in similar contexts. Issues, such as latent needs and cultural sensitivities, that managers are not familiar with, take on importance in subsistence marketplaces.

Additionally, several unique aspects must be carefully considered when developing products for subsistence marketplaces, many of which are related to the adage of doing more with less. Less expensive and more robust products that can withstand harsh operating conditions and misuse, with user-friendly interfaces for low levels of literacy, are key elements. Innovative solutions extend beyond the engineering design phase, to include many aspects of manufacturing and marketing as well in light of the lack of basic infrastructure assumed in developed contexts. Anticipating unconventional usage situations borne out of necessity is another important aspect of product design. In traditional marketplaces in developed economies, products have an established (and streamlined) approach to market, using established infrastructure for functions such as distribution and promotion.

In contrast, marketing activities in subsistence marketplaces from promotion to distribution represent significant challenges and must be considered during product development and not as an afterthought or sequentially after product design and development. Rather, these issues must be considered simultaneously with product design and development and be an integral part of a coherent, holistic development plan. Issues in various marketing functions include:

- market research (e.g., contextual product testing);

- promotion (social network mediated communications, visualization of customer benefits);

- distribution (developing partnerships and reaching fragmented rural locations);

- pricing (explicating the value proposition); and

- relationships with diverse organizations (Viswanathan et al. 2008; Sridharan and Viswanathan 2008).

Another important aspect of product development in subsistence marketplaces is in engaging subsistence communities at every stage in the design and development process, and not treating them solely as end consumers (Murcott 2007). Such an approach builds on immersion to understand life circumstances described above in maintaining continuous learning from people living in subsistence. It is essential to treat customers and communities as partners, enabling local entrepreneurship, improving education and health, and conserving resources.

Finally, we emphasize sustainable solutions that place personal and community welfare and the local environment front and center. Our nuanced approach emphasizes designing solutions that fit within the pre-existing marketplaces while carefully envisioning the role of business, in concert with governmental and nonprofit organizations, in enabling such marketplaces to move toward being economically, socially, and ecologically sustainable marketplaces. In this regard, we have argued that a focus on social good in a product-relevant sense should be a central aspect of business processes including product development (Viswanathan et al. 2009).

Our learning experience provides a platform that engages students and companies to create detailed insights about product development in subsistence marketplaces. We list a number of insights from juxtaposing the product development process in the subsistence context in the form of questions, as our learning is ongoing. These questions are tied to the projects and have emerged as we developed and executed this course:

- How should managers and researchers unfamiliar with subsistence educate themselves through immersion?

- How should market research be conducted as a basis for product development, promotion, distribution, and pricing?

- What should the product development process for subsistence marketplaces look like?

- How should interfaces be designed for low-literate subsistence consumers?

- How should the design process anticipate local manufacturing opportunities of the opportunity to incorporate small entrepreneurs into the value chain?

- How should existing infrastructure or lack of infrastructure be incorporated into the product development process?

- How should usage situations be envisioned in the product development process?

- How should products be designed at low cost while being of good quality and high reliability in hostile working conditions?

- How can conventional products be used as vehicles to improve welfare (e.g., nutritional additives in food)?

- How should packaging be ecologically friendly and sustain the local environment?

- How should product benefits be visualized and communicated to low-literate consumers?

Professional Responsibility Through Sustainable Global Businesses for Subsistence Marketplaces

This five-week module is an offshoot of the year-long class already described in this chapter that has been scaled to all the approximately 600 first-semester business undergraduates (see Table 12.2). It focuses on the twin issues of sustainability and poverty alleviation to highlight professional responsibility, and is organized around developing a sustainable business for a subsistence context.

We have framed it within a larger course on professional responsibility, aptly described as being about "me," "us," and "more than us," or self, profession (or organization or any other collective unit), and global society, with the emphasis of the latter on the important role that businesses can play in addressing global problems. Students participate in a poverty simulation, and analyze interviews and videos to understand subsistence contexts (see Table 12.2). Using a number of assignments and class discussions to understand subsistence and sustainability, groups generate product ideas, develop a short business plan, make presentations, and participate in a poster session.

The course is facilitated in small sections run by juniors and seniors previously trained through videos of the instructor covering topics, structured assignments, etc. Students analyze interviews of subsistence consumers and entrepreneurs before the first meeting, which involves either a poverty simulation described earlier, or a regular class, for logistical reasons. Regular class sessions are structured around a video-based introduction, allowing for a section leader to lead a discussion on the topic. A video-based lecture on poverty and low literacy in the US and India provides insights about low-literate, low-income consumers in the US and subsistence consumers and entrepreneurs in India.

In the second part of this same class session, students go through an immersion exercise with images and videos. Students in assigned groups are asked to write observations from scenes in subsistence marketplaces to identify unique characteristics of the larger context and needs of individuals and households. Subsequently, students use this exercise as a basis to generate product ideas at the end of the class.

In the ensuing week, students move from a general focus on understanding life circumstances in subsistence marketplaces to generating product ideas. Their next assignment is to analyze videos and further reflect on subsistence contexts, and then to generate additional product ideas that would serve subsistence consumers, emphasizing the need for solutions and for confronting challenges. This structure allows section leaders to serve as peer facilitators of the learning experience rather than teachers. In fact, what we emphasized both to section leaders during training and to students in the course is the general lack of answers to these problems and topics and the need for a collaborative learning environment.

After the first two weeks, we emphasize student presentations and group assignments. In the third class, a video-based lecture covers the example of one company involved in balancing people, planet, and profit by engaging in subsistence marketplaces, covering the needs served, products, competition, aspects of marketing, and performance metrics. We intersperse the slide presentation with video of some relevant material to bring the topic to life.

Table 12.2: Overview of Sustainable Businesses for Subsistence Marketplaces Module

Table 12.2 lists assignments preceding class sessions, the class sessions, their philosophical orientation, their substantive orientation, and their methodological orientation.

Assignments Preceding Sessions	Class Sessions	Philosophical Orientation	Substantive Orientation	Methodological Orientation
Analysis of interviews Reflections on simulation Analysis of videos	Session 1 and 2 - Poverty simulation Session 1 and 2 - Understanding subsistence marketplaces and envisioning solutions • Immersion exercise • Idea generation exercise* • Small group idea generation	Emphasis on envisioning a more sustainable global society as a central element of professional responsibility and associated challenges	Focus on understanding subsistence marketplaces	Bottom-up learning from interviews, simulation and videos
Presentation of product idea Write-up of part of business plan	Session 3 - Creating sustainable products for subsistence marketplaces • Presentation of product idea • Business plan elements generation exercise* • Small group discussion with emphasis on ecological issues	Designing solutions that incorporate larger vision including poverty alleviation and ecological sustainability and consider challenges Confronting challenges through a focus on core business functions and processes, such as product development Developing mission and code of ethics for organization to incorporate larger vision and detailed plans that reflect challenges and trade-offs	Solutions customized to subsistence marketplaces Organization designed for subsistence marketplaces	Project-based bottom-up learning Learning by doing and bottom-up learning

Presentation/write-up of business plan	Session 4 - Developing sustainable business plans for subsistence marketplaces	Confronting challenges through a focus on core business functions and processes	Solutions customized to subsistence marketplaces	Learning by doing
		Building on synergies and balancing trade-offs between different elements of sustainability	Organization designed for subsistence marketplaces	
		Balancing stakeholder perspectives		
Poster presentation	Session 5 - Poster session			

*Elements being designed for next offering of module.

In this class, we cover the topic of environmental sustainability, emphasizing the need for ecologically sustainable business solutions, and we show many specific product examples. Students are thus challenged to consider both people (living in poverty) and planet (by considering ecologically sustainable solutions). Such sequential treatment facilitates student learning and translation into their project as well. We encourage section leaders to stop the presentation at points that can facilitate discussion.

This part of the class is followed by group presentations, with time built in for questions and feedback from section leaders, and small group discussions. We structure the assignment to enable groups to cover relevant topics for their projects, such as needs served, and description of solutions. Again, the key here is to structure the class with a mix of listening and doing, with the important issues of content and administration covered by the instructor on video.

The next group assignment involves a written documentation of part of the business plan over the course of the week before Thanksgiving in the United States. We provide immediate feedback on the business plan through email to enable incorporation into revisions. The final class involves a video-based summary, linking the experience to broader themes, including sustainability and professional responsibility.

We emphasize the need to view a business in a broader context as well in terms of global problems that can be addressed and in terms of seeing beyond compartmentalized notions of profit, ecological good, and social good. Students make final presentations and then prepare for a poster session organized as a large public event a few days later, where they take the role of a startup company seeking investors.

The essence of the learning is for students to be able to integrate seemingly disparate notions of social good and ecological good into the notion of a business, thus, broadening the notion of what a business is for the realities of the 21st century under the umbrella notion of sustainability. In this regard, a typical student reaction goes something like, "Until now, I thought a business was about making money and nothing else." This five-week module includes a very condensed version of virtual immersion and the design of solutions.

Again, the emphasis has been on economically sustainable solutions reflective of a business perspective rather than an NGO; whereas the occasional student group may want to take on projects such as building hospitals or transportation systems and argue for economic viability from grants, we encourage self-contained products and economic sustainability, with the end user paying at least some and usually all of the final price.

Thus, we follow through on our philosophical orientation in moving beyond a broader vision for a business to confronting the challenges in implementing it. Students have come up with, or modified, interesting ideas that cover the gamut from eco-friendly, non-inflammable housing alternatives, to flooring material for hygiene in subsistence dwellings, and many iterations of water purification devices.

This module focuses on the subsistence context to bring out issues of sustainability, adopts a bottom-up orientation to students learning about the context and generating solutions, and highlights the central role of envisioning a better world and the role of business for a sustainable global society as well as the challenges that would need to be confronted. We are able to impart a significant early experience on a large scale, although we continue to develop the overall model and administrative support each year as an ongoing process.

With the right mix of structured tasks and educational materials available online, along with a motivated group of section leaders, and investment and administrative support for a larger course such as this on professional responsibility or on a related topic, we believe that the topic of sustainability can reach all business majors through such a modular approach. Note the first semester time slot, which emphasizes the importance of sustainability in the very first business course that students take and reaches them at a formative period in their business education, as they begin to learn about the program and the career that lies beyond.

As noted, we implement this course in small classes, using section leaders. The section leaders are typically juniors or seniors who have taken the course themselves in their first semester. We select them through an application and interview process. We conduct training sessions for section leaders in the previous semester, taking them through each aspect of the course and building a team dedicated to delivery of the learning experience. In recent go-arounds, we have converted this training into a formal course.

During the delivery of the 101 course (including this module), we schedule weekly meetings with section leaders. A number of issues are central here, foremost being the recognition that student section leaders are not teachers. Thus, we prepare very detailed teaching material needs, including video presentations by the instructor, teaching materials for specific classes, and in-class exercises. With experience, we have found the need to provide minute details to enable consistency among section leaders while also allowing for their creativity.

Whereas our experience with section leaders has been very positive, the occasional problems we face include the very busy schedules of section leaders and consequent inability to spend time focusing on the week-to-week tasks. We also find the need to create a very detailed organizational/procedural roadmap that lays out pathways of communications for different contingencies, such as attendance records or missed assignments. At a broader level, we need to constantly find solutions to the fundamental issue of placing a junior or senior in the role of facilitator—one who does not have the authority or experience to decide on issues that may arise in a classroom setting.

Through this early experience, we set the stage for junior- and senior-level courses that provide a further integrative experience. We have offered an experimental course for juniors and seniors on sustainability modeled around the graduate-level course described earlier. However, the challenge now is to create additional learning experiences as well as have sustainability percolate into other course offerings.

In more recent iterations of the course, we have used concepts developed from our year-long course to involve sponsor organizations and challenge students to develop a professional responsibility stakeholder engagement plan for introducing a new product in an emerging market. This approach provides for concepts that organizations are considering for actual launch as well as a closer alignment with topics of professional responsibility through a more tightly structured project experience.

Global Business Horizons

This course on Global Business Horizons for the Executive MBA program engenders an appreciation for the global challenges as well as opportunities that lie ahead and the important role that businesses can play in addressing these challenges. This course consists of two immersive and interactive modules organized around understanding global challenges and designing business solutions on the topics of poverty and environmental sustainability. The first module entitled Sustainable Businesses for Subsistence Marketplaces focuses on understanding subsistence marketplaces and designing business solutions for the four billion people living in poverty in the global marketplace. To develop understanding of subsistence marketplaces, we use exercises to enable participants to view the world from the eyes of subsistence consumers and entrepreneurs, facilitate bottom-up understanding generated by participants, and provide insights from extensive research. To envision solutions for subsistence marketplaces, we use group assignments as well as a project involving the development of a solution and a business plan to serve a need. The second module entitled Sustainable Businesses Enterprises explores current challenges and opportunities facing firms in the area of environmental sustainability. Through interactive exercises and discussions and a project, we examine topics such as unsustainable consumer behavior, sustainable product design, and sustainable supply chains, and develop a sustainable business plan. Tying the two modules together is the arena of emerging markets with poverty alleviation, upward mobility, and burgeoning middle-class segments, and associated issues of consumption and sustainability.

Engineering for Global Development

This course for first-semester undergraduate engineering students focuses on developing products to serve the needs of those living in low-income communities, domestically and internationally. Rather than begin with a predetermined technology, this course teaches students to be bottom-up in beginning with life circumstances and cultural issues and then using such understanding to design engineering solutions.

First-year engineering students are introduced to concepts of product development and designing for unfamiliar concepts in order to give them a global perspective where people's needs are not consistent with their own. They develop an understanding of subsistence marketplaces, design solutions, and develop brief business plans. As they progress through the engineering curriculum, this concept provides them with a wider perspective of the world and their potential future within it.

Outcomes

The year-long course has been extremely well-received by students, partially reflected by extremely high evaluations, and more fully captured by word of mouth and unsolicited comments that simply describe the course as life-changing or transformative, no less. Here are a few brief quotes from students who have gone through the course:

> The immersion trip was an incredible experience—a chance to see business at its best. Interacting with consumers, entrepreneurs, and nonprofit workers helped me to understand how to design products and programs for maximum impact. I was amazed at the resourcefulness and creativity I witnessed on the trip.

> The trip to India is the capstone to my MBA experience. In India, I was able to take the knowledge gathered in the classroom and apply it in a context of one of the most important markets in the near future: subsistence marketplaces. Our project team includes engineers, industrial designers, and MBAs. The challenge of making a multi-disciplinary solution to real-world problems in subsistence markets has been the best project that I have been involved with in my graduate school career.

The impact of the year-long course on subsistence marketplaces is evident at the university and is used as a model of interdisciplinary, integrated learning experiences. Businesses and social enterprises that sponsor our class projects and receive detailed prototypes and business plans at the end of the course are also impacted by our teaching and have provided consistently positive feedback. We are also beginning to see outcomes being put into practice or being moved to the next stage of development by some of our sponsors (e.g., working models of prototypes). Prospective instructional cases are being developed out of several reports, examining possible products that do not currently exist.

We have similarly received very positive feedback on the module for first-year undergraduates, as reflected from feedback from both section leaders and students and also in the quality of the work presented in project reports and poster sessions, the latter having received positive feedback from the larger community that attends. Students come up with innovative ideas and attempt to develop a business plan that addresses economic, ecological and social sustainability. Similarly, all our other courses have received very positive feedback and affected actual practice in some instances (e.g., course projects on environmental sustainability).

Philosophical, Substantive, and Methodological Orientations

We present the foundational principles of our approach in a framework for educational endeavors on management and sustainability, covering philosophical, substantive, and methodological elements (see Figure 12.1). Philosophically, our approach is very much in line with "envisioning a better world." However, we jointly emphasize understanding the challenges that lie ahead, thus moving beyond "talking the talk" to "walking the walk." We combine the central role of envisioning a better world with an approach that lays out the challenges in getting there.

Thus, our vision is not left at an abstract level of discussion and accepted unquestioningly. Rather, we carefully evaluate the challenges associated with implementing the vision, with an emphasis on practicing sustainability. In tune with this practical emphasis, our approach is interdisciplinary in a very broad sense—going beyond areas of business to engineering, design, and other technical areas, as well as international, and providing an integrative learning experience. Our offerings all culminate in business solutions that are economically sustainable in addition to other forms of sustainability. Our focus is on core business processes and solutions through deliverables, such as product design and business plan development.

Thus, we treat subsistence contexts and issues of sustainability as being central to the business rather than a peripheral activity, confronting central challenges and moving beyond the abstract visioning level. Our approach is consistent with Dart (2008), who makes a case for addressing issues of poverty centrally in management education. Central to challenges is understanding different stakeholder perspectives, a feature of our offerings (please also see Reade, Todd, Osland, & Osland, 2008).

Substantively, we began with a sharp focus on subsistence marketplaces, thus using the most resource-constrained and ecologically-affected circumstances as our laboratory and providing a distinct window to sustainability in management education in general. By doing so, we emphasize the people dimension and highlight the interlinkage with the planet dimension of sustainability. Thus, we construe sustainability in a broad sense, setting up explicit considerations, synergies, and trade-offs between people and planet elements.

Methodologically, we adopt a bottom-up orientation in executing the courses— from learning mindsets, to research, to assignments and the nature and design of solutions. We use the dictionary meaning of bottom-up—"an approach to a problem that begins with details and works up to the highest conceptual level." Rather than emphasize top-down delivery of knowledge and concepts, we adopt a bottom-up discovery from "data."

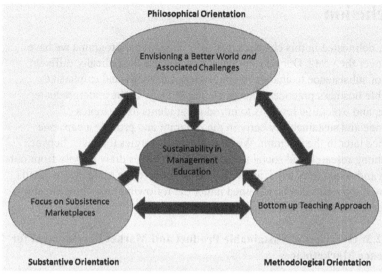

Figure 12.1: Philosophical, Substantive, and Methodological Elements of Educational Endeavors on Management and Sustainability.

The topic of sustainability is most conducive to such an orientation, creating a true discovery process in the classroom. This orientation is also implemented through such means as projects and assignments. In terms of learning, we begin with the stakeholders often neglected in top-down approaches, such as poor consumers and entrepreneurs, through reading interviews and participating in simulations. We also begin with learning from our own experiences as consumers, such as in the arena of unsustainable consumption.

This learning mindset also applies to issues such as the meaning of sustainability. Rather than accept top-down definitions, students are encouraged to understand sustainability in terms of elements they see and how these elements interact. The bottom-up research mindset emphasizes speaking to customers, including impoverished people, in the course about subsistence marketplaces, through qualitative interviews, observations, and virtual and actual immersion. Moreover, such research is conducted with a mutual learning mindset acknowledging the expertise of respondents in surviving in subsistence. The idea is to create solutions that resonate at this level to the extent possible, and are thus socially sustainable as well.

Finally, in terms of designing solutions, the focus is very much on incorporating aspects that "sustain" for the communities who would use the product. Thus, this approach comes full circle in terms of a bottom-up orientation. It also leads to an aggregation of bottom-up insights in a way that leads to unique solutions.

Conclusion

We have delineated in this chapter a series of educational programs we have created over the years. Our educational initiatives use the radically different context of subsistence to challenge conventional thinking and emphasize sustainable business practices. Our curricular strategy at the undergraduate, graduate, and executive levels is to introduce students to the topics of subsistence and sustainability early in the program and provide a capstone experience later in the program. We reiterate the synergies that exist between our teaching, research and social initiatives. Our courses draw heavily from our research and social initiatives, and in turn contribute to the same. More details regarding the courses can be obtained under the following link: (http://business. illinois.edu/subsistence/teaching/)

Table 12.3: Overview of Sustainable Product and Market Development for Subsistence Marketplaces

Table 12.3 provides an overview of the class session activities for the course. For each session activity, the table provides the philosophical orientation, substantive orientation, and methodological orientation.

Class Sessions	Philosophical Orientation	Substantive Orientation	Methodological Orientation
Fall Semester *Virtual Immersion* • Week 1 - Poverty simulation • Weeks 2-4 - Analysis of interviews and videos • Week 2 - First person summaries and discussions • Week 3 - Models of poverty • Week 4 - Models of needs, products, and markets • Week 5 - Critiques of papers	Course introduction with emphasis on envisioning a better world and understanding related challenges	Focus on subsistence marketplaces and a global view of sustainability	Bottom-up learning from interviews, videos, and simulation to derive conceptual models Classroom as space for learning without "expert" view
Fall Semester *Emersion* 6 weeks of emersion of ideas and concepts unique to subsistence marketplaces • Cases from Prahalad (2005) • Guest speakers – entrepreneurs, technologists, social workers	Role of vision and values in organizational strategies and associated challenges with elements of business as key points of analysis Balancing different stakeholder perspectives Synergies and trade-offs between economic, social, and environmental sustainability	Focus on organizations working in subsistence marketplaces – vision and challenges	Learning from examples and case studies rather than beginning with traditional concepts Implicit comparison and contrast with existing concepts emerging from approach

Fall Semester Group Project	Role of vision and associated challenges for organizational sponsors	Solutions focused on subsistence marketplaces	Open-ended generation of needs and ideas
• Group formation for projects with commercial or social enterprises • Generation and screening product ideas • Market research plan for family of ideas			Bottom-up market research plan through unstructured interviews
Winter International Immersion Experience	Emphasis on individual and community welfare	Actual immersion in subsistence marketplaces	Unstructured interactions to facilitate bottom-up learning
• Broader immersion in subsistence marketplaces through first-hand observation of the influences of poverty, literacy, and culture • Individual and group interactions in urban and rural settings; observations in urban and rural settings • Market research for projects Individual and group interviews in rural and urban settings • Discussions with company sponsors regarding projects • Learning about a diverse set of organizations and their initiatives in subsistence marketplaces	Interaction with organizations that explicitly incorporate social values	Learning from subsistence marketplaces Learning from commercial and social organizations serving subsistence marketplaces	Bottom–up research methods to learn from and then design solutions for Communication on an equal plane with subsistence consumers and entrepreneurs with mindset of mutual learning Bottom-up learning from field examples
Spring Semester Product Design and Business Plan Development	Explicit incorporation of values into all elements of design and business plan	Solutions designed based on learning from subsistence marketplaces	Contextualized product design and business plan development processes based on bottom-up learning
• Concept generation and evaluation • Conceptual Design, Prototyping and Testing • Business Plan Development	Confronting challenges through a focus on core business functions and processes, such as product development rather than as peripheral area for business to pay attention to Balancing different stakeholder perspectives		

Appendix 12.1: Overview of Global Business Horizons—Sustainable Businesses for Subsistence Marketplaces

Assignments

- Analysis of interviews / videos
- Poverty simulation
- Live interactions with subsistence consumers / entrepreneurs
- Case analyses
- Product idea generation
- Development of business plan

Sessions

- Understanding subsistence marketplaces
  o Virtual immersion—understanding context and needs
  o Poverty simulation
- Designing Solutions for Subsistence Marketplaces
  o Case analysis
  o Virtual immersion—generating ideas
  o Product innovations for subsistence marketplaces
- Developing Business Plans for Subsistence Marketplaces
  o Case analysis
  o Exercises—generating aspects of business plan
  o Marketing and business model innovations for subsistence marketplaces
  o Understanding emerging middle-class markets
- Final Presentation and Report

Appendix 12.2: Overview of Engineering for Global Development

Week 1 Monday

- Orientation/Introduction to the Course
- Group Formation Exercises
- Poverty Simulation

Week 1 Wednesday

- Understanding the Subsistence Context—Individuals, Groups, and Society
- Analysis and Profile of Interviews and Videos
- Developing Conceptual Models of Poverty

Week 2 Monday

- Understanding the Subsistence Context—Local environments
- Analysis and Profile of Interviews and Videos
- Developing Conceptual Models of Ecology and Poverty

Week 2 Wednesday

- Understanding the Subsistence Context
- Products and Markets
- Analysis of Interviews and Videos
- Developing Models of Needs, Products, and Markets

Week 3 Monday

- Understanding the Subsistence Context—Summary
- Comparison and Contrast of Literacy and Poverty in the US versus India
- Analysis of Readings

Week 3 Wednesday

- Product Design Primer
- Reading
- Group Projects—Idea Generation

Week 4 Monday

- Group Projects—Idea Generation
- Reading

Week 4 Wednesday

- Group Projects—Idea Screening and Evaluation

Week 5 Monday

- Group Presentation of Idea Screening and Evaluation
- Group Projects—Concept Generation

Week 5 Wednesday

- Group Projects—Concept Generation and Evaluation

Week 6 Monday

- Concept generation and selection

Week 6 Wednesday

- Customer needs and engineering specs
- Student presentation of criteria and narrower set of concepts
- Assignment to develop detailed design/specs
- Reading

Week 7 Monday & Wednesday

- Prototyping

Week 8 Monday & Wednesday

- Business plan development/Prototyping

Week 9 Monday & Wednesday

- Business plan development/Prototyping

Week 10 Monday

- Final Presentations

Appendix 12.3: Outline of Sustainable Business Plan

This is an excerpt from the business plan outline for the year-long course on Sustainable Product and Market Development for Subsistence Marketplaces. The business plan for the Sustainable Marketing Enterprises course is largely similar.

Executive Summary (Synopsis and major aspects of the business plan)

    I. Situation Analysis
        A. Internal Strengths and Weaknesses (including strengths and weaknesses in the arenas of sustainability and subsistence)
        B. External Opportunities and Threats (including ecological issues, such as depletion of natural resources, and challenges in subsistence marketplaces)
          a. Field research and learning
          b. Macro environment
          c. Market (for product)—Size and growth potential

    d. Competition
    e. Customer information—Profile, benefits to customers, needs served, segments

II. Mission/Objectives in terms of Profits, People, and Planet

III. Field Research and Product Development
  A. Discussion of learning from virtual immersion and emersion
  B. Description of idea generation and screening—Discussion of process and outcomes and appendix of matrix
  C. Market Research
    a. Detailed discussion of planned market research method and findings
    b. Detailed appendix with field notes, images, and video
  D. Learning and Reflection from Field Research
    a. Discussion of broader insights about consumer behavior based on Market research
    b. Learning from the Fall semester
  E. Concept generation and evaluation
    a. Focused generation of concepts
    b. Evaluation
  F. Technical specifications and Detailed Drawings
  G. Prototype

IV. Marketing Strategy
  A. Target Market Selection—Rationale based on market research and consumer behavior
  B. Sustainable Marketing Mix (Sustainable Product design or redesign with life cycle analysis, Sustainable value chain, Designing and communicating a sustainable value proposition)

V. Action Plans
  A. Targeting and Positioning Statement Including Sustainability Issues
  B. Sustainable Product Design
  C. Sustainable Value Chain
  D. Design of the Value Proposition
  E. Communication of the Value Proposition
  F. Manufacturing Plan, Product Forecast and Launch Schedule
  G. Financial Forecast
  H. Ecological (Planet) Impact Forecast
  I. Societal (People) Impact Forecast

VI. Implementation, Controls, and Evaluation
  A. Measures of performance—meeting triple bottom lines
  B. Monitoring and evaluating performance on multiple dimensions

References

Apple, L. and D. Vanier. 1988. Product development: An assessment of educational resources. Journal of Product Innovation Management 5 (1): 70-75.

Ashby, M. and K. Johnson. 2003. The art of materials selection. Materials Today, December, 24-35.

Cardozo, R., W. Durfee, A. Ardichvili, C. Adams, A. Erdman, M. Hoey, P. Iaizzo, D. Mallick, A. Bar-Cohen, R. Beachy, and A. Johnson. 2002. Perspective: Experiential education in new product design and business development. Journal of Product Innovation Management 19 (1): 4-17.

Chick, A. 1997. The 'freeplay' radio. Journal of Sustainable Product Design 1: 53-56.

Dart, R. (2008). A commentary on "piercing the bubble"737. Journal of Management Education, 32(6), 731-737.

Donaldson, K. 2006. Product design in less industrialized economies: constraints and opportunities in Kenya. Research in Engineering Design 17 (3): 135-55.

Ehrenreich, B. 2002. Nickel and dimed. New York: Henry Holt.

Eppinger, S. and M. Kressy. 2002. Interdisciplinary product development education at MIT and RISD. Design Management Journal 13 (2): 58-61.

Geschka, H. 1986. From experience creativity workshops in product innovation. Journal of Product Innovation Management 3 (1): 48-56.

Giacalone, R. A., & Thompson, K. R. (2006). Business ethics and social responsibility education: Shifting the worldview. Academy of Management Learning & Education, 5(3), 266-277.

Green, M., J. Linsey, C. Seepersad, K. Wood, and D. Jensen. 2006. Frontier design: A product usage context method. Proceedings of the ASME Design Engineering Technical Conference. Philadelphia, PA: Paper Number: DETC/ DFM 2006-99608.

Hannukainen, P. and K. Holtta-Otto. 2006. Identifying customer needs—disabled persons as lead users. Proceedings of the ASME Design Engineering Technical Conference. Philadelphia, PA: Paper Number: DETC/DFM 2006-99043.

Hargadon, A. and R. Sutton. 2000. Building an innovation factory. Harvard Business Review, 78 (3): 157-66.

Hauser, J. and D. Clausing. 1988. The house of quality. Harvard Business Review 66 (3): 63-73.

Herstatt, C. and Eric von Hippel 1992. From experience: Developing new product concepts via the lead user method: A case study in a "low tech" field". Journal of Product Innovation Management 9 (3): 213-21.

Horan, J. 2004. The one page business plan. Berkley, CA: The One Page Business Plan Company.

Murcott, S. 2007. Co-evolutionary design for development: Influences shaping engineering design and implementation in Nepal and the global village. Journal of International Development 19 (1): 123-44.

Prahalad, C. (2005). The Fortune at the Bottom of the Pyramid: Eradicating Poverty through Profits. Upper Saddle River, NJ: Wharton School Publishing.

Prahalad, C. K. and A. Hammond. 2002. Serving the world's poor profitably. Harvard Business Review, 80 (9): 48-57.

Prahalad, C. K. 2005. The fortune at the bottom of the pyramid: Eradicating poverty through profits. Upper Saddle River, NJ: Wharton School Publishing.

Pugh, P. 1991. Total design: Integrated methods for successful product engineering. NY: Addison-Wesley.

Reade, C., Todd, A. M., Osland, A., & Osland, J. (2008). Poverty and the multiple stakeholder challenge for global leaders. Journal of Management Education, 32(6), 820-840.

Rodriguez, J., J. Diehl, and H. Chistiaans. 2006. Gaining insight into unfamiliar contexts: A design toolbox as input for using role-play techniques. Interacting with Computers 18 (5): 956-76.

Sahlman, W. 1997. How to write a great business plan. Harvard Business Review 75 (4): 98-08.

Schumacher, E. F. 1973. Small is beautiful: Economics as if people mattered. London: Blond & Briggs.

Society of Manufacturing Engineers (SME) 2004. Fundamental Manufacturing Processes Sampler DVD.

Society of Manufacturing Engineers (SME) 2003. Plastic Injection Molding DVD.

Sridharan, S. and M. Viswanathan. 2008. Marketing in subsistence marketplaces: consumption and entrepreneurship in a south Indian context. Journal of Consumer Marketing 25 (7): 455-62.

Stone, R., K. Wood, and R. Crawford. 2000. A heuristic method for identifying modules for product architectures. Design Studies 21 (1): 5-31.

Taguchi, J. and D. Clausing. 1990. Robust quality. Harvard Business Review 68 (1): 65-75.

Tybout, J. 2000. Manufacturing firms in developing countries: how well do they do, and why? Journal of Economic Literature 38(1): 11-44.

Ulrich, K. and S. Eppinger. 2007. Product Design and Development. (4th ed.). NY: Irvin/McGraw-Hill.

Viswanathan, M., J. Rosa. and J. Harris. 2005. Decision-Making and Coping by Functionally Illiterate Consumers and Some Implications for Marketing Management. Journal of Marketing, 69(1): 15-31.

Viswanathan, M. 2007. Understanding product and market interactions in subsistence marketplaces: A study in south India. In: Product and Market Development for Subsistence Marketplaces: Consumption and Entrepreneurship Beyond Literacy and Resource Barriers, (Advances in International Management Series), Joseph Cheng and Michael Hitt (Eds.), 21-57. NY: Elsevier.

Viswanathan, M. and J. Rosa 2007. Product and market development for subsistence marketplaces: Consumption and entrepreneurship beyond literacy and resource barriers. In: Product and Market Development for Subsistence Marketplaces: Consumption and Entrepreneurship Beyond Literacy and Resource Barriers (Advances in International Management Series), Joseph Cheng and Michael Hitt (Eds.), 1-17. NY: Elsevier.

Viswanathan, M., S. Gajendiran, and R. Venkatesan. 2008. Enabling Consumer and Entrepreneurial Literacy in Subsistence Marketplaces. The Netherlands: Springer.

Viswanathan, M. and S. Sridharan 2009. From subsistence marketplaces to sustainable marketplaces: A bottom-up perspective of the role of business in poverty Alleviation. Ivey Business Journal, March/April.

Viswanathan, M., A. Seth, R. Gau, and A. Chaturvedi. 2009. Internalizing social good into business processes in subsistence marketplaces: The sustainable market orientation. Journal of Macromarketing. 29 (4): 406-425.

Chapter 13

Social Initiatives in Subsistence Marketplaces: The Marketplace Literacy Program[32]

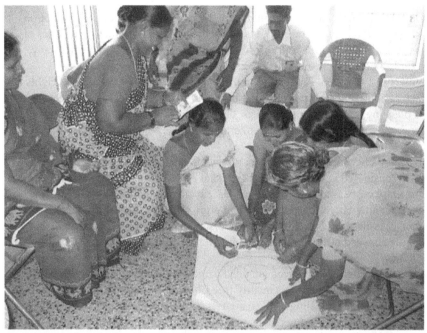

Image 13.01: An exercise in marketplace literacy education, Tamil Nadu, India.
Photograph courtesy of Marketplace Literacy Communities, India, and Marketplace
Literacy Project, USA.

---

[32] This chapter includes material adapted from the following previously published works:

Viswanathan, Madhubalan, Srinivas Sridharan, Roland Gau, and Robin Ritchie (2009) "Designing Marketplace Literacy Education in Resource-Constrained Contexts: Implications for Public Policy and Marketing," Journal of Public Policy and Marketing, 28 (1), 85–94. DOI: 10.1509/jppm.28.1.85

Viswanathan, Madhubalan, S. Gajendiran, and R. Venkatesan (2008), "Understanding and Enabling Marketplace Literacy in Subsistence Contexts: The Development of a Consumer and Entrepreneurial Literacy Educational Program in South India," International Journal of Educational Development, 28 (3), 300-19. DOI: 10.1016/j.ijedudev.2007.05.004

In this chapter, we discuss an educational program on marketplace literacy aimed at people living in subsistence. An exemplar of social initiatives in subsistence marketplaces, this initiative also represents an illustration of the bottom-up approach described in this book. The program aims to build life skills in the economic realm. Whereas there has been considerable attention on microfinance (Hertz-Bunzl, 2006; Stix, 1997), our focus on enabling generic skills about the marketplace complements these important efforts.

Our research provided rich insights into the lives and marketplace interactions of low-literate, low-income buyers and sellers. There were many examples of innovative practices that our informants educated us about along with many pitfalls where people are vulnerable and suffer negative consequences as buyers and as sellers. Vulnerabilities ranged from lack of awareness of rights to lack of confidence or lack of skills for day-to-day consumer tasks. Tasks such as planning, creating shopping lists, checking prices, checking products, or requesting a bill were often not undertaken.

Trade-offs between get and give components of an exchange were often not fully considered in terms of travel time and other non-monetary or indirect monetary costs. Similarly, as sellers, people did not analyze the marketplace or consider alternatives before starting enterprises. Lack of clear accounting was another issue, as was lack of a full understanding of the costs of doing business. People also had difficulty understanding return on investment.

As buyers, effective practices included bargaining, checking weights, checking prices, and checking product quality (see Chapter 4). As sellers, effective practices included dealing with customers in difficult situations, responding to demands from customers, managing word of mouth among customers, and researching the marketplace.

These innovative practices, which represent adaptation to the adverse conditions of subsistence marketplaces, informed the design of the educational program as much as the vulnerabilities. Our research enabled us to develop a detailed list of issues that people face as buyers and as sellers, as well as a deeper understanding of life in the economic realm.

Implications for Marketplace Literacy Education

The research was invaluable in educating us on a wide range of issues. A striking issue is the complex social environment in which marketplace exchanges occur, with myriad one-to-one interactions. Individuals seek help from people on the street, develop relationships with shops, and engage in constant conversations with other buyers and sellers. Skills, such as communication through spoken language, verbal counting, or bargaining, develop through these interactions as well as through experience as vendors, despite low levels of literacy. Central to the development of any educational program is the need to leverage these existing skill sets in the social domain.

Another issue relates to buyers and sellers in the environment of one-to-one interactions being two sides of the same coin. This is in contrast to the customer-to-large-corporation interaction in western countries. Skills associated with being a buyer versus a seller are mutually reinforcing. Nevertheless, we found some sellers with little experience as buyers and buyers with no experience as sellers.

Learning how to assess the value of an exchange as a buyer can lead to learning how to provide value as a seller. Many people make a living by being sellers. Moreover, buyers and small sellers share similar life circumstances and learn from each other's roles about the marketplace at large through one-to-one interactions. Marketplace literacy education that addresses both sides of the exchange can capitalize on their mutually reinforcing nature.

Another issue that was apparent from our research was the transformational effect that practical adult education in the marketplace realm could have on people. Some of the individuals we interviewed had practically no marketplace skills for much of their adult life. Yet the effect of enrolling in an adult literacy program that addressed the consumer realm was extraordinary in enabling self-confidence in the shopping realm, leading to bargaining, switching, questioning shopkeepers, and so on.

Our research provided a basis from which to develop an educational program that would benefit people living in subsistence. The next sections describe the development and implementation of the consumer and entrepreneurial literacy educational program.

Marketplace Literacy Education

Our research gave us a deep appreciation of the pre-existing traditions of subsistence marketplaces: embedded, symbiotic, and long-standing ecosystems of equally poor consumers and sellers who demonstrate both significant vulnerabilities and strengths. This led us to focus on an educational goal of facilitating the development of marketplace literacy in subsistence individuals.

Although market access (Prahalad, 2005) and financial resources, such as microcredit (Yunus and Yusus, 1998), have been identified as two core elements that subsistence individuals need for marketplace participation, we believe that marketplace literacy is a third and complementary element that can lead to successful use of the first two. Marketplace literacy exists at three levels of abstraction. The lowest level is vocational or occupational and consumer skills acquired through everyday experience or very basic training and resulting in learned behaviors (e.g., completing a purchase or engaging in specific trades). This level should be distinguished from higher levels of marketplace literacy, where procedural and conceptual marketplace knowledge develops.

The distinction is commonly made between knowledge and skills, which relates to performance of specific tasks on dimensions such as accuracy. Although this distinction is not a clear one due to such factors as the interactions between knowledge and skills, it is useful in this context to differentiate the lowest level of marketplace literacy from higher levels. Skills have been defined as "goal-directed, well-organized behavior that is acquired through practice and performed with economy of effort" (Proctor and Dutta, p. 18). The lowest level of marketplace literacy includes vocational elements required for workplace performance, often resulting from "engagement in everyday, goal-directed activity" (Billett, 1998, p.258).

A higher level is tactical or procedural knowledge as consumers and as entrepreneurs (e.g., how to design or promote a product, how to find a discount). The highest level of abstraction is conceptual/strategic marketplace knowledge, or "know-why" (e.g., how/why to seek value in exchanges, how/why marketplace exchanges work, how/why products and technologies evolve, why customer orientation is important, how a business should be chosen for start-up).

Procedural knowledge has been argued to be tied to specific types of problems and not widely generalizable and defined as the "ability to execute action sequences to solve problems" (Rittle-Johnson et al., 2001, p. 346). Conceptual knowledge has been argued to be generalizable and defined as "implicit or explicit understanding of the principles that govern a domain and of the interrelations between units of knowledge in a domain" (Rittle-Johnson et al., 2001, p. 346-47). Though procedural/tactical and conceptual/strategic levels of marketplace literacy are distinct, an iterative process leads to the development of both procedural and conceptual knowledge, similar to findings in the educational psychology literature (e.g., Rittle-Johnson et al., 2001).

Our review of existing entrepreneurial development and adult literacy programs uncovered many programs that addressed vocational skills (Bennell and Segerstrom, 1998; Johanson and Adams, 2004; Oxenham et al, 2002; Singh, 2005), related to the lowest level of marketplace literacy described a few paragraphs earlier, in addition to programs that addressed basic literacy, i.e., reading and counting skills. However, we found few programs that focused on imparting business skills and addressing business know-how-oriented tasks that relate to procedural/tactical marketplace literacy (e.g., how to keep accounts, how to promote a product), and none that focused on conceptual/strategic marketplace literacy (which we will refer to as know-why).

In other words, many programs focused on vocational skills, fewer on procedural/tactical marketplace knowledge, and none on conceptual/strategic marketplace knowledge or know-why. The reasons for this are unclear, but, given the concrete orientations and abstracting difficulties of low-literate people (Luria, 1976; Viswanathan et al., 2005), a choice of education focusing on a high level of abstraction may seem counterintuitive to many. Yet in spite of this, achieving some degree of know-why offers the greatest potential to envision different realities and develop lifelong learning and empowerment among subsistence consumers.

For example, a poor woman skilled in cooking may decide to open an eatery after being trained on how to start a business. However, with an understanding of know-why, she would have the ability to expand her horizons and sell different foods in different locations, or even become a supplier to other, larger restaurants. Or, she may envision a different enterprise altogether. Such ability to envision beyond the immediate is likely to be a critical determinant of the survival of micro-enterprises in subsistence populations, faced as they are with significant impediments associated with life in poverty. With this in mind, we designed a marketplace educational program that began with know-how as the basis for gaining consumer and entrepreneurial literacy.

Development of the Marketplace Literacy Educational Program

Using the research as a basis, we developed a curriculum for an educational program in entrepreneurial and consumer literacy for low-literate, low-income people. The curriculum grew out of extensive discussions of learning goals, content to be covered, and methods for conveying the content. Our team drew from experience in business education, vast experience in developmental work in low-income communities, and our own extensive research.

These three sources of knowledge were continually used to develop a research-based educational program that addressed the realities that subsistence individuals negotiated on a day-to-day basis. A key here was to avoid imposing "known solutions" from the outside; instead, we used our immersive research and data that was largely based on the words of our informants to design a program that combined relevant broader concepts with localized knowledge.

Overview

The method we employed in developing an educational program involved several phases. In the first phase, we undertook a search and review of educational materials and programs for both customers and sellers. Two team members had direct experience and involvement in an entrepreneurial development program targeted to low-literate, low-income women, and an adult literacy program. Entrepreneurial development programs cover such topics as understanding costs, understanding product design, making safe and clean products, packaging, delivering customer service, and determining fair pricing.

Such training empowers people to explore options for starting a business and gives them the confidence and basic skill sets to be successful. Adult literacy programs may also address day-to-day functional skills that people need in their roles as customers, in addition to focusing on basic reading and counting skills. As discussed, our research suggests that such classes can be transformational experiences that open the door to an altogether different existence where people are aware of their rights as customers, are willing to bargain and argue, and are willing to take action against unfair practices.

In the second phase, we developed the educational program and materials. As discussed, our approach was unique in beginning with the know-why and then moving to the know-how, enabling coverage of abstract concepts by leveraging the social skills that people bring to the program and relating the concepts back to their experiences. Thus, our approach runs counter to traditional approaches that are more concrete in orientation, consistent with the difficulties that low-literate people may have with abstract thinking (Luria, 1976; Viswanathan et al., 2005). However, our approach aims to provide deeper understanding of the marketplace and can enable people to be aware of the choices available to them and potentially place themselves on a path to lifelong learning.

In this phase we used generic business principles from contemporary education, yet customized it and generated new educational material that fit the unique context, using our research as a basis. Rather than a one-size-of-business-education-fits-all-contexts approach, our aim was to combine relevant business principles with localized research. Such an approach allows for modifications and extensions of existing business principles as well as the development of new business principles. We drew a variety of concepts and approaches from the business literature, a few of which are cited here for illustrative purposes (Kotler, 2003; Howard and Sheth, 1969; Porter, 1998; Blackwell, Miniard and Engel, 2001; Monroe, 2002).

The third phase involved first piloting the educational program and then offering it regularly for purposes of assessment, and for making further modifications as needed. In this phase, observations and discussions were used to gauge responses to aspects of the educational program. Both urban and rural settings were chosen to deliver the program and customize it. We used follow-up sessions a few months after each program to evaluate its impact on people's experiences as buyers and sellers.

Development of Curriculum and Instructional Methods

The process of developing the educational curriculum and materials began a year after we began to interview buyers and sellers. Our research provided a rich basis, in terms of concepts as well as concrete examples, to design the content and instructional methods. In terms of curriculum development, we considered four levels: learning goals, topics, instructional methods, and instructional material. Learning goals referred to broad educational objectives of professionalism and ethics, consumer literacy, and entrepreneurial literacy.

We listed, in detail, topics within these learning goals. Entrepreneurial literacy covered broad areas such as the basics of marketplace exchanges and philosophies of conducting a business and specific functions within business such as marketing and finance and sub-functions, e.g., product design, pricing, promotion, and distribution within marketing. Through top-down listing of topics and concepts and bottom-up considerations from data and experience, these four levels of curriculum development were explicated.

We took several issues into consideration in designing instructional methods and materials, given our target audience. The group of people who typically live in the same neighborhood and go through the educational program together can be construed as a self-help group that provides a sample set of customers, a source of ideas, financial resource, and a source for potential business partners.

Our pedagogical methods were innovative and built on the social skills and ability with spoken language that participants possessed to varying degrees, combining games and tasks and transferring home management skills to management elsewhere. We modified and conveyed concepts at a common-sense one-to-one level to enable the audience to relate to the idea. The aim was not to convey a concept for its own sake as much as to convey useful, understandable concepts that are relevant to the reality that participants face. Thus, we tempered concepts and their presentation by the practical constraints people faced.

For instance, people may live in the here and now and focus on a skill they possess that they may have acquired growing up, such as cooking. Through our educational program, we tried to broaden their approach to consider possibilities such as variations in product offerings or location. Our educational goal was to shift thinking from the very specific and immediate to the somewhat less specific, more general, through the iterative process of covering business concepts and examples.

In this regard, some researchers have argued that low literacy leads to living in the here and now, or the immediate, and thinking in situational, concrete, graphic terms (Luria, 1976; Viswanathan, Rosa, and Harris, 2005). Therefore, notions and abstractions have to be introduced carefully to broaden situational thinking incrementally.

This exercise in curriculum development was, in one sense, to seek the meeting point between relevant business concepts in a top-down approach, with know-how that addressed reality on the ground in a bottom-up approach. This required filtering business education to its very essence to convey the core topics, and perhaps, more importantly, the approaches to thinking in the domain of the marketplace in general. At the same time, the use of business concepts for their own sake was eschewed in favor of relevance.

Moreover, we needed to be open to modifying concepts or creating new concepts based on the localized knowledge that our research provided. Modification was also necessary not just in terms of the relevant content but from an instructional viewpoint for purposes of conveying these concepts to a low-literate audience. We developed a thorough list of topics from the data, representing a bottom-up approach. We followed the iterative process of matching bottom-up and top-down approaches.

In terms of the process, communication among team members, each with unique experiences, in itself was a microcosm of the educational program and an important source of learning. We took a sequential approach in developing the program to cover topics, guided by our four-tiered model of learning goals, topics, methods of teaching, and instructional material.

Details of the Educational Program

As noted, subsistence marketplaces are complex social environments, driven by personal interaction and long-term social relationships. Hence, marketplace literacy education in such settings is likely to be most effective when it develops social skills and addresses both sides of the consumer-seller dyad. We customized concepts and approaches from the business literature that were applicable to fit the context (e.g., Kotler, 2003; Howard and Sheth, 1969; Porter, 1998; Blackwell, Miniard and Engel, 2001; Monroe, 2002).

In direct contrast to a top-down one-size-fits-all delivery of predetermined content, we relied on three bases from which our program iteratively developed: field level knowledge of subsistence contexts, drawn from two of our core team members; grounded research of buyers and sellers; and my experience with business education. Thus, we designed the program by learning from both the vulnerabilities and the strengths of subsistence buyers and sellers.

As described below, rather than emphasize specific concepts for their own sake, we aimed to convey useful, understandable concepts, with a bottom-up approach beginning at a concrete level. We assumed that the typical participant could not read or write, and thus placed a heavy emphasis on visual, conversational, and social teaching methods (e.g.., picture sorting, group discussion, and role-playing). Although we have developed programs of varying lengths, we describe our five-day version here for sake of simplicity.

Day 1

Day 1 focuses on the process of marketplace exchange and its evolution over time. We cover the concept of a value chain from production of products to consumption. We start out with activities planned to first help participants feel comfortable, and then we discuss and clarify expectations. We address the nature of the program, which is to provide generic consumer and entrepreneurial literacy rather than specific trade skills.

We then cover the basics of marketplace exchanges and the centrality of exchange. We convey various concepts through discussion, exercises, and games, rather than through lectures. We use a discussion of historical evolution of goods and services in arenas such as energy and transportation to highlight the centrality of finding a demand and serving it better than the competition.

We also introduce the notion of a value chain as comprising of multiple exchanges. One task in particular is illustrative, involving a number of pictures relevant to one value chain (say, a farmer growing fruits through wholesaler and retailer to a customer) along with a picture of money. We ask participants to place the pictures on a chart with concentric circles, placing the most important picture in the middle and so on. Often in the beginning, participants place money at the center. When we repeat this task later in the program, most participants place the customer at the center, emphasizing the importance of satisfying consumer needs to run a business.

Day 2

In Day 2, participants assume the role of customers. As discussed, our research identified a host of innovative practices and vulnerabilities. We use the notion of value for a product as the guiding concept to communicate the importance of informed consumer behavior. Simulated shops and role-playing by instructors are used to "cheat" participants or to make them commit mistakes. We carefully designed the tasks to reflect pitfalls for consumers.

We use a quiz, where stimuli are recorded audio statements covering different situations faced by consumers, to cover various issues. These issues include bargaining, weighing, buying wholesale versus retail, making versus buying, saving, understanding interest rates, switching stores and questioning sellers, being aware of consumer rights, understanding discounts, paying in installment versus cash, checking prices and totals, planning purchases and preparing shopping lists, checking expiry on packages, and understanding MRP (maximum retail price).

Days 3-5

In Days 3-5, participants assume the role of sellers. We emphasize a customer-oriented philosophy of doing business that makes a profit on the basis of satisfying customer needs and providing a valuable product. This orientation flows from the exchange focus of Day 1 and the customer focus of Day 2 and the importance of value in a product. We start out with a discussion of how sellers can evaluate business opportunities based on customer needs served, competitors, and strengths and weaknesses of individual entrepreneurs. Following through on a customer-oriented business philosophy, the next step is to begin to understand the customer need to be served.

We provide a general introduction to consumer behavior in terms of steps in decision-making such as need recognition, search for alternatives, and evaluation of alternatives, and the various influences on consumer decision-making. Following this is the notion of a market segment (a subset of consumers with similar needs and exhibiting similar behaviors). A situational definition, such as people living nearby, has to be expanded to an improved understanding of who the customers are, what describes them, and what their needs are. Such expansion of individual instances can lead to broader understanding of segments and more specific descriptions of customers.

The next topic we cover is information gathering and research. We emphasize the importance of carefully collecting and evaluating information. Included here are ways of gathering information, such as through talking to people, observing the competition, conducting an analysis of costs, or obtaining feedback on specific ideas. We also cover basic issues in asking questions when gathering information, such as planning questions to ask beforehand, avoiding leading questions, and attempting to obtain an accurate picture. We role-play to bring out these issues. We emphasize the importance of asking oneself tough questions and looking for accurate information.

The next major topic we cover is product design. Here, we cover some basics such as what a product is and what consumers look for in specific products.

Our purpose here is to help participants understand how physical product characteristics and ingredients translate to psychological benefits to consumers.

It's also important to understand the relatively abstract benefit beyond the physical product itself. Thus, through application in several specific arenas of running an enterprise, we illustrate the abstract notion of customer orientation and serving customer needs. We also bring out the distinction between goods and services. In addition, we go over the importance of packaging to preserve the product and provide an attractive exterior. Participant groups take part in exercises where they choose a product and decide on its design.

We cover distribution by using the concept of a value-chain, as introduced in the first day. Again, we ask participant groups to focus on a particular product and work out various steps in the value chain from purchase of ingredients all the way to distribution to wholesalers, retailers, and end users. Under pricing, we cover factors to consider when setting price, the notion of value from the consumer's perspective, the relationship between price and quality, and the relationship between price and volume. We discuss different types of promotions, ranging from store signs to fliers, and relate them to different promotional objectives such as gaining awareness, generating interest, and encouraging purchase.

We cover a number of miscellaneous issues on the final day, including the basics of accounting. We discuss ethical issues in business within the broader philosophy of balancing seller and buyer needs with societal good, with an emphasis on sustainability and the environment. We also discuss opportunities and threats that result from globalization and the changing marketplace, giving examples that encourage participants to proactively shape the economic world around them.

In an ideal sense, by beginning with basic understanding of the marketplace, our program highlights the choices available to participants, emphasizes proactivity in creating opportunities, and serves as a basis for continued learning. A focus exclusively on how-to skills, in contrast, may lead to a more reactive attitude among participants. Moreover, our entire program is characterized by free-flowing discussion to allow participants to question assumptions, express ideas freely, and develop confidence in their inherent marketplace abilities.

Program Implementation

To assess and refine our educational program, we tested it in various urban and rural settings. We used a number of approaches to recruit participants: We recruited from neighborhoods where members of our team have worked, we collaborated with community-based organizations that identified members who could benefit from enhanced marketplace skills, and we worked with larger non-governmental organizations that helped us to identify participants.

We conducted our pilot effort with 20 low-income, low-literate women in an urban neighborhood, and it was a highly encouraging first attempt, judging from the feedback we received from participants. One assignment mentioned earlier serves to illustrate this. On the first day, we asked participants to complete a picture-sorting task with pictures of several participants in a certain value chain such as farmers, retail outlets for food, consumers, and money. When asked to place the most important element at the center, most chose to place money. By the third day, the same groups placed the customer at the center, fully realizing the importance of customer needs and a customer orientation.

We deliberately conducted our pilot tests in challenging neighborhoods so we could rigorously test our methods. Our cumulative experience in piloting and then offering the program spans a decade. However, considerable challenges relate to sustaining our effort while maintaining continuity and buy-in from communities in a context of uncertainty and impoverishment on multiple fronts. Given the costs and challenges associated with a five-day commitment, we have since offered a one-day marketplace/consumer literacy program that covers the first two days of the five-day program and a two-day entrepreneurial literacy program that covers the last three days.

We covered all educational expenses, expected our participants to give us time and attention in return, and depended on a community-based or larger nongovernmental organization to provide physical space, while sharing in miscellaneous expenses, such as the cost of electricity and refreshments. Thus, our value proposition was to provide an educational experience in return for investment of time and some community-level resources. We offered no other incentive, reasoning that our approach leads to the recruitment of cohort groups committed to the educational experience we offer. In turn, participants exhibited near-perfect attendance across our multi-day programs, despite facing significant problems such as water shortages or illnesses in the family.

Qualitative and Quantitative Assessments

We conducted several programs in urban and rural settings, modifying aspects based on feedback. We also conducted follow-up sessions with participants three to six months later to judge the relatively longer-term impact on their lives. The feedback was overwhelmingly positive. All participants reported making considerable savings as consumers, typically saving several hundred rupees per month. They reported grouping their resources to buy staples such as rice wholesale, collectively saving thousands of rupees.

Nearly all participants reported significant positive developments, including standing up for consumer rights and bargaining with shopkeepers, switching shops, and taking over purchasing duties from husbands. As one shopkeeper in a village reportedly told one of our participants, after observing the program's effects on others, "You are a woman who participated in the program. Here! I will give you a good deal, go away." Participants also reported sharing what they learned with many others in their neighborhoods.

On the entrepreneurial literacy side, participants reported considerable learning as well, though behavioral outcomes were more limited (typically, about four or five women in each cohort of 20 to 25 women of our program started, or at least experimented with, microenterprises). Others appeared more open to starting a business or expanding an existing business after participating in our educational program. Starting a new business, of course, involves a number of uncontrollable factors. There are, however, many more challenges beyond the typical participant's control in starting a microenterprise, such as difficulty obtaining permission from her husband or other family members, lack of financial resources, and a lack of time due to her considerable household responsibilities.

In the broadest sense, continuous assessment of the program represents an ongoing field test of basic theory, providing valuable data that, in turn, enriches our research.

The evaluation of our educational program continued by documenting the details in the form of a book (Viswanathan, Gajendiran, and Venkatesan, 2008). The process of articulating the details and the rationale led us to revise the educational program, as did ongoing basic research.

Our program also allowed for flexibility in its duration. We provided a different configuration of a one-day marketplace and consumer literacy program and a two-day entrepreneurial literacy program, with the latter sometimes offered to those who express interest after completing the former. We also offered a combined two-day consumer and entrepreneurial literacy program, reflecting the flexibility of content developed here.

Quantitative assessments of the educational program were conducted, primarily to gauge improvements in skill and confidence. We administered pre-program surveys to participants a few days prior to the program, and a post-program questionnaire one to six months afterward. Questions varied according to the focus of the particular program, but generally addressed shopping behavior, self-reports of skill and confidence levels on various attributes as consumers and sellers, and self-reports of improvement in individual skills or confidence as a result of the program.

In a number of studies, we found an increase in self-rating of skills and confidence in most aspects of consumer interactions with the marketplace. We also found an increase in many aspects of entrepreneurial literacy. The pattern of results on specific attributes also enabled us to pinpoint areas that require attention and improvement in our program (e.g., checking prices at several stores, buying correct amounts).

Challenges and Limitations

We acknowledge the challenges and limitations inherent to our approach. Some of our most significant challenges revolved around how to increase the reach or scale of our program. Rather than view it as a module that needed to be implemented with minimal modification, we favored a flexible approach that applied the principles of marketplace literacy in different situations ranging from face-to-face training, to video or computer-based educational materials. We demonstrated the program to a wide variety of nonprofit agencies, and worked with several large organizations in India to scale the program to reach many participants.

Our foray into scaling considered training "trainers of trainers" (e.g., training a group of people, who in turn train trainers in many villages), or creating video-based learning modules and video-based community television programming, with the latter gaining traction.

Following extensive piloting and assessment through face-to-face informal educational approaches, the program is being scaled through large social enterprises with plans for implementation in other countries and contexts (www. marketplaceliteracy.org). Working with one of the largest microfinancing companies in the world, video-based marketplace literacy education has been created, organized around a movie specifically produced to bring out challenges with a storyline of a woman striving to empower herself through the marketplace. This is an educational innovation in itself for any audience that is accentuated in light of its intended audience of low-literate individuals. This program has just been launched regionally with planned reach in the hundreds of thousands, using a franchise model for the larger public as well as providing the program to microfinancing clients. Working with a Foundation in the state of Andhra Pradesh, community-based television programs have been created and computer centers are being used to reach women living in subsistence.

In order to be community-centric and learn continuously in addition to engaging in scaling efforts with other organizations, almost 100 self-help groups of women have been formed in Chennai and villages nearby, providing benefit to approximately 2,000 families through an organization named the Marketplace

Literacy Communities. Plans to expand to other parts of India and to other countries and continents are also in process. Marketplace literacy educational content has also been used by student organizations in the Dominican Republic and Uganda and provides a curriculum for a number of student organizations that conduct international trips. More information is available through the web portal.

Other issues relate to conceptual or strategic knowledge, or "know-why" knowledge, which is not always practical or actionable, particularly for people with low levels of literacy or those living in extreme and multifaceted deprivation. Livelihood programs that serve immediate needs may be more appropriate in situations when even the near-term future cannot be envisioned. Thus, we need to investigate the impediments and boundary conditions to the effectiveness of our program.

However, we should also note that many efforts at providing livelihood opportunities fail precisely because of a lack of understanding of know-why, leading to questions about how products conceived without sufficient attention to customer needs should be marketed. In our scaling as well, we have assessed the program at a micro level or are working with larger organizations in reaching people. However, it will also be important to study the program in the context of communities to study how this aspect interacts with other aspects of life in subsistence.

Another limitation was reflected in our qualitative assessments. Whereas all participants appear to benefit as consumers, a number of factors beyond our control led to a lack of similar outcomes on the entrepreneurial side. This, of course, is the reality of subsistence contexts, where entrepreneurs need many elements to participate in the marketplace. We have attempted to address this weakness by working with larger organizations that provide the necessary market access and financial resources. Finally, our quantitative assessments which relied in the early stages largely on self-reports, now captures actual behavioral outcomes as well as improvements in ability.

Empowering People through Marketplace Literacy

Financial resources, market access, and marketplace literacy are all required for people in subsistence populations to successfully engage in marketplace exchanges. Although progress has been made on the first two elements, fewer advances have been made in providing marketplace literacy. Our educational program aims to make a contribution in this regard.

In particular, we help people overcome the limitations associated with low literacy by equipping them with a deeper understanding of marketplace exchanges–the conceptual/strategic knowledge or know-why, which forms the basis for the procedural/tactical knowledge or know-how, because of its value in facilitating lifelong learning. The program seeks to alleviate participant difficulty in understanding abstract concepts by transposing them onto familiar experiences–for instance, conveying the importance of customer orientation by referring to the common practice of sellers demonstrating empathy for the personal circumstances of their customers.

As noted, in direct contrast to conveying a predetermined set of business-related concepts, we designed the program and its content using a bottom-up approach, by learning from both the vulnerabilities and the strengths of subsistence buyers and sellers. Rather than teaching a conventional set of basic and functional literacy skills, the program also endeavors to impart a socially embedded form of marketplace literacy, underscoring the importance of interpersonal skills in navigating a relational marketplace environment.

Thus, our approach echoes the growing recognition in consumer and other domains that literacy in its fullest sense must be rooted in a socio-cultural context, and constitutes more than a predetermined set of reading and writing skills (Adkins and Ozanne 2005; Viswanathan et al. 2005). Finally, the program emphasizes both consumer and entrepreneurial literacy, as many people are both buyers and sellers and can use one set of experiences to inform the other.

As we aim to enable participants to envision different realities and seek to improve their self-confidence and awareness of rights, in addition to skills, it is useful to briefly discuss the concept of empowerment in the context of this work. Empowerment has been defined as "a process by which people gain control over their lives, democratic participation in the life of their community" (Rappaport, 1987), and "a critical understanding of their environment" (Zimmerman, Israel, Schulz, Checkoway, 1992; Perkins and Zimmerman, 1995, p. 570).

In our context, we seek to enable people to gain control over their roles as consumers or as entrepreneurs, participate in the marketplace as informed buyers and sellers, and gain understanding of their marketplace environment. Working with others to reach goals, gaining access to resources, and understanding the socio-political environment have been discussed as being aspects of empowerment (Perkins and Zimmerman, 1995). Our qualitative and quantitative assessments suggest that participation in our program led to group buying, sharing of information in the community, accessing and using resources wisely, and gaining understanding of the marketplace environment.

A perspective on the process of empowerment education developed by Freire (1970, 1973) emphasizes those being educated defining problems and developing beliefs about influencing personal and social realms. According to this perspective, empowerment education extends beyond enhanced self-esteem or self-efficacy to individual, group, and systemic change. Our emphasis on know-why stems from the larger goal of empowering subsistence consumers and entrepreneurs through education to envision and shape different realities and influence the world around them.

Implications for Education

Our discussion to this point has been grounded in the research and in the development of the educational program. In this section, we draw out some broader issues relevant to education and discuss them in the context of the literature where relevant. We start out with a brief discussion of linkages with research and practice documented in the literature. We then emphasize some of the key distinctions in our program.

Linkages with Research and Practice

Generic issues that we highlight in our educational program have been used and written about in numerous contexts in education and more specifically, in adult and non-formal education. In designing instruction for adult learners, researchers have presented numerous frameworks. For example, one framework emphasizes assessing one's own skills, developing content knowledge, learning about learners, and understanding the learning contexts (Dean, 2002), all elements of our approach. In learning about learners, Knowles (1980) distinguishes between basic and educational needs. An understanding of these two categories of needs and their relationship is critical in a subsistence context, where needs are often basic and immediate and education may offer a means to address these needs.

Similarly, many methods can be used to assess learner needs. We used in-depth interviews and observations and immersion in the context as the basis for guiding our educational program. A variety of learning methods have been discussed in the literature, including role-play and simulation (Galbraith, 1998), which we use in our program. We also emphasize cohort and collaborative learning (Drago-Severson, 2004). In terms of our focus on informal education in a developing context, there are numerous examples in the literature (e.g., Singh, 2005). We highlight some distinct aspects of our educational program below.

Working With Existing Skill Sets and Literacy

Our philosophy in one sense was to take the participants as-is in terms of their levels of literacy and work through an educational program. We did not require basic literacy in any form, nor did we teach it; rather, we assumed that our participants could not read or write. Many programs are similar in emphasizing, say, technical skills, rather than basic literacy (e.g., Krishna, 2006). We worked with the skill sets that participants brought to the program, which were unconventional but considerable, and often derived from the social context of frequent one-to-one interactions.

Participants, individually and collectively, bring skills to the program that we build on, such as spoken language skills in the native language and pattern recognition skills. Some possess writing skills in the native language, although we do not assume this to be the case. As the program evolves, participants in various small groups pool their skills together to complete assignments, performing tasks that include assigning spokespersons and preparing charts for presentation.

In a longer time frame, if women we train are from a community or a self-help group, this sharing continues, as we observed in their efforts three to six months later to pool resources to buy staple items wholesale or to run a business. In a larger sense, women who participate in the educational program report sharing knowledge by informing others about their learning. Unique to these resource-poor but network-rich contexts is that a small educational effort can go a long way.

From Functional Literacy to Basic Literacy

The consumer and entrepreneurial literacy program can in turn facilitate basic literacy. Numerical and verbal skills play out in the economic realm, and learning to bargain in a consumer setting, or learning to analyze costs in a business setting, can in turn enable basic literacy. Functional skills in the economic realm may lead to acquisition of basic skills. The economic realm provides a rich context where counting and reading skills play out and where people can draw on their experience. In this regard, researchers have noted the ease of adding among low-literate people when dealing in dollars rather than abstract numbers (Viswanathan et al., 2005). Similarly, skills relating to budgeting, accounting, and other topics covered may lead to enhancement of basic counting skills. Some participants report developing confidence to read and count.

Some skills may be inherent and unrecognized, emerging in a context-rich setting such as shopping. A key issue here appears to be difficulty transferring across domains, which is not surprising, given that the use of analogy and transfer has traditionally been considered the behavior of those who are comfortable with using structural information (Gentner, 1983), likely due to their well-developed schemas (Gick and Holyoak, 1983). Requirements to complete transactions, to avoid getting cheated, and so forth, may lead to developing skills in marketplace contexts that may not transfer to basic settings, similar to the findings of Viswanathan and Gau (2006). By highlighting these skills, our educational program can serve to reinforce the notion that people possess some level of basic literacy and can build on it.

Breaking Barriers Between Individuals and Groups

A tendency in designing an educational program may be to assume that people will interact among each other, an assumption that is reasonable in many contexts. In fact, a homogeneous class may even be desirable (Carr-Hill, 2001). However, our effort, like other such efforts, is at the confluence of poverty and low literacy as well as culture. Although our classes to date have mostly been homogeneous in terms of gender (i.e., usually exclusively women), participants may be from different strata or different castes. Barriers that exist at the beginning of the program may come down over time, emphasizing the need for educators to understand the cultural context.

For instance, we conducted training in a village where women from different strata based on caste came from different locations in the village. Although they started out the program staying with their respective groups, over time, they mingled and interacted with women from different castes as the program ensued. We are, of course, not claiming that our program led to a social revolution in the village. Rather, it was interesting to observe the breaking of barriers in a small microcosm of social interactions, presumably through a learning environment with emphasis on equal treatment and respect for ideas.

A lesson learned here is the need to understand the underlying social relationships that exist, which may have to be overcome to some degree during the educational program. Learning about learner characteristics as well as the learning context is important to the design of an educational program (Dean, 2002).

Rights and Functional Skills

The rights approach versus the functional approach to literacy has been discussed in the literature (Robinson-Pant, 2003; EFA Global Monitoring Report, 2003; Verhoeven, 1994). In reality, these two approaches are intermingled in our educational program. Our follow-up qualitative assessment suggests that much of the learning relates to self-confidence and awareness of rights. Following participation in our program, some women reported taking over purchasing duties from their husbands, bargaining, and switching shops, leading shopkeepers to identify them as the ones who received training and provide them with better treatment and service.

Consumer literacy education focuses on both functional skills and rights. In fact, the two are inseparable in that the exercise of a functional skill may follow from awareness of a right. For example, at a broader level, making well-informed purchase decisions involves seeking information and being aware of several rights. The use of functional skills is in the context of being aware of one's rights. Acquiring functional skills and learning about rights combine to reinforce self-confidence.

The interrelationships between these elements are accentuated in the social context of myriad face-to-face interactions among individuals. Self-confidence is central to engage in conversations and negotiate the marketplace of one-to-one interactions. Whereas the contrast between the rights approach and the functional approach is an important one, our program necessarily emphasized both.

Relevant here is also the emphasis on "education for living and education for making a living" (p., 2, Singh, 2005; Gerasch and Duran, 2005). Also relevant is a holistic view of education in terms of learning to know, to do, to live together, and to be (UNESCO, 2006; Singh, 2005). Rights embedded in consumer education and in awareness about the marketplaces have implications for both of these important objectives.

Curriculum Choices

Our focus at the lowest levels of literacy and income was the guiding principle in deciding on curriculum issues. How do we convey the central and most important concepts to people who generally have the lived experience but are at the lowest level of literacy and income? This was the guiding question that led to our choice of the concepts we describe in the program. In terms of content, our approach is guided by a customer-oriented philosophy of doing business based on mutually beneficial exchanges.

There are numerous business issues we could have covered, such as managing human resources and so forth. However, for the audience we were targeting, an appreciation of exchanges, value chains, and most importantly, customer needs, is critical as a starting point. We start at the basic level of an exchange. We use multiple exchanges to illustrate a value chain. These are fundamental and intuitive concepts and provide the building blocks for then discussing the desirable nature of these exchanges. Our focal concepts included value in exchanges, viewed from both buyer and seller perspectives. We address the importance of a customer-oriented philosophy of doing business based on mutually beneficial exchanges.

Such knowledge would enable conception of products and enterprises, with more specialized knowledge for carrying on these enterprises in terms of managing human resources perhaps following suit. Moreover, the notion of mutual fairness in exchanges resonates at a human level, as does the right of every person to make a livelihood. Understandably, abstract economic and business principles relating competition and other issues are not usually contemplated, nor particularly relevant. Similarly, rudimentary financial and accounting knowledge is sufficient, whereas much of the business literature aims to address the issues faced by large organizations.

We covered the broader issue of identifying a business by evaluating ones' strengths and weaknesses, the competition, and customer needs, a translation of notions from business strategy tempered by reality on the ground. Our specific issues on the entrepreneurial side ranged from product design and distribution to pricing and promotion. However, our discussions of these topics were not restricted to the perspective of any single area of business, such as marketing. Rather, we discussed logistics and operations when covering distribution, and production when covering product design. And throughout the treatment of these topics and particularly in discussing pricing, costs were front and center.

As noted earlier, we cover societal responsibility and issues of sustainability and the environment. We also address threats and opportunities in globalization. Our emphasis on basic understanding of the marketplace would ideally open up choices for participants. Coupled with our use of open discussions, our program can potentially encourage a proactive attitude toward the marketplace rather than a reactive one. Such an attitude may result in participants shaping and altering the economic reality that they face.

Conceptual Treatment of Content

Another broad issue relating to education is our emphasis on conceptual treatment. Researchers have argued that low-literate individuals have difficulties with abstractions, and engage in concrete thinking in the visual, graphic world of usage, rather than the more abstract world of concepts (Luria, 1976; Viswanathan et al, 2005).

Our goal was to enable longer-term learning and essentially, to enable learning how to learn. Therefore, we organized the material around some key concepts. One concept was value and valuable exchanges, to organize much of the material about buyer and seller behaviors. Other concepts included the philosophical orientation of a business. The key to implementing such an approach has been to relate the content and instructional methods of the program to participants' lived experiences and leverage their social skills through our classroom exercises.

There are many challenges in trying to illustrate the concepts. For example, when we use simulated vegetable shops to demonstrate how prices, quality, and weighing may differ, participants often draw conclusions that one type of shop was bad and the other was good. We reiterate that our conclusions are not about types of shops, but that these are just examples created to illustrate broader issues, such as the need to make informed choices based on value in specific exchanges.

When using the notion of value, which essentially involves a judgment of what is given and what is obtained in return, people may equate what is given with price. This requires elucidation in terms of the various give-and-get components, such as price and travel effort and costs versus convenience and quality products. Understandably, people often do not consider the non-monetary and indirect monetary costs associated with purchasing a product, given severe income constraints. Therefore, it is important to be vigilant in tempering the outcome of specific examples to avoid concrete conclusions and illustrate more abstract issues.

Both low income and low literacy can create a short-term orientation that is often practical but sometimes counterproductive. The importance of abstracting across time needs to be emphasized. For example, return on investment is an important issue, but sellers may often not think beyond the next day and may not consider profits in proportion to investment.

One seller noted that whether he invested Rs. 300 or Rs. 100 in buying vegetables, a profit roughly equivalent to his daily monetary needs was sufficient because "that is all that he needed," a refreshing lesson in contentment, but nevertheless, one that may be disadvantageous in the near future. Buyers may not plan ahead for the month and buy at cheaper prices from a large reseller for many reasons, such as buying daily at retail due to the credit offered and out of fear of the next crisis. However, a longer-term orientation would enable them to switch buying habits when circumstances allow.

Customizing Concepts

There are, of course, many assumptions built into the program design, based on the unique context that we researched. Needless to say, actual customization in a variety of diverse settings is bringing out many issues, both in the content and in the delivery of the program. At a concrete level, depending on the context, we need to adjust many examples.

Perhaps most important are the unique set of products and markets encountered in South India. They form the underpinning for materials used throughout the program. Our material showing evolution of products across long periods of time are generic enough to use in most contexts. We use generic images of value chains, such as starting out with farmers and moving to consumers. However, images that are close to the reality that participants face, including appearances of people and objects in the educational materials that they see, would go a long way toward helping them relate to the program.

Important here is the need to relate the content back to participants' lived experiences. Materials, shops, and procedures used for the consumer literacy program would need to be modified to capture different realities. For the elements of the entrepreneurial literacy program, examples of products and value chains that are from the context where the program is run would be necessary.

Relevant to customization is translation into other languages. Our limited experience suggests that translation would require creating terminology to describe concepts and marketplace phenomena as well as stimuli that are relevant to specific cultures. Because spoken language is central to our approach, the need to capture the essence of the content would require careful translation with a full understanding of curriculum issues.

At a broader level, our conceptual treatment and an emphasis on the know-why provides an organizing framework, while our procedures provide one exemplar of a viable program. Our orientation in terms of viewing buyers and sellers as two sides of the same coin applies to marketplaces characterized by small buyers and sellers and frequent one-to-one interactions. Our emphasis on conveying concepts also generalizes, provided appropriate attention is paid to leveraging lived experiences and skills that participants bring to the program.

The larger purpose of enabling people to learn how to learn and move themselves toward a path of lifelong learning is central here. Ideally, such an orientation enables people to understand the larger context, exercise choice, and proactively interact with the marketplace. The specific concepts we use are fundamental and apply in a variety of settings. For instance, the broader notion of value would be very useful to organize a number of issues around. Our approach in terms of a research-based program is consistent with first educating ourselves about the potential recipients of an educational program before designing it. This is consistent with successful literacy programs that have first researched the potential beneficiaries (Robinson-Pant, 2003; Rogers et al., 1999).

In advanced societies such as the United States, there is much that can be done to provide marketplace literacy to low-literate, low-income individuals. Adult education programs provide excellent examples of providing people with marketplace skills. Similarly, other programs, such as nutritional education, provide skills in specific domains. Our experiences to date include a research-based approach to teaching marketplace literacy that recognizes the constraints people face due to low literacy and low income, customized to the customer-to-large-corporation context, as well as to the nature of entrepreneurial opportunities available.

Conclusion

This chapter discusses an educational program on marketplace literacy, aimed at people living in subsistence, that addresses an important gap in practice. In the economic realm, considerable attention has been devoted to micro-financing. However, our focus on enabling generic skills about the marketplace complements these important efforts. Among our unique contributions is the distinct focus on consumer and entrepreneurial literacy. We describe an approach grounded in basic research that combines broader business concepts with localized understanding.

Rather than a one-size-(of consumer and entrepreneurial education)-fits-all (contexts) approach, we customize our approach to the subsistence context in which we worked. As discussed, our approach is also unique in beginning with the know-why and then moving to the know-how, despite the audience being low literate. We cover abstract concepts by leveraging the social skills that participants bring to the program and relating the concepts back to their lived experiences. Our approach aims to provide deeper understanding of the marketplace that can enable people to potentially place themselves on a path to lifelong learning.

This work has a number of implications for educational research and practice, particularly for areas such as non-formal education, adult literacy, conceptual treatment of material, and educational programs in subsistence contexts. Generic issues relating to adult literacy include the linkages between functional literacy and basic literacy, and the balance between rights and functions. Issues specific to the realm of consumer and entrepreneurial literacy range from the concepts covered to the instructional method.

Beyond traditional nonprofit organizations, this work has implications for other types of organizations as well, such as corporations. The type of educational program we outline can be useful for corporations interested in training low-literate individuals as employees, or for training other partners in the value chain, such as producers (e.g., farmers) or resellers.

In addition to the program being offered in two states in India through video-based approaches, pilot efforts are in progress in Africa and South America. In closing, the design, delivery, and scaling of this educational program presents the most fully developed exemplar of following the bottom-up approach described in this book.

References

Arnould, E. and J. Mohr (2005) Dynamic Transformations for Base-of-the-Pyramid Market Clusters. Journal of the Academy of Marketing Science 20, 1-21.

Banerjee A.V. and E. Duflo (forthcoming, winter 2007) The Economic Lives of the Poor. Journal of Economic Perspectives.

Bennell, P. and J. Segerstrom (1998) Vocational education and training in developing countries: Has the World Bank got it right? International Journal of Educational Development 18, 271-287.

Blackwell, R., P. Miniard, and J. Engel (2001) Consumer Behavior, 9th Edition. Harcourt College Publishers. Belmont, CA.

Carr-Hill, R.A. (ed.) with A. Okech, A. Katahoire, T. Kakooza, A. Ndidde, and J. Oxenham (2001) Adult Literacy Programs in Uganda, Human Development Africa Region. The World Bank: Washington, DC.

Dean, G. (2002) Designing Instruction for Adult Learners. Kreiger. Melbourne, FL.

Drago-Severson, E. (2004) Becoming Adult Learners: Principles and Practices for Effective Development. Teachers College Press. New York.

Dyer, C. (2000) "Education for All" and the Rabaris and Kachchh, Western India. International Journal of Educational Development 33, 241-251.

EFA Global Montoring Report (2003) Gender and Education for All: The Leap to Equality.

Galbraith, M.W. (1998) Becoming an effective teacher of adults. In Adult learning methods: A guide for effective instruction, ed. M.W. Galbraith. Krieger. Malabar, FL.

Gerasch, P. and A. Duran (2005) Training in Modest Housing Construction for Those Who Need it Most: An Examples from Nicaragua. In Meeting Basic Learning Needs in the Informal Sector, ed M. Singh. Springer. The Netherlands.

Gentner, D. (1983) Structure Mapping: A theoretical framework for analogy. Cognitive Science 7, 155-170.

Gick, M. L. and K.J. Holyoak (1983) Schema induction and analogical transfer. Cognitive Psychology 15, 1-38.

Hart, S. (2005) Capitalism at the Crossroads: The Unlimited Business Opportunities in Solving the World's Most Difficult Problems. Wharton School Publishing. University of Pennsylvania.

Hertz-Bunzl, N. (2006) Financing Hope–Improving Microfinance. Harvard International Review 2006, 32-34.

Howard, J., and J. Sheth (1969) The Theory of Buyer Behavior. John Wiley & Sons. New York.

Johanson R., and A. Adams (2004) Skills Development in Sub-Saharan Africa. World Bank Regional and Sectoral Studies.

Knowles, M.S. (1980) The modern practice of adult education: From pedagogy to andragogy. Cambridge. New York.

Kotler, P. (2003) Marketing Management, 11th edition. Prentice Hall. Upper Saddle River, NJ.

Luria, A. (1976) Cognitive Development: Its Cultural and Social Foundations. Harvard University Press. Cambridge, MA.

Monroe, K. (2002) Pricing: Making Profitable Decisions. McGraw-Hill Higher Education. Columbus, OH.

Oxenham, J., A. Diallo, A. Katahoire, A. Petkova-Mwangi, and O. Sall (2002) Skills and Training for Better Livelihoods: A Review of Approaches and Experiences. The World Bank.

Perkins, D. D., & Zimmerman, M. A. (1995). Empowerment theory, research, and application. American Journal of Community Psychology, 23(5), 569-579.

Porter, M. (1998) Competitive Strategy: Techniques for Analyzing Industries and Competitors. Free Press. New York.

Prahalad, C.K (2005) The Fortune at the Bottom of the Pyramid. Wharton School Publishing. University of Pennsylvania.

Rappaport, J. (1987). Terms of empowerment/exemplars of prevention: Toward a theory for community psychology. American Journal of Community Psychology, 15(2), 121-148.

Robinson-Pant, A. (2003) Overview of learning programmes for literacy and more general life/vocational skills for women. Paper prepared for UNESCO EFA Monitoring Report Team.

Rogers, A., B. Maddox, J. Millican, K. Newell Jones, U. Papen, and A. Robinson-Pant (1999) Re-defining post-literacy in a changing world. DfID Education Research Serial No. 29. DfID. London.

Saini, A. (2000) Literacy and Empowerment: An Indian Scenario. Childhood Education 76, 381-384.

Singh, M. (2005) Meeting Basic Learning Needs in the Informal Sector. Springer. The Netherlands.

Singhal, A. and B. Duggal (2002), Extending Banking to the Poor in India.

Stix, G. (1997) Small (lending) is beautiful. Scientific American 276, 16-17.

UNESCO (2006) Literacy for life. EFA Global Monitoring Report. Verhoeven, L., (1994) Modeling and promoting functional literacy. In Functional Literacy: Theoretical issues and educational implications, ed. L. Verhoeven. John Benjamins. Amsterdam.

Viswanathan, Madhubalan (2007) Understanding Product and Market Interactions in Subsistence Marketplaces: A Study in South India. In Product and Market Development for Subsistence Marketplaces: Consumption and Entrepreneurship Beyond Literacy and Resource Barriers, Editors, Jose Rosa and Madhu Viswanathan, Advances in International Management Series, Joseph Cheng and Michael Hitt, Series Editors. Elsevier.

Viswanathan, Gajendiran, and Venkatesan (2008), Enabling Consumer and Entrepreneurial Literacy in Subsistence Marketplaces: A Research-Based Approach to Educational Programs, Springer.

Viswanathan, M. and R. Gau (2006) Functional Illiteracy and Nutritional Education in the United States: A Research-Based Approach to the Development of Nutritional Education Materials for Functionally Illiterate Consumers. Journal of Macromarketing 25, 187-201.

Viswanathan, Madhubalan, and Jose Rosa (2007) Product and Market Development for Subsistence Marketplaces: Consumption and Entrepreneurship Beyond Literacy and Resource Barriers, Editors, Jose Rosa and Madhu Viswanathan, Advances in International Management Series, Joseph Cheng and Michael Hitt, Series Editors, Elsevier.

Viswanathan, M., J. Rosa, and J. Harris (2005) Decision Making and Coping of Functionally Illiterate Consumers and Some Implications for Marketing Management. Journal of Marketing 69, 15-31.

Yunus, M., and Yusus, A. J. M. (1998). Banker to the Poor. Penguin Books India.

Zimmerman, M. A., Israel, B. A., Schulz, A., & Checkoway, B. (1992). Further explorations in empowerment theory: An empirical analysis of psychological empowerment. American Journal of Community Psychology, 20(6), 707-727.

Chapter 14
Lessons Learned in Moving from Basic Research to Practice in Subsistence Marketplaces[33]

Image 14.01: The author talks with a man from the local community in Tamil Nadu, India. Photograph courtesy of the Subsistence Marketplaces Initiative.

Following a brief overview of our work, this chapter focuses primarily on the lessons learned in moving from basic research to applications designed to create impact in practice. These lessons comprise such topics as designing research methods, making the important transition from research to practice, and benefiting from the feedback loop between practice and research. Chapter 11 discussed issues with designing research methods in this arena. Chapter 12 discussed our educational initiatives, and Chapter 13 described our social initiatives. This chapter is about our journey in a broader sense, while emphasizing synergies between research and practice. As such, it covers a number of intangibles that span issues covered across the preceding chapters.

---

[33] This chapter includes material adapted from the following previously published work:

Viswanathan, Madhu (2011), "Conducting Transformative Consumer Research Lessons Learned in Moving From Basic Research to Transformative Impact in Subsistence Marketplaces," Transformative Consumer Research for Personal and Collective Well-Being, Editors, David Glen Mick, Simone Pettigrew, Cornelia Pechmann, and Julie Ozanne, Routledge/Taylor & Francis.

A Summary of Our Journey to Date

Our work began with the study of low-literate consumer behavior in the US (see Figure 14.1), using a variety of methods and working with students at adult education centers (Viswanathan, Rosa, & Harris, 2005). Striking here was the lack of work in this area across disciplines, particularly regarding such issues as marketplace interactions and decision-making. This was less true at the macro or societal level—where, in fact, numerous studies examine literacy rates—but it was strikingly true at the level of individual decision making and behavior.

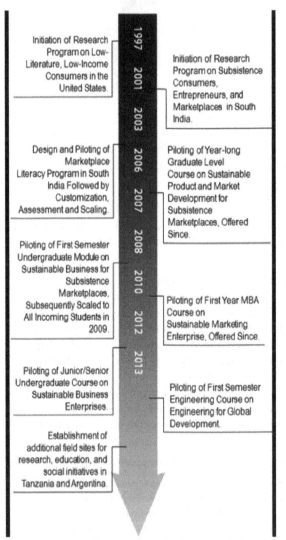

Figure 14.1: Timeline of Research, Social, and Teaching Initiatives

In the US, working with the Cooperative Extension program at the University of Illinois, we developed educational materials that were user-friendly for low-literate audiences, and at the same time reflected the reality they faced during shopping trips (Viswanathan & Gau, 2005). We did so by listening to clients and teachers, and observing teacher-client interactions. We then moved into a phase of using our "Big Picture" understanding in the US to seek in-depth insight into specific issues—for example, through experimental studies of nutritional labeling for low-literate consumers, and of literacy and consumer memory (Viswanathan, Hastak, & Gau 2009; Viswanathan, Torelli, Xia, & Gau, 2009).

A few years after launching our program in the US, we expanded our research to subsistence marketplaces in India, where we built a small team consisting of two core members who had grown up in the contexts we were studying, and who had extensive experience in community development. As we listened and learned during the early Indian research phase, the idea of an extended engagement with an educational program on consumer and entrepreneurial literacy (which we came to call "marketplace literacy") took preliminary shape. Ultimately, it led to the creation of a nonprofit dubbed the "Marketplace Literacy Project."

As the name implies and as we described in Chapter 13, our focus was not on basic literacy. Rather, it was on what we now describe as a socio-culturally embedded form of marketplace literacy—one that is a necessity in an intensely one-to-one interactional environment. Similarly, we focused not so much on concrete vocational skills, but rather on know-how in running a business, and know-why to adapt to changing circumstances (e.g., why be customer-oriented, why choose a business, how and why value chains work, etc.). And while we certainly turned up numerous programs focusing on vocational skills, our search for programs on know-how was relatively unsuccessful, and programs with the starting point of know-why appeared to be nonexistent. These were the gaps that we set out to fill.

Once we had several years of experience on the ground in India, we began documenting and assessing the project. The iterative documentation, editing, and fine-tuning process that ensued over several years culminated in a book recently published by Springer (in an education series in alliance with UNESCO) that describes the project and its implications for different sectors of society (Viswanathan, Gajendiran, & Venkatesan, 2008a; see also 2008b).

Meanwhile, we continued to offer our programs in an increasingly broad variety of settings and configurations. We developed, for example, a day-long marketplace and consumer literacy program, and a two-day entrepreneurial literacy program. These and similar experiments were conducted in cooperation with community-based organizations, such as local women's groups, in a given locality.

Our approach was (and is) problem-centered, rather than program-centered, emphasizing a customized approach to creating educational programs rather than using our existing program as a hammer as we look for nails. We emphasized know-why—again, to enable people to learn and adapt to the changing marketplace—and treated buyers and sellers as two sides of the same coin.

In the next phase, we began seeking ways to scale the project. We are convinced that, given sufficient commitment and customization, our programs are highly effective, and this encourages us to push for broader reach and more impact. This scaling effort is ongoing. We have also created focused involvement in some communities where we facilitate marketplace interactions through facilitation and support of self-help groups, linkages to financial institutions, and provision of marketplace literacy education.

We also continue to work on multiple levels. Our approach in India—again, based on previous learning in the US—was to operate at the micro level as we moved through different communities during the development and customization phase. Those impacts were almost entirely local. But we also continued to work at the macro level, partnering with larger organizations whose impact is felt over a far broader base.

Each approach informs and supports the other. Individual communities are our platforms for change; we need to stay in close touch with them to develop a holistic understanding of the issues they face, and to get ongoing feedback on our educational programs and their impact. This helps us paint the "Big Picture," and the big picture, in turn, lends rigor and system to our local efforts. In parallel, similar to our progression in the US, research grew from big-picture understanding to specific projects encompassing experimental, survey, and qualitative approaches (Viswanathan, Rosa, & Ruth, 2010; Chaturvedi, Chiu, & Viswanathan, 2009).

More recently, we have expanded to countries in Africa and South America, with pilot efforts in marketplace literacy in parallel with basic research.

Lessons About Methodological Issues

In this section, we describe lessons that we have learned about methodological issues, including local partnerships, understanding motivations of partners, and contextualizing research methods.

Develop Diverse Skills Through Local Partnerships

In venturing into the arena of low-literate consumer behavior in the US, it was not clear how we were going to move forward (research methods, samples, etc.), or even what we expected to find. Obviously, this was not a discrete research project with a circumscribed outcome; rather, our goal was to understand and educate ourselves as a first step—a process that we now readily describe as "immersion."

We began by attending a required training session to serve as volunteer tutors at the local adult education center, and we subsequently tutored students and observed classroom activities. This required reaching out to the staff at the adult education center, communicating to them about our objectives, and—drawing on their expertise—emphasizing the need to build relationships with organizations.

The classes at the adult education center were roughly divided into three grade-equivalent levels: 0-4, 5-8, and 9-12. Although we observed a range of classes, we began by interviewing students in levels 5-12, and teachers from all levels. We used unstructured approaches, essentially aiming to learn in different ways. (Clearly, with low-literate participants, tools such as surveys did not seem to hold much potential, at least as a starting point.)

We were more cautious with 0-4 level students; we spent more than a year building rapport with them before attempting to interview them—a delay that, in retrospect, may have been unnecessary. In those intervening months, we interacted with these students in classroom settings, and observed them on group shopping trips.

Although unearthing the stories of these individuals was a slow process, and one that took us well out of our comfort zone—that is, conducting experiments with US students in a campus setting—it was more than worth the effort. Above all, we found ourselves learning about the many things that we take for granted as a result of our literacy. In many ways, our educational levels made us least qualified to study those with low levels of literacy: it was difficult for us to "unlearn" what we already knew, and see the world as they saw it.

Over time, as we tried to disentangle literacy from related issues, we moved to studying comparison groups through in-depth interviews, including literate but poor people and students of English (as a second language) at adult education centers. But in retrospect, it is clear that our focus was still one of developing the Big Picture—that is, understanding this realm in a broad way. Going into parts of the picture in greater depth, and expanding our methodological "tool kit," would come later.

Driving our methodological approach was the need to accumulate a diverse set of skills—through working with organizations in the field—and developing our research team's own skills, through activities like volunteer training and tutoring. One point of satisfaction and pride is that we have developed relationships with teachers and staff that continue to this day. Central to building such relationships has been our practice of informing our partners of our research goals—and doing so on a regular basis.

Their goals and ours, without exception, are well aligned; we all seek to improve the lives of low-literate, low-income consumers. The currency that sustains these relationships is not money, but rather, a shared sense of purpose, and a habit of sustained communication about the research, its anticipated outcomes, and the social initiatives that might grow out of those outcomes.

This collaborative approach has been duplicated in our work in India. That work initially was construed by our team somewhat narrowly: we saw ourselves simply as studying low-literate consumer behavior in a different setting. It soon expanded in new directions, to comprise research on subsistence consumers, entrepreneurs (or consumer-merchants), and marketplaces.

Our initial contact in India was a large NGO, which recommended an employee of theirs to assist us on a part-time basis with interviews. We began with in-depth interviews in neighborhoods where our associate had worked with families on a variety of initiatives, and our research method evolved as we began to understand the constraints under which we would operate, and also the limits on what feasibly could be implemented. Our associate, who had grown up in the same subsistence contexts we studied, spoke little English, but was fluent in the native language and had worked with the communities we studied.

More than anything else, our goal was to listen and learn in a relatively bottom-up way, without specific research goals and the associated in-depth study of the relevant literature. Again in retrospect, this was well suited for our larger objectives of creating a broad program of research and social initiatives, with the goal of educating ourselves being the first step. It would be less well suited for researchers at the stage of their careers where time is scarce, and during which it is important to be both grounded in the phenomenon and having an understanding of the theoretical lenses that can be applied to make the research more efficient.

To sum up, our interviews were sincere conversations: nothing more, and nothing less. Growing up middle-class in India meant that I had some understanding of the culture, but a sustained study of people who live in subsistence was for me an eye-opening experience. In a sense, all that we do begins and ends with the generosity of people in sharing their life-experiences, and thereby educating us.

Participants generously opened up their lives to us, often relating the saddest of circumstances with deep emotions. We thereby gained a window into a previously unknown world—one that was resource-poor but network-rich, in which the people survived through their ability to communicate orally. These social connections offered people a stepping stone to learn and develop skills, but—as it turned out—there were significant downsides, as well.

We soon realized that to take our research to the next level, we needed a trained team on the ground. We therefore hired our part-time associate and another person, both of whom had employment (at the NGO mentioned earlier) that was coming to an end. They had grown up in the cultural contexts we studied, and had spent decades in community development. The fact that they did not possess a business background has been, in our view, an advantage, because it has helped us to jointly approach projects without preconceptions, and to honestly assess our progress.

Also important was our decision, early on, to view the field team as partners, rather than simply data collectors. They do serve multiple important functions—a fact that needs to be recognized. Their role as cultural brokers within communities, for example, has been highlighted in the literature (Molyneaux et al., 2009).

In these settings, the support of local organizations such as NGOs and CBOs (community-based organizations) is vital. As noted elsewhere, such organizations tend to have deep understanding of local communities, and can facilitate research and other initiatives in a number of ways (Molyneaux et al., 2009).

A note of caution should be sounded here, however: conducting the kinds of research described herein requires a trained team—one that a given NGO may not be able to field, or may not have the capacity to share. Thus, a central methodological lesson is that examining complex social phenomena requires diverse skills best embodied by teams of researchers, field workers, and alliances with indigenous organizations.

We design and adapt methods in the field and implement them through an array of relationships on the ground. Developing and nurturing relationships is paramount as well. Understanding capabilities and limitations in these relationships is also essential in this regard. Conceptual understanding of research is an important area where communication with the field team is critical, an issue highlighted in the literature (Molyneaux et al., 2009).

A key challenge is to communicate about the nature of academic research and the need for abstract understanding. Training through means such as role-play is important in administering data collection procedures. Language is another arena in which understanding capabilities and limitations is critical. We try to adhere closely to the original statements made by our research participants, but this is not always a simple task. Of the two core members of our team, the junior associate was learning English, while the senior associate had moderate English skills (oral and written). The process of translation has involved transcribing work (in Tamil) by the junior associate and then translation to English by the senior associate. Similar issues arise in translating survey measures from English to Tamil, and in our writing and editing efforts. More recently, our team has changed and expanded to three research associates and five field workers but the underlying guiding principle of nurturing relationships is remains central.

We should stress that there is significant give and take in these partnerships that moves the academic researcher out of his or her traditional role. Inevitably, one builds relationships that comprise a deep understanding of the life circumstances and constraints faced by one's colleagues. Individually and collectively, working in subsistence contexts, we face personal adversity. We learn to support each other.

At the same time, the relationships that we build with people in the organizations we work with are also critically important. In the social arena, ultimately, it is individuals who act as champions of specific goals and broader programs. The relationships we build with individuals are, therefore, extraordinarily important.

Understand Motivations of Partners

We turn now to a related lesson in implementing methods and social initiatives. When one seeks to study complex phenomenon through relationships with a diverse set of partners, it may prove necessary to develop a system of incentives well beyond those traditionally associated with academic research. Perhaps the most important question in gauging the potential for relationships is that of motivation: What are the prospective partners looking for?

The answer is likely to vary widely. The participants in our surveys, interviews, and other research efforts seek a meaningful interaction from which they gain a broader vision—whether it be in educating their communities through marketplace literacy education, or in creating a climate where quality goods and services become available. The community-based organizations, obviously, are looking for our core "product": marketplace literacy education. The local socio-political leadership looks to us to help them provide community welfare. Larger social enterprises want the chance to engage in collaborative work that furthers their mission, and to derive the benefits of relevant research findings. Local educational institutions also seek new knowledge, and see benefit in participation in public events.

The question of incentives and motivations quickly brings us back to the importance of relationships. As in most realms of collaborative human activity, participants are unlikely to make satisfactory progress when those organizations have significantly different agendas. Alignment is key. When the researcher nurtures strong relationships, well beyond the traditional role of the researcher, he or she is well positioned to make decisions about potential partners.

"Drilling down" on this issue of incentives, early on, we decided not pay participants to attend our educational program, but instead, to create other appropriate incentives. This approach mitigated issues of fair selection when incentives are offered, as has been highlighted in the literature (Molyneaux et al., 2009). We also decided not to pay "recruiters," because we did not want to risk muddying the incentives of a participant who has been recruited (e.g., attendance in exchange for receiving a portion of the recruiting fee). Similarly, paying community-based organizations to run educational programs gave us pause, although, after negotiation, we often agreed to help pay the cost of renting community halls, serving refreshments, and so on.

Our overall aim in setting up incentives was to recruit participants who wanted to be educated, while also asking the communities to make at least a modest investment in the local effort. We believed that signaling our guiding values— in part through our incentives—was important both to the core team and the communities we worked with. At the same time, however, we understood the need for enough flexibility to accommodate the complex realities of subsistence.

Invest Time to Understand Local Context and Develop Appropriate Methods

Implicit in the methodological issues discussed above is the challenge of immersion in the local context: in order to understand that context, to develop teams and relationships, and to design more tailored methods.

We took this challenge seriously as our own backgrounds may not prepare us for an easy understanding of our target communities. Our open-ended venture into low-literate, low-income consumer behavior as well as subsistence consumer, entrepreneur, and marketplace behavior was intended, in part, to educate myself in an intensive (and thereby efficient) way. As anticipated, this immersion provides a reasonably powerful "bottom-up" set of insights into local life circumstances. It also makes it possible to change our methods more or less in real time, based on what we are learning.

At the same time, immersion in the field also helped build a team, and establishing relationships with partners—not only for research purposes, but also for creating targeted social initiatives. Finally, time in the field enables working closely with a team, setting both direction and tone. Human capital was, and is, our most important asset, and it can only be developed through sustained, in-person interactions. Immersion, for us, was a sine qua non.

Engage in Healthy Disbelief to Refine Methods to Local Needs

We have mentioned several times the importance of refining methodologies in response to on-the-ground learning, to ensure that maximum benefits are delivered to target beneficiaries. Moving our focus of investigation from the US to India made this lesson immediately obvious to us, as we sought to serve at-risk people in dramatically different contexts.

In the US, for example, our methods evolved to reflect the particular needs of our participants there: from tutoring and observations in classrooms to open-ended interviews, group shopping observations (based on a class assignment), and one-on-one shopping observations (supplemented with interviews), as well as surveys and experiments. Similarly, in India, we conducted observations, interviews, and experiments in different settings—ranging from community centers to people's houses—that emphasized the comfort and needs of the participants. In both contexts, logistical issues needed to be addressed, such as providing participants with transportation to grocery stores.

Beyond that, the specific methods we designed were carefully customized. Interviews in India emphasized learning about larger life circumstances through empathetic conversations. Experiments minimized "text-anxiety" issues through realistic tasks and stimuli, personal administration, and verbal responses (Viswanathan, Gau, & Chaturvedi, 2008). We believe that this is a generalizable lesson, given the nature of phenomena that are in focus, and also given the constraints of participants. Several cases in point may help illustrate the need for local knowledge combined with iterative design, assessment, and modification.

The use of translated statements with seven-point response categories, for example, was a complex task that sometimes led to the same response being given across multiple items. One associate devised the approach of asking which side of the scale respondents fell into ("agreement" or "disagreement"), and then asking for finer discriminations within those broader categories. Similarly, when administering a questionnaire to female participants, we changed the focus of a scale item from "romance" to "affection.", for cultural appropriateness.

Our methodological explorations also extended to the design and assessment of the marketplace literacy program. Simply stated, we were attempting to create an education program that drew on (a) my own experience with business education, (b) my associates' extensive local background, acquired both through growing up in similar contexts and through their work in community development, and (c) our ongoing research, including interviews and observations. We sketched out some initial ideas on broader objectives, specific topics, instructional methods, and specific details.

Certain conclusions seemed obvious from the outset, such as assuming our audience could not read or write. (This was almost definitional: we were aiming for the lower levels of literacy and income.) Given the anticipated background of our participants, it seemed likely that even before we attempted to cover specific topics, ice-breaking exercises would be very important. We had to make them comfortable with an educational setting with which they would not be familiar, and we had to shape and inform their expectations for the program (i.e., that the program was not about livelihood skills, and would not involve advice on a specific business idea).

Our team members clearly complemented each other as we carried out two key tasks: developing our core topics, and identifying the life circumstances— including low literacy—that had to be taken into account. A sharp and exclusive focus on topics to be covered would have been counterproductive, at that stage and in that context. Drawing on our different life experiences in these contexts, my associates and I were able to design, assess, and iteratively adapt our educational program.

For example, as discussed in Chapter 13, we used picture sortings, simulations of situations, an audio quiz, and small group assignments and discussions to cover a number of issues. We asked small groups to organize a set of pictures depicting a value chain (e.g., a farmer growing fruit, a retail outlet selling it, and consumers buying it) and money (represented by a currency bill) into concentric circles, in such a way that the element that is most important to running a successful business wound up in the innermost circle. Many groups first placed "money" in the middle. Gradually, though, most amended their "universe" to put the customer at the center. This and other exercises evolved almost continuously.

Similarly, the qualitative and quantitative methods we used for assessment purposes also evolved to suit the preferences of participants, and to reflect our ongoing learning. For example, we learned to take into account the paradoxical outcome that many participants experienced decreased confidence, at least temporarily, in the wake of their educational program, evidently because they realized for the first time how much they didn't know.

The researcher should assume that there is no particular "right" way to do things, and that a healthy skepticism about precedent is essential throughout the research process. Our methods continue to evolve as we try to scale our program to reach more people. Each setting offers unique challenges, ranging from the logistical to the cultural; and yet, we feel duty-bound not to reinvent the wheel in each locale. For example, should different social strata living in different hamlets within a village be combined into one educational program, or should each hamlet be treated separately? There are no easy answers, so it remains an important question.

The literature makes reference to elements of these methodological lessons in different contexts. For instance, in the context of collaborative research with disadvantaged communities, difficulties due to time-consuming and diverse tasks (e.g., communicating with different stakeholders, offering expertise and advice to help the community, etc.) and management of community sensitivities (e.g., conflicts regarding who represents the community) have been noted (MacLean, Warr, & Pyett, 2009).

The need to use multiple methods has been emphasized in field research in such areas as health, as has the need to design research based on learning from participants (Israel et al., 2005). The importance of social relationships between researchers and field teams, and also between field teams and communities, has been emphasized in the context of conducting research ethically in low-income settings (Molyneaux et al., 2009).

A number of issues we discuss have been highlighted in the context of developing partnerships with communities in participatory research (e.g., Wallerstein et al., 2005), reflecting on the research organization's strengths and weaknesses, listening and learning about power dynamics, identifying partners through participation in relevant networks, determining the benefits for the community of working with outside organizations, figuring out the unique needs and imperatives of partners, and understanding the time-intensive nature of relationship building.

Lessons About Impact

In this section, we discuss lessons we learned about impact, including the transformative role of education, the differences between theoretical and practical impact, the role of the researcher in scaling, and the importance of a research mentality.

Education Can Be Transformative

One of the central lessons that we have learned involves the power of education. This may sound like an odd statement, coming as it does from a long-time business educator (see Figure 14.2). Starting from a vantage point of skepticism and relative unawareness—and, to be sure, a position of relative privilege—coming to understand how non-formal educational programs can have real impact has been an eye-opening experience.

It has underscored how education can change not only people's skills, but also their self-confidence—and, by extension, their awareness and exercise of their rights. It reminds us of all the things we take for granted as educated individuals, and how the very act of being treated with dignity in a learning environment, even for a few days, can bring with it enormous benefits. For example, a woman in our program thanked us for not just educating her, but also her entire family. Particularly when women are the "change agents," that kind of impact tends to spread beyond the family as well, as people share what they learn with others in their community.

The viral nature of "information spread" became evident to us during qualitative assessments a few months after conducting our pilot educational program. Women in our feedback session talked about sharing their learning throughout their community, particularly in the consumer realm. They told us that they had passed along to friends and acquaintances their learning on such issues as checking prices, buying wholesale, and switching shops. The women in one village talked about the local shopkeeper offering them good deals because they were the "women who had received training."

Obviously, in a one-to-one interactional world of intense personal communications—often face-to-face— there exists a powerful potential for the spread of new ideas. When combined with life skills that are immediately relevant and practical for those living in extreme resource constraints, this potential is realized and accentuated.

Combining the powers of research and education places the academic researcher with expertise in each of these areas at the center of research-based educational initiatives. The potential for consumer research that translates into transformative impact through education is tremendous. What researchers can produce—socially relevant knowledge based on rigorous research—in turn can provide the basis for creating powerful educational programs, which are powerful in part due to their "viral potential."

Also noteworthy is the power of education that is aimed at "know-why," and helping people learn and adapt to changing circumstances. We teach people to proactively shape their marketplaces, rather than simply "fit into" them. Two strands in the literature are noteworthy in this regard. The path from self-perception as an object reacting to reality to a subject shaping it has been described as "conscientization" (Freire, 1970). This certainly resonates with our work.

Similarly, pragmatic learning theory (Dewey, 1910; Elkjaer, 2004; Jayanti and Singh, 2010) emphasizes how experiences lead to awareness of problems (e.g., why something happens), which then leads to inquiry about how problems can be solved, which in turn mobilizes the person to productive action, and ultimately creates a self-reinforcing cycle (Jayanti and Singh, 2010). Central to this approach is that thinking is instrumental to action, which in turn, is rooted in situations (Dewey, 1910; Elkjaer, 2004). Our emphasis on know-why, relating to marketplace situations that subsistence consumers and entrepreneurs experience, aims to trigger inquiry and productive action, thereby enabling people to gain experience-based knowledge.

Practical and Theoretical Impact May Not Align

Also noteworthy is the issue of what translates, and—perhaps—transforms. Disseminating our findings in a nuanced research article certainly has its value, but it seems evident that the best way to have a substantial impact is through the proactive pursuit of social initiatives based on the broader research program. The research article, by its very nature, tends to involve a "funneling" of discoveries into a more pointed set of theoretical insights, with the conventional set of "implications" at the end.

In our case, the implications that led to the most important social initiatives flowed out of the dedicated immersion. We are certainly not arguing against rigorous or nuanced thought. But in this particular realm, what translates from research to practice tends not to overlap with what is central to the typical academic article; instead, it grows out of a more inclusive effort to understand the phenomenon in context.

What really creates impact? (For us, at least, this is the key question.) Our experience is certainly not one of a research project leading to publishable insights, the implications of which were then acted on to create impact. Again, ours is an experience in which a broad understanding through research preceded, but then paralleled, our educational initiatives. This was perhaps because, in many ways, we were seeking big-picture understanding to educate ourselves. Once the research-to-social-initiative translation efforts are in place, however, the latter lead to nuanced insights that in turn spur research questions. Immersion leads to learning, which aids in the design of an application to improve consumer welfare, which opens the door to deeper and richer insights.

The nature of education in our projects is also noteworthy in this regard. As noted, it is more than "skills"; it extends to self-confidence and awareness of rights. Our focus on know-why helps participants learn how to learn. Researchers occupy a unique vantage point, in this regard, because their research experiences create nuggets of insights that can be translated into educational efforts. Our (understandable) instincts to cover concepts in the education we designed had to be tempered by contextual factors.

For example, as noted in Chapter 13, when working with adults who have not been in a formal educational setting in many years—if ever—their anxieties about what will transpire in the "classroom" have to be taken into consideration. Thus, exercises to make participants feel comfortable and discussions to set expectations are very important. Socio-cultural factors, such as social hierarchy, may also need to be taken into account. For example, in one of our programs, there were three distinct groups that were based on social hierarchy and associated areas of residence within their village. Those groups began their experience with us as substantially separate entities that gradually intermingled as time passed—a process that happened at its own pace.

Also paramount in making the translation from research to education is design from the vantage point of end-beneficiaries. This is particularly challenging for the academic who focuses primarily, or exclusively, on writing for research journals and teaching university students. Translation, in that case, means turning theory into classroom content for the benefit of a group of students with backgrounds and literacy levels comparable to their professors.

This is fine, as far as it goes; but we university-based educators tend to be under-qualified when it comes to working with low-literate people. For one thing, we have to strive to overcome the presumptions that accompany a high level of literacy. In designing programs for low-literate poor audiences, for example, we have to keep in mind their unfamiliarity and difficulty with abstractions, and instead, emphasize concrete learning experiences.

We use local examples from people's daily lives, making it easier for them to relate to the concepts at hand. Because our participants possess strong oral language and social skills, we emphasize learning through social interactions. Consistently, we focus on providing benefits in the near term, which underscores the relevance of our "product" to their life circumstances.

Again, we don't mean to suggest research only exerts its influence through practical application, or that there are no synergies with core research. In fact, we are convinced that our learning through intuitively designing and administering a program can and does lead to ideas for new specific research projects. Our engagement in social initiatives provides grounded knowledge that can and should be used to gauge potential research projects for their social relevance. More insights on this feedback loop are discussed later in the chapter.

Researchers Can Play a Central Role in the Challenge of "Scaling"

In understanding the challenge of creating large-scale impact, it seems clear that researchers can contribute significantly to that scaling process, and also can design new kinds of research as opportunities arise during scaling.

Scaling, though, is not the preferred term here, because it connotes "one size fitting all." Our purpose is perhaps better expressed as maximizing reach. We have been actively involved in this phase for many years now, and it is very much a work in progress. Based on our experience to date, however, we can point to several key steps along the way, including: identifying an important need that is not being served, finding an innovative way to serve it, creating the right technology to deploy to maximize reach, and—eventually—developing an enterprise model. The need for patient human capital, paralleling the need for patient financial capital, which is discussed eloquently by Novogratz (2009), is critical.

Of all of these, developing an enterprise model is the most elusive—and in some ways, the most important. Identifying a need is not sufficient; finding a solution is not sufficient; innovating in its delivery is not sufficient; and finding the right technology to maximize reach is not sufficient. Developing an enterprise model for large-scale application—and, of course, a way to conduct a careful assessment of impact—are essential. Pilot programs are an important learning medium, but unless the learning leads to larger-scale application, the real potential for impact is not fully realized. This is particularly true for an educational program.

Given our limited resources, our approach has been to present our program to organizations already capable of wide reach. For example, one of our early scaling efforts involved working with a large foundation that reached some 200 villages. With that foundation, we first attempted to "train trainers" who would conduct subsequent programs. The costs of this approach proved prohibitive, and we next decided to focus on video-based education. People from such communities created video episodes that we scripted, embedding key aspects of marketplace literacy into the situations that our characters confronted. This process underscores the unique role played by the researcher, who contributes on levels ranging from the conceptual to the operational.

The effort continues. We have launched a program after multiple pilots whereby facilitators show videos and run classes with assignments and feedback. The challenge here is that video alone doesn't create an in-depth educational experience. The actual learning occurs in interactions among participants, such as through small-group exercises in which they apply their learning to their own villages. The involvement of the researcher in such issues of design can be invaluable in gauging effectiveness of educational approaches and limitations of technologies, guiding the scaling process while balancing pragmatic constraints.

Not surprisingly, a host of logistical issues tend to arise. Villages often have a place to meet, but only about 20 of the approximately 200 villages can be reached through computer centers with facilitators that our partner foundation operates. For the remaining villages, a mobile van may be needed with a TV and DVD player, and then using the local community centers to administer modules. Large-screen capability with the van would allow us to play the video in some central location, in an effort to reach others in the village. As noted, many of these villages are divided into different hamlets, reflecting various social strata. This compels us to consider whether to organize classes on a hamlet-by-hamlet basis.

We incorporate immediate and delayed assessments to understand the efficacy of our educational programs, as well as the factors that inhibit or enable entrepreneurship. We can, therefore, incorporate differences in groups of villages, social strata, and gender of participants to understand the relationships among socio-cultural factors and the scaling of in-depth entrepreneurial literacy. Some of the factors we could explore include access to financial resources, membership in social networks, local infrastructure, local livelihood opportunities, governmental support, and family support. Thus, even our scaling process—mainly aimed at increasing our transformative impact—serves as a research endeavor that may lead to new insights.

Concurrently, we are working with one of the largest micro-finance organizations in the world, embedding marketplace literacy issues in a movie that has now been produced. The movie revolves around a woman who joins a self-help group to overcome personal problems and realize her aspirations as an entrepreneur. This movie has served as a launching platform for a video-based educational program with 14 modules we designed that addresses marketplace literacy. The program is self-administered by groups of women, with a small role for a facilitator. It includes both in-class assignments—based on the movie—and out-of-class assignments aimed at applying the learning to their own villages. This program has also been extensively piloted and launched in limited scale.

To envision scaling and to have our own community platform, we formed a non-profit organization, Marketplace Literacy Communities. Through this entity, we have formed, reactivated, or work with existing self-help groups, totaling approximately 100, each consisting of 15-20 women in urban settings. We provide linkages to financial institutions and assist groups with financial records required to maintain good standing. We also work in a cluster of villages nearby, aiming to reach about 500 women. We conduct base-line surveys to assess needs as they relate to the marketplaces and skill and confidence levels in marketplace literacy. We also conduct pre-and post-cost program surveys to assess its effectiveness. We offer the video-based modules described above and assess marketplace literacy before and after. Our short-term goals are to provide marketplace literacy education to the self-help groups in our communities through video and activity-based methods and provide support to enterprises that are started up. Using a research-based approach, this community platform is offering unique ways to advance our understanding as well.

To reiterate a lesson discussed earlier about the importance of relationships, scaling is greatly enabled by people in organizations who serve as champions and with whom we have developed relationships over time. Challenges in scaling include 1) identifying the appropriate technology, and 2) adapting educational content accordingly. Similarly, creating the enterprise model, incentivizing people, and working out logistical issues all impact the educational goals, and can benefit from the perspective of the researcher.

Finally, scaling in itself offers special opportunities for large-scale field research. Again, the researcher has a particularly useful vantage point from which to help design the scaling process. He or she is in a position to preserve the integrity of the planned application—education, in the case above—while also making difficult trade-offs. With deep grounding in the underlying research and involvement in the design of the application, the researcher has much to offer larger social-enterprise partners.

A Research Mentality is Key

In our work, we emphasize a particular kind of inquiry—what might be called our "research mentality." That mentality suspends preconceptions (as much as humanly possible). It aims to rigorously analyze the data, strive for new insights, and avoid reinventing the proverbial wheel. For instance: the power of social networks in subsistence contexts is not a new discovery, but our ability to "peel the onion" in a more refined manner has led to novel insights.

Our research mentality is also reflected in how our findings provided the basis for our educational programs. We depended on the listening and immersion phase to design our original educational program. Over time, our research has progressed in parallel with the educational program, in part because a process of continuous assessment of the program also involves a research mentality.

Our determination to view our research program as a set of varied insights that can be customized to different situations is another manifestation of the particular research mentality we endorse. This research mentality is also crucial in designing the scaling process and its assessment, and in detailing new research projects that stem from such fieldwork, as elaborated in the next section.

Above all, our focus on real impact—rather than the kind of self-perpetuating publicity that all too often predominates in these contexts—captures the research mentality that our program has sought to engender. This is our most important yardstick: Is it hype, or is it real impact? Real impact is also the strongest test of the underlying research, and drives our research mentality.

Lessons on the Loops Between Research and its Practical Impact

Moving from research to positive impact has enriched our research, and these lessons—relating to forward and backward loops—are discussed in this section (see Figure 14.2).

Synergies Between Research and Social Initiatives

Perhaps the most important lesson we have learned to date is that rich synergies can develop across coordinated research, teaching, and social initiatives. In fact, each of these activities has enriched the others. Research informed the design of the educational program in India. The design and administration of the program has shed light on important research issues, and provided nuanced insights. Careful documentation and assessment of the education program also reflects such synergy. As noted, scaling our educational program in turn offers opportunities for new field research.

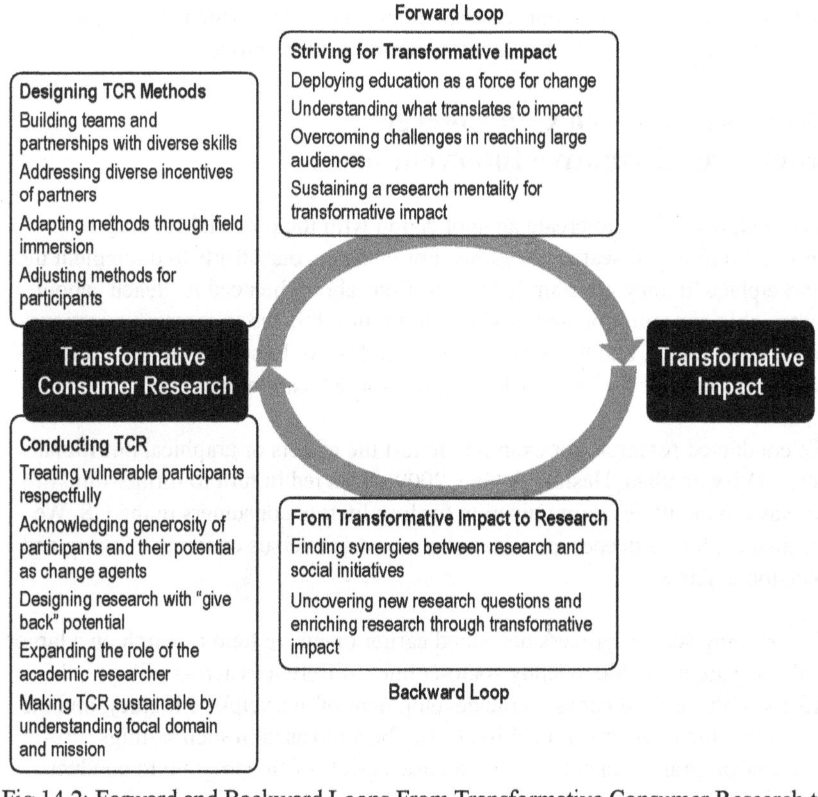

Forward Loop

Striving for Transformative Impact
Deploying education as a force for change
Understanding what translates to impact
Overcoming challenges in reaching large audiences
Sustaining a research mentality for transformative impact

Designing TCR Methods
Building teams and partnerships with diverse skills
Addressing diverse incentives of partners
Adapting methods through field immersion
Adjusting methods for participants

Transformative Consumer Research

Transformative Impact

Conducting TCR
Treating vulnerable participants respectfully
Acknowledging generosity of participants and their potential as change agents
Designing research with "give back" potential
Expanding the role of the academic researcher
Making TCR sustainable by understanding focal domain and mission

From Transformative Impact to Research
Finding synergies between research and social initiatives
Uncovering new research questions and enriching research through transformative impact

Backward Loop

Fig 14.2: Forward and Backward Loops From Transformative Consumer Research to Transformative Impact.

The relationships and partnerships we developed for social initiatives greatly increase our effectiveness in research, by addressing a number of issues such as shared purposes and incentives among the organizations and people with which we work. As noted earlier, our ability to demonstrate the larger practical purpose of our research—while also developing activities on the ground that help communities, and that are aligned with the goals of the organizations with which we work—opens up research opportunities. Explaining and demonstrating the practical implications of our research to our participants increases cooperation.

Looking more broadly, communicating to different audiences also enriches one's research. We communicate to a range of audiences. These include participants of a wide range of ages, and also practitioners in social and commercial enterprises. We view each interaction as an opportunity to strengthen the relevance of the research, and to develop deeper insights.

Similarly, writing for different audiences helps us improve our communication to the academic audience (among others). Working with different groups enriches research by providing a variety of real-world feedback. It also leads to new insights, as managers and social entrepreneurs pose tough questions that force us to be clear about what we are trying to do—which may in turn necessitate more research. These are, in short, virtuous circles.

Relevant Research Can Emerge from Transformative Interventions

As noted, our efforts to create an application with the potential for social impact led to new research questions. For instance, our efforts to implement the marketplace literacy program led to questions about the need to "teach" about sustainable consumption and production. In turn, this led to research questions about these topics, and the need to understand them. Research on low-literate consumers provided a basis to design nutrition-education materials.

We conducted research, for example, to test the effects of graphical nutritional labels (Viswanathan, Hastak, & Gau, 2009). This led in turn to further thinking on ways to facilitate communication for low-literate consumers in the US. We are also exploring deeper questions about abstract versus concrete thinking and decision making.

The ongoing scaling process described earlier opens up field research on a larger scale. We are now able to study socio-cultural differences across villages, the effects of those differences on the development of marketplace literacy, and the extent to which new theoretical issues can be addressed in such settings. Pre- and post-program data collections can use aspects of the program to conduct theoretical tests of such topics as creativity and efficacy. It is worth reiterating that such new directions stem from the bottom-up opportunities that arise out of our field work, rather than a top-down examination of a predetermined set of variables.

Lessons on the Conduct of Research

A number of lessons we learned relate to the conduct of research covering respect for at-risk participants, affirming participants as agents of changes, designing research for give-back, recognizing research as transforming the researcher, and forging sustainable initiatives.

Respect At-Risk Participants

We have strived to maintain the highest level of integrity in conducting research and imparting education, especially in the way we treat our participants. Despite the recurrent temptation to sidestep procedures and incentives—for example, when locals tell us that payment or informed-consent forms are not needed—we have carefully adhered to procedures.

Our guiding principle is that we respect the inherent dignity of every human being with whom we interact. By that standard, a subsistence participant can't be treated any differently than an affluent one. In rural settings, it is not uncommon for a group of people to gather and for several of them to volunteer information about the interviewee, requiring additional effort on the part of the researcher to follow procedures and ensure confidentiality. (This is not a trivial issue, as men interviewing women in a closed room is not culturally suitable; and yet, issues of privacy and confidentiality can't be ignored.)

In our international immersion experiences, we ensure that every individual who shows up to be interviewed by our students is interviewed. In our educational program, we emphasize that what participants have to say is of great value, and that they are the experts on their life circumstances.

In fact, some arrive on our doorstep—which is actually their doorstep—expecting to be scolded for their "incorrect views"; they are pleasantly surprised by our non-judgmental approach. Bridging the perceived status gap is a huge challenge for researchers—indeed, one of the biggest. We take pride when community members decide to trust us, just as we later take pride when they inform us that they benefited from participation in the program.

Our experience underscores the need to follow the spirit of IRB (Institutional Review Board) procedures and the conduct of ethical research (Wood, 2006). Invariably, field research leads to new situations that require moral judgments on the part of the researcher, such as in avoiding exploitation of participants as they relate emotion-laden events or in sidestepping procedures simply because we can get away with it. We can see the need to go beyond documented informed-consent procedures to ensure that our participants understand their rights. It is safe to predict that this will be an area of increasing concern and study.

Affirm Participants as Agents of Transformation

Our entire program is based on what might strike some as an unlikely foundation: the generosity of people in opening their homes to us and sharing their lives with us. In the space of an hour or two, they relate their life stories to a stranger. One woman, telling us about the extraordinary adversities she faced, stated that she only normally confided in God on some of these topics.

A second woman explained the driving motivation in her life—that no one else should suffer the way she has—as she related overcoming the loss of her husband and her son to support her family. A third woman who had managed a household of abject poverty for 15 years literally became an entrepreneur overnight when her husband became dysfunctional. Some of these interviews go back more than a decade, but we remember them as if they took place yesterday.

Why should people open up their homes and hearts to us? We explicitly and frequently pose this question to ourselves, and thereby remind ourselves that our work is built entirely on the generosity of participants in our research, teaching, and social initiatives. At the grassroots level, this is not due to the expectation of concrete rewards. Rather, it is because people respond at the human level to requests from members of our team with whom they are personally acquainted. Secondarily, it is because of an appreciation for our larger objectives, and perhaps even a sense of shared purpose.

What is that shared purpose? There seem to be several answers. We hear from communities that they benefited from participating in our research. Similarly, we receive positive feedback about the impact of our educational program. As hoped and anticipated, the program enables people to be agents of change, by spreading their learning to their communities. In our qualitative assessments, women relate how they have spread the word to many others on issues such as buying wholesale, and buying staples like rice at discounts by grouping their purchases. Our participants learn, benefit, and become agents of transformation, and that is our shared purpose.

Design Research to Give Back

Our foray into low-literate consumer behavior in the US stemmed from a desire to understand groups that are often left out of policy and business solutions.

Equally, it stemmed from a perceived potential to empower people and thereby change their status, although there was much uncertainty about how to achieve such outcomes. Our core belief, at the outset, was that understanding low-literacy-related marketplace phenomena could lead to the design of solutions that would enable low-literate consumers to participate more effectively in the marketplace.

A similar belief preceded the work on subsistence marketplaces in India. We chose projects not based on anticipated research outcomes, but rather on their potential for actual impact through the insights generated, as well as their inherent potential for educating ourselves. Of course, we are far from perfect in our foresight. But we do ask these kinds of tough questions in formulating our research objectives.

A case in point is a current project on understanding what "sustainability" means to those living in subsistence. "Planet, profit, and people" is a top-down rendering of this notion, but what are the real elements of sustainability for subsistence consumers and entrepreneurs (or consumer-merchants), and what is the interplay among these elements? What are they actually striving to sustain, each day? Livelihood? Culture? Social networks? What began as a throwaway line is stimulating deeper conversations, although the outcome is very uncertain, and is likely to range from restating the obvious to deeper insights. Such uncertainty of outcome is, of course, an exciting aspect of this work.

We also deemphasize repetitive studies that show the vulnerabilities of low literacy and poverty. This grows not so much out of wishful thinking, but rather, out of our determination to avoid studying the obvious, and to seek more nuanced insights about the circumstances in which low-literate people can perform better. For instance, we have identified conditions under which low-literate consumers perform as well as literate counterparts (Viswanathan, Xia, Torelli, & Gau, 2009). In a similar vein, our educational program focuses on overcoming the difficulties posed by abstract thinking by leveraging people's inherent social skills to enable learning.

Research Transforms the Researcher

A number of lessons learned have related to our roles in bridging different worlds, and point to the expanded role of the academic researcher. At the outset, we should state that there is no experience we would substitute for our own journey over more than 15 years. This experience has truly been transformative, at so many levels—including our own conception of research and how it can and should be conducted. But the intent here is not so much to prescribe as to describe, in the hope that aspects of this journey can strike a chord in others, and perhaps even be useful to them.

Looking again to our own experience, an academic is ideally positioned to shape an educational program, follow through on the administration of that program, and attempt to develop an enterprise model around it. Being responsible both for the dissemination of one's research and its translation into social initiatives gives a rare opportunity to communicate insights and to shape the way the work is used.

Moreover, just as effective communication of research is critically important in academic research—with writing being emphasized—so is the dissemination and translation of ideas into social actions. We tell our students that if they don't communicate their work, no one else will. This is no less true for us: if we don't champion the educational program we design by demonstrating it and by serving as a resource in its implementation, any inherent transformative potential is not likely to be realized. Thus, our experience and inclination has been toward a very proactive approach to social action, especially as it flows from the research.

Results, not surprisingly, have been mixed. At the very least, we have ensured responsible communication of our work and illustrated socially relevant applications (see Viswanathan, Seth, Gau, & Chaturvedi, 2009, for an example of the centrality of individual and community welfare for businesses). We continue to strive to maximize the reach of our approach. Success in this context would mean not only wide reach, but also the demonstration of real impact through bettered lives. This is still a long way from where we are currently.

A primary issue relates to one's own role as an academic versus running a social enterprise. Here, issues have included keeping the mission of the nonprofit clear (i.e., disseminating rather than creating knowledge), and thus not interfering with one's academic role at a university. A common issue raised in these circumstances is being an advocate for something versus researching it. For us, this has not been a central concern, at least in the conventional sense of pushing for a given outcome—i.e., poverty alleviation—versus conducting research.

If anything, having a research orientation has been essential to our "cause." Conducting research has enhanced our social initiatives, and vice versa. It has also enabled us to constantly focus on assessing the efficacy of our educational program. As we have worked with marketplace literacy over the years, our own proximity to it and its effectiveness need to be constantly questioned through assessment.

Our flexibility is important, especially in thinking more expansively about the nature and effects of marketplace literacy. In this regard, we are wedded to a few special issues: that consumer and entrepreneur are two sides of the same coin (as illustrated by our use of the term, subsistence consumer-merchant, Viswanathan, Rosa, and Ruth, 2010), that know-why is an important starting point, and that educational experiences need to be concretized, localized, and socialized. However, these guidelines are general, and provide ample room for customization based on thorough understanding through research.

In short, viewing ourselves as a learning organization with a research mentality is very useful, indeed. This does not devalue the importance of complete freedom in making choices; in fact, it underscores the importance of freedom (and the associated integrity) of decision making. Important issues such as funding sources and the requirements of journals have been highlighted in the literature on participatory action research in this regard (David, 2002; Ozanne and Saatcioglu, 2008). Our funding sources have not proven restrictive in any way, although a clear delineation between research and social initiatives based on the intent of grants is very important.

Another potential area of separation is between funding from businesses devoted to specific projects in our program versus basic research. With respect to the requirements of journals, this research has largely been initiated without specific regard to this issue, other than acknowledging the need to conduct research with the highest level of rigor and relevance, both of which have a significant bottom-up flavor. With progress in a series of experiments or qualitative interviews, further understanding has led to the crafting of a potential paper for an academic outlet.

The day-to-day activities and decisions involved in such work point to an expanded role for the academic researcher well beyond the traditional comfort zones. In-depth understanding of what lies ahead is essential for any researcher who chooses to walk down this path.

Forge Sustainable Initiatives

A final lesson in the conduct of such research is simply that it must be sustainable.

There are many forms of sustainability, not the least of which is financial. But the financial capital invested in these efforts pales in comparison to the human capital committed. As we traverse new paths, extrinsic rewards are not apparent, and they therefore aren't available to sustain such human capital. What ultimately can sustain it is a belief in the larger purpose of a specific program, and the ability to flow around obstacles, rather than march through or over them.

For this to happen, each researcher has to define his or her larger purpose, and decide up front what "success" or positive impact will look like. Impact can mean the degree to which we have given people who have not had a chance a chance, especially to improve their well-being.

First and foremost, this means giving that chance to people living in poverty. Our impact has been minuscule when held up to the millions who live in poverty. Therefore, our tasks remain infinitely large.

Second, this means reaching out to diverse audiences. Here we mean not only our participants, but also students, many of whom who have not had the benefit of opportunities to work toward a sustainable global society. We provide those opportunities. Another related responsibility is to create opportunities for junior researchers to work in this arena without having to clear the same kinds of hurdles that we did.

Third, this means disseminating our learning and implications responsibly to commercial and social enterprises, as well as to policy makers. This kind of careful dissemination—in which the researcher is directly involved in both communicating the research and designing applications—increases the likelihood of organizations responsibly serving impoverished communities.

A central focus on mission and domain is important in deciding which paths to go down, and which paths to turn away from. For example, our focus could be expanded to adjacent areas, such as health care, which overlap with marketplace activity and consumption. The risk, of course, would be an overall dilution of outcomes—which our central focus on marketplace/consumption perspective might help head off, if not entirely preclude.

Conclusion

A final leg in this journey has been in bringing subsistence marketplaces into the classroom, creating synergies with research and social initiatives in the last six years. As noted earlier in Chapter 12, our field team has executed international immersion experiences as a part of the learning experiences we offer. Such education was made possible through research and social initiatives.

In turn, this has led to a number of synergies: research has provided the academic foundation for designing education, and, in turn, the educational platform has provided a basis for research articles, such as on product development. Our initiatives on the ground have enabled education, and, in turn, our educational immersion experiences where students interact with the community have strengthened our relationship on the ground and provided our partners with an understanding of who we are and what we do.

Our approach should be put in perspective as it relates to the literature on relevant topics such as action research. Our approach does bear resemblance to action research in some ways, such as the concurrence of research with action (Coghlan, 2004). We began with practical problems that low-literate people face, which is another characteristic of action research (Ozanne and Saticioglu, 2008). Our approach blurs the division between theory and practice (Ozanne and Saticioglu, 2008).

Aspects of our approach—such as the focus on specific contexts and the emphasis on solving problems therein, the emergent nature of the research based on local conditions, enrichment of research through experiences of participants, and the notion that the larger test of theory is in its ability to have a positive impact on social problems—also have been discussed in the context of action research (Greenwood and Levin, 1998).

However, as the preceding description makes clear, we don't claim anything close to full collaboration with participants, nor have we shaped a collaborative process for authority over and execution of research, as has been discussed with participatory action research (Greenwood, Whyte, and Harkavy, 1993).

We conclude by pointing to the uncertainty that still surrounds our endeavors. Our journey is an attempt, and nothing more. While we derive some measure of satisfaction from our research and curricular outcomes, we strive to reach larger audiences. By the metric of changing lives on the ground, we have succeeded qualitatively, but there is much work that remains quantitatively. If this writing leads to visions for larger-scale impact, then the positive reactions they engender are ones we have not yet fully earned. If those visions are realized, our own investments will in some small way be validated. In the meantime, the journey continues.

References

Chaturvedi, A., Chiu, C. Y., & Viswanathan, M. (2009). Bounded agency and analytical thinking among low literate Indian women, Journal of Cross-Cultural Psychology, 40 (5), 880-893.

Coghlan, D. (2004). Action research in the academy: Why and whither? Reflections on the changing nature of research. Irish Journal of Management, 25 (2), 1-10.

David, M. (2002). Problems of participation: the limits of action research. International Journal of Social Research Methodology, 5 (1), 11-17.

Dewey, J. (1910). How we think: A restatement of the relation of reflective thinking to the education process. Lexington, MA: Heath.

Elkjaer, B. (2004). Organizational learning: The 'third way.' Management Learning, 35 (4), 419-434.

Freire, P. (1970). Cultural action for freedom. Cambridge, MA: Harvard Educational Review.

Greenwood, D. J. & Levin, M. (1998). Action research, science, and the co-optation of social research. Studies in cultures, organizations & societies, 4 (2), 237-261.

Greenwood, D. J., Whyte, W. F., & Harkavy, I. (1993). Participatory action research as a process and as a goal. Human Relations, 46 (2), 175-192.

Jayanti, R. K. and Singh, J. (2010). Pragmatic learning theory: An inquiry-action framework for distributed consumer learning in online communities. Journal of Consumer Research, 36 (6), 1058-1081.

Novogratz, J. (2009). The blue sweater: Bridging the gap between rich and poor in an interconnected world. New York: Rodale Books.

MacLean, S., Warr, D., & Pyett, P. (2009). Was it good for you too? Impediments to conducting university-based collaborative research with communities experiencing disadvantage. Australian & New Zealand Journal of Public Health, 33 (5), 407-412.

Molyneux, C., Coudge, J., Russell, S., Chuma, J., Gumede, T., & Gilson, L. (2009). Conducting health-related social science research in low income settings: Ethical dilemmas faced in Kenya and South Africa. Journal of International Development, 21 (2), 309-326.

Ozanne, J. L., & Saatcioglu, B. (2008). Participatory action research. Journal of Consumer Research, 35 (3), 423-439.

Viswanathan, M., Gajendiran, S., & Venkatesan, R. (2008a). Enabling consumer and entrepreneurial literacy in subsistence marketplaces. Dordrecht: Springer.

Viswanathan, M., Gajendiran, S., & Venkatesan, R. (2008b). Understanding and enabling marketplace literacy in subsistence contexts: The development of a consumer and entrepreneurial literacy educational program in south India. International Journal of Educational Development, 28 (3), 300-19.

Viswanathan, M., & Gau, R. (2005). Functional illiteracy and nutritional education in the United States: A research-based approach to the development of nutritional education materials for functionally illiterate consumers. Journal of Macromarketing, 25 (2), 187-201.

Viswanathan, M., Gau, R. & Chaturvedi, A. (2008). Research methods for subsistence marketplaces. In P. Khandachar & M. Halme (Eds.), Sustainability challenges and solutions at the base-of-the-pyramid: Business, technology and the poor (pp. 242-260). Sheffield, UK: Greenleaf Publishing.

Viswanathan, M., Hastak, M. & Gau, R. (2009). Enabling processing of nutritional labels among low-literate consumers. Journal of Public Policy & Marketing, 28 (2), 135–145.

Viswanathan, M., & Rosa, J. (2007). Product and market development for subsistence marketplaces: Consumption and entrepreneurship beyond literacy and resource barriers. In J. Rosa & M. Viswanathan (Eds.), Product and market development for subsistence marketplaces: Consumption and entrepreneurship beyond literacy and resource barriers (pp. 1-17). Advances in International Management Series, J. Cheng & M. Hitt (Series Editors), Oxford: Elsevier.

Viswanathan, M., & Rosa, J. (2010). Understanding subsistence marketplaces: Toward sustainable consumption and commerce for a better world. Journal of Business Research, 63 (6), 535-537.

Viswanathan, M., Rosa, J. A., & Harris, J. (2005). Decision-making and coping by functionally illiterate consumers and some implications for marketing management. Journal of Marketing, 69 (1), 15-31.

Viswanathan, M., Rosa, J. A., & Ruth, J. (2010). Exchanges in marketing systems: The case of subsistence consumer merchants in Chennai, India. Journal of Marketing, 74 (3), 1-18.

Viswanathan, M., Seth, A., Gau, R. & Chaturvedi, A. (2009). Internalizing social good into business processes in subsistence marketplaces: The sustainable market orientation. Journal of Macromarketing, 29, 406-425.

Viswanathan, M., & Sridharan, S. (2009). From subsistence marketplaces to sustainable marketplaces: A bottom-up perspective of the role of business in poverty alleviation. Ivey Business Journal, 73 (2).

Viswanathan, M., Sridharan, S., Gau, R. & Ritchie, R. (2009). Designing marketplace literacy education in resource-constrained contexts: Implications for public policy and marketing. Journal of Public Policy & Marketing, 28 (1), 85-94.

Viswanathan, M., Xia, L. Torelli, C. & Gau, R. (2009). Literacy and consumer memory. Journal of Consumer Psychology, 19, 389–402.

Wallerstein, N., Duran, B., Minkler, M., & Foley, K. (2005). Developing and maintaining partnerships with communities. In Israel et al. (Eds.), Methods in community-based participatory research for health (pp. 31-51). San Francisco, CA: Jossey Bass.

Wood, E. (2006). The ethical challenges of field research in conflict zones. Qualitative Sociology, 29 (3), 373-386.

What This Means: Designing Solutions For Subsistence Marketplaces[34]

Given the micro-level insights presented in the previous pages, how do we leverage this bottom-up perspective to develop a greater understanding of business development in subsistence marketplaces (see Figure S2.1).

First, we need to acknowledge our own weaknesses in understanding subsistence contexts (see Outline: A Bottom-Up view of BOP Marketplaces). Most managers cannot personally relate to poverty, particularly the poverty that characterizes those living in subsistence. Added to this are preconceptions that need to be unlearned, such as the presumed "dependence" of the poor on governmental program when, in fact, lack of such programs and lack of dependence is more common. (There is little to depend on.) The preconceptions of middle-class or lower-middle-class people not deeply exposed to the subsistence context often prevent visualization of solutions, and may even lead to dismissal of innovative approaches. Perhaps most counterproductive is the attitude that solutions need to be imported from advanced contexts (Hart, S.L., 2011).

Second, we need to acknowledge that those living in subsistence have significant experience in surviving it, either as consumers or entrepreneurs or both. That learning can serve as an invaluable foundation.

At the same time, we have to understand their limitations, including their understandable difficulties in envisioning beyond the challenges of the moment. It is important to understand both strengths and vulnerabilities, without romanticizing the former or exaggerating the latter.

---

[34] This chapter includes material adapted from the following previously published work:

Viswanathan, Madhubalan (2010), "A Micro-Level Approach to Understanding BoP Markets," Next Generation Business Strategies for the Base of the Pyramid: New Approaches for Building Mutual Value, Editors, Ted London and Stuart Hart, FT Press.

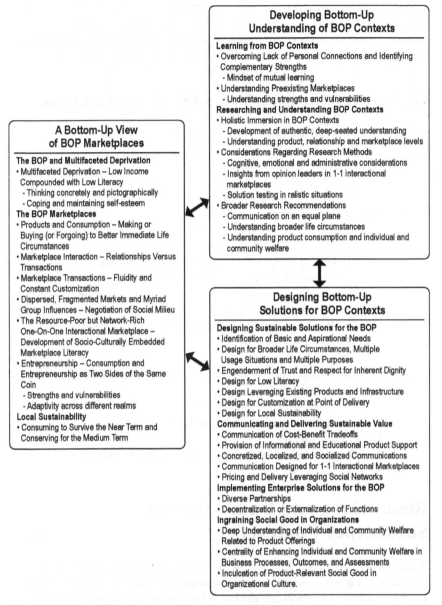

Developing Bottom-Up Understanding of BOP Contexts

Learning from BOP Contexts
• Overcoming Lack of Personal Connections and Identifying Complementary Strengths
  - Mindset of mutual learning
• Understanding Preexisting Marketplaces
  - Understanding strengths and vulnerabilities
Researching and Understanding BOP Contexts
• Holistic Immersion in BOP Contexts
  - Development of authentic, deep-seated understanding
  - Understanding product, relationship and marketplace levels
• Considerations Regarding Research Methods
  - Cognitive, emotional and administrative considerations
  - Insights from opinion leaders in 1-1 interactional marketplaces
  - Solution testing in ralistic situations
• Broader Research Recommendations
  - Communication on an equal plane
  - Understanding broader life circumstances
  - Understanding product consumption and individual and community welfare

A Bottom-Up View of BOP Marketplaces

The BOP and Multifaceted Deprivation
• Multifaceted Deprivation – Low Income Compounded with Low Literacy
  - Thinking concretely and pictographically
  - Coping and maintaining self-esteem
The BOP Marketplaces
• Products and Consumption – Making or Buying (or Forgoing) to Better Immediate Life Circumstances
• Marketplace Interaction – Relationships Versus Transactions
• Marketplace Transactions – Fluidity and Constant Customization
• Dispersed, Fragmented Markets and Myriad Group Influences – Negotiation of Social Milieu
• The Resource-Poor but Network-Rich One-On-One Interactional Marketplace – Development of Socio-Culturally Embedded Marketplace Literacy
• Entrepreneurship – Consumption and Entrepreneurship as Two Sides of the Same Coin
  - Strengths and vulnerabilities
  - Adaptivity across different realms
Local Sustainability
• Consuming to Survive the Near Term and Conserving for the Medium Term

Designing Bottom-Up Solutions for BOP Contexts

Designing Sustainable Solutions for the BOP
• Identification of Basic and Aspirational Needs
• Design for Broader Life Circumstances, Multiple Usage Situations and Multiple Purposes
• Engenderment of Trust and Respect for Inherent Dignity
• Design for Low Literacy
• Design Leveraging Existing Products and Infrastructure
• Design for Customization at Point of Delivery
• Design for Local Sustainability
Communicating and Delivering Sustainable Value
• Communication of Cost-Benefit Tradeoffs
• Provision of Informational and Educational Product Support
• Concretized, Localized, and Socialized Communications
• Communication Designed for 1-1 Interactional Marketplaces
• Pricing and Delivery Leveraging Social Networks
Implementing Enterprise Solutions for the BOP
• Diverse Partnerships
• Decentralization or Externalization of Functions
Ingraining Social Good in Organizations
• Deep Understanding of Individual and Community Welfare Related to Product Offerings
• Centrality of Enhancing Individual and Community Welfare in Business Processes, Outcomes, and Assessments
• Inculcation of Product-Relevant Social Good in Organizational Culture.

Figure S2.1: A Bottom-Up View of BOP Marketplaces.

A somewhat paradoxical insight is that those who cannot personally relate to poverty and low literacy, but have an openness and willingness to learn, are ideally positioned to envision new and innovative solutions. Herein lies a strength of managers and researchers that complements the weakness of those close to the subsistence context. With a willingness to learn from these contexts, managers and researchers can complement the strengths and weaknesses of subsistence consumers and entrepreneurs. Indeed, a mindset of mutual learning can lead to innovative and contextually relevant solutions, as well as learning that is transferable to advanced economies (Simanis, E., 2011).

Outline: A Bottom-Up View of BOP Marketplaces

- The BOP and Multifaceted Deprivation
  - o Multifaceted Deprivation—low income compounded with low literacy
    - Thinking concretely and pictographically
    - Coping and maintaining self-esteem
- The BOP Marketplaces
  - o Products and Consumption—making or buying (or forgoing) to better immediate life circumstances
  - o Marketplace Interaction—relationships versus transactions
  - o Marketplace Transactions—fluidity and constant customization
  - o Dispersed, Fragmented Markets and Myriad Group Influences—negotiation of social milieu
  - o The Resource-Poor but Network-Rich One-to-One Interactional Marketplace—development of socio-culturally embedded marketplace literacy
  - o Entrepreneurship—consumption and entrepreneurship as two sides of the same coin
    - Strengths and vulnerabilities
    - Adaptivity across different realms
- Local Sustainability
  - o Consuming to survive the near term and conserving for the medium term

Researching and Understanding Subsistence Contexts

If we seek to undertake a fundamental shift in thinking about people living in subsistence, a holistic immersion in that context is extremely important. Such an immersion would help overcome individual and organizational deficits in subsistence contexts, including the lack of knowledge, expertise, and personal connection. It would help us unlearn prior notions—such as what appears to be rational decision-making and efficient problem-solving in affluent settings—that may not be applicable in subsistence conditions.

Holistic immersion in the daily lives of subsistence consumers and entrepreneurs should aim for authentic, deep-seated understanding of a number of specific issues. For instance, at the product level, issues would include how a portfolio of products fit into consumers' life circumstances, what the usage situations are, and whether such usage can lead to individual and community welfare. At the relationship level, issues would relate to the nature of one-to-one interactions, the role of opinion leaders, word-of-mouth effects, and the development of consumer skills. Issues at the marketplace level would include the socio-political structures, varied group influences, and livelihood opportunities that can sustain the local economy and create wealth.

The need for holistic immersion should not be viewed as being in contradiction with gaining general understanding of subsistence contexts, as reflected in the earlier discussion. Rather, holistic immersion should aim to gain nuanced understanding of specific subsistence contexts, given the myriad differences across these contexts.

Disseminating Marketplace Literacy Education

A real-world example from the social realm that we have been involved in is developing and disseminating marketplace literacy education, elaborated in Chapter 13. We would identify a key need through extensive immersion and research, such as in-depth interviews and observations of subsistence consumers and entrepreneurs. Through the initial listening process, which occurred over the course of a year, we would identify a critical need for people living in subsistence to participate more effectively in the marketplace as consumers and as entrepreneurs—that is, a need for marketplace literacy—in addition to other needs, such as market access and financial resources. This marketplace literacy enables subsistence consumers and entrepreneurs to better negotiate the marketplace.

Marketplace literacy was categorized at three levels: a concrete level of livelihood skills, a more abstract level of knowhow as consumers or entrepreneurs, and a meta-level of "know-why" that provides deeper understanding of marketplace dynamics—and, by extension, adaptability to changing circumstances (e.g., how and why do exchanges work, how do exchanges add up to a value chain, why should enterprises be customer-oriented, and so on).

Our immersion provided a window into both the strengths and vulnerabilities of subsistence consumers and entrepreneurs. This enabled us to develop an educational program that harnesses the strengths and addresses the vulnerabilities of subsistence consumers and entrepreneurs. The program employs concrete examples and visual content in order to be accessible to low-literate participants. Further, the delivery of the program hinges upon social interactions and peer learning, leveraging the rich tradition of orality and social interactions in the local context.

In addition to reviewing recent literature, learning about the subsistence marketplace should incorporate the insights of subsistence "experts," ranging from small vendors and retailers to self-help group leaders, non-governmental organizations, and community-based organizations. The network-rich nature of the subsistence context emphasizes the need to gain insights from opinion leaders, and to understand how word of mouth works in specific marketplaces.

At the same time, we need to avoid relying exclusively on "filtered" views of the subsistence marketplace, such as those that may be presented by middle- or upper-income people working for NGOs or non-local companies. This can't be overstated: direct interaction with subsistence consumers and entrepreneurs is essential.

In many respects, the missing insights have to be stitched together from the bottom up—that is, through localized studies from select communities—rather than through top-down sampling methods that tend to be based on unrealistic assumptions about homogeneity in these marketplaces. They have to be gleaned in ways that reflect the subsistence reality. For example, in the realm of product testing: given the reliance that low-literate consumers have on holistic experience with a product, the use of actual products is likely to be far more effective than the testing of products along the kinds of abstract attributes common in product testing in affluent contexts.

And to extend the example further: Product testing may have to take on dimensions rarely seen in affluent settings. For example: How can the consumption of this product enhance personal and community welfare? How does it foster a constructive interplay between marketplace activity and social good?

How else should we think about the "missing" subsistence research? One answer, also implied in previous pages, is the need to engage in interactions with our research subjects on a more or less equal footing. We can't see ourselves as possessing solutions for what are fundamentally unfamiliar problems and settings. More so than many research settings, this requires empathy, and the ability to engage in a sincere conversation. It also requires a sincere focus on individual and community welfare. Also important is "big-picture" thinking: that is, an understanding of the rich contextual setting in which subsistence marketplace exchanges and consumption tend to play out. In contrast to a transaction in a context of affluence—the purchase of a single product, in isolation, using a small proportion of one's discretionary income, in impersonal settings—the subsistence marketplace and life circumstances are inextricably intertwined. Solutions succeed and fail based on the depth of their understanding of life circumstances. And such understanding requires a bottom-up orientation that relies on micro-level insights as a foundation for designing solutions.

The How: Designing Solutions for Subsistence Marketplaces

Given a micro-level orientation to understanding subsistence contexts, how do we build on what we know and design for a better future? Our recommendations, not surprisingly, emphasize designing solutions from the bottom-up (see Outline: A Bottom-Up view of BOP Marketplaces), delivering sustainable value propositions, implementing enterprise solutions, and ingraining social good in the core business processes and offerings of the organization.

Designing Sustainable Solutions

At the risk of stating the obvious, the biggest challenge for an enterprise that seeks to operate in the subsistence niche is identifying a central need that can be met affordably. It is a universe of far too many needs and far too few resources.

But people in this world do consume. They strive to meet their basic needs. They seek healthier alternatives for their children. They aspire to own (or at least, have access to) higher-quality products that won't fail them. The ubiquity of cell phones in the subsistence context attests to the centrality of one vital need—communication—which sometimes helps overcome isolation, and at other times may provide a literal lifeline in a medical emergency. Other aspirational needs revolve around the driving motivation to create a better life for one's children—for example, through education—or acquiring skills for themselves to improve their life circumstances.

The fundamental challenge is to envision life circumstances, and—more specifically—flexible product-usage situations. Rather than responding to a fixed set of usage conditions, the effective "subsistence design" allows for the many different and unanticipated ways in which the product will be used, depending on situation and need. Again, this is made possible by a rich understanding of the household activities of consumers and the kinds of fluid point-of-sale conditions faced by subsistence entrepreneurs (e.g., on bicycles and carts). The nature of usage in harsh conditions needs to be factored in, as well.

The transactional context of constant customization discussed earlier suggests the need for product design to allow for different configurations and perhaps determination of final configuration by local entrepreneurs. Communications solutions may call for different local language and dialect interfaces, which may best be done at the local level. Food products may call for value addition at the point of purchase by local entrepreneurs, who may customize the product by adding different ingredients for different segments, such as the elderly versus children. Such localization may be sound like heresy to those in charge of standardization and quality control in large organizations, but nevertheless, relinquishing control in this way may be essential to success.

Solutions should address livelihood opportunities and explore potential partnerships to co-create products through business relationships. Solutions should sustain the local economy, the local ecology, and the local culture (Hart, S., 2011). Solutions need to address the myriad differences among fragmented small markets, and the demand for customization in an intensely one-to-one environment. Solutions have to grow out of transparent and fair processes that both engender trust and respect the inherent dignity of subsistence consumers and entrepreneurs.

We emphasize the need to concretize, localize, and socialize solutions (Viswanathan, et al. 2009). For example, packaging, communication, and education should be concrete, in light of the low-literate audience. Localizing solutions range from using local language in designing product interfaces to involving local entrepreneurs. In the one-to-one interactional and relational marketplace, the socializing of solutions entails both involving the community and leveraging the inherent social and oral language skills of subsistence consumers and entrepreneurs.

This means, for example, engaging in community-level interaction in informational and educational products; involving local entrepreneurs in final assembly and communication of value and benefits to low-literate consumers; and packaging, communication, and education that can be disseminated through word of mouth.

Product interfaces and packages should be designed for concrete thinking and pictographic thinking. Also central to the design is the need to visualize and communicate benefits. Equally, the design of solutions should address the issue of multi-faceted deprivation. For example, educational aspects can be a central aspect of the packaging, covering topics like benefits or proper usage.

Existing products can serve as vehicles for important add-ons (e.g., staples serving as vehicles for nutritional additives, and cell phones serving as platforms for educational and informational products). Leveraging existing infrastructure and products and services is also important, rather than thinking in terms of a unique device and a micro-financing plan for every seemingly discrete need. Leapfrogging the lack of infrastructure is another important facet, as with cell phones in the absence of landlines. Solutions should show sensitivity in sustaining local culture in an intensely social world—for example, in the realm of cooking products and associated cultural beliefs.

At the broadest level, designing solutions calls for a micro-level, bottom-up approach, wherein each step in the process involves immersion in the field. It also draws upon insights from nonprofit organizations, small vendors and retailers, and self-help group leaders, thus deriving expertise from those most experienced in the context.

Delivering Sustainable Value Propositions for the Subsistence Marketplace

Communications must help potential customers visualize benefits. Despite their limited resources, subsistence consumers are sometimes willing to pay a small premium for quality products that serve core needs (e.g., communication, staple food, and education) and better their life circumstances. It is therefore critical to design and communicate the value proposition to emphasize costs and benefits, in a context where consumers may undervalue or even ignore non-monetary resources such as time, costs, and benefits beyond the immediate term (e.g., interest rates), or hidden outcomes such as enhanced health.

In marketplaces with lacking informational and educational resources, communications should be envisioned and initiated from the bottom up, rather than relying on top-down, mass media-based approaches, and aim to provide product-related support. Communication strategies can leverage the intensely social interactions, use of word of mouth, and develop partnerships with opinion leaders to share information and obtain feedback, and conduct dialogue with the community. Social networks should be integrated with communications to maximize impact and adoption through product trials (see "Concretize, localize, and socialize your communication").

Concretize, Localize, and Socialize Communication

The marketplace literacy educational program discussed earlier was designed entirely around low-literate audiences, using concrete materials, localized content, and methods that leveraged participants' inherent social skills, using role-plays, pictorial tasks, and other such means. Thus, this program represents an illustration of the need to concretize, localize, and socialize communication.

We designed the program around cultural sensitivity, given the unfamiliarity of educational settings for our participants. It addresses aspirational needs of people to seek nontraditional education to better themselves and find a way up and out economically. We based the ongoing process to scale these programs to reach larger audiences on using existing infrastructure, audiovisual media, or community-based television, depending on the situation.

The educational program serves multiple purposes, with the potential to be customized more narrowly to emphasize employability training in areas such as customer service, entrepreneurial opportunities in specific arenas, or consumer education on nutrition, or more broadly as a stepping stone for advanced education.

What about distribution?

As noted, the one-to-one interactional marketplace is characterized by trust and patronage between small, local retailers or service providers and local customers. An effective distribution model understands and draws upon these social networks. The distinctive services offered by local vendors—such as extending credit to consumers in times of need—creates loyalty, and there are parallels in the relationships between entrepreneurs and their suppliers. Pricing and distribution practices can be designed to build on these relationships, allowing for retailers to extend credit, adjust prices, and offer different product configurations (e.g., local production, final stage of manufacture, or central value added at the retail level). The broad point about communicating value propositions also applies here: the most effective distribution methods are those which are developed from the bottom up, rather than from the top down.

Implementing Enterprise Solutions for the Subsistence Marketplace

Enterprise solutions in the subsistence marketplace require the successful negotiation of widely diverse conditions and socio-political environments across small geographic regions, and along such challenging dimensions as language and culture. Enterprises should therefore consider decentralizing, working with diverse organizations, and even "externalizing"—in other words, forming partnerships with local entities and empowering them to make decisions (Ritchie, R., and Sridharan, S., 2007).

These approaches are likely to bring several benefits, including increased access to marketplace knowledge, high responsiveness, livelihood creation, the involvement of local communities, and a more symbiotic relationship between enterprises and subsistence consumers and entrepreneurs (see "Sun Ovens International").

Sun Ovens International

An interesting and illustrative example of a small company working with the subsistence marketplace is provided by Sun Ovens International Inc., which makes solar ovens around the world, discussed in Chapter 9. The company has considerable experience in subsistence contexts, having spent time understanding the life circumstances in these contexts. Its CEO, Paul Munsen, adopts the mindset of understanding how business can fit into preexisting traditions in a profitable manner that also sustains the local economy, culture, and environment.

The product is designed to address a lack of firewood and high fuel prices. Portable solar ovens are produced by local entrepreneurs, with a key component being licensed. The company works with diverse organizations—including local NGOs and entrepreneurs—to reach their customers. The product is priced carefully to enhance affordability, with innovative financing schemes also part of the package. Along the way, of course, a number of local challenges have to be overcome, given the culturally ingrained nature of cooking and eating.

Contrast Sun Oven's approach to the extended transactional relationships that characterize affluent markets. Through these economic-centered relationships, enterprises can work within and across different communities. But the assumption that dominates in affluent markets—that certain types of institutions (e.g., credit bureaus) are required to facilitate marketplace exchange—generally does not hold in subsistence marketplaces. Nor are the types of institutions that play a role in exchange necessarily clear-cut or fixed. Family, neighborhood, and village play a subtle but important role in exchanges. Children may help run enterprises; neighborhoods may come together to establish savings plans; villages may organize marketplace activities.

Ingraining Social Good in the Organization

Another key implication is that "social good," in a product-relevant sense, is essential for economic success in subsistence marketplaces (Viswanathan, M., et al. 2009).

An overriding characteristic of subsistence marketplaces is that traditional boundaries become permeable. In a context of severe resource constraints, product needs become intertwined with the betterment of basic life circumstances. Economic relationships overlap substantially with human relationships. The larger social milieu blends into marketplace activities, and vice versa.

The prescription? Enterprises have to run in a similarly nuanced way, reflecting the permeable border between commercial purpose and social good. A compartmentalized approach to products and functions—in other words, one that puts the business in one box and the social context in another—is unlikely to work. In most cases, a holistic approach holds far more promise. Products and related communications have to go beyond their (necessary) focus on the betterment of immediate life circumstances. They also have to provide support that improve individual and community welfare.

Such a focus on individual and community welfare may be a prerequisite for subsistence consumers to spend their scarce resources. Similarly, an emphasis on the human dimension in relationships—a key aspect of life in subsistence contexts—can help make the organization and its product offerings a more credible "community member." Enterprises that develop a reputation for enhancing individual and community welfare, and for reinforcing individual relationships and the social fabric, are likely to prevail and succeed.

Negotiating a complex social milieu also entails working with diverse organizations, often through the common denominator of "social good." Geographically dispersed and fragmented markets come under a wide variety of influences. In an era of increasing connectivity, the small groups that focus on compelling issues—ranging from women's rights to ecological concerns—provide both a connection to subsistence marketplaces and a counterweight to unfair or exploitative practices that harm personal and community welfare.

This is rarely easy. Embedding an organization into a community through embracing social good requires a deep understanding of individual and community welfare as they relate to product offerings. That thinking must be ingrained in the organization. With such ingraining, product-relevant social good becomes a fundamental orientation for the enterprise, affecting its knowledge, processes, outcomes, performance, and culture. Again, it is not easy; but it may be essential for economic success in subsistence marketplaces.

Conclusion

This micro-level approach also emphasizes that subsistence contexts are preexisting marketplaces. Social and commercial practitioners must begin by understanding existing dynamics. They must also, however, realize that subsistence contexts are much more than parallel markets for existing products or solutions.

This means there are many opportunities for learning. What exactly, then, should we try to learn? We can learn how appropriate solutions can be designed within the context of rich, existing marketplace dynamics. We can learn how such solutions can enable these marketplaces to become ecologically, socially, and economically sustainable, while also generating profit for the outside enterprise. And finally, we can learn how solutions that arise in these adverse settings can be transferred, profitably, to other contexts.

But—going full circle—before we can create solutions for subsistence marketplaces, we must first understand those marketplaces–at a micro level.

Yes, this is true in any context, but it is even more true in the subsistence context, for all the reasons articulated in the preceding pages. The typical researcher or manager who has not spent much time in that context—and to date, only small numbers have—has many preconceptions to set aside, and much learning to do. That learning requires communication on an equal footing. It requires a mindset of learning from in order to design for. Almost certainly, it will reflect an inescapable truth: that individual and community welfare are deeply intertwined with effective solutions.

References

Hart, S.L. (2011). Taking the Green Leap to the Base of the Pyramid. In T. London and S. Hart (Eds.), Next Generation Business Strategies for the Base of the Pyramid (pp 79-102). Upper Saddle River, N.J.: FT Press.

Ritchie, R., and Sridharan, S. (2007). "Marketing in Subsistence Markets: Innovation through Decentralization and Externalization," Product and Market Development for Subsistence Marketplaces: Consumption and Entrepreneurship Beyond Literacy and Resource Barriers, Jose Rosa and Madhubalan Viswanathan (Editors), Elsevier, Vol. 20, 195–214. See also Ted London's chapter in this book.

Viswanathan, M., Sridharan, S., Gau, R., and Ritchie, R. (2009). "Designing Marketplace Literacy Education in Resource-Constrained Contexts: Implications for Public Policy and Marketing," Journal of Public Policy and Marketing, 28 (1), 85–94.

Viswanathan, M., Seth, A.,,Gau, A., and Chaturvedi, A.(2009). "Ingraining Product-Relevant Social Good into Business Processes in Subsistence Marketplaces: The Sustainable Market Orientation," Journal of Macromarketing, 29: 406–425.